While conceptions of "global journalism" may be relatively new, journalism has long been globalizing in its ambitions to forge communicative networks across national borders. This excellent volume disrupts Western, ethnocentric assumptions in media research, its impressive range of chapters affording important insights into questions of power, influence, and social change recurrently denied the attention they deserve. Highly recommended for scholars, students, and journalists alike.
—Stuart Allan, Author of The Future of Journalism: Risks, Threats, Opportunities, School of Journalism and Communication, Cardiff University

In this era beset by misinformation, quality journalism has never been more important. Dimitrova and colleagues convincingly show that there is more than one definition of quality and more than one way to achieve it. This cosmopolitan compendium will open some eyes!
—Rodney Benson, New York University

This inspiring book takes the reader on a world tour of journalism practices, touching on theories and current issues that describe, explain, and predict the evolution of global journalism cultures from the local perspective. It is a must-read for journalism students in higher education.
—Lindita Camaj, Director of Graduate Studies, Valenti School of Communication, University of Houston

One of the key challenges for journalism research is to identify, map, and articulate issues that cut across national boundaries while keeping our eye on local particulars. This book provides an essential road map for navigating such truly global journalism studies.
—Mark Deuze, Author of Media Life, University of Amsterdam

There is no one work that provides the breadth and depth of understanding the technological changes and their impact on all aspects of global journalism as Dimitrova does here. Global Journalism generates a fresh and complex view of timely case studies and theoretical models featured by contributors from twelve different countries. This book will arouse interest and provide a scholarly foundation for understanding world media systems and key issues facing international communication today.
—Shahira S. Fahmy, Associate Editor, Journal of Communication, The American University in Cairo

Global Journalism is the textbook global communication scholars have been waiting for. Its truly global approach, clear-cut language, success placing complex processes into non-judgmental context, and seventeen well-chosen, comprehensive chapters makes it an ideal text for upper-level undergrads and grad students alike.
—Robyn S. Goodman, Professor Emerita of Communication Studies, Alfred University, Alfred, New York

It's not easy to capture the rich diversity of contexts in which journalism exists. This book does so brilliantly, providing an accessible, up-to-date and truly global analysis of the key questions and issues that confront journalism at a time of fundamental transformations. It is a must-read for anyone who wants to gain a better understanding of journalistic cultures and practices.

—Folker Hanusch, Editor-in-Chief of Journalism Studies and Co-editor of Worlds of Journalism: Journalistic Cultures Around the Globe, University of Vienna

It's widely acknowledged that finding journalism books that truly take an international focus has long been a remarkable challenge. Thanks to extensive and innovative dispatches masterfully put together by Daniela Dimitrova, this book is to become the go-to volume for anyone interested in theoretical, methodological and epistemological developments in international journalism or broadly, international communication. The editor has the world-leading, sought-after track-record to speak about these issues.

—Bruce Mutsvairo, Professor in Journalism, Auburn University

A robust and breathtaking look at global journalism practices, this book showcases diverse views from more than twenty global media experts from twelve different countries unpacking pivotal issues snatched from today's headlines. Topics range from the refugee crisis, press freedom to journalism culture, and media ethics. Scholars and students alike benefit from this panorama rooted in the classical theories but fresh with new ideas and insights. Excellent as a textbook, it belongs on every global news scholar's shelf.

—B. William Silcock, Emeritus, Former Assistant Dean for Research and International Programs, Walter Cronkite School of Journalism and Mass Communication, Arizona State University

At last, here is a global journalism textbook that accounts for the worldwide ascendance of digital platforms and the spread of populism and authoritarianism. What a fantastic collection!

—Miglena Sternadori, book review editor, *Journal of Magazine Media*, Texas Tech University

Global Journalism is an exceptional volume, offering both a broad scope and nuanced detail. It takes digitalization seriously and fundamentally revisits how to think about global journalism in the digital age. It promises to set the agenda for the field by highlighting key themes while also exploring overlooked but important topics.

—Tim P. Vos, President, Association for Education in Journalism and Mass Communication (AEJMC), Director, School of Journalism, Michigan State University

This excellent volume provides a comprehensive, state-of-the-world examination of global journalism's practices and characteristics. An explication of key concepts and topics is combined with more context-specific perspectives from all regions of the world to provide a multiperspectival view.

—Melissa Wall, California State University, Northridge

Global Journalism

Global Journalism

Understanding World Media Systems

Edited by Daniela V. Dimitrova

ROWMAN & LITTLEFIELD
Lanham • Boulder • New York • London

Acquisitions Editor: Natalie Mandziuk
Assistant Acquisitions Editor: Sylvia Landis
Sales and Marketing Inquiries: textbooks@rowman.com

Credits and acknowledgments for material borrowed from other sources, and reproduced with permission, appear on the appropriate pages within the text.

Published by Rowman & Littlefield
An imprint of The Rowman & Littlefield Publishing Group, Inc.
4501 Forbes Boulevard, Suite 200, Lanham, Maryland 20706
www.rowman.com

6 Tinworth Street, London SE11 5AL, United Kingdom

British Library Cataloguing in Publication Information Available

Library of Congress Cataloging-in-Publication Data

ISBN: 978-1-5381-4684-2 (cloth)
ISBN: 978-1-5381-4685-9 (paperback)
ISBN: 978-1-5381-4686-6 (electronic)

To Journalists Worldwide

Contents

Acknowledgments

A book is by default a group effort. This is especially true for edited volumes. Simply put, this book would not exist without the twenty-one amazing chapter authors who contributed their expertise, time, and energy to this book project. They come from twelve different countries, representing a diverse set of institutions and educational backgrounds. I would like to thank each and every one of them for their exceptional contributions and professionalism working on the book during a global pandemic.

The book took shape during several AEJMC conventions, in conversations with expert editor Elizabeth Swayze, now Senior Editor at MIT Press. Elizabeth not only saw potential in this book project, but enthusiastically endorsed it and convinced me to give it a go. Recognition is also due to my current editor at Roman & Littlefield—Natalie Mandzuik—who supported the endeavor with prompt feedback and expert advice from the draft manuscript stage to proofs and production. Her editorial assistant Sylvia Landis offered technical and logistical assistance as part of the R&L publishing team.

Two people at my institution, Iowa State University, deserve special recognition: Dr. Michael Bugeja, Distinguished Professor at the Greenlee School of Journalism and Communication, whose mentorship and support as well as vast book publishing experience was instrumental in the creation of this book; and Dr. Dianne Bystrom, Director Emerita of the Catt Center for Women and Politics, whose assistance during the final stages of book completion was invaluable.

I also wish to recognize Claudia Kozman, a colleague, friend, and chapter contributor from Lebanese American University who joined the book project early on. Claudia not only provided valuable input as a content expert but also raised questions and served as a sounding board as the book progressed, thus shaping the structure and content of the final version.

The majority of this book was completed during my sabbatical at the University of Vienna, where my host University Professor Dr. Jörg Matthes provided a welcoming work environment. University Professor Dr. Roland Burkart and Dr. Petra Herczeg also deserve special recognition for making my stay both productive and enjoyable. Iowa State University and the Greenlee School of Journalism and Communication made the sabbatical possible. Partial support for the publication of this book was provided by the ISU Foundation through the Iowa State University Publication Endowment.

It is a bit of a cliché to say thanks to one's family, but the truth is this book would not have been possible without them. My parents Velichka and Veselin instilled in me love for books at an early age and always supported my educational endeavors, even when those took me far away from them. And a big thank you to the boys in my life—Alexander and Philip—who provided a loving and supportive environment to do my work across cities, countries, and continents. They remain my grounding and inspiration.

Preface

This book is a collaborative effort that provides an overview of the key concepts, media developments, and pertinent issues in global journalism. My own research on global journalism topics has examined media coverage of political issues and events such as the Iraq War, the Syrian refugee crisis, national elections, and global migration across countries and regions. It was always fascinating to see how the same news event would be covered differently—or not covered at all—in global media outlets, which begged the question: Why? Finding answers to this question became one of the main motivations for this book.

Two other concerns guided the structure and content of the book. One was the frequently cited criticism that existing publications and communication scholarship, in general, are based on Western theoretical and epistemological perspectives. To avoid such ethnocentrism, special care was taken to invite contributors who are not only established experts in their scholarly areas but could also infuse the book with a global outlook. To this end, the book features contributions from twenty-two chapter authors representing twelve countries. The other issue was the explosive growth of new communication technologies. Simply put, the significance of social media and other communication platforms—from Telegram to Weibo—cannot be overstated. Therefore, technological change and its impact on all aspects of global journalism are interwoven throughout the book.

A basic premise in this book is that there is no ideal media system. While it may be easy to see the media in dichotomous terms—free versus censored, open versus closed, one-sided versus diverse, or objective versus subjective, the book cautions against simple generalizations. Global media systems range from tightly controlled authoritarian systems to highly liberal systems with no media restrictions, with most countries being somewhere in between. We see examples of media being used as propaganda tools or as vehicles for promoting national development, political stability, national cohesion, or economic growth, often at the expense of media freedom. Other countries encourage a marketplace of ideas and place little restrictions on commercial media, which may lead to sensational and entertainment content at the expense of public service news and information. The "right balance" between media freedom and media responsibility changes over time and is determined by the specific sociocultural environment.

A noteworthy feature of the book is the inclusion of timely case studies. These include the killing of journalists at the satirical magazine *Charlie Hebdo* by religious extremists in France and the murder of Ján Kuciak for mafia investigations in Slovakia, both of which show that journalism remains a dangerous profession. Also featured are case studies about social media and the Arab Spring, the Facebook-Cambridge Analytica data scandal, cultural imperialism and Japanese cartoons, and the media's role in global health pandemics. The spread of disinformation through Russian troll factories and the use of social media channels by political populists to disseminate "fake news" are also highlighted as case studies.

It is important to remember the primary audience of the book. While the text is informed by the latest scholarly research on global journalism, it provides accessible content geared toward upper-level undergraduate and post-graduate students. Thus, the book is intended to serve as an all-encompassing textbook for courses on global journalism, international communication, world media systems, foreign news reporting, global communication, and media and globalization. A number of features have been added to assist with learning the material. These include succinct chapter summaries, discussion questions at the end of each chapter, case studies in separate callout sections as well as regional maps and other visuals where appropriate. A comprehensive bibliography in each chapter also allows for further exploration of any topic, theory, or case. Lastly, the book cautions against cultural relativism or judging another country's media based on one's own perspective.

The book is structured in three parts. The introductory chapter summarizes the dominant theoretical models that guide our understanding of global media, from the classic Four Theories of the Press to more nuanced media models. The introductory chapter also establishes a framework for the study of world media systems that builds upon previous research and positions each national media system as embedded within a distinct macro-level context that both enables and constrains how media function. The framework includes the following factors: the economy and level of economic development; political system, media policy, and government factors; existing technology and infrastructure; cultural characteristics such as language and cultural norms; and journalism characteristics such as journalistic autonomy and level of professionalization. This framework demonstrates that media institutions and practices are impacted by these factors simultaneously and that they evolve over time. It offers an easily accessible visual model to contextualize media differences across nations and provide consistency across the book chapters.

The book's first part—**Key Concepts**—addresses the foundational concepts in global journalism. Starting with global news flows, chapter 2 by Elad Segev traces the historical imbalances in information and communication between the global North and the global South, highlighting the importance of the MacBride Commission report and the New World Information and Communication Order recommended by the commission. Using sophisticated online search data analysis, the chapter outlines the similarities and changes in international news flow in today's digital age. It shows that there are more opportunities for people from geographically or culturally closer countries to get information about each other and that the dominance of more powerful countries—while undermined by social media—is still an issue.

Chapter 3 delves into the critical role of technology in global journalism and communication, which has become increasingly important for both media producers and media consumers around the world. Denis Wu offers a comprehensive look at current phenomena such as misinformation, disinformation, and post-truth public diplomacy. The author emphasizes that, in this day and age, our awareness and understanding of what happens in foreign places is largely dependent on communication technologies. The chapter also includes a poignant case study of the Facebook-Cambridge Analytica data scandal.

Chapter 4 by Jane Whyatt discusses the many challenges and threats to media freedom around the world—not only in the so-called developing nations but also across Europe and North America. She presents global statistics from organizations such as the Freedom House, the Committee to Protect Journalists, and Reporters without Borders to illustrate that journalism remains a dangerous profession. The powerful case study about the murder of Slovakian investigative journalist Ján Kuciak offers a chilling example of what can happen in a European Union (EU) nation in the twenty-first century. The chapter ends with a call to heed the warning signs and act on them early on rather than wait for more memorials to murdered journalists around the world.

In chapter 5, Patric Raemy and Lea Hellmueller offer a critical perspective on defining and measuring global journalistic cultures. The chapter includes current examples of journalistic perceptions in widely different countries—from China to Switzerland and Tanzania to the United States. It raises questions about how individual journalists negotiate their institutional and organizational roles vis-à-vis their personal identity. The chapter concludes that journalistic culture goes beyond survey ratings of professional norms and journalistic role performance.

The next chapter shifts the focus to global journalism education. In chapter 6, Tudor Vlad offers a thorough overview of media education in different world regions, contrasting two main models: the so-called Missouri model and the Wisconsin model. The former model focuses on teaching applied skills while the latter emphasizes introducing students to conceptual knowledge. This tension between applied journalistic skills versus conceptual understanding of phenomena has manifested itself across universities around the world. The chapter stresses that the two models are not mutually exclusive and have evolved to embrace advertising and public relations, in addition to journalism, and adapt to the dramatic technological changes in the media industry.

From global journalism education, we shift gears to journalistic ethics and responsibilities. In chapter 7, Katerina Tsetsura and Dean Kruckeberg provide a rigorous review of the underlying dimensions of journalism ethics in the twenty-first century. They argue that navigating the uncharted waters of journalistic responsibilities is especially challenging in the Information Age and that technological change has put the relevance of the journalistic profession on the line. The chapter concludes that the role of professional journalists in the digital era may be to digest, condense, and evaluate vast amounts of information for the public, rather than simply present raw facts.

The second part of the book—**World Regions**—takes the reader on a journey around the globe. Chapters 8 through 14 feature discussions of current trends in journalism practice and media use across seven world regions. These chapters offer insights into the main factors that affect media development around the world, utilizing the macrolevel framework outlined in chapter 1.

Starting with sub-Saharan Africa in chapter 8, Yusuf Kalyango traces the evolution of journalism as an institution during the postcolonial transition in the region where the practice of muzzling the press to tow state propaganda was widespread. The changing political and economic environment as well as the infusion of communication technologies has liberalized sub-Saharan media. The chapter examines both traditional media platforms such as terrestrial television, radio, newspapers, and magazines and contemporary digital media and social media platforms. A case study about the role of news media during global health pandemics is especially relevant in the COVID-19 era.

Chapter 9 examines the media in the Middle East and North Africa—the so-called MENA region. Claudia Kozman provides a detailed overview of how the interplay of different macro-level factors has shaped Arab journalism. Far from being a homogenous region, MENA encompasses different types of governments as well as different perceptions of media roles. Political conflict and consolidation of power, in addition to Arab identity, are particularly influential in journalism practice in the region. The chapter ends with an interesting case study about the media's role during the Arab Spring.

Another diverse region with shared historical roots is Central and Eastern Europe. In chapter 10, Ioana Coman and Christopher Karadjov position journalism as part of the overall post-communist transition. Political liberalization and commercial expansion, in addition to dramatic changes in journalism education, have led to uneven media practices. Some resemble the *authoritarian* media model while others fit under the *liberal* media model with unfettered freedom, political autonomy, and economic sustainability. The chapter illustrates the vulnerability of media outlets at the hands of authoritarian rulers who may choose to stop state funds or introduce legislation to limit media freedom. A case study about the spread of "fake news" and disinformation campaigns orchestrated by Russian troll factories shows the dark side of social media.

Moving from Central and Eastern Europe to the media in Western and Northern Europe, Elisabeth Fondren underscores the importance of the EU to understanding journalism in the region. In chapter 11, she positions the media in this region as primarily falling under the *democratic corporatist* and *polarized pluralist* media models. Individual idiosyncrasies notwithstanding, the countries in this region have experienced turmoil as a result of global migration. This has presented challenges to media institutions and has resulted in threats and even the murder of journalists, as the cases of the Muhammad cartoons controversy in Denmark and the *Charlie Hebdo* satirical magazine in France demonstrate.

The push and pull of globalization are also evident in Asia and the Pacific. In chapter 12, Namho Kim fittingly observes that a key concept to understanding media in the region is the notion of developmental journalism, which sees journalism as a vehicle to facilitate national development. That means economic growth, political stability, or the promotion of Asian values are commonly used as justifications of state interference and government control across the region. The chapter stresses the importance of online platforms for boosting investigative journalism efforts and citizen-driven alternative journalism. The spread of Japanese Manga comics worldwide provides an illustrative case study about the concept of cultural imperialism.

Chapter 13 focuses on media developments in Latin America. As Manuel Alejandro Guerrero aptly articulates, Latin America is a land of contrasts, not only because of its rich geographic diversity but also because of stark economic inequalities where liberal democracies exist alongside authoritarian countries. The region as a whole also remains one of the most dangerous for journalists who are often threatened by organized crime or by corrupt government officials. Politicians across the region do not shy away from suing journalists; they also tend to withdraw state funds or, in some cases, refuse to protect journalists who are perceived to be too critical of the government. While it is hard to generalize, the best fit for the media in the region might be a blended *captured liberal* media model.

The last chapter of Part II zooms in on media developments in North America, focusing on Canada and the United States. Zac Gershberg and D. Jasun Carr show that while historically the media in the region have been prototypical examples of the *liberal* media model, they have incorporated elements of the *polarized pluralist* media model in recent years. Nevertheless, media freedom has remained a core feature of journalism in both countries. Two major challenges for traditional media organizations have been economic consolidation and technological change. The growth of social media and the declining credibility of legacy media outlets are also germane. Existing concerns about the use of social media by populist politicians are summarized in the chapter case study.

Part III of the book—**Current Issues**—addresses important topics that have deeply affected media audiences on a global scale. In chapter 15, Terhi Rantanen and Anthony Kelly trace the evolution and transformation of global news agencies from the so-called Big Five to today. These organizations have had to grapple with technological globalization and resulting financial challenges, propelling diversification of their operations—although their ownership and type of governance have not changed. As representatives of institutional journalism, global news agencies have shown resistance to change despite new developments in society at large. The chapter concludes that global and national news agencies need to continue to adapt in order to stay competitive and remain viable as information sources to global audiences.

Another important consideration from the perspective of global audience members is the coverage of international news. Foreign correspondence is the focus of chapter 16 by Raluca Cozma. She traces the evolution of foreign correspondence from its golden age with Edward R. Murrow to today. The chapter shows that international news coverage has declined steadily since the end of the Cold War, with media organizations grappling with declining budgets and staff to cover what happens in other parts of the world. Not surprisingly, interest in foreign news tends to spike during international crises such as military conflicts and natural disasters. Cozma cautions against stereotypical coverage, which tends to favor elite sources and episodic framing of events, both of which ultimately affect how people around the world perceive other nations. The chapter incorporates an instructive case study of the news coverage of the Syrian civil war.

The last chapter in the book, chapter 17, focuses on public diplomacy and international communication. Offering a comprehensive definition of what public diplomacy is, Suman Lee underscores the importance of soft power in today's global world. He uses the COVID-19 global pandemic as a backdrop to discuss China's public diplomacy efforts as well as Japan's handling of the Tokyo Olympics. The chapter argues that it takes a long time to build a strong national reputation, but a very short time to undermine it. Digital channels have made public diplomacy efforts more important and more elusive at the same time, showing the intricacies of maintaining soft power and retaining a nation's positive image among the world publics.

Taken together, the chapters in this book provide a significant contribution to scholars, students, and practitioners interested in global journalism. The book offers a thorough overview of media developments in all world regions, capturing their unique political, cultural, and economic context as well as the role of journalistic factors and technological change across media industries. This makes it a valuable resource for anyone interested in learning about the practice, growth, and impact of global media.

Daniela V. Dimitrova
January 2021

1

A Framework for the Study of Global Media Systems

Daniela V. Dimitrova

This chapter proposes a framework for the study of global media systems by combining different media models, starting with the classic Four Theories of the Press by Siebert, Peterson, and Schramm to Hallin and Mancini's pivotal work about differences in national media systems in the Western world and more nuanced global media typologies that have recently emerged in the literature. Contextual factors in terms of economic system, political system characteristics, technology and infrastructure, as well as cultural differences that affect journalism at the national level, are explained along with journalistic factors such as journalistic autonomy and professionalization. This chapter concludes with the notion that global media systems are intricately embedded within their specific socioeconomic context and range from very authoritarian at the one end to very liberal on the other. Students and scholars are reminded that global media systems should be evaluated from a local perspective, avoiding cultural relativism, and need to take into account regional idiosyncrasies and historical trends.

DEFINING GLOBAL JOURNALISM AND MEDIA SYSTEMS

The notion of global journalism is relatively new since the concept itself emerged in conjunction with the process of globalization. As such, we can trace the term "global journalism" to the twenty-first century, following its precursor "international journalism." These terms are sometimes used interchangeably, although international journalism generally refers to foreign news reporting while the term global journalism is linked to the borderless nature of media production and consumption in the era of globalization. Berglez (2008, p. 845) notes that the concept of global journalism "transgresses and transcends the traditional domestic-foreign dichotomy" and acknowledges that the term remains elusive and hard to define. For this book, we define global journalism as *journalism produced within a specific media system, which is typically a national-level media system, embedded within a regional and global network.*

Despite the existence of a diverse set of global media systems, there is no single, clearly defined framework that allows us to categorize the media system in every single country. There are existing models and theoretical frameworks, however, that can help us categorize and better understand how the media differ between countries across different world regions. Some of these theories are normative—they tell us how journalism should be. Other theories are non-normative and focus on observations of how media operate within a society (McQuail, 2005).

A systems perspective is especially useful to the study of global media since it allows us to understand how different contextual elements affect the media in any nation as well as compare different media systems across nations and across time. Seethaler (2017, para. 1) defines media systems as "a set of media institutions and practices that interact with and shape one another" and identifies two general approaches to the study of media systems, as follows:

> normative-critical approaches, which aim at generalizing particular concepts of how media systems should function within society, and . . . analytical approaches, which attempt to explain the emergence of and changes to media structures and institutions and their impact on media performance and audience behavior.

Rooted in sociology, media dependency theory posits that a country's media system is dependent upon other social systems while, at the same time, itself affecting those systems (Ball-Rokeach & DeFleur, 1979). Ball-Rokeach and DeFleur (1979) establish that media systems at the macro level are dependent upon two main systems—the economic and political system—in addition to what they term secondary systems such as educational and religious systems. Similarly, Hallin (2016) sees media systems as "embedded within wider social, political, economic, and cultural systems." Guerrero and Márquez-Ramírez (2014) emphasize the importance of commercialism and marketization, in addition to communication policies, as key. Applying a macro-level approach to the Internet era, technological factors have also emerged as critical for media development (Dimitrova, 2003).

This chapter proposes a framework that builds upon previous research and utilizes a functionalist approach that positions the media as part of a larger social system. Building on the core principles of previous models, it aims to present a comprehensive, multidimensional model that captures the effects of several macro-level factors simultaneously, while acknowledging that additional elements may be at play at the micro level. This type of approach is fluid and enables scholars to determine relationships between systems while, at the same time, identifying regional patterns.

At a most basic level, the world's media systems can be arranged on a continuum from most restrictive to most open. They range from strictly authoritarian and monolithic to libertarian and pluralistic. Focusing on the political system, Benson (2008, p. 2592) astutely observes that "there are as many normative theories of journalism as there are political systems, from Marxism—Leninism to diverse conceptions of democracy." It is clear from these examples that a nation's political system exerts paramount influence on the national media system. Another way to classify media within a specific country is by evaluating its rankings on a global media freedom scale and then compare that to the existing levels of media responsibility. While some countries, particularly in the Western world, prioritize journalistic freedom, others put an emphasis on media ethics and social responsibility, which tends to be more common among consolidated democracies. In developing nations, another approach called developmental journalism, which emphasizes social, political, and economic development, has predominated.

Although scholars acknowledge that all theories are artificial constructs to a certain degree, they underscore the importance of theory for understanding journalism practice around the world. One of the cornerstone theoretical models that guide our conception of global media systems is the so-called Four Theories of the Press.

THE FOUR THEORIES OF THE PRESS

In 1956, Siebert, Peterson, and Schramm published the now widely cited and frequently criticized book titled *Four Theories of the Press: The Authoritarian, Libertarian, Social Responsibility, and Soviet Communist Concepts of What the Press Should Be and Do*. This was the most systematic classification of world media systems at that time and, not surprisingly, journalism and mass communication professors often use this classification as reference points for any scholarly discussion of global journalism (see Nerone, 2002).

Under the Authoritarian Theory of the press, according to Siebert, Peterson, and Schramm (1956), the state has direct control of the country's media and nothing that undermines the state's ideology can be published or aired. Although the media can be privately owned under this system, criticism of the government or its supreme leader is not allowed. Different forms of media control exist in such a press model—for example, licensing of the media organizations, strict libel laws, and resulting self-censorship. Under these conditions, journalists tend to be part of society's elite and lapdog loyalty is expected from them by the state. This theory was seen as "most pervasive both historically and geographically" at the time of writing (1956).

At the other end of the spectrum is the Libertarian Theory. Freedom of the press is a key characteristic of that media system. Journalists have complete autonomy from the state and tend to perceive themselves as a watchdog of the government and those in power. Therefore, criticism of the state and its representatives is encouraged and journalists are expected to keep the government accountable. The U.S. First Amendment is a quintessential example of how media freedom is perceived and valued under a libertarian media system. Other key characteristics of such a media system include marketplace competition and objective reporting, and the media is touted as the Fourth Estate.

At the time Siebert, Peterson, and Schramm proposed their categorization—back in 1956—the Cold War was still in full swing. It is not surprising then that they included a Soviet Communist Theory of the press. Under this system, the communist government owns the media and the goal of journalism is not commercial success, but rather promoting Marxist–Leninist ideology. All media are public and the media as an institution carries an educational and propagandistic role, serving as a collective agitator and a guard dog for dominant ideology. Simply put, media organizations are used as a megaphone for distributing and amplifying communist party ideas and policies.

The fourth theory of the press is the Social Responsibility Theory. It emerged in the aftermath of the findings of the *Commission on Freedom of the Press*, also known as the Hutchins Commission (1947), which showed that mass media have become subservient to big business and are resistant to social change (McQuail, 2005). This model is very similar to the Libertarian press model, but emphasizes the media's responsibility to provide objective and balanced news coverage through self-regulation. Journalistic codes of ethics and other professional standards are developed to ensure the media address public concerns and offer a representative picture of a diverse society, giving the public sufficient information to make informed decisions. The model underscores that the media are accountable to the public and places value on journalistic responsibility rather than media freedom.

Each of the classic press theories is implicitly based on four common principles of normative media theory, as follows: (1) freedom, (2) diversity, (3) truth, and (4) social or cultural order. As McQuail (2005) notes, each principle is relatively more or less important under different press models.

Shortcomings of the Four Theories of the Press

The Four Theories of the Press have faced much criticism. As normative theories, they are based on how things should be in an ideal press model and do not necessarily reflect how media operate in practice. Additionally, they lack explanatory power and appear to be valid for a limited period. Especially with the end of the Cold War, the Soviet Communist press model has limited applicability and perhaps can be seen as a specific sub-category of the Authoritarian Press model.

A good theory is simple, yet complex enough to be fruitful. Some have argued that the four press models proposed by Siebert, Peterson, and Schramm back in 1956 are too simplistic to be particularly useful (Nerone, 2002). They focus primarily on news and information rather than other kinds of media content (Downing, 2020). Furthermore, the typology carries an implicit bias toward the Libertarian and Social Responsibility models and implies that they are more desirable. An objective categorization, however, should not favor one specific system. Thus, the Four Theories of the Press reveal a Western bias.

Lastly, since the focus is on the political system, the agency of the audience or the individual journalist is missing from the categorization. As Ostini and Fung (2018) argue, journalism should be viewed as a "relatively autonomous" cultural production dependent on both the journalistic level of professionalization and the level of state control. Therefore, journalistic autonomy, while constrained in itself by the contextual political system and existing media policies in the country, still plays an important role.

Despite its many criticisms, the Four Theories of the Press remain a useful and trendsetting taxonomy and a reference point for research and scholarly investigations of media worldwide (Seethaler, 2017), and their core principles should be understood by journalism students and future media professionals.

DEVELOPMENT MEDIA THEORY

Some authors have argued that, for developing nations, a different type of media model is most applicable. Sometimes dubbed the fifth theory of the press, the so-called Development Media Theory is employed in nations with lower levels of economic development, which are typically located in the global South (McQuail & Deuze, 2020). The purpose of the media under this model, simply put, is to aid national development. Improving economic conditions and facilitating the political and social development of the nation is of higher value than media freedom. Radio campaigns against the spread of HIV/AIDS in Africa are given as typical examples.

This media model can be seen as part of the so-called Development Communication approach advocated by organizations such as the World Bank and USAID. Development communication focuses on social transformation and economic development, where meeting the basic needs of the local population is of utmost importance. While the media are important tools for development, this approach also incorporates information dissemination in the areas of health, agriculture, and education, and relies on social mobilization and community participation, enabled through both the media and interpersonal channels. Other terms used under this umbrella include Developmental Journalism and Communication for Development (C4D). The focus of C4D is on empowering the local community to take care of their needs and the media as a whole are conceived as "magic multipliers" that can not only facilitate but also accelerate development (Servaes, 2002, p. 4). Under the Development Media Theory, journalistic freedom can be restricted and media can be sanctioned by the government in the name of national development.

DEMOCRATIC-PARTICIPANT MEDIA THEORY

A sixth theory called the Democratic-Participant Media Theory has been added to the existing media models (McQuail, 2005). This theory juxtaposes top–down traditional media institutions with flatter, non-hierarchical, and smaller-scale media operations. Community media that offer local information and enable participation, social action, and two-way communication between producers and consumers are preferred (Downing, 2020). Under this theory, the media are pluralistic and decentralized and encourage ground-up participation.

Community-run radio stations or local public access TV channels are good examples of this approach. Some see mobile technology and interactive communication tools as fulfilling such a democratic participation function in less-developed countries. The emphasis is on giving equal and unhindered access to information to all individuals regardless of their status and wealth. The Democratic-Participant Media Theory advocates for cultural pluralism and encourages citizen participation in community affairs.

THREE MODELS OF MEDIA AND POLITICS IN WESTERN EUROPE AND NORTH AMERICA

Another well-established typology comes from Hallin and Mancini's (2004) work, which proposed three models of media and politics based on the characteristics of eighteen countries located in Western Europe and North America. They ranked those countries on four dimensions, as follows: (1) media commercialization and market circulation; (2) government/state intervention; (3) journalism professionalization; and (4) political parallelism. Based on similarities along these four dimensions, they grouped the countries into three models, as follows:

The Polarized Pluralist Model of media and politics is typical across the Mediterranean region and is characterized by a press with limited circulation that is oriented toward society's elite. In this type of media system, advocacy journalism is common and journalists feel they need to take a stand so journalism and political activism may mix as a result. The state can be an owner and regulator of the media and centralized broadcast electronic media is common, especially historically. Typical examples of the Polarized Pluralist Model include Southern European nations, such as France, Greece, Italy, Portugal, and Spain.

The Democratic Corporatist Model is common for North/Central European nations and is characterized by strong professionalization of journalism and emphasis on neutral journalism. The countries with such a media model tend to have high levels of media freedom and well-established journalistic organizations with strong professional boards and codes of ethics. Countries such as Austria, Belgium, Denmark, Germany, Switzerland, and the Scandinavian nations are prototypical examples of this media model.

Lastly, Hallin and Mancini (2004) propose the Liberal Model of media and politics as quintessential for the North Atlantic region. High, well-established media freedom is characteristic of this model. Commercialism dominates and there is a clear emphasis on information and news reporting rather than advocacy. High level of professionalization among journalists is also typical while, at the same time, featuring low-level of organization among media professionals. Countries that fall under the Liberal model include Canada, Great Britain, Ireland, and the United States.

Criticisms of Hallin and Mancini's typology have emerged, the main one being that the three models have a Western focus, raising questions about their applicability to other world regions. Furthermore, the models are based on observation and empirical data rather than theory so scholars have also questioned the ability of this framework to predict media behavior in the future. Several attempts have been made to extend the Three Models of Media and Politics beyond Western Europe and North America—for example, to Eastern Europe or newly established democracies (Hallin & Mancini, 2011). Such attempts have shown the challenges of applying this framework beyond the Western world. For instance, Dobek-Ostrowska (2015) combined different elements to describe media in post-communist countries: the Hybrid Liberal, the Politicized Media, the Media in Transition, and the Authoritarian, observing that only parts of existing typologies may be relevant in the region. Others have noted that Hallin and Mancini's models may need to be adapted for transitional democracies (Voltmer, 2013) or specific regions such as Latin America (Guerrero & Márquez-Ramírez, 2014). Scholars have also observed that the models may converge over time within a specific country, arguing for a Polarized Liberal model for contemporary U.S. news media, for instance (Nechushtai, 2018).

OTHER MODELS OF GLOBAL MEDIA SYSTEMS

Other frameworks for understanding journalism practice around the world have been developed and proposed. The *Worlds of Journalism* study, for example, emphasizes the question of how journalists in different countries perceive their professional roles and responsibilities (Hanitzsch, Hanusch, Ramaprasad, & De Beer, 2019). Based on standardized surveys with journalists, they show that individual perceptions differ widely across nations.

Another typology relies on two dimensions of media freedom—state intervention and media mission (Meyen, 2017). The typology incorporates concepts such as patriotism, clientelism, and cartelism to the study of media systems, resulting in classifying a diverse set of countries such as Turkey, Japan, and Mexico under the same group. Others have tried to distinguish between individual and cultural characteristics, on the one hand, and institutional and country-level factors, on the other, as determinants of journalism practice (Hanitzsch & Vos, 2017). Most of these models acknowledge the need to take into account the national context and include a range of system-level factors in order to understand how media professionals do their jobs (Raemy, 2020).

IMPORTANCE OF CONTEXT

The media as an institution does not exist in a vacuum—the context surrounding the media in any country is of vital importance. Hence, it is imperative to position journalism in the national context where journalists operate and where media organizations function within specific boundaries. As we will trace later in the book, each country's media are bound by macro-level factors, which include but are not limited to political factors, economy, culture, and technology and infrastructure. These are coupled with journalistic factors such as journalistic autonomy and level of professionalization. The interplay between these factors exerts a critical influence when it comes to media development, as demonstrated in the following section.

Students and scholars are reminded that global media systems should be evaluated from a local perspective and need to take into account regional idiosyncrasies and historical trends. For example, a country in the Middle East may rank low on media freedom when compared to a Western European nation; however, that same country could have increased its media freedom index over time. Local journalists may also aspire to keep the government accountable, despite existing constraints. Reverse trends are also possible, as recent cases of infringing on journalistic freedom across Europe, highlighted in the following chapters, show. Among them, the murder of Maltese journalist Daphne Galizia stands out. She was uncovering corruption at the highest levels of government and her murder investigation was stalled. It is important not to use one country's "measuring stick" when judging another; in other words, it is essential to avoid the danger of cultural relativism and resist the temptation of evaluating another country's media from the perspective of one's own culture. Rather, we should take into account the local cultural context and compare the current media situation relative to historical trends.

DETERMINANTS OF NATIONAL MEDIA DEVELOPMENT

When discussing media development around the world, we include all means of communication such as newspapers and magazines, radio, television, satellite, Internet and online media, books, movies, and other types of media that transmit information and entertainment to (mass) audiences. As suggested in the previous section, multiple factors influence media development in any country. Some authors call these factors determinants of media development, while others use the term "barriers" or "antecedents." Combining existing theories and models, several of these determinants are used to develop a multidimensional macro-level framework (Ball-Rokeach & DeFleur, 1979; Dimitrova, 2003; Guerrero & Márquez-Ramírez, 2014; Hallin, 2016). The proposed framework includes five contextual factors that can be utilized to explain as well as predict the development of global media systems. Figure 1.1 illustrates the proposed framework and its components. Media development encompasses existing journalistic practices and the diversity, quantity, and quality of media within a nation.

Political System and Government Factors

As the models reviewed above show, political factors exert a significant influence on journalism in any country. The type of political system, level of government control over the media, as well as existing media laws and regulations inadvertently affect journalistic practices and routines (Dimitrova & Kostadinova, 2013). Restrictive governments around the world use legal tools such as libel laws, licensing of outlets, or direct media censorship to punish specific media outlets and journalists who criticize the government. In Latin America, for example, libel laws protect government officials from media criticism. Laws can also facilitate journalistic reporting. In the United States, several states such as Florida, for instance, have adopted the so-called *sunshine* laws that require official records to be made public.

Autocratic rulers around the world try to stifle media freedom. A notorious case from the Philippines is the trial of Maria Reza who was arrested on "cyber libel" charges as a result of being critical of Duterte's government in her online publication *Rappler*. The United Nations High Commissioner for Human Rights observed that Reza's arrest illustrates a consistent

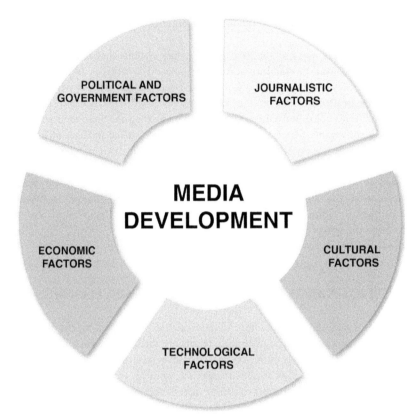

Figure 1.1.   Macro-level factors that influence a nation's media development

pattern of government intimidation of Philippine media, which ranks 136th out of 180 countries according to the Reporters Without Borders rankings (Ratcliffe, 2020).

Politicians can put pressure on journalists directly or indirectly. Recent trends in Central and Eastern Europe, for example, show that journalistic independence is under threat across this region. In Hungary, Viktor Orbán's government has been gradually and consistently trying to stifle critical journalism. In Slovakia, the murder of investigative journalist Ján Kuciak and his fiancée represents a sad example of the dangers journalists who investigate corruption and organized crime still face. Lack of protection for media practitioners facing intimidation and death threats are among the tools used by repressive governments. Other tactics of government control include limiting media access, tax investigations, travel restrictions, and even jail. Accusations of "fake media" are another strategy utilized by populist politicians around the world.

The relationship between political control and media freedom is not so simple or clear-cut, however. Research has shown that some advanced democratic societies have government-controlled media while some autocratic regimes tend to have relatively free media (Whitten-Woodring, 2009). Such examples underscore the fact that additional factors beyond political system or government type influence media behavior within a nation. According to the Freedom House (2019), almost 80 percent of Hungarian media are owned by government allies, which shows that politics and economics are often intertwined.

Economic Factors

Multiple economic factors play a role when it comes to media development. Economic pressures on journalists, especially those with low wages, may make them more susceptible to financial "favors" offered by outside companies or powerful elite. In some countries, it is not uncommon to purchase favorable coverage directly from the media outlet. According to Barboza (2012), getting a profile of a chief executive in the Chinese version of Esquire costs about $20,000 a page while appearing on the state-run China Central Television costs $4,000 a minute. This type of prepaid "soft news" is not uncommon in other parts of Asia as well.

Media outlets in a free market system are heavily dependent on advertising. Thus, large corporations may use the threat of withdrawing advertising revenue to influence editorial decisions. Such cases happen not only in developing nations but also in well-established democracies. Media conglomerates can also stifle airing certain types of stories. In the United States, for example, ABC News has been criticized for not covering and even withdrawing unfavorable coverage of their parent company, Disney, although direct censorship has been denied by both organizations (Davis & Stark, 2001). Nevertheless, the possibility of self-censorship remains high because of economic dependency.

Journalists across many world regions face rising job insecurity as well as increasing media consolidation and concentration of ownership. Transnational media conglomerates, which are financially stronger, may enter a local media market and push independent outlets out of business. Sometimes, truly independent media can only afford to exist in an online format. Some examples, according to the Committee to Protect Journalists (2020), include investigative journalism outlets such as bivol.bg in Bulgaria, madamasr.com in Egypt, Revista Factum in El Salvador, and slidstvo.info in Ukraine. These types of media outlets often investigate government corruption and have experienced harassment and multiple attempts to be shut down by the government and/or by organized crime groups.

Commercial pressures and competition among media to reach more "eyeballs" may also lead to more entertainment-focused content rather than news. Reality TV shows and soap operas have gained popularity across continents, from Latin American *telenovelas* to Bollywood *masala* movies. Global media empires such as News Corp. dominate the world media landscape and continue to bring in increasing revenues. The impact of such Transnational Corporations (TNCs) on both local media and local audiences is explored further in this book.

Technological Factors

The growth of digital media and online communication around the world has been unprecedented. Digital technologies and social media networks have truly changed how people communicate with each other and also dramatically affected the media industry in multiple ways, as discussed throughout this book. Global technological advancements, however, have been uneven within and across regions. Recent statistics show that the gap in Internet access and use of online technologies—the so-called digital divide—remains stark. Nevertheless, the Internet has made information available to more people in more corners of the world than ever before and has been seen as a lifeline during crises.

One such crisis resulted from the quick spread of the COVID-19 virus around the world in 2020, which made the World Health Organization classify it as a global pandemic. Communication technologies played a critical role during the pandemic. First, online platforms allowed quick access to information when traditional media, such as newspapers, faced significant challenges in terms of access and physical delivery during the period of social isolation. Online media offered constant updates and were regularly used by the public to get news and share the latest information about the virus (Iwai, 2020). Perhaps more importantly, social media enabled individuals to stay connected with family members and communities and better cope with self-distancing and quarantine.

At the same time, the COVID-19 crisis also showed the challenges with online information when it comes to spreading fake news and misinformation on social media, sometimes making it hard to distinguish trustworthy sources (Iwai, 2020). Without critical thinking or verification of information, some people shared unproven "tips" and quick "solutions" that downplayed the severity of the crisis. This example shows that when it comes to technology, human capital and digital literacy skills are critical. That is why international organizations such as UNESCO have developed lengthy guides and tutorials about detecting disinformation (Ireton & Posetti, 2018). The COVID-19 pandemic also reinforced the need for trustworthy news sources and the value of traditional media, with online news sites as well as television news seeing a surge in audience attention during the pandemic.

Lack of infrastructure and the cost of Internet access present additional barriers to media development. There are countries around the world where the Internet is not easily accessible or has been blocked for political reasons. Countries such as China and Ukraine, for instance, see the Internet as a political threat. As a result, sophisticated digital tracking and screening technologies have been developed to monitor public expression online. Even large multinational companies such as Google and Facebook have agreed to screen their content and block certain types of information from their sites in certain countries.

Cultural Factors

Perhaps most obvious and also most easy to overlook is the role of cultural factors in media development. Broadly defined, culture refers to the underlying social norms, values, traditions, and beliefs that exist in any society. These include language, religion, customs, and other social norms that guide social behavior. Needless to say, cultural barriers are difficult to overcome since they are ingrained in the fabric of society and have been established over long periods.

When it comes to media development, social mores make certain topics or subjects less acceptable in different cultures. The type of media content that is considered acceptable in Amsterdam may be widely different from the content considered acceptable in Riyadh, for example. Walking down the streets of Sofia one may see a lot of sensational headlines and nudity openly displayed on newspaper kiosks. This may not happen on the streets of Cairo, however.

In addition to cultural norms, language is another barrier to media development. Many societies across Africa, for example, are multilingual. That presents clear challenges for media communicators. This is the case not only in Africa but also in several Asian and European nations. Belgium and Switzerland represent two examples where media content is offered and consumed in multiple languages. Another example is the city–state of Singapore, which itself has four official languages—English, Malay, Mandarin, and Tamil.

Even when a story is printed in one's native language, it won't be of much use if the person cannot read. Illiteracy remains an issue on a global scale and is especially evident in the so-called developing world. In a country such as Niger, the literacy rate is barely above 19 percent as of 2020. Compare that with Russia where the literacy rate is almost 100 percent. Literacy remains an issue in many African nations that have witnessed ethnic conflict. Interestingly, in such areas, cell phone subscription rates tend to be higher than literacy rates. According to Statista (2019), Niger has 40.63 mobile subscriptions per 100 people. Such audience characteristics open the door to online and audio–visual media, including radio and television. This example demonstrates that the same macro-level factor can be an impediment and, at the same time, facilitate media growth (Haider, Mcloughlin, & Scott, 2011).

Journalistic Factors

Journalistic factors encompass several dimensions at the institutional, organizational, and professional identity levels, such as the level of autonomy and professionalization, journalistic perceptions, professional training, and education. As you will see in the following chapters, some societies such as Sweden have developed strong professional organizations for ethical conduct and protection of journalists. Many countries around the world offer specialized journalism curricula and options for university degrees in journalism and mass communication. In countries where journalism education is lacking, organizations such as *USAID* and *Open Society* provide in-country training and workshops.

It is also important to note that, regardless of educational background, journalistic perceptions of what media's role in society should vary widely around the world. The *Worlds of Journalism* project has demonstrated how professional norms and understanding of journalism's place in society, as well as journalistic ethics and level of autonomy, differ significantly around the globe (Hanitzsch et al., 2019). Comparative analysis shows a wide range of attitudes toward journalistic duties and the nature and meaning of journalistic work. Inevitably, such differences lead to different types of media practices and journalistic performances across nations. These, coupled with organizational roles and identities, influence media development.

In addition to different perceptions, professional education and training, and level of autonomy in their work, journalists have different backgrounds in terms of race, ethnicity, and gender. Issues such as lack of diversity in the profession and concerns about social justice have become more prominent in recent years. Across U.S. newsrooms—ranging from *The Washington Post* to the *LA Times* and the *Philadelphia Inquirer*—had hard conversations about racial inequalities continue with their own "racial reckoning" (Farhi & Ellison, 2020).

CHAPTER SUMMARY

This chapter concludes with the notion that global media systems range from extreme authoritarianism on the one end to extreme libertarianism on the other end and that media are intricately embedded within their specific context. The role of contextual factors in terms of political system, economic system, technology/infrastructure, cultural differences, as well as journalism characteristics that affect media development at the national level was explained in a proposed general framework that can be used for the study of world media. In the end, it is the interplay of multiple factors that shapes world media. The proposed framework also establishes that as contextual factors change over time so does the practice of journalism around the globe.

But why does global journalism and media development around the world matter? Even more pointedly, why should you read this book? The reasons are eloquently summarized by Haider et al. (2011, p. 37):

> The media can be a powerful force for change in both developed and developing countries. In developing countries, it can have an important role in advancing a pro-poor development agenda, as well as supporting economic growth by stimulating consumer markets. Where it is able to effectively fulfill the roles of watchdog, gatekeeper and agenda-setter, it can improve governance by raising citizen awareness of social issues, enabling citizens to hold their governments to account, curbing corruption, and creating a civic forum for debate.

DISCUSSION QUESTIONS

1. What are the five main factors that influence media development?
2. Choose one of the factors and discuss how it has impacted journalism and media within a specific nation.
3. Which theory described in the chapter seems most applicable to the media in the country you live in? Provide examples to support your opinion.
4. Do you think that the Four Theories of the Press are still applicable today? Why or why not?
5. If you had to propose your own media model to explain media differences around the world, which dimensions would you include?

BIBLIOGRAPHY

Ball-Rokeach, S. J., & DeFleur, M. L. (1979). A dependency model of mass-media effects. In Gumpert, G. & Cathart, R.S. (Eds.), *Inter/Media: Interpersonal communication in a media world* (pp. 81–96). Oxford University Press.

Barboza, D. (2012, April 3). In China press, best coverage cash can buy. www.nytimes.com/2012/04/04/business/media/flattering-news-coverage-has-a-price-in-china.html

Benson, R. (2008). Journalism: Normative theories. In W. Donsbach (Ed.), *International Encyclopedia of Communication* (pp. 2591–2597). Wiley-Blackwell.

Berglez, P. (2008). What is global journalism? Theoretical and empirical conceptualisations. *Journalism Studies, 9*(6), 845–858. DOI: www.tandfonline.com/doi/abs/10.1080/14616700802337727

Committee to Protect Journalists (2020). News alerts. cpj.org/news/

Davis, M., & Stark, A. (2001). *Conflict of interest in the professions.* Oxford University Press.

Dimitrova, D.V. (2003). Internet adoption in post-communist countries: A proposed model for the study of Internet diffusion (Publication No. 3096613). [Doctoral dissertation, University of Florida]. ProQuest Dissertations & Theses Global. search.proquest.com/pqdtglobal/docview/305326167/fulltextPDF/D092EE34DA3F42E6PQ/86?accountid=10906

Dimitrova, D.V., & Kostadinova, P. (2013). Identifying antecedents of the strategic game frame: A longitudinal analysis. *Journalism & Mass Communication Quarterly, 90*(1), 75–88.

Dobek-Ostrowska, B. (2015). 25 years after communism: Four models of media and politics in Central and Eastern Europe. In Dobek-Ostrowska, B. & Głowacki, M. (Eds.), *Democracy and media in Central and Eastern Europe 25 years on* (pp.11–44). Peter Lang.

Downing, J. D. H. (2020). Drawing a bead on global communication theories. In Kamalipour, Y. R. (Ed.) *Global communication: A multicultural perspective* (pp. 56–71). Roman & Littlefield.

Freedom House (2019). *Media freedom: A downward spiral.* freedomhouse.org/report/freedom-and-media/2019/media-freedom-downward-spiral

Guerrero, M. A., & Márquez-Ramírez, M. (2014). *Media systems and communication policies in Latin America.* Palgrave Macmillan.

Haider, H., Mcloughlin, C., & Scott, Z. (2011). *Topic guide on communication and governance.* Governance and Social Development Resource Centre (GSDRC), University of Birmingham, UK. gsdrc.org/wp-content/uploads/2010/04/CommGAP2.pdf

Hallin, D. C. (2016). Typology of media systems. *Oxford Research Encyclopedias.* doi.org/10.1093/acrefore/9780190228637.013.205

Hallin, D. C., & Mancini, P. (2004). *Comparing media systems: Three models of media and politics.* Cambridge University Press.

Hallin, D. C., & Mancini, P. (2011). *Comparing media systems beyond the Western world.* Cambridge University Press.

Hanitzsch, T., Hanusch, F. Ramaprasad, J., & de Beer, A. S. (2019). *Worlds of journalism: Journalistic cultures around the globe.* Columbia University Press.

Hanitzsch, T., & Vos, T. (2017). Journalistic roles and the struggle over institutional identity: The discursive constitution of journalism. *Communication Theory, 27*(2), 115–135. DOI: doi.org/10.1111/comt.12112

Ireton, C., & Posetti, J. (2018). *Journalism, "fake News" & disinformation: Handbook for journalism education and training.* United Nations Educational, Scientific and Cultural Organization (UNESCO).

Iwai, Y. (2002, April 7). Harnessing social media for the COVID-19 pandemic campaigns such as #See10Do10 can make a sometimes frivolous way of communicating socially useful. blogs.scientific american.com/observations/harnessing-social-media-for-the-covid-19-pandemic/

Farhi, P., & Ellison, S. (2020, June 13). Ignited by public protests, American newsrooms are having their own racial reckoning. www.washingtonpost.com/lifestyle/media/ignited-by-public-protests-american-newsrooms-are-having-their-own-racial-reckoning/2020/06/12/be622bce-a995-11ea-94d2-d7bc43b26bf9_story.html

Nechushtai, E. (2018). From Liberal to Polarized Liberal? Contemporary U.S. news in Hallin and Mancini's typology of news systems. *International Journal of Press Politics, 23*(2), 183–201. DOI: doi.org/10.1177/1940161218771902

Ostini, J., & Fung, A.Y.H. (2018). Beyond the four theories of the press: A new model of national media systems. In Ran, W. (ed.), *Advances in foundational mass communication theories* (pp. 62–77). Routledge.

McQuail, D. (2005). *McQuail's mass communication theory* (5th ed.). Sage.

McQuail, D., & Deuze, M. (2020). *McQuail's mass communication theory* (6th ed.). Sage.

Meyen, M. (2017): Beyond both Hallin & Mancini and Freedom House. What *Mapping Media Freedom* is all about. In Meyen, M. (Ed.), *Mapping media freedom.* LMU Munich. mappingmediafreedom.de/about-us/

Nerone, J. C. (2002). The Four Theories of the Press four and a half decades later: A retrospective. *Journalism Studies, 3*(1), 133–136. DOI: 10.1080/14616700120107374

Ratcliffe, R. (2020, June 4). Trial of journalists to deliver 'existential moment' in Philippines: Editor of news website Rappler could face prison if convicted under 'cyber libel' law. www.theguardian.com/world/2020/jun/14/trial-of-journalists-rappler-philippines

Raemy, P. (2020). A theory of professional identity in journalism: Connecting discursive institutionalism, socialization, and psychological resilience theory. *Communication Theory, 54*(4). DOI: doi.org/10.1093/ct/qtaa019

Seethaler, J. (2017). Media systems theory. *Oxford Bibliographies.* DOI: 10.1093/OBO/9780199756841–0185

Servaes, J. (ed.). (2002). *Approaches to development communication*. UNESCO. www.unesco.org/new/fileadmin/MULTIMEDIA/HQ/CI/CI/pdf/approaches_to_development_communication.pdf

Siebert, F. S., Peterson T., & Schramm, W. (1956). *Four Theories of the Press: The Authoritarian, Libertarian, Social Responsibility and Soviet Communist concepts of what the press should be and do*. University of Illinois Press.

Voltmer, K. (2013). *The media in transitional democracies*. Polity.

Whitten-Woodring, J. (2009). Watchdog or lapdog? Media freedom, regime type, and government respect for human rights. *International Studies Quarterly, 53*(3), 595–625. DOI: 10.1111/j.1468–2478.2009.00548.x

I

KEY CONCEPTS

2

International News Flow in the Digital Age

Elad Segev[1]

The unequal flow of information has been one of the greatest concerns among international communication scholars. In terms of news, only a few international agencies covered a selected number of world events relevant to the richer countries. Poorer countries were completely ignored. Yet with the growing use of social media, local content production, and the rapid transformations in the news industry, the question is how much of this debate is still valid. Is there still inequality in the representation of our globalized world, where the United States and the West dominate the scene and peripheral countries are completely ignored? Is it still possible at all to ask questions about global news coverage when everyone reads different news tailored to their information behavior and interests? The current chapter attempts to address these questions based on the findings of recent studies in the field.

NEWS CONSUMPTION

Every morning I turn on my smartphone, swipe the home screen to the right, and get the news: a mixture of local and international news, technology, science, and even culture and history. Based on my online searches, e-mails, and website visits, the news items that appeared on my Android phone are tailored by Google's algorithm to cater my changing interests and information needs. This is comfortable to sink into my own personal filter bubble, but very soon I feel disconnected. I then turn to traditional news outlets, local or American, which give me the feeling, perhaps the illusion, of being "globally" informed. If an unusual event pops up, I sometimes look at the English edition of Al Jazeera, just to get another point of view. Consciously or not, I attempt to break my filter bubble to connect to other imagined communities, shape my identity and my sense of belonging.

Am I a typical user? Next door sits my wife. Coming from a family where news is an inevitable part of life, she actively reads the news at least three times a day. Though she mostly uses her mobile phone as well, she never lets Google decide for her what to read, but rather sticks to three news sources, which she believes to be credible. She starts with local and soft news and then moves to national and international news. She invests much more time in selecting the items of her interests, but at the same time feels confident in her news environment that enables her both to connect to other imagined communities and to disconnect from her everyday life.

In the attempt to fulfill similar needs, it seems that my wife and I roughly represent two types of news consumption strategies. One type of news consumers, which studies show to be associated with the younger generation, is based on customization algorithms (Stolero & Segev, 2017). Many users increasingly depend on algorithms to get more relevant news based on their interests or friends' interests. This often comes at the price of being detached from broader topics and the larger imagined community, and the difficulty to control the quality and credibility of the sources. The other types of news consumers, which are associated with more traditional and older generations, are loyal to specific, often traditional, news sources. They may even get familiar and accustomed to certain journalists, and enjoy a broader outlook of their surrounding news environment, yet they must invest more time in selecting in advance the relevant news sources they wish to consume, be that television channels or specific websites.

Luckily, my wife and I share this information in order to broaden our perspectives (and hopefully) think critically about our surroundings and about the motives behind the stories that the media tell us. Still, although we have completely different practices of news consumption and read them in different languages, we end up getting a very similar, partial, and some may add "unbalanced" picture of the world. This picture depends not only on our location, knowledge of news sources and languages, and personal preferences, but also on global economic hierarchies, the popularity and dominance of certain information sources, and the algorithms and social mechanisms that constantly organize and prioritize them.

INTERNATIONAL NEWS FLOW

The global news flow literature regards information inequalities as a major concern. Research in this field became important after the Second World War, when people began realizing how crucial global media could be (Cutlip, 1954; Hart, 1966; Markham, 1961; Smith, 1969). Two descriptive studies conducted by the International Press Institute (1953) and UNESCO (1954) displayed the unequal flow of international news and inspired scholars to further explore the possible reasons behind it. In a detailed review, Mowlana (1985) found around 300 publications over more than a century between 1850 and 1969 dealing with the global information flow. Immediately after, during less than a decade, the number of studies increased significantly.

Both Wilbur Schramm (1964) and Herbert Schiller (1969) are known to be critical of the global monopoly of U.S. media. Schiller even compared the American media to a global Empire, which provides the basis for its political and economic expansion around the world. Inequality in global media and the representation of the world certainly reflect the global economic structure, tapping directly into Wallerstein's (1974) World System Theory. This theory suggests that bilateral trade (and consequently also media and information) flows hierarchically from the richest and largest countries (core countries) to the peripheries. Core countries not only produce and export more information products but also control their global dissemination through transnational corporations.

Together with the rapid growth of the global media industry, including news agencies, books, films, music, and television during the 1970s, these inequalities were intensified and prompted UNESCO to establish an international committee chaired by Seán MacBride to study the asymmetry in global information flows, its implications, and possible solutions.

SEÁN MACBRIDE AND THE NWICO

It was not by chance that Seán MacBride was chosen to chair UNESCO's committee on information inequalities. Seán was born in Paris in 1904 to Maud Gonne and John MacBride, both Irish republican activists. As a young boy, his father was executed by the British firing squad for his participation in the 1916 Irish Easter Rising in Dublin. Seán returned to Ireland and by the age of 15 joined the Irish Volunteers, which fought against the British in the Irish War of Independence. It seems that growing up in such a revolutionary environment shaped his later life as a politician with a strong affinity for international affairs, human rights, and global equalities. MacBride served as Minister for External Affairs between 1948 and 1951 and was a founding member of Amnesty International. In 1974, despite or perhaps because of his belligerent attitude toward peace, MacBride was awarded the Nobel Peace Prize for his ability to "mobilized the conscience of the world in the fight against injustice" (Lionaes, 1974).

In 1980, MacBride was appointed as the president of UNESCO's International Commission for the Study of Communications Problems. The final report of his committee, entitled "Many Voices, One World" and published by UNESCO (MacBride, 1980), outlined some of the core problems and possible steps to be taken by the international community to achieve the New World Information and Communication Order (NWICO). The term NWICO referred to international attempts to take measures against global information inequalities. These inequalities are related to: (1) the direction and volume of information flows across the globe, (2) the dominance of certain content and countries, (3) the lack of representation of poorer countries, or when mentioned, their overall negative or biased coverage, (4) the commercialization of content, and (5) the monopolization of global media. Most of the criticism focused on the dominance of Western countries and the division of the world into "developed" and "developing" countries, but the report also discussed differences in political and social systems and disparities within countries.

The impact of MacBride's report was immense as it signified the global movement toward democracy and stressed the role of communications (Nordenstreng, 2005). It was also the first time an official document by the United Nations systematically showed structural biases in communication and offered steps to diminish them (Mattelart, 2005). Many of MacBride's recommendations are valid today more than ever before. In particular, media commercialization and the advertisement industry promote consumption at the expense of other values, may hinder professional and critical journalism, and most alarmingly, turn each one of us into a passive, irrational consumer. In the spirit of MacBride's report, Wikipedia and other global commons initiations are required to counterbalance global inequalities and our profit-driven world.

Considering the stark differences between core countries and periphery identified in MacBride's report, it is important to ask what the possible implications of this imbalance are. In other words, why is it so important to strive for more equal global information flows? The claim is that those disparities deepen other political and economic inequalities, as they enable global corporations to exploit markets and eliminate any possible competition. It is also argued that the dominant Western media tend to produce and disseminate a distorted picture of economically less developed countries, typically located in the global South. This virtuous circle enables Western governments and global corporations to justify their economic expansion, and further promote their own political and economic interests. Global Western companies make use of the local resources in poorer countries, for example, by hiring much cheaper labor for producing hardware and software, while the exploited local population is unable to access viable information in their languages or access reliable local media outlets.

The main criticism raised by UNESCO over the years concerns the concept of "free flow," which means letting the market forces shape the global media landscape. During the 1980s, this policy was embraced by Ronald Reagan in the United States and Margaret Thatcher in the United Kingdom along with other economic reforms. For most other countries, however, this "free flow" policy rather limited media freedom. It is the sole luxury of richer countries to produce and disseminate information through a global media monopoly. Until today many people around the globe are not free to choose what information to consume and can certainly not reach global audiences. If at all, they can mostly access the one-way flow of information mostly produced in the West. "Freedom," critics would argue, is an empty word that is used by economically dominant countries such as the United States and the United Kingdom to justify their global influence. It is therefore not surprising that both the United States and the United Kingdom resigned from UNESCO in 1984, claiming that it was hostile to their interests. They re-joined many years later after UNESCO had implemented considerable organizational reforms.

IS THE FLOW OF INTERNATIONAL NEWS MORE EQUAL IN THE DIGITAL AGE?

In many ways, these global information "inequalities" remain relevant today, corresponding to the current discussion of the global digital divide and the growing influence of transnational corporations (TNCs). While the first-level digital divide refers to the exclusion of people at the international and national level, the second-level divide refers to the quantity and quality of information available (Segev, 2019), the dominance of the English language, the commercialization of content, and digital literacy and skills. UNESCO's World Summits on Information Society in 2003 and 2005 are thus a direct continuation of its ambition to reach an NWICO, which aimed to equalize the global news flow. Similar to previous debates, one of the most heated issues was the idea of establishing an Internet Governance Forum to handle domain name allocation. Not surprisingly, the United States strongly rejected this initiation, and the administration of domain names at the global level is still in the hands of an American organization (Constantinou, 2008). Hence, despite the ongoing criticism over American media dominance, the ability to counterbalance it is rather limited.

In 1977, Jeremy Tunstall published a book titled *The Media Are American*. He systematically demonstrated how the global market forces of the American media industry—movies, television, news—dominated many parts of the world. In the past decades, however, Tunstall (2008) argues that this dominance has been challenged with the emergence of local and regional media production in Africa, Asia, Europe, the Middle East, and South America. Tunstall does not completely refute the existence of global inequality but rather shows that as the larger and more populated regional centers like China, India, Russia, Brazil, and Mexico have become independent, they gradually decreased their media imports below 10 percent. At the same time, these countries serve as media hubs for the smaller countries in the region.

Tunstall's findings seem to echo a more general claim that started materializing during the 1990s on media globalization and the emergence of contra-flows (Boyd-Barrett & Thussu, 1992; Thussu, 2000, 2006; Straubhaar, 1997, 2002). These authors argue that the presence and share of American media in many countries have declined as they develop local and regional content. Together with the growing globalization of international trade, tourism, and migration, people increasingly produce and consume more information from various local and regional sources and more diverse information channels as well.

Still, when looking at the development of the BRICS (Brazil, Russia, India, China, and South Africa) in terms of economy, technology, and the communication industry, Fuchs (2015) maintains that not much has changed. Indeed, many countries develop their own information and communication services. People in China and Russia, for example, use their own national search engines (Baidu and Yandex respectively) and social media services (Tencent QQ and VK respectively). Yet the same commercial principles that govern the United States penetrate across the globe and produce local and global economic and informational inequalities that become larger than ever before.

One way to demonstrate global inequalities in the information flow today is through search engine data. Studying the scope of international searches in Google, Segev (2018) identified three types of flows that constantly influence one another: people (tourism and immigration), products (shopping) and services, and information (news and entertainment). In line with the contra-flow thesis, he showed that users often search for information related to countries in their regions. Still, there were clear indications for inequalities in global flows as economically leading countries and particularly the United States attracted far more searches from other countries. Indeed, several regional hubs in Africa, Asia, and America emerged, but rather as information gateways, connecting more peripheral countries in their region with former colonial powers in Europe.

While the lower barriers to produce and disseminate content may have counter-balanced the unequal global flow in some domains, such as international searches, the question is whether *international news* displays similar contra-flows trends. For many years, international news around the world has been particularly dependent on American and European international agencies such as AP, Reuters, or AFP. Together with the adoption of the Internet in the early 1990s, the local production and global dissemination of information, including news, have become simpler and cheaper. Thus, in the global news industry, there is a similar chance for more local production, which can further spread through social media, bypassing the traditional gatekeepers and global organizations and institutions. We would therefore expect to find that international news has also become more regional in focus. Yet even Tunstall (2008) acknowledges that international news is still dominated by American and increasingly also European news agencies, particularly in the Middle East, Africa, and South Asia.

When looking at the distribution of countries mentioned in mainstream media today (print news, television, and major online news outlets), research indicates that very little has changed (Cohen, 2013; Segev, 2016; Wu, 2007). In line with the patterns outlined in MacBride's report, numerous studies over the past decades have repeatedly reported on an unbalanced picture, in which the United States is by far the most mentioned country followed by its European allies and competitors or foes (Segev & Blondheim, 2013). The global narrative told by most mainstream media around the world is almost always related to the narrative told by U.S. media, and the similar "usual suspects": Afghanistan, China, Iran, Iraq, and North Korea, the prime concern of U.S. foreign affairs, feature as the main actors of most international news around the world from Asia, Africa, the Middle East, and Europe to the Americas.

Studies examining foreign news coverage in the United States have documented some alarming recent trends. For example, Jones, Van Aelst and Vliegenthart (2013) compared the representation of the world in U.S. news over a 57-year period. They showed that the number of countries mentioned in the news decreased over the years, despite the growing number of countries in the international system. Similar to others (Norris, 1995; Riffe, Aust, Jones, Shoemaker, & Sundar, 1994), they maintained that the international scope of the U.S. news media has shrunk, even though the country has become more globally connected politically and economically.

One of the reasons for this imbalance is certainly related to the fact that changes in the patterns of international news flows are slower as they still heavily rely on traditional structures of international news organizations dominated by Western international news agencies such as AP and Reuters. Almost all local news organizations purchase their world news from international agencies rather than employ foreign correspondents around the world. Yet, when comparing at different types of news sources (international news agencies, national newspapers, broadcast channels, and news aggregators), Segev (2017) revealed that international news agencies were the most representative of all news sources. News aggregators such as Google News collect and customize news from a variety of national sources, which have a narrower international scope, and thus further perpetuate and even deepen the narrow representation of the world.

Among social media channels, Twitter has attracted scholarly attention due to its affordance and data abundance. While realizing its important role for journalists, Golan and Himelboim (2016) studied the structure of the international news flow on Twitter. They found general hierarchies and also identified the new role of non-institutional actors as a bridge between news sources and audiences. They maintained that together with the growing use of social media to mediate news, the global news flow will get both more diverse and more fragmented over time.

It seems that today, as globalization processes continue, there are more types of information flows and, therefore, also more opportunities for contra-flows. This does not mean that the world is getting flatter, as Thomas Friedman (2007) anticipated. Indeed, some local and regional centers have emerged as important media players in the past decades due to the relative ease of producing and disseminating information content locally. Yet, at the same time, the general network structure remains very hierarchical, where the most powerful economies attract the highest attention, and the local hubs serve as regional gatekeepers to the center. In the global flows of international news, compared, for example, to that of online searches, these hierarchies are even stronger, as a handful of international news agencies dominate the production and dissemination of information. Moreover, news aggregators further intensify these hierarchies since their customization mechanisms reproduce a narrow and unbalanced picture of the outside world.

THE POWER-PROXIMITY MODEL
OF INTERNATIONAL NEWS FLOW

When attempting to summarize the arguments above, it seems that two main principles—power and proximity—govern the flow of information from one country to another. The power of the country in which the information is produced is related to a range of aspects, including its economic power, political influence, military power, dominance of media and entertainment industry as well as its attractiveness as a tourism destination. Similarly, the proximity between countries, which can be geographic but also historical, social, and cultural proximity, plays an important role.

Information can further flow in different directions. When it comes to international news or the media industry (movies, games, television programs, etc.), it is the so-called Western countries that push information abroad to less-developed countries, using market mechanisms. This can be seen, for example, when the United States promotes and advertises its own media and information products abroad. International searches and social media reflect these trends, but here people from the less powerful countries actively pull information originating from the West. They search for a popular travel destination, news about prominent countries, and information on products and media produced in dominant countries. They also follow popular social media accounts. Based on these premises, figure 2.1 offers a model to describe how the principles of power and proximity shape the direction of global information flows.

The principle of proximity tends to work in both directions. There are more chances for people from geographically or culturally closer countries to get information about each other. People often get news and search for information about countries in their region (Segev, 2018). Still, the economic and political power differences between countries play a vital role. The chances that Canadians read and search about information coming from the United States, or that the Swiss read and search about information coming from Germany are much higher than vice versa.

While international news is "pushed" from powerful countries and online searches are "pulled" from the less powerful countries, social media flows encompass both push and pull practices. People using social media platforms such as Twitter or Facebook experience the "push" principles as they get the news about powerful countries or information about popular tourist destinations from their peers as well as from advertisements and algorithms aiming to promote the agendas of powerful actors. At the same time, people can actively "pull" information by asking questions, search and customize their information on social media platforms, or follow popular social media accounts. Customization mechanisms work in line with the proximity principle, as the information in social media is often based on language, location, and peer preferences (see also Segev, 2019).

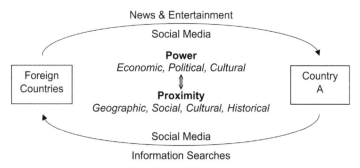

Figure 2.1. The Power–proximity model of global information flow

GLOBAL FLOWS OF NEWS AND ONLINE SEARCHES

The following section offers some empirical evidence for the power-proximity model of the global information flow based on data from international news and Google searches. The news data presented here were collected daily for one year from more than fifty most popular news sites in seventeen countries (China, Egypt, France, Germany, India, Iran, Israel, Italy, Japan, Mexico, Russia, South Africa, South Korea, Spain, Switzerland, the United Kingdom, and the United States). The sample of countries and news sites was designed to reflect some of the most influential media hubs (print, broadcast, online news services, and aggregators), the number and proportion of Internet users in each country, and variety of cultural backgrounds and ideologies (see Segev, 2016 for more details).

A total of 192,910 news items were collected during January 1, 2019, and December 31, 2019, and the number of news items mentioning each of the seventeen countries was calculated. For this purpose, a database of country names with all their possible spellings and derivations in twelve different languages (Arabic, Chinese, English, French, German, Hebrew, Italian, Japanese, Korean, Persian, Russian, and Spanish) was built, and computer software was developed to count their occurrences. Finally, a directed network was created to portray how frequently Country A was mentioned by Country B. The strength of ties between countries was standardized, ranging from 0 to 100 to be comparable with the search data. For example, the United States was mentioned in 10.26 percent of U.S. news items, while China was mentioned in 4.17 percent of U.S. news items. Accordingly, the weighted directed link of United States to the United States was 100, while China to the United States was 40.64.

International searches were based on Google Trends data for country-related searches (see also Segev, 2018). The seventeen countries mentioned above were searched in Google Trends as entities for the entire year of 2019. A list of the available sixteen other countries from which users searched was extracted. Google Trends data are similarly standardized relative to the country from which the percentage of searches was the highest. Thus, for example, in 2019 Germany was searched mainly by German users (scored 100), and then by Swiss users (scored 58). The weighted directed link Germany to Germany was 100, while Switzerland to Germany was 58. In the final networks, self-mentions in the news and Google searches were removed.

Figure 2.2 portrays the directed network of international news and searches based on ties with a standardized weight of ten and above. Countries are the nodes, while international

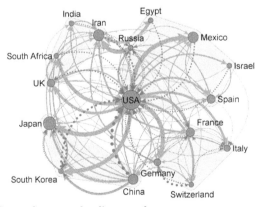

Figure 2.2. Global flows of news and online searches

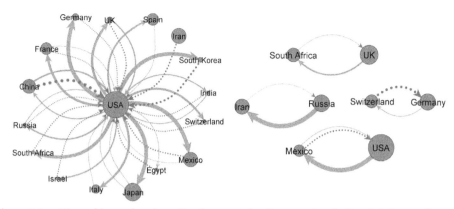

Figure 2.3.   Hierarchies and reciprocity of news and online searches in the global news flow

news (in solid line) and Google searches (in dotted line) are the directed links between them. The size of the nodes reflects their betweenness centrality (the extent of being in between other countries), and the width of the ties reflects their standardized weight. Clusters of countries were automatically assigned using the Louvain method (Blondel et al., 2008), which is based on the density of edges inside communities.

As can immediately be observed from figure 2.2, the United States is at the absolute center of the network of global flows. It is the most prominent country in the news of others, reflecting the "push" principle (as indicated by the thick solid ties going out from the United States to all other countries). It is also the most searched country, reflecting the "pull" principle (as indicated by the thick dotted ties coming into the United States from all other countries). Another interesting pattern that can be observed is the regionality and language divide in the flow of news and searches. The patterns of information flow among countries correspond to common regions and languages. Thus, there is more flow of news and searches among East Asian countries (at the bottom-left) and European countries (at the bottom-right). Similarly, English-speaking countries (on the top-left, except for Iran) share more news and information searches. Finally, a mixed cluster (on the top-right) of countries that share news and information searches with the United States, including Spain and Mexico.

Figure 2.3 further demonstrates the clear patterns of hierarchies in the global flow and the reciprocity between international news and searches. First, it highlights the ego network of the United States (on the left), revealing the systematic global flow pattern in which news goes (pushed) out and searches come in (pulled). Second, it shows for selected dyads in the network (on the right): the United Kingdom and South Africa, Russia and Iran, Germany and Switzerland, and the United States and Mexico, a systematic political and economic dependency and reciprocity. A greater share of international news flows from the respective stronger country, while a greater share of online searches is initiated by the smaller and more dependent countries.

CHAPTER SUMMARY

The analysis of global flows of news and searches reveals three important patterns. First, inequalities and hierarchies exist today even in online environments. These imbalances often reflect other political and economic inequalities in the world. It seems therefore that the same concerns raised by Schramm (1964), Schiller (1969), and Wallerstein's (1974) about the dominance of the United States and the West, which were later addressed by UNESCO in an attempt to establish a New World Information and Communication Order, are still valid today. In the digital age, algorithms and news aggregators such as Google News perpetuate and even intensify a narrow and unequal view of the world, which is led by the United States. This was observed in the current analysis and the unidirectional global flow, where the United States is mentioned in international news by far more than any other country, with no significant competitor on the horizon. Online searches in Google further mirror this trend as users from most countries continue to search information mainly about the United States.

The second pattern is related to the regionalization of global flow. When looking beyond the overarching power of the United States in shaping the global information flow, it is possible to observe patterns of local interactions, which reflect geographic and cultural proximity, and consequently the local flows of people (global migration and tourism) and products (bilateral trade). Together with traditional editorial decisions for relevance, algorithms for customization push information based on language and location, and thus people get more news about countries that are geographically, culturally, and historically connected.

The last and most interesting pattern in the global flow of information is the combination of the previous two. When looking at the patterns of global flows in a network, the remarkable role of certain regional information hubs appears. In line with Tunstall's (2008) observations on the rise of regional media centers in Africa, Asia, the Middle East, and South America, it seems that the global flows of news, searches, and possibly also social media relies on some rising gatekeepers. When analyzing the patterns of international searches in all countries, Nigeria and South Africa emerged as hubs for the African region as did the UAE for the Middle East. Based on the direction and volume of international searches, information was found to flow from the United States and Europe to these gatekeepers, and then to the smaller countries in the region. To complete the picture, the current analysis revealed a clear reciprocity of information and dependency between bigger and smaller countries with geographic, cultural, or even political and economic proximity. Thus, when looking respectively at the dyads of Germany–Switzerland, the United Kingdom–South Africa, or Russia–Iran, it is easy to see a similar pattern. The stronger country "pushes" news-related information, while the dependent country "pulls" back information through online searches.

The debate on equality in the global flows remains as valid today in the digital age as it was earlier, and perhaps even more. Precisely because it seems that, at the microlevel, people get different information customized to their personal interests, there is a greater illusion of information access, freedom, and equality. A systematic analysis at the macro level, however, including numerous studies on the global flow presents a rather hierarchical pattern. Global inequalities are perpetuated and tend to reflect existing economic, political, and historical dependencies between countries. Distributed technologies and social media, despite their potential, will not and cannot solve the global information imbalance by themselves. Apart from presenting the power-proximity model to understand the patterns in global information flow, this chapter hopes to raise attention to the severity of the imbalance and to encourage scholars to continue to unveil global inequalities and students to propose ideas for making the global news flow a little bit more even.

DISCUSSION QUESTIONS

1. What is the New World Information and Communication Order (NWICO)? Describe its origins and main propositions.
2. Do you think there is still a discrepancy in information flow at a global level? Why or why not?
3. How can online technologies such as search engines, news aggregators and social media services affect international news flow from core countries to the periphery and vice versa?

BIBLIOGRAPHY

Blondel, V. D., Guillaume, J. L., Lambiotte, R., & Lefebvre, E. (2008). Fast unfolding of communities in large networks. *Journal of Statistical Mechanics: Theory and Experiment, 10*, 10008.

Boyd-Barrett, O., &. Thussu, D. K. (1992). *Contra-flow in global news.* John Libbey.

Cohen, A. A. (Ed.) (2013). *Foreign news on television: Where in the world is the global village?* Peter Lang.

Constantinou, C. M. (2008). Communications/excommunications: An interview with Armand Mattelart. *Review of International Studies, 34*(S1), 21–42.

Cutlip, S. M. (1954). Content and flow of AP news: From trunk to TTS to reader. *Journalism Quarterly, 31*, 434–446.

Friedman, T. (2007). *The world is flat: A brief history of the twenty-first century.* Farrar, Straus and Giroux.

Fuchs, C. (2015). The MacBride Report in twenty-first-century capitalism, the age of social media and the BRICS countries. *Javnost-The Public, 22*(3), 226–239.

Golan, G. J., & Himelboim, I. (2016). Can World System Theory predict news flow on Twitter? The case of government-sponsored broadcasting. *Information, Communication & Society, 19*(8), 1150–1170.

Hart, J. A. (1966). Foreign news in U.S. and English daily newspapers: A comparison. *Journalism Quarterly, 43*, 443–448.

International Press Institute (1953). *The flow of news.* International Press Institute.

Jones, T. M., Van Aelst, P., & Vliegenthart, R. (2013). Foreign nation visibility in U.S. news coverage: A longitudinal analysis (1950–2006). *Communication Research, 40*(3), 417–436.

Lionaes, A. (1974). *Award ceremony speech for the Nobel Peace Prize 1974.* Available at: www.nobelprize.org/prizes/peace/1974/ceremony-speech/

MacBride, S. (1980). *Many voices, one world: Communication and society today and tomorrow.* UNESCO.

Markham, J. W. (1961). Foreign news in the United States and South American press, *Public Opinion Quarterly, 25*, 249–262.

Mattelart, A. (2005). The Stammering Discovery of the Processes of Internationalisation. *Quaderns del CAC, 21*(38), 53–54.

Mowlana, H. (1985). *International flows of information: A global report and analysis.* UNESCO.

Nordenstreng, K. (2005). A Milestone in the Great Media Debate. *Quaderns del CAC 21*(38), 45–48.

Norris, P. (1995). The restless searchlight: Network news framing of the post—Cold War world. *Political Communication, 12*(4), 357–370.

Riffe, D., Aust, C. F., Jones, T. C., Shoemaker, B., & Sundar, S. (1994). The shrinking foreign news hole of the New York Times. *Newspaper Research Journal, 15*(3), 74–88.

Schiller, H. I. (1969). *Mass communications and American empire.* Beacon Press.

Schramm, W. L. (1964). *Mass media and national development: The role of information in the developing countries.* Stanford University Press.

Segev, E. (2016). *International news online: Global views with local perspectives*. Peter Lang.

Segev, E. (2017). From where does the world look flatter? A comparative analysis of foreign coverage in world news. *Journalism, 20*(7), 924–942.

Segev, E. (2018). Googling the world: Global and Regional information flows in Google Trends. *International Journal of Communication, 12*, 2232–2250.

Segev, E. (2019). Volume and Control: The Transition from Information to Power. *Journal of Multicultural Discourses, 14*(3), 240–257.

Segev, E., & Blondheim, M. (2013). America's global standing according to popular news sites from around the world. *Political Communication, 30*(1), 139–161.

Smith, R. F. (1969). On the structure of foreign news: A comparison of the New York Times and the Indian White Papers, *Journal of Peace Research, 6*, 23–35.

Stolero, N., & Segev, E. (2017). "It's not how I use it, but what I believe about it": The role of experience in the online information seeking behavior. *AoIR Selected Papers of Internet Research*. Available at: firstmonday.org/ojs/index.php/spir/article/view/10201

Straubhaar, J. D. (1997). Distinguishing the global, regional and national levels of world television. In A. Sreherny-Mobammadi, D. Winseck, J. McKenna, & O. Boyd-Barrett (Eds.), *Media in a global context* (pp. 284–298). Edward Arnold.

Straubhaar, J. D. (2002). (Re)asserting national media and national identity against the global, regional and local levels of world television. In J. M. Chan & B. T. McIntyre (Eds.), *In search of boundaries: Communication, nation-states, and cultural identities* (pp. 181–206). Ablex.

Thussu, D. (2000). *International communication: Continuity and change*. Arnold.

Thussu, D. K. (Ed.). (2006). *Media on the move: Global flow and contra-flow*. Routledge.

Tunstall, J. (1977). *The media are American: Anglo-American media in the world*. Constable.

Tunstall, J. (2008). *The media were American: U.S. mass media in decline*. Oxford University Press.

UNESCO (1954). *How nations see each other?* UNESCO.

Wallerstein, I. (1974). *The modern world system I: Capitalist agriculture and the origins of the European world-economy in the sixteenth century*. Academic Press.

Wu, H. D. (2007). A brave new world for international news? Exploring the determinants of the coverage of foreign news on US websites. *International Communication Gazette, 69*, 539–551.

3

Technology's Role in Global Journalism and Communication

H. Denis Wu

Our awareness and understanding of what happens in locales outside our communities or beyond national borders often rely on communication technologies. Imagine people who have never traveled to a given nation, they would have to depend on the media—including broadcast news, tourism advertisements, travelers' comments and reviews, and even bots-generated posts—to obtain any information about that nation. Essentially, our perception of the world is, to a great extent, dependent on the type and amount of media we consume—because we cannot be everywhere at all times. What's more, our directly observed, literal reality under certain circumstances can be less important than the counterpart presented and discussed in the media. Given the increased penetration of communication technologies around the world and the different types of new media platforms, a wide variety of important issues have come to the fore and warrant new discussion. This chapter offers a brief introduction of key technologies and developments that have taken place in the past few decades and addresses several pressing issues related to their influence on journalism and communication around the globe.

As communication across national borders relies greatly on the media, it is vital to examine the role technology plays not only at the personal but also at the aggregate level. The 2018 Facebook-Cambridge Analytica data breach, which leaked private data of 50 million users to third parties, led to an international outcry about privacy and surveillance issues worldwide (Rosenberg, Confessore, & Cadwalladr, 2018)—and this case merely shows the tip of the iceberg. The 2019 Mueller Report unveiled Russian interference in the U.S. election campaign through targeting social media users and brought transnational distribution of disinformation, misinformation, and alternative facts to the fore. With the rising penetration of social media networks in almost every corner of the world and the increasing influence of global technology juggernauts such as Alphabet, Facebook, and Tencent, communication scholars have raised questions about the credibility of myriads of online information sources, their sophisticated operation, and nefarious manipulation of public opinion at the global level (Jones, 2019). While technology companies have largely avoided public scrutiny, how do journalism entities cope with ongoing technological advancement and how does the Internet-based, computational operation affect communication across national borders (Woolley & Howard, 2019)? This chapter addresses the role of technology in content creation, dissemination, and automation and its impact on how we understand the world. The following also explores the implications of technologies and cyberspace for media professionals and policymakers to improve the flow of accurate, credible information between countries.

EVOLUTION OF COMMUNICATION TECHNOLOGIES

Before we address current developments, it is beneficial to look back, briefly, at the past century to inspect the impact of a few technologies on global journalism and communication. The impressive list of major media technologies invented in the twentieth century includes radio, television, computer, digitization, satellite, smartphone, and the Internet, each of which has affected what, when, where, and how people from different parts of the world communicate. One of the most researched media technologies is television, primarily due to its omnipresence and capacity to instantly transmit not only audio but also video content. The term "global village" was first coined (McLuhan & Powers, 1989) to reflect the interconnected lives and shared experiences of the world's different locations, thanks to television. In a way, television contributes to the abatement of geographical distance and extension and homogeneity of human consciousness, profoundly affecting people's sense of place (Meyrowitz, 1986). Most apparent examples would include large global sports events like the Olympics or the World Cup that are immediately shared by viewers all over the world. Undoubtedly, television as a medium has propelled the speed of globalization.

Yet, on the other hand, the dispersion of information, cultures, and national images shown on the very medium can be considerably uneven and inaccurate. For one thing, the cost of television content production, transmission, and needed infrastructure may prevent poor countries from competing with those with more financial, technological, and human resources. This imbalance between the haves and have-nots among the world's nations has resulted in uneven flow of information and cultural products across national borders (Mowlana & Roach, 1992); in other words, certain parts of the world are less likely to be covered by the news media (Stevenson & Shaw, 1984) and their entertainment output is more difficult to circulate globally. Additionally, a disadvantaged nation's reliance on media content from elite nations might yield negative influence, including undermining its indigenous culture and self-identity (Aslama & Pantti, 2007) rather than being economically beneficial, as development communication scholars originally envisioned and predicted (Lerner, 1958; Schramm, 1964). The effects from the global export of television content can range from inundation with national stereotypes and clichéd images of foreign destinations to formulaic reality and game shows adopted worldwide (e.g., *America's Got Talent*).

The palpable influence of television, a global medium (Lule, 2015), can also be examined together with other connected technologies, such as cable, satellite, video streaming, and so forth. Each of the aforementioned technologies may have accentuated different aspects of impact on global communication. For example, thanks to the advent of cable news and its insatiable need for news content, more comments and opinions have been included in news programming than hard facts. The constant and instantaneous live coverage of disruptive events outside national borders has forced national leaders to accept interview invitations and make prompt responses—or even take immediate action that would otherwise have needed far more diplomatic deliberation and consultation. Without the hasty policy announcement, they run the risk of looking weak and indecisive to their domestic supporters and worldwide stakeholders. This phenomenon was termed "CNN effect" to epitomize the significant impact that television coverage of international events such as civil wars or humanitarian crises has on foreign policymaking, forcing national leaders to intervene due to public pressure (Gilboa, 2005). Similar to cable and satellite television, digitally transmitted, online-based media have also exponentially increased, allowing for more partisan and divisive perspectives about individual nations to percolate into global discourse. With more access and capacity, media technologies have paved the way for more heterogeneous, voluminous, and valenced (even polarized) discourse about world affairs and global issues. For example, the dramatically different angles adopted by MSNBC and Fox News when covering global warming and climate change illustrate the point; so do other globally distributed television channels such as Al Jazeera, BBC (British Broadcasting Corporation), and CCTV (China Central TV). Their impact on the nature and characteristics of global communication will be discussed later in the cyberspace section.

Communication infrastructure such as satellites, fiber optic cables, and cellular towers should be considered key technologies that have also transformed how journalism is practiced and its produced content accessed/consumed worldwide. Most people probably are not aware of their extensive contribution but many existing communication and media services that the entire world enjoys rely on them. Pelton (2010) pointed out the crucial role satellites have been playing in facilitating globalization, making nations intricately interconnected and interdependent. Satellites beam down to almost every corner of the world at all times to transmit information, meet the demands for entertainment, facilitate business transactions, and much more. Another significant unintended consequence of satellites is allowing global access to instantaneous information around the clock, which has many ramifications for global commerce, international relations, and policy-making, including the "CNN effect." All of these aforementioned aspects of changes undoubtedly bolster globalization.

Aside from infrastructural technologies, personalized mobile phones and their direct and collateral benefits and impacts at the global level cannot be overstated. Mobile phones (a broad category that may include smartphones and tablet computers connected via a cellular system) have provided critical communication services for countries with scarce resources in the latter half of the twentieth century and were found to have elevated quality of life and counterbalanced uneven information flow patterns in the global South (Ling & Horst, 2011). With its potential leapfrogging impact on economic performance, education, health, and culture in the South (Hyde-Clarke & Van Tonder, 2011), there was much hope that mobile phone technology would provide a level playing field. However, it remains to be seen whether the potential for increasing access, level of participation, and contra-flow of information originating from the Global South will be fulfilled in the future.

Other technologies also have generated a profound impact on how individual nations connect. Online technologies that take advantage of artificial intelligence so far have only shown the beginning of the major global transformation that lies ahead (Davenport, 2018). While it is challenging for us to foresee future trends, technologies will undoubtedly make the world even more connected and integrated. As we have witnessed, each of the platforms created on the Internet has brought various types of influence on the world: for example, blogs were found to give rise to the demands of the "voiceless" for more freedom, self-identity, and power (Russell & Echchaibi, 2009). Additionally, transnational strategic use of social media has been linked to initiating or sustaining the Arab Spring (2010) and the Occupy (2011) protests, and the globalized #MeToo (2019) movement would not otherwise have been thought possible.

CHALLENGES OF GLOBAL COMMUNICATION

Before the advent of the Internet and Web 2.0, international news carried by mass media had been the primary source upon which communication between nations was based. News produced at a locale or region, primarily controlled by international news agencies (e.g., AFP, AP, Bloomberg, and Reuters) and transmitted through national borders to various parts of the world mattered tremendously. The volume, valence, characteristics, and dissemination of the news about a given nation, culture, people, or region can introduce vital issues, which have been vigorously debated by scholars and are discussed in other parts of the book. The following section introduces three interconnected issues that pertain particularly to communication technologies that pose serious challenges for global communication.

One critical component of global communication nowadays stems from governmental, corporate, and non-governmental organizations' efforts in enhancing their influence and gaining the support of the international public. The channel of influence is beyond traditional journalism practice and orchestrated by industry-backed, professional execution. The execution of reaching out to the international public can be technologically sophisticated, financially compelling, and psychologically savvy. Public diplomacy is often used to describe such operations (Manheim, 1994) and has become more important than traditional diplomatic work that has been firmly grounded in official communication, interpersonal relationships, and diplomatic protocol. The emphasis of public diplomacy today is placed on mediated persuasion that is targeted directly at foreign publics (Entman, 2008) and is intended to win "the hearts and minds" of global constituencies (Nye, 2004; Servaes, 2012). Public diplomacy, in addition to issues related to cyberspace and post-truth, deserves further discussion.

PUBLIC DIPLOMACY

This subfield of international communication tends to be more practitioner oriented and overlaps significantly with public relations and international relations. It has been used by governments, NGOs, and the private sector (Manheim, 1994) to inform and influence foreign publics in order to gain support for the sponsoring entity's goals, policies, and interests (Tuch, 1990). Public diplomacy deserves a rekindled attention in the context of technological change for several reasons. For one thing, public diplomacy is no longer a mere supplement to conventional diplomacy. It goes beyond making splashy advertisements for foreign audiences or maintaining international broadcasting operations, which are still keenly practiced by global powers such as China and Russia (Massoglia & West, 2018). Now, technologies like AI algorithms and geosocial targeting can generate unprecedented, superbly tailored messaging for individuals worldwide. How nations communicate today with international publics is deeply affected by media technologies. Throughout history, one can see the distinct influence from different mediums during different points in time. Radio, for example, was strategically utilized during World War II by both the Allies and Axis nations that transmitted their propaganda messages. Currently, the frequent use of social media, such as Twitter, by prominent political leaders has resulted in unfathomable impact on cross-national relations and foreign policy and has facilitated direct communication with global audiences (Duncombe, 2017). This practice of "Twitter diplomacy" and its impacts on public opinion around the world needs to be thoroughly ascertained.

Traditionally, promotional information and images of individual nations have been clearly labeled as promotional content and/or placed in a distinct section of news media. However, the distinction between editorial and sponsored content, due to business pressure, has blurred. That is to say, audiences would have tremendous difficulty in distinguishing editorial content or entertainment from promotion, because ads can be equated with news (naked advertising) and movies and games can use long-format or interactive ads that feature a place on earth (product placement). Tiffany's, a jewelry store, centered in *Breakfast at Tiffany's* or Dubrovnik, Croatia featured prominently in *Games of the Thrones* are just two examples. The combination of public diplomacy and unscrupulous, profit-driven media practices should lead us to trace and question how people's opinion and evaluation of foreign nations really come about.

While public diplomacy efforts to create content appropriate for foreign nations are usually accepted, their interference with creative and journalistic works can be frowned upon and encroach on freedom of expression. Hollywood's financial clout that eyes in the gigantic Chinese market, for example, has been reported to directly intervene in the production process, including rewriting scripts for movies or changing the villains' nationality (Qin & Carlsen, 2018). Given this, one needs to examine not only text-based information, but also images, visuals, and effective memes associated with nations from comprehensive sources, including movies and social media (Elasmar & Groshek, 2017).

POST-TRUTH FLOW

Traditionally, the volume of information and the direction of news flows from one part of the world to another has been a critical issue in international communication. As discussed in chapter 5, the long-term concern about the imbalance of information flow between the North and the South sparked debates about a New World Information and Communication Order (NWICO) and raised discussion about the potential of communication technologies to empower and strengthen smaller media organizations in the developing world. There has been a great body of empirical works devoted to investigating the pattern and genres of international news coverage (Golan, Johnson, & Wanta, 2010; Hester, 1973) and many editorial and contextual determinants have been identified (Segev, 2016; Wu, 1998). However, the news is merely one facet of content that flows across borders; other types of content of interest include infotainment (Thussu, 2007), entertainment content (Walter, Sheafer, Nir, & Shenhav, 2016), film (Fu & Sim, 2010), and recently, post-truth.

The concept of post-truth is broad (Beckett, 2017; Mcintyre, 2018) and includes misinformation, disinformation, "junk news" and "fake news" (Howard, 2020). These terms generally refer to false content deliberately created to sway public opinion toward an issue, organization, or country. Such content quickly spreads across national borders via multitude means of strategic sharing and delivery, often relying on social media channels. Russia's targeted use of social media in an effort to influence U.S. voters' perceptions and possibly voting outcomes during the 2016 presidential election provides a vivid example (Allcott & Gentzkow, 2017; Grinberg, Joseph, Friedland, Swire-Thompson, & Lazer, 2019). Recently, many other nations, including Iran and Saudi Arabia (Reuters, 2019), have also resorted to social media to troll and fabricate tactically tailored content to generate sociopolitical impact in various nations.

The widespread of false information, especially online, has been a challenge for journalists who are expected to solve the thorny problem for the public (Mitchell, Gottfried, Stocking, Walker, & Fedeli, 2019). The task of fact-checking content on the myriads of media platforms is critical to democracy and public health, but average users do not have the expertise necessary to do this—thus, media literacy training would not suffice and industry regulations may be urgently needed. However, social media platforms, where most disinformation originates, have faced complex and evolving laws and regulations and have taken different stances when it comes to flagging false and potentially harmful information on their platforms. As a case in point, Facebook and Twitter took opposite actions in May 2020 when facing Donald Trump's social media posts (Isaac & Kang, 2020).

The Chinese control of and intervention on the Internet and ingenious ways of disseminating self-benefiting messages to other countries are also worth discussing (Cook, 2019). Because of China's highly controlled communication system, Mokry (2017) reports that the most frequently quoted sources in Western mainstream media are from the Chinese central government. The Freedom House's Annual Report says that the Chinese endeavor may "undermine key features of democratic governance and best practices for media freedom" (Cook, 2019, p. 10). The most significant human resource invested in monitoring online content and steering social media discourse is the so-called 50 cent army, composed of government employees whose task is to screen all online information (King, Pan, & Roberts, 2017). The well-orchestrated cyber program has utilized multiple methods to shape foreign public's perception of China. For example, China-backed efforts to reach soybean farmers via mainstream media were made in order to influence the 2018 midterm election (Cook, 2019). Similarly, twenty-three websites registered in Taiwan were found to disseminate fake news directly from China's government to influence Taiwan's presidential election in 2020 (Chung-shan, Hsin-fang, & Hetherington, 2019). These anecdotes unveil that technologically advanced communication apparatus has been implemented by nation-states or their proxies in order to affect political outcomes in another nation.

Social media automation through the use of algorithms, artificial intelligence, and bots can have a marked impact on another nation. The Russian Internet Research Agency (IRA), according to the Mueller (2019) report, strategically intervened through social media:

> The IRA conducted social media operations targeted at large U.S. audiences with the goal of sowing discord in the U.S. political system. These operations constituted "active measures," a term that typically refers to operations conducted by Russian security services aimed at influencing the course of international affairs.
>
> (Mueller, 2019, p. 14)

According to the report, by the end of 2016, the IRA had produced 80,000 Facebook posts and reached 126 million people. Twitter reported that 3,814 accounts were controlled by the IRA and 1.4 million may have been in contact with an IRA-controlled account. This trend of reaching out to foreign nationals with disinformation is likely to worsen (Davis & Mazzetti, 2019). Recently, Twitter took down 23,750 accounts linked to China that tweeted 348,608 times, 1,152 Russian accounts that tweeted 3,434,792 times, and 7,340 Turkish accounts that tweeted 36,948,524 times (Observatory, 2020), indicating a regular practice for some countries.

The above cases should shed light on what lies ahead. The era of post-truth (Mcintyre, 2018) has facilitated the practice of spreading emotion-stimulated disinformation and complete falsehood to advance sponsoring nations' interests. Capitalizing on the openness of cyberspace and unfettered connections on social media, countries can and have bypassed traditional news gatekeepers and communicated directly with foreign publics and stakeholders around the world. Moreover, the transmitted content can be meticulously—and automatically—tailored to achieve individual targeting, creating the intended effects the sponsor envisions. News reported that Russian's online operation unit based in St. Petersburg (MacFarquhar, 2018) served exactly this purpose. The old-fashioned cultural events used during peace times or blatant propaganda operations during war times have been transformed into a far more high-tech, large-scale, and covert manipulation in cyberspace.

CYBERSPACE

Although the majority of international communication scholarship focuses on traditional mass media, a significant volume of global communication takes place in cyberspace. This artificial space arguably has exerted more influence than other types of media in the twenty-first century—it enables a multitude of communication activities and transforms how people access, process, and act on information originating from other countries. It is notable that under certain circumstances the cyber version of the world can overwhelm and overpower the counterparts covered by mass media (Rainie & Wellman, 2014; Turkle, 2011). The combined impact of platform functionality, information creation and sharing, and participation in cyberspace can cut through all the research topics addressed above and has resulted in tremendous changes—both welcoming and challenging. It is therefore no surprise that countries were found to have resorted to cyberspace to skew reality outside their borders (Alba & Satariano, 2019). As Choucri and Clark (2018) indicate, the ease of access to online information has been a great equalizer, enabling weaker actors to influence or even threaten stronger actors in the world. Cyberspace also provides a level playing field for all levels of participants—not only nation-states, but also individuals, private sector companies, and other communities—to voice, collaborate, network, and advocate for their interests, representation, and possible actions. Given these positive indications, does cyberspace really make global communication more transparent, diversified, and horizontal?

Because of various levels of participants (content providers, commenters, opinion leaders, and so forth) involved in cyberspace, the degree of complexity increases exponentially. The term "lateral pressure" was coined to explain cyber entities' behavior and influence beyond established boundaries (Choucri & Clark, 2018). The #MeToo movement that started in the United States has spread to many other countries and exerted influence in various domains is one case in point. Alt-right and extremist messages, initiated and propagandized on the Internet, also know no national borders and have been blamed to wreak havoc on traditional democracies (Benkler, Faris, & Roberts, 2018). The point here is that nation-states traditionally are the unit of analysis in the communication domain. Yet the Internet has significantly empowered its participants in the cyber communication process. How can individuals be part of and analyzed in international communication? Do/should individuals represent the nation in which they are recognized/come from? These questions can be extended to include alternative participants, such as issue-based online groups or even bots (Veale & Cook, 2018). The issue of participants in cyberspace and their impact on global communication awaits further exploration and clarification.

Zeroing in on "participants" of cyberspace, one can anticipate that certain actors with superior technological know-how and better networks can exert a much greater influence than others. For example, WikiLeaks enjoys unparalleled access to critical information on key leaders and global security; its operation—completely circumventing mainstream media's mechanism—has been able to create political bombshells worldwide. Tencent's WeChat messaging service that reaches an estimated 100 to 200 million users outside China can offer a large platform but is closely monitored and censored by the Chinese government (Cook, 2019; Xiao, 2020). The cyberspace ecosystem along with other issues such as sovereignty, legality, technical management, and online censorship affect global communication greatly. Furthermore, while journalism and mass communication scholars may not be keen on the issues of cybersecurity or warfare—which mostly fall into the realms of data science and international relations (Flournoy & Sulmeyer, 2018)—monitoring of and interfering in communication content and process by foreign nations via cyberspace should be an area of concern. Policy experts and lawmakers therefore should take proactive, sweeping actions.

CHAPTER SUMMARY

This chapter set out to examine the recent interplay between technology and global communication. Cyberspace presents a huge challenge as well as a potential opportunity to transform global communication for the next decades. It could potentially be a great enabler and equalizer for the world's communication participants and enhance the efficiency and magnitude of global communication, despite the unrelenting issues of unequal resources and access. It is also a nexus for the other two critical topics: post-truth and public diplomacy. As explained above, misinformation and the spread of deceptive content online shows some alarming trends, which have been observed in both domestic and international settings. Public diplomacy aims at communicating directly to foreign publics via all types of media in the hope of benefitting sponsoring agents. Merging the two concepts, post-truth public diplomacy (PTPD) strategically disseminates fabricated content across national borders to sway public opinion and bolster the sponsor's interests and goals. PTPD is more than a propaganda apparatus witnessed during world wars, including the Cold War; it is far more sophisticated, technically advanced, and harder to detect by target participants. It has been embraced and implemented by nations of all regions for quite some time and can engender a gargantuan impact on how the world is communicated, understood, and perceived.

One of the major trends in global communication has been Anglo-American influence—in language, pop culture, and media ownership (Stevenson, 1992). The influence in these three areas remains noticeable even today, although it seems to have shifted toward the technology side. Current media technology juggernauts such as smartphone producer (Apple), Internet search engine (Google), content streaming services (Amazon, Apple+, Disney+, and Netflix), and social networking sites (Facebook and Twitter) are all based in the United States. The questions then are whether the prevailing communication system worldwide remains fundamentally uneven and whether these major conglomerates should establish effective mechanisms to curb PTPD and safeguard universal values such as democracy, equal access, and individual privacy and well-being.

The underlying issues from a few media conglomerates that control key technologies are multifaceted, complex, and definitely deserve more attention. For one thing, representativeness, accuracy, and diversity and plurality (of the world's nations, identities, and cultures) in produced and distributed content are always a concern when ownership and management are increasingly centralized. Moreover, the practice of post-truth public diplomacy via the platforms controlled by the conglomerates is one urgent issue as companies wrestle to find solutions how to handle highly deceitful content such as deep fake within civil, open societies (Dowdeswell & Goltz, 2020). Systematic fact-checking and detection of harmful online content by independent, credible entities should be a necessity in order to protect the general public from being misled or deceived. Making sound, effective laws and policies regarding these complex issues should be another feasible pathway for solutions. Lastly, the identified trends have important implications for journalism practice. At the basic level, news professionals working in highly competitive markets need to resist the temptation to simply repackage stories expediently gathered via the social media or other convenient online sources (Lambert & Wu, 2018). In addition, journalists need to be more prepared and embrace new technologies in order to excel in their jobs and serve the world's information needs (International Center for Journalists, 2018). This might be the best time for them to win back their audiences' trust and attention.

FACEBOOK-CAMBRIDGE ANALYTICA DATA SCANDAL

Christopher Wylie, a whistleblower who worked at Cambridge Analytica based in the United Kingdom, unveiled in 2018 that Facebook violated its privacy consent decree and shared more than 50 million users' private information with third parties, including Cambridge Analytica. The research firm, founded by Robert Mercer, a wealthy Republican donor, and headquartered in London, was involved in crafting effective online strategies for Donald Trump's 2016 presidential campaign. Facebook's violation of its commitment to user privacy is particularly damaging to democratic process because it included not only private data on its own services, but also all types of user information across the web, enabling the so-called psychographic modeling. With this trove of private data from Facebook, Trump's campaign team could effectively custom-build its messages to influence key American voter segments. *The Economist* concludes that "targeting based on Cambridge Analytica's data may have helped Mr. Trump win the presidency, although how much cannot be known" ("The Facebook scandal could change politics as well as the internet," 2018). Additionally, the fact that the Facebook platform—during the same period—was penetrated by Russia's advertisements and trolls that disseminated disinformation and misinformation in an attempt to influence the 2016 U.S. presidential election led the public to believe that the social media giant crossed ethical and legal boundaries, and resulted in increasing distrust among its users and even shareholders.

DISCUSSION QUESTIONS

1. What can average users do to prevent disinformation and misinformation about another nation from impacting their social networks?
2. Should governments and/or social media firms systematically sift, label, or purge falsehood from media platforms? Why and why not?
3. Can you identify any content or message that can be categorized as "post-truth public diplomacy"? Do you know which country it comes from (or which country sponsors it)?
4. What type of technology do you think is most critical to enhancing global communication and improving the representation of the Global South, in particular?

BIBLIOGRAPHY

Alba, D., & Satariano, A. (2019, September 26). Turning to 'cyber troops' to skew global reality. *New York Times*, pp. B1, B6.

Allcott, H., & Gentzkow, M. (2017). Social media and fake news in the 2016 election. *Journal of Economic Perspectives, 31*(2), 211–236. doi:10.1257/jep.31.2.211

Aslama, M., & Pantti, M. (2007). Flagging Finnishness: Reproducing national identity in reality television. *Television & New Media, 8*(1), 49–67. doi: 10.1177/1527476406296263

Beckett, C. (2017). Truth, trust and technology. *Media Asia, 44*(2), 98–101. doi:10.1080/01296612.2017.1455571

Benkler, Y., Faris, R., & Roberts, H. (2018). *Network propaganda: Manipulation, disinformation, and radicalization in American politics*. Oxford University Press.

Choucri, N., & Clark, D. D. (2018). *International relations in the cyber age: The co-evolution dilemma*. MIT Press.

Chung-shan, H., Hsin-fang, L., & Hetherington, W. (2019, July 14). Taichung city councilor says 23 local web sites spreading TAO's fake news. *Taipei Times*, p. 3. www.taipeitimes.com/News/taiwan/archives/2019/07/14/2003718648

Cook, S. (2019). *The implications for democracy of China's globalizing media influence*. freedomhouse.org/report/freedom-media/freedom-media-2019

Davenport, T. H. (2018). *The AI advantage: How to put the Artificial Intelligence revolution to work*. MIT Press.

Davis, J. H., & Mazzetti, M. (2019, July 24). Highlights of Robert Mueller's testimony to Congress. *New York Times*. www.nytimes.com/2019/07/24/us/politics/mueller-testimony.html?searchResultPosition=3

Dowdeswell, T. L., & Goltz, N. (2020). The clash of empires: Regulating technological threats to civil society. *Information & Communications Technology Law, 29*(2), 194–217. doi: 10.1080/13600834.2020.1735060

Duncombe, C. (2017). Twitter and transformative diplomacy: Social media and Iran—US relations. *International Affairs, 93*(3), 545–562. doi: 10.1093/ia/iix048

Elasmar, M., & Groshek, J. (2017). A historical overview and future directions in the conceptualization of country images. In J. A. Fullerton & A. Kendrick (Eds.), *Shaping international public opinion: A model for nation branding and public diplomacy* (pp. 27–38). Peter Lang.

Entman, R. M. (2008). Theorizing mediated public diplomacy: The U.S. case. *International Journal of Press/Politics, 13*(2), 87–102. doi:10.1177/1940161208314657

The Facebook scandal could change politics as well as the internet. (2018, March 22). *The Economist*. www.economist.com/united-states/2018/03/22/the-facebook-scandal-could-change-politics-as-well-as-the-internet

Flournoy, M., & Sulmeyer, M. (2018). Battlefield Internet: A plan for securing cyberspace. *Foreign Affairs, 97*(5), 40–46. ezproxy.bu.edu/login?qurl=https%3A%2F%2Fsearch.proquest.com%2Fdocview%2F2094369619%3Faccountid%3D9676

Fu, W. W., & Sim, C. (2010). Examining international country-to-country flow of theatrical films. *Journal of Communication, 60*(1), 120–143. doi:10.1111/j.1460-2466.2009.01455.x

Gilboa, E. (2005). The CNN effect: The Search for a communication theory of international relations. *Political Communication, 22*(1), 27–44. doi:10.1080/10584600590908429

Golan, G. J., Johnson, T. J., & Wanta, W. (Eds.). (2010). *International media communication in a global age*. Routledge.

Grinberg, N., Joseph, K., Friedland, L., Swire-Thompson, B., & Lazer, D. (2019). Fake news on Twitter during the 2016 U.S. presidential election. *Science, 363*(6425), 374–378. doi:10.1126/science.aau2706

Hester, A. (1973). Theoretical considerations in predicting volume and direction of international information flow. *International Communication Gazette, 19*(4), 239–247. doi:10.1177/001654927301900404

Howard, P. N. (2020). *Lie machines: How to save democracy from troll armies, deceitful robots, junk news operations, and political operatives*. Yale University Press.

Hyde-Clarke, N., & Van Tonder, T. (2011). Revisiting the 'Leapfrog' debate in light of current trends of mobile phone Internet usage in the greater Johannesburg area, South Africa. *Journal of African Media Studies, 3*(2), 263–276. doi:10.1386/jams.3.2.263_1

International Center for Journalists. (2018). *ICFJ survey: The state of technology in global newsrooms.* www.icfj.org/sites/default/files/2018-04/ICFJTechSurveyFINAL.pdf

Isaac, M., & Kang, C. (2020, May 29). While Twitter Confronts Trump, Zuckerberg Keeps Facebook Out of It. *New York Times.* www.nytimes.com/2020/05/29/technology/twitter-facebook-zuckerberg-trump.html?action=click&block=more_in_recirc&impression_id=486679771&index=0&pgtype=Article&region=footer

Jones, M. O. (2019). Propaganda, fake news, and fake trends: The weaponization of Twitter bots in the Gulf crisis. *International Journal of Communication (19328036), 13*, 1389–1415. search.ebscohost.com/login.aspx?direct=true&db=ufh&AN=139171770&site=ehost-live&scope=site

King, G., Pan, J., & Roberts, M. E. (2017). How the Chinese government fabricates social media posts for strategic distraction, not engaged argument. *American Political Science Review, 111*(3), 484–501. doi: j.mp/2ovks0q

Lambert, C. A., & Wu, H. D. (2018). Journalists in Taiwan: Marketplace challenges in a free media system. In E. Freedman, R. S. Goodman, & E. Steyn (Eds.), *Critical perspectives on journalistic beliefs and actions* (pp. 57–68). Routledge.

Lerner, D. (1958). *The passing of traditional society: Modernizing the Middle East.* Free Press.

Ling, R., & Horst, H. A. (2011). Mobile communication in the global south. *New Media & Society, 13*(3), 363–374. doi: 10.1177/1461444810393899

Lule, J. (2015). *Globalization and media: Global village of Babel.* Rowman & Littlefield.

MacFarquhar, N. (2018, February 18, 2018). Inside Russia's troll factory: Turning out fake content at a breakneck pace. *New York Times.*

Manheim, J. B. (1994). *Strategic public diplomacy and American foreign policy: The evolution of influence.* Oxford University Press.

Massoglia, A., & West, G. (2018). Foreign interests have spent over $530 million influencing U.S. policy, public opinion since 2017. www.opensecrets.org/news/2018/08/foreign-interests-fara-lobby-watch-exclusive/

Mcintyre, L. (2018). *Post-Truth.* MIT Press.

McLuhan, M., & Powers, B. R. (1989). *Global village: Transformations in world life and media in the 21st century.* Oxford University Press.

Meyrowitz, J. (1986). *No sense of place: The impact of electronic media on social behavior.* Oxford University Press.

Mitchell, A., Gottfried, J., Stocking, G., Walker, M., & Fedeli, S. (2019, June 5, 2019). Many Americans say made-up news is a critical problem that needs to be fixed. www.journalism.org/2019/06/05/many-americans-say-made-up-news-is-a-critical-problem-that-needs-to-be-fixed/

Mokry, S. (2017). Whose voices shape China's global image? Links between reporting conditions and quoted sources in news about China. *Journal of Contemporary China, 26*(107), 650–663. doi: 10.1080/10670564.2017.1305480

Mowlana, H., & Roach, C. (1992). New world information and communication order: Overview of recent developments and activities. *Few voices, many worlds: Towards a media reform movement.* World Association for Christian Communication.

Mueller, R. S., III. (2019). *Report on the investigation into Russian interference in the 2016 presidential election.* U.S. Department of Justice.

Nye, J. S. (2004). *Soft power: The means to success in world politics.* Public Affairs.

Observatory, S. I. (2020). Analysis of June 2020 Twitter takedowns linked to China, Russia and Turkey. cyber.fsi.stanford.edu/io/news/june-2020-twitter-takedown

Pelton, J. N. (2010). Satellites as worldwide change agents. In D. K. Thussu (Ed.), *International communication: A reader* (pp. 13–35). Routledge.

Qin, A., & Carlsen, A. (2018, November 18). How China is rewriting its own script. *New York Times.* www.nytimes.com/interactive/2018/11/18/world/asia/china-movies.html

Rainie, L., & Wellman, B. (Eds.). (2014). *Networked: The new social operating system.* MIT Press.

Reuters. (2019, August 1). Facebook says it dismantles covert influence campaign tied to Saudi government. *New York Times.* www.nytimes.com/reuters/2019/08/01/world/01reuters-facebook-saudi.html?searchResultPosition=1

Rosenberg, M., Confessore, N., & Cadwalladr, C. (2018, March 17). How Trump consultants exploited the Facebook data of millions. *New York Times*. www.nytimes.com/2018/03/17/us/politics/cambridge-analytica-trump-campaign.html?searchResultPosition=10

Russell, A., & Echchaibi, N. (2009). *International blogging: Identity, politics, and networked publics*. Peter Lang.

Schramm, W. (1964). *Mass media and national development: The role of information in the developing countries*. Stanford University Press.

Segev, E. (2016). *International news flow online: Global views with local perspectives*. Peter Lang.

Servaes, J. (2012). Soft power and public diplomacy: The new frontier for public relations and international communication between the US and China. *Public Relations Review, 38*(5), 643–651. doi: doi.org/10.1016/j.pubrev.2012.07.002

Stevenson, R. L. (1992). Defining international communication as a field. *Journalism Quarterly, 69*(3), 543–553. doi:10.1177/107769909206900302

Stevenson, R. L., & Shaw, D. L. (Eds.). (1984). *Foreign news and the new world information order*. Iowa State Press.

Thussu, D. K. (2007). *News as entertainment: The rise of global infotainment*. Sage Publications.

Tuch, H. N. (1990). *Communicating with the world: U.S. public diplomacy overseas*. St. Martin's Press.

Turkle, S. (2011). *Alone together: Why we expect more from technology and less from each other*. Basic Books.

Veale, T., & Cook, M. (2018). *Twitterbots: Making machines that make meaning*. MIT Press.

Walter, D., Sheafer, T., Nir, L., & Shenhav, S. (2016). Not All Countries Are Created Equal: Foreign Countries Prevalence in U.S. News and Entertainment Media. *Mass Communication and Society, 19*(4), 522–541. doi:10.1080/15205436.2016.1170853

Woolley, S. C., & Howard, P. N. (Eds.). (2019). *Computational propaganda: Political parties, politicians, and political manipulation on social media*. Oxford University Press.

Wu, H. D. (1998). Investigating the determinants of international news flow: A meta-analysis. *International Communication Gazette, 60*(6), 493–512.

Xiao, E. (2020, May 8). World News: WeChat Monitors Foreign Users. *Wall Street Journal*, p. A9.

4

Media Freedom Around the World

Jane Whyatt

A shot rings out. A car bomb explodes. The secret agent re-arranges the reporter's lifeless body so that it looks like a suicide. The rapist's throttling fingers close around the journalist's neck and she stops breathing. The whistleblower hears the key turn in the lock and knows he is never going home.

These examples of extreme censorship have all happened in real life, in recent years. Journalists around the world continue to lose their lives because of their work—either in war reporting or by assassination. Most of them were killed in conflict zones or unrest. Yet even in peaceful Western democracies, there is a significant death toll. Here are the names of journalists who have been killed in North America and Europe since 2015: Alison Parker and Adam Ward, shot on live TV (Virginia, USA, 26.8.2015); Pavel Sheremet, car bomb (Ukraine, 20.7.2016); Kim Wall, raped, murdered and dismembered (Denmark, 10.8.2017); Daphne Caruana Galizia, car bomb (Malta, 16.10.2017); Viktoria Marinova, raped and murdered (Bulgaria, 6.10.2018); Ján Kuciak and Martina Kušnírova, shot dead (Slovakia, 22.2.2018); Gerald Fischmann, Wendi Winters, John McNamara, Rob Hiaasen, shot dead (Maryland, USA, 28.6.2018); Jamal Khashoggi, murdered and dismembered (Saudi Embassy, Turkey, 2.10.2018); Antonio Megalizzi, killed in a terrorist attack (France, 11.12.2018); Lyra McKee, shot dead (Northern Ireland, 18.04.2019); and Vadym Kumarov, beaten into a coma (Ukraine, 20.6.2019).

These are not even the worst cases. In 2015, twelve writers, editors, and cartoonists were massacred at the editorial office of the French satirical magazine *Charlie Hébdo* and eleven other people were injured. The Committee to Protect Journalists notes that worldwide 1,369 journalists were killed between 1992 and 2020 (CPJ, 2020).

Mafia death threats against media workers mean that at least twenty reporters and TV presenters live under permanent 24-hour police guard in Italy. The Rome-based monitoring organization Ossigeno per l'informazione (Oxygen of information) has created a tribute website honoring Italian journalists who have been killed because of their work (see www.giornalistiuccisi. it/en/homepage/). The public also mourns their loss, as shown in the photo of Slovakian journalist Kuciak and his fiancée (see figure 4.1).

Figure 4.1.   Bratislava Shrine to Ján Kuciak. Photo Credit: Jane Whyatt. Source: Original/Self-generated

These journalists all died because criminals and corrupt politicians tried to silence their critics. They believed they could do it with impunity. They would get away with murder. The extent to which they enjoy that impunity in different countries is a litmus test for press freedom.

JOURNALISM IS NOT A CRIME

Many journalists around the world are behind bars because of their work. Turkey is one of the world's worst offenders for locking up critical writers. They are held on charges such as "supporting terrorism," "insulting the president" or "spying," all arising from their journalistic work.

Murder and imprisonment are relatively rare. More common are physical beatings, blocked access, gender-based violence, online trolling, and the most insidious of all—self-censorship. This happens when threats are internalized, so that a reporter knows instinctively that a certain subject is too dangerous to cover, or a chill of fear strikes the heart of a publisher.

Political leaders who wish to weaken press freedom often denigrate particular journalists, or smear certain media outlets as "fake news." There are recent, frequent examples of this in the United States of America, Turkey, Zimbabwe, Slovenia, Hungary, Greece, and the United Kingdom.

THE KILLING OF KUCIAK

Ján Kuciak was an investigative reporter on the Slovakian news website Aktuality.sk. He was working on alleged corruption involving government politicians, grants from the European Union and an Italian mafia gang, the 'Ndrangheta.

Kuciak lived with his fiancée Martina Kusnirova in the town of Velka Maca. They were both 27 years old and making preparations for their wedding. On 21 February 2018, a hired assassin broke into their home. He shot Jàn through the head and Martina through the heart. Those shots reverberated through Slovakian society, triggering a wave of protests against corruption with tens of thousands of people on the streets. A new movement was formed, calling itself "For a decent Slovakia" (Za slusne Slovensko). Press freedom missions went to Slovakia to offer support and solidarity to the bereaved families and pressure the authorities to find the killer. Prime Minister Robert Fico and his entire cabinet resigned. Yet still, the assassinations went unpunished. Then police chief Tibor Gašpar quit and his replacement began to question suspects.

Five were arrested: Zoltan Andrusko who organized the killings and Miroslav Marcek who pulled the trigger were tried first after pleading guilty. They are serving jail terms of 15 and 25 years, respectively. Their evidence framed the alleged mastermind behind the plot, business owner Marian Kočner who was already in jail. He was sentenced in 2019 to 19 years for financial crimes including falsifying promissory notes (see MFRR, 2020). The United States Treasury Department had added Kočner's name to its international corruption watchlist and frozen his company assets on December 10, 2019 (Human Rights Day). On September 3, 2020, he was acquitted of commissioning the murders of Ján Kuciak and Martina Kušnírova. Kočner's alleged accomplice Alena Zsuszova, who was accused of handing over 70,000 euros ($82,000) to pay for the killings, was also cleared. Tomas Szabo, the getaway driver, was found guilty and sentenced to 25 years in prison for his part in the murders.

The case had far-reaching consequences. Thirteen judges, including the Acting Supreme Court President, were arrested in a police raid in March 2020 by police investigating their communications with Marian Kočner in the Threema encrypted app. Slovakia elected a new president just two days after Marian Kočner was jailed for financial crimes. She is Zuzana Čaputovà and she chose as her first official duty as President to visit the shrine in the capital Bratislava where fresh flowers, photos, and candles honor the memory of Ján Kuciak and Martina Kušnirova.

Meanwhile Kuciak's colleagues continue his work and a new investigative journalism center has been established in his name. They know the risks involved, and in June 2020 came a grim reminder: *Atkuality.sk* reporter Peter Sabo received a bullet in the post.

FROM AREOPAGITICA TO ALGORITHMS AND ANALYSERS

Yet the concept of press freedom is contested and has different meanings in different contexts. Attempts to define it started in 1644 with poet John Milton's *Areopagitica,* the Latin form of the Greek "Areophagus." That is the name of a large rock near the Acropolis temple in Athens, the capital of Greece. There the ancient censors met and courts were held—including the one which sentenced to death the philosopher Socrates.

In Milton's case, he had been refused permission by the church to divorce his wife. All the pamphlets he had written, urging divorce law reform, had been censored. So the motivation for this founding document *Areopagitica* was not so much free speech as free love. (Milton wished to be free to marry another woman, known to history as "Miss Davis"!). The English House of Commons passed a Bill of Rights in 1766, following agitation by journalist and MP John Wilkes, but it only granted the freedom to publish in full the proceedings of the House of Commons without risk of libel suits (Mellen, 2015).

More than 100 years passed before the French Revolution of 1789 and the First Amendment to the Bill of Rights, ratified by the State of Virginia in 1791, both enshrined freedom of speech and the press for all citizens. In France, the writer Madame (Germaine) de Staël, who had lived through that Revolution, described press freedom as *"The right on which all other rights depend."* She showed more enthusiasm than the self-serving John Milton. He was later employed as a government censor on the government newspaper *Mercurius Politicus.*

France continues to honor the freedom of the press at La Maison des Journalistes (The House of Journalists), a museum and refuge for journalists in trouble. The U.S. First Amendment is displayed at the National Constitution Center in Philadelphia, Pennsylvania, and celebrated at a museum in Augusta, Maine.

Given this history and ongoing reverence, it is no surprise that the twenty-first century's leading global arbiters of press and media freedom are based in the United States and France, respectively. *Freedom House*, substantially funded by the U.S. government with additional recent grants from the Canadian, Norwegian, and Netherlands governments, has published an annual assessment of freedom across the globe since 1941. And *Reporters sans Frontières (RSF)* or *Reporters Without Borders* also produces a detailed set of rankings displayed on a map of the world (see figure 4.2). Another useful mapping of countries with most censored media is produced by the Committee to Protect Journalists (see figure 4.3). RSF's work began in 1985. It receives 50 percent of its funding from the French government, gets grants from philanthropic organizations, and generates its own income from selling books and pens (The WEApen retails at 100 euros or $109).

Both the Freedom House and the RSF rankings are open to criticism for alleged Western bias. This is not surprising, since only Western democracies see press freedom as a public good and put a strong emphasis on it. Other forms of government rely on restricting press freedom to sustain unelected leaders in power through propaganda and might argue that the role of the press is to promote their policies, national development, or economic growth.

Other monitoring systems share an American version of freedom: Ralph Lowenstein's Press Independence and Critical Ability (PICA) Index, developed in the 1960s, maintains that any financial assistance from government subsidy or reliance on state advertising revenue severely compromises the freedom of the media outlet (Lowenstein, 1970).

Dutta and Roy (2009) emphasize, as Lowenstein does, that financial independence is a key determinant that allows media outlets to be free. However, their 2009 study of 115 countries insists that foreign direct investment is the best means to that end. Sobel et al. (2010)

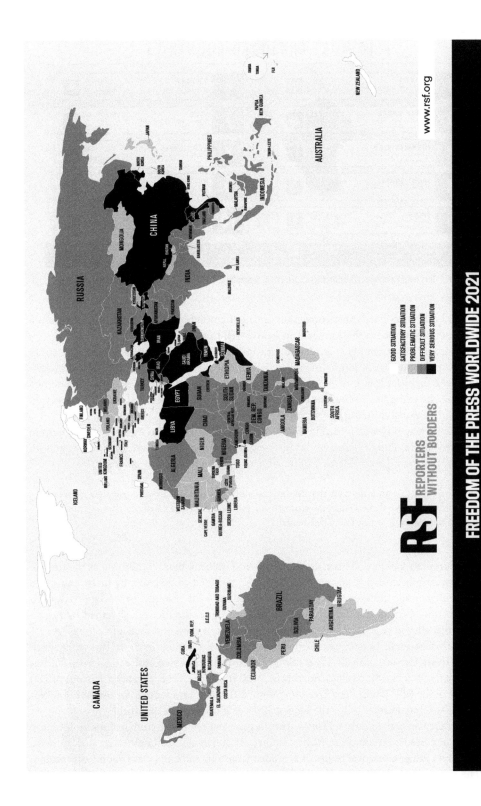

Figure 4.2. Freedom of the press worldwide. Source: Reporters Without Borders, 2021. www.rsf.org

Figure 4.3.   Ten most censored countries. Source: Committee to Protect Journalists, 2020. cpj.org/

discovered that press freedom is contagious and that contiguous countries benefitted from a "spillover effect" if the neighboring nation scored well in the rankings.

Apart from these attempts at academic scrutiny, most assessments generally consist either of counting the number of journalists killed, jailed, threatened or sued, or of a holistic assessment of the financial health of the independent media and the state of democracy. The two approaches are embodied in the United States/Freedom House versus RSF/France stereotypes and dominate global thinking on press freedom.

In 2009, a new player arrived. The European Charter of Freedom of the Press was written and signed in Hamburg, Germany, by forty-eight editors-in-chief from nineteen European countries. European Union Media Commissioner, Viviane Reding, welcomed it:

> The Charter is . . . an important step towards reinforcing these basic values and rights allowing journalists to invoke them against governments or public authorities whenever they feel the freedom of their work is unjustifiably threatened.
>
> (EC, 2009, para. 2)

The European Union (EU) is a single market and political bloc, comprising at the time of writing twenty-seven nation-states. Membership is regarded as desirable by many countries. The EU offers trade deals and international protections—for example, in workers' rights. To qualify for membership, candidate countries need to show that they are governed by rule of law and that they have achieved international standards of press and media freedom.

So the Charter can be seen as a sort of meal ticket for nations such as Turkey, a North Atlantic Treaty Organization (NATO) military pact member, which aspire to join the EU but fail to live up to democratic values, notably on press freedom. Turkey is ranked 154 out of 180 countries in the RSF World Press Freedom league 2019, and Freedom House assesses it as Not Free and—as noted earlier—it is the biggest jailer of journalists in the world.

One of the Charter's founders, Hans-Ulrich Jörges, went on to co-found the European Centre for Press and Media Freedom (ECPMF), a non-governmental organization that aims to make the Charter's values a practical reality. It is funded largely by the European Union Commission.

The question of who pays for NGOs that promote press and media freedom in Europe is highly significant. A good score in the international rankings of RSF and Freedom House can open the door to membership of the European Union, or other trading blocs, or bring interim rewards, such as emergency relief funds or the relaxation of visa requirements. By funding certain NGOs to deliver specific projects, the paymasters can strengthen certain elements in civil society and influence policy.

ALGORITHMS

Algorithms are mathematical constructions that can be trained to produce or reproduce data and to find patterns in it, which resemble the raw material of what we call "news." They are widely used in media production today, but not widely understood. Nor are they closely monitored, since commercial confidentiality means that their workings are regarded as "trade secrets" so that they exist in what is known as a "black box."

However, algorithms have consequences for freedom of the press. A 2017 experiment by U.S. social network Facebook included two European countries—Serbia and Slovakia—among its "lab rats." Suddenly newspapers there found that their articles were no longer included in their Facebook followers' regular feed. Instead, users were forced to switch instead to a "Rocket Feed" to continue reading their favorite articles (The Daily Disruptor, 2018). This resulted in a sudden massive loss of advertising revenue for local news outlets, since they could no longer prove to advertisers that thousands of users had engaged with their articles. Now they got only a handful of clicks and shares.

Still, who would dare to suggest that Facebook and its GAFA counterparts (Google, Amazon, Facebook, Apple) should not be free to deliver factual content differently, by tweaking their algorithm? This technology is just a tool. Newsrooms are also using it to empower investigative reporting and training algorithms to become, for example, sports reporters (Thurman et al., 2017).

Algorithms are also being applied to the study of press freedom. The ECPMF and the University of Leipzig, Germany, are developing an innovative approach to monitoring press and media freedom. Based on an interactive map by Ushahidi, it will use Artificial Intelligence (AI) to identify and log, for example, attacks on journalists, censorship, new restrictions, and gender-based hate speech. The map will be known as Mapping Media Freedom 2.0. Automatically generated and crowd-sourced alerts will be verified and categorized by a network of human researchers before they are uploaded to the map. The statistics will be used to trigger help for journalists in trouble in an international partnership of seven organizations called the Media Freedom Rapid Response. In its first three months of operation, the Media Freedom Rapid Response charted 152 violations of press and media freedom across a range of legal, physical, and online threats (MFRR, 2020).

Those human researchers live in-country and are native speakers of the local languages. They belong to the European Federation of Journalists, representing 300,000 trade union journalists and paid for by members' subscriptions) and the International Press Institute (IPI). Based in the Austrian capital Vienna, IPI has grassroots media freedom campaigners and lawyers and is funded by the governments of Austria and Sweden, the European Union Commission, and philanthropic foundations.

ANALYZER

More far-reaching—but less technologically advanced—is the new Media Freedom Analyzer proposed by University of Hamburg postdoctoral researcher Laura Schneider (2020).

She evaluates existing methods of assessing press and media freedom, noting that empirical research into these is in its infancy. Schneider replaces traditional monitoring systems such as Freedom House and RSF's with an in-depth survey, to be answered by in-country journalists and experts. Schneider explains:

> Almost 1,000 worldwide experts determined which factors should be included in the new instrument and how those indicators should be weighted. The structure of the set of indicators was also empirically supported by the experts' evaluations. Consequently, the aim of developing an empirically-based measuring instrument to reduce subjectivity and potential bias was achieved.
>
> (Schneider, 2020, p. 6)

FREEDOM OF THE MARKET

In addition to ensuring freedom from political control, economic freedom is crucial to press freedom. For if a newspaper receives state subsidies (as in France) or is owned by a political party's educational trust (as in Denmark), how can it bite the hand that feeds it? Across Europe, media have flourished thanks to free-market economics. There was a gap of a few decades for countries under communist control after World War II, but they reverted to free-market economies around 1990.

In a free market, anyone can start a newspaper, a blog, a YouTube channel, or a podcast. However, to make a living from it and to achieve a professional quality of journalism is prohibitively expensive. This is still the case even today, with access to the Internet and easy-to-use, affordable means of filming, recording, editing, and publishing. The free market favors multimedia, multinational corporations that can afford to cross-subsidize loss-making news outlets with profits from, for example, a luxury luggage business like Louis Vuitton. It is owned by French tycoon Bernard Arnault's LMVH group, which lists his media interests *Le Parisien, Les Echos*, and *Radio Classique* under "other activities" on its website, as though two major national newspapers with a combined readership of almost 24 million people are of little importance, compared to the latest trend in bags.

Similarly, the massive farming concern Agrofert is the powerhouse of a business empire built up by the Prime Minister of the Czech Republic, Andrej Babiš, now controlled by a trust. It also owns the biggest media house in the country, Mafra (Sykorova, 2018).

Perhaps the most famous example of a media-owning political leader is Silvio Berlusconi, who has been Italy's Prime Minister four times. His business assets include the Mediaset TV companies and AC Milan football club. Media magnates reach across national boundaries too: Ireland's Mr. Big, Denis O'Brien, owned over the past decade most of Bulgaria's private radio stations, as well as stations in Hungary, Latvia, Finland, and Estonia. Competition rules meant his Communicorp companies had to divest from those countries. Now he has Communicorp U.K. which controls eight radio stations in Britain. Meanwhile Australian-born U.S. citizen Rupert Murdoch's News Corporation owns the U.S. influential Fox News and dominates the British TV news and print newspaper markets. Setting aside the academic thesis of Dutta and Roy (2009) that foreign investment promotes press freedom, this concentration of media ownership is regarded by most observers as inimical to press freedom.

At the European University Institute in Fiesole, Italy, the Centre for Media Pluralism and Freedom (CMPF) scrutinizes individual countries in the Media Pluralism Monitor. This is less well known than the Freedom House and RSF press freedom monitoring systems, but in many ways more relevant. The in-country monitors are media academics, working with journalists on the ground in the local language(s). Among other criteria, they assess the safety of journalists (including job security), the state of professional development of journalism, and the social inclusiveness of the media (for example in allowing a voice for minority languages and critical reporting). The extent of political or proprietorial interference in editorial decision-making is also measured (see cmpf.eui.eu/).

FREEDOM FROM POLITICAL INTERFERENCE

The owners of national and international news media can use their outlets to promote their favorite politicians. They do so in the hope that politicians would return the favor, for example by passing laws that make it easier to maximize profits, to destroy the journalists' and printers' trade unions, to acquire new titles, TV and radio networks, or avoid paying taxes (Greenslade, 2004).

In the United Kingdom, some newspaper owners were granted seats in the House of Lords and so became politicians themselves. They were known as "the press barons." The U.K. current Prime Minister Boris Johnson is a journalist by profession.

In France, the owner of the *Figaro* newspaper is weapons manufacturer Serge Dassault. Naturally, the company receives defense contracts from the French government. Not so natural: Serge Dassault's son Olivier is a deputy in the Assemblée Nationale, the lower house of parliament. Politics, business, and media activities that overlap in this way are known as "conflicts of interest" and raise questions about corruption.

On the Mediterranean island of Malta, where many such questions have been raised by investigative journalists, the TV stations are each owned and controlled by a different political party. The CMPF Media Monitor (2020, p.14) assesses this as a 90 percent risk of political interference and comments that this system is unique in Europe: "both political parties represented in the House of Representatives own, control and manage their own media enterprises consisting of different media outlets."

By contrast, in Germany "mainstream media" (the local term for the politically centrist quality newspapers and public service broadcasters) try to visibly distance themselves from political figures because of long-standing criticism from the right- and left-wing parties. They are accused of being "Systemmedien"—media mouthpieces for "the system"—the coalition of parties that has governed Germany since the 1989 fall of the Berlin Wall and the re-unification of communist East and capitalist West Germany (Krüger, 2016). In this way, the German attitude is more akin to the American view of the proper relationship between politicians and journalists, immortalized by *Baltimore Sun* writer H.L. Mencken: Journalism is to politician as dog is to lamp-post and exemplified by the Watergate scandal, in which reporters revealed wrong-doing that led to the impeachment of President Richard Nixon.

The weapon of choice for autocratic politicians wishing to manipulate the mass media into supporting their parties is public service media (PSM). As the name suggests, PSM is meant to serve the public by providing accurate, impartial, and up-to-date news that reflects the nation's social, political, and religious diversity so that citizens can make well-informed democratic choices. As examples, Poland and Hungary show how the ruling parties, Law and Justice (PiS) in Poland and Fidesz in Hungary, have dismissed broadcast journalists who challenged their political views, or who tried to exercise the impartial objectivity that is required in public TV and radio. To make the changes stick, they have both reformed the regulatory structures that govern public broadcasting, putting their candidates in leading positions.

Similar trends can be observed across Eastern Europe, including the Czech Republic. In Hungary, this party-political takeover, known as "state capture" was completed in November 2018. According to the government, media owners "donated their assets to KESMA, a new conglomerate" (ECPMF, 2018). It was headed by one of the Prime Minister Viktor Orbàn's greatest supporters, the media owner Gabor Liszkay. Further "consolidation" followed, as a joint media freedom fact-finding mission led by International Press Institute found in 2019.

Poland is "re-polonising" its media markets by excluding foreign owners and using state advertising budgets to favor government-friendly media at the expense of the main opposition newspaper *Gazeta Wyborzca*. Both Hungary and Poland are subject to Section 7 sanctions by the European Commission because of unconstitutional reforms of the judiciary and political moves that restrict press freedom and media plurality.

FREEDOM OF INFORMATION

However, independent and investigative journalism is not yet extinct.

New technological tools such as data science and AI-powered reporting are helping journalists to hold politicians to account. They work best when harnessed to a legal instrument called Freedom of Information. That gives journalists (and citizens) the right to request and receive official information that has not been published.

The American investigative journalist Heather Brooke (now Professor Brooke at London's City University, United Kingdom) championed the public's right to know as a guiding principle, setting citizens and taxpayers at the heart of the debate (Brooke, 2006).

Her campaign for a U.K. Freedom of Information Act was successful and coincided with the *Daily Telegraph*'s exposé—based on leaked government documents—of massive fraud by hundreds of Members of the House of Commons and Lords (the lower and upper houses of Parliament). They were cheating on their expenses, paid for by the taxpayer. Seven went to prison, one had a mental breakdown and dozens were forced to resign, including Sir Peter Viggers who claimed £1,645 ($1,800) for building a house for the ducks that lived on the lake at his country house.

Freedom of Information (FOI) requests, enshrined in the 2000 Act became a powerful tool for journalists to hold politicians and bureaucrats accountable to those they are supposed to serve: "we the people," as the United States Constitution states.

In the Spanish capital Madrid, a non-governmental organization called *Access Info Europe* attempts to enforce freedom of information across the whole continent. In 2019, they scored a notable victory, obliging the European Parliament to reveal details of Members' expenses which had previously been kept confidential.

WHISTLEBLOWERS

Still, FOI does not always deliver the goods. So reporters must rely on information from sources. How the leakers and whistleblowers are treated by governments and public opinion provides a further important indicator for the health (or sickness!) of freedom.

Whistleblowers are vital to journalism in its function as democracy's watchdog. For this reason, all journalists' ethical codes insist that sources must be protected, their identities must not be revealed and a good reporter should be prepared to go to jail rather than betray a source. Trainee reporter Bill Goodwin came close to a jail term in 1996 (Davies, 2011) and Suzanne Breen took her right to keep sources secret to the High Court in Belfast in 2009 (Dowell, 2009).

In both these cases, it was the United Kingdom—the historic inventor of press freedom—that tried to prosecute those journalists. The United Kingdom is equally repressive with whistleblowers:

- The founder of the WikiLeaks secure online platform, Julian Assange, is currently held in solitary confinement in a maximum security prison near London, awaiting extradition on spying and computer misuse charges to the United States.
- Maria Bamieh, a judge, was sacked from her job at the EU mission to Kosovo after revealing wrongdoing in the court system there, first internally and then to the press.
- Katharine Gun, an analyst at the GCHQ spy center, was prosecuted and facing 20 years in jail for leaking an e-mail to the *Observer* newspaper that showed the case for a US and UK invasion of Iraq was based on lies. The case was dropped at the last minute. It is now a Hollywood film *Official Secrets* starring Keira Knightley.

Elsewhere in Europe, whistleblowers are also suffering. These include

Rui Pinto, who leaked the data that led to the Football Leaks soccer bribes scandal and the Luanda Leaks political corruption exposé is awaiting trial in Portugal, after being extradited from Hungary, and Aleksandr Obradovic, who revealed corruption and sanctions-busting in the Serbian state-owned arms company and was put under house arrest.

GENDER-BASED THREATS

Just as in the Hollywood movie industry where the #MeToo allegations of sexual harassment emerged in 2018, female journalists in the United States are sometimes treated disrespectfully as sex objects and offered promotion in return for sexual favors. The story of the Fox News women newscasters who teamed up to denounce this practice is now itself a Hollywood movie, *Bombshell*.

It happens in Europe too, and there is currently an investigation underway at France Télévisions of sexist abuse against female sports reporters.

More serious is the violence provoked by online hate speech that targets women in the media. At least two women have fought back successfully, enhancing their reputation while the haters were made to suffer. Jessikka Aro, a Finnish TV reporter, tracked down her trolls to a "hate factory" in St. Petersburg, Russia. One of them was jailed for two years in 2018 and Ms. Aro was awarded the Courage in Journalism Prize 2020.

Alexandra Pascalidou, a Swedish TV journalist of Greek heritage, suffered death threats, threats to rape her young daughter and a neo Nazi demonstration outside the TV station where she works. It was prompted by her reporting on refugees, homeless people, and marginalized groups in society. She faced them down, writing a play and posting a YouTube video about her experience. Eventually one neo-Nazi contacted her to apologize, saying he had quit the movement. Pascalidou met him and wrote his story as a front page article in the *Dag Nyter* newspaper.

There are also trolls in high places. They are harder to denounce. The President of the Czech Republic Milos Zeman made a speech in 2018 denouncing journalists as "hyenas and whores" and Slovenia's Prime Minister Janez Jansa has been hit with a 6,000 euro fine for a 2018 tweet in which he called two female reporters "prostitutes you can have for 30 euros."

As gender-based violence against female workers becomes more visible, the United Nations has appointed a Special Rapporteur and opened a consultation on this problem. The Media Freedom Rapid Response (MFRR, 2020) has a Women's Reporting Point and other services are offering help. A smartphone app called JSafe is in Beta testing, and U.S. journalist Michelle Ferrier has founded an online community called Trollbusters.com.

SLAPP! YOUR NEWSPAPER'S FINISHED AND SO IS YOUR CAREER

Some of the most potent weapons against journalistic freedom are totally legal. The laws of libel and insult exist to allow a right of redress to people who are unjustly defamed. However, they can be abused to devastating effect by filing abusive lawsuits through the courts. They are intended to intimidate critics, thwart investigative reporting and ultimately cause the financial collapse of the news outlet that is their target. That is why they are known as Strategic Litigation Against Public Participation (SLAPPs). Typically, they are brought by politicians or wealthy business owners to cover up their dealings by frightening away the media.

EMERGENCY REGULATIONS

Governments use states of emergency to curb freedom of thought and expression, just as they restrict freedom of movement by curfews and bans.

In France on 13.11.2015, a state of emergency was declared following the Islamist terrorist attacks on the Stade de France and the Bataclan concert venue, both in the capital Paris. It was renewed after the deadly Islamist attack in Nice on 14.7.2016 and repealed after five extensions in November 2017. In 2018, there was a terrorist shooting rampage in Strasbourg in which an Italian journalist was among five people killed. The state of emergency was not renewed. Observers such as RSF believe that this is because its provisions have already been quietly transformed into normal police practice.

In Turkey after the failed military coup on 15.7.2016, President Erdoğan's government started closing down news media outlets and arresting the journalists on suspicion of supporting the "Gülenist terrorism conspiracy to overthrow the democratically-elected government" (Committee to Protect Journalists, 2018). Since then more than 150 journalists, editors and writers have been detained. Eight-five are still in jail (European Federation of Journalists, 2020).

The emergency decree in Hungary gave the government the power to jail media workers or anyone spreading "false information" for up to five years. Spain's Royal Decree also criminalized the publication of false information. In Slovenia and the Czech Republic, governments used the pandemic as a platform to vilify journalists and accuse them of "spreading panic." The Greek Health Minister banned health editors from attending government briefings, allowing them only to submit online one written question each. Serbia stepped back from restrictions like these after reporter Ana Lalić was arrested outside a hospital and her camera and mobile phone were confiscated by police. It caused an outcry from media freedom campaigners. Later Lalic was released and her equipment was returned, and the Prime Minister Ana Brnabic withdrew the emergency provisions.

Governments used the 2020 Corona virus pandemic to bring in emergency restrictions that affected the work of journalists (MFRR, 2020). In China, where the Corona virus outbreak was first diagnosed, tight control of the media by a totalitarian government meant that only the official version of the health crisis was widely known. Jane Li, a Hong Kong-based reporter at Quartz, told an International Women in Media Foundation webinar about how she feared for the safety of her sources in China who used social media to communicate facts and figures that contradicted the Chinese government messages.

A similar situation exists in Turkey, where in 2020 a new social media law and repeated blocking of individual Twitter accounts are being used to strangle even the tiny amounts of critical reporting that can be spread by microblogging. And in Belarus and Bulgaria, two east European countries where popular protests in the streets continued for weeks, social media are used to disseminate dissent because of the government crackdown on mainstream media, which can no longer be regarded as free.

Civil unrest caused by the lockdown restrictions brought new threats to press freedom in Germany: demonstrations dubbed "Hygiene Demos" brought together disparate groups of anti-vaxxers (people opposed to vaccination), populists, and neo-Nazis who believed the mainstream media were "lying" about Corona virus. In Stuttgart and the capital Berlin, they attacked camera crews who were filming the protests. The "lying press" ("Lügenpresse" in German) is a term of abuse frequently hurled at camera crews covering right-wing marches. It is the subject of a long-term monitoring project by the European Centre for Press and Media Freedom.

Financial ruin inflicted on many freelance journalists and photographers by the cancellation of normal life, travel, sport and politics can turn a crisis into an economic emergency. Press freedom campaigners lobby for funding to alleviate this distress, because it is dangerous to press freedom. If journalists' jobs or contracts are insecure, they are less likely to take risks or to upset the boss, the boss's political friends, or the advertisers. Insecurity breeds self-censorship.

GLIMMERS OF HOPE

In 2019 an international team of fact-finders went to Denmark and Sweden, neighboring countries that are consistently ranked in the top five in the world for press freedom. They produced a report outlining best practices, which enable a supportive environment for press and media freedom: a high level of trade union organization among media workers, state subsidies delivered at "arm's length" to newspapers and a concerted effort to involve local audiences in the newsgathering operations of the public service broadcaster (ECPMF, 2019).

The European Parliament and Commission, recognizing the importance of press freedom for defending European values, use tax euros funding the Media Freedom Rapid Response and the IJ4EU cross-border investigative journalism project. In Italy, a well-developed police protection scheme, with political backing from the Anti-Mafia Commission, ensures that media workers facing credible death threats from organized criminals can do their jobs as journalists in safety. Working with the journalists' trade unions and the police federations, the European Centre for Press and Media Freedom has devised a new Press Freedom Police Codex, as the basis for dialogue, aiming toward better mutual understanding and an end to police violence against journalists.

These are practical initiatives that tackle press and media freedom violations as they happen. For a more considered perspective on the best way to measure and assess progress, trends, and needs, more work clearly needs to be done. This should synthesize the 360-degree Laura Schneider Media Freedom Analyser (Schneider, 2020) with accurate statistics about violations and trends, for example, from the Mapping Media Freedom 2.0 project (mappingmedia freedom.org) and add the political and financial filters provided by the Media Pluralism Monitor (cmpf.eui.eu/media-pluralism-monitor/). Special consideration should also be given to particular threats such as gender-based violence, vexatious lawsuits, and the protection of sources and whistleblowers. All these together give a true panorama.

CHAPTER SUMMARY

This chapter shows that the Western view of press and media freedom is contested, complex, and even contradictory. Yet in the end, it comes down to courage. It's the courage that murdered Maltese investigative reporter Daphne Caruana Galizia showed in challenging corruption: "*Speak the truth, even if your voice shakes*" is the title of a collection of her writings published to honor her memory (Caruana Galizia & Saviano, 2020). Her other work was completed in The Daphne Project, an award-winning cross-border journalistic investigation. Her widower Peter and three sons continue to defend her reputation against posthumous SLAPP lawsuits in the Maltese courts and at the public inquiry into her death. The Daphne Caruana Galizia Foundation stands as her legacy, together with the Kim Wall Foundation, the Ján Kuciak Center for Investigative Journalism, the Lyra McKee Award and the Slavko Ćuruvija Foundation, and others.

Perhaps the best way to monitor the press and media freedom in the future is not to wait for more memorials to murdered journalists to join the roll of honor, but to note the warning signs, track the trends, and act on them.

DISCUSSION QUESTIONS

1. How do sources and whistleblowers contribute to press and media freedom?
2. Research the case of one of the journalists named in the chapter and explain what this case tells us about press freedom.
3. Why do you believe that the United States ranks lower in the RSF World Press Freedom chart than Sweden?
4. What would you do to improve the fairness and accuracy of international monitoring systems that are used to measure the state of press and media freedom in a given country?

BIBLIOGRAPHY

Brooke, H. (2006). *Your right to know: A citizen's guide to the Freedom of Information Act* (2nd ed.). Pluto Press.

Centre for Press and Media Freedom (2000). *Media pluralism monitor*. cmpf.eui.eu/media-pluralism-monitor

Committee to Protect Journalists. (2018, Dec. 13). *Hundreds of journalists jailed globally becomes the new normal*. cpj.org/reports/2018/12/journalists-jailed-imprisoned-turkey-china-egypt-saudi-arabia/

Committee to Protect Journalists. (2020). *32 Journalists killed in 2020.* cpj.org/data/killed/2020/?status=Killed&motiveConfirmed%5B%5D=Confirmed&type%5B%5D=Journalist&start_year=2020&end_year=2020&group_by=location

Caruana Galizia, D., & Saviano, R. (2020, Oct. 19). *Di la verità anche si la sua voce trema.* Munizioni.

Davies, P. (2011, Oct. 23). European court backs journalist who hid source. *The Independent.* www.independent.co.uk/news/european-court-backs-journalist-who-hid-source-1344436.html

Dowell, B. (2009, June 11). Suzanne Breen: Defending journalists' right to protect sources. *The Guardian.* www.theguardian.com/media/2009/jun/11/suzanne-breen-profile

Dutta, N., & Roy, S. (2009, April 15). The impact of foreign direct investment on press freedom. *Kyklos,* *2*(2), 239–257.

European Federation of Journalists. (2020). *Turkey: Can Dündar sentenced to over 27 years in prison.* europeanjournalists.org/blog/2020/12/23/turkey-can-dundar-sentenced-to-over-27-years-in-prison/

European Centre for Press and Media Freedom. (2018). *Media freedom in Hungary is no more.* mailchi.mp/ecpmf/press-release-media-freedom-in-hungary-is-no-more

European Centre for Press and Media Freedom. (2019). *Identifying best practices for journalism and press freedom in Sweden and Denmark.* www.ecpmf.eu/mission-to-find-best-practice-in-scandinavia-2019/

European Commission. (2009, June 9). *Commissioner Reding welcomes new European Charter on Freedom of the Press.* ec.europa.eu/commission/presscorner/detail/en/IP_09_891

Greenslade, R. (2004). *Press gang: How newspapers make profits from propaganda.* Pan Macmillan.

Krüger, U. (2016). *Mainstream: Warum wir den Medien nicht mehr trauen* (Vol. 6232). CH Beck.

Lowenstein, R. (1970). Press freedom as a political indicator. In H.D. Fischer & Merrill, J.C. (Eds.). *International communication: Media channels, functions* (pp. 129–142). Hastings House.

Media Freedom Rapid Response (MFRR). (2020). *Mapping media freedom: Monitoring report.* www.mfrr.eu/wp-content/uploads/2020/07/MFRR-Monitoring-Report-FINAL.pdf

Mellen, R.P. (2015). John Wilkes and the constitutional right to a free press in the United States, *Journalism History, 41*(1), 1–9.

Schneider, L. (2020). The five international media freedom indices: A critical analysis. In Schneider, L., *Measuring global media freedom* (pp. 89–121). Springer. doi.org/10.1007/978-3-658-28095-6_4

Sobel, R., Dutta, N., & Roy, S. (2010). Beyond borders: Is media freedom contagious? *Kyklos, 63*(1), 133–143.

Sykorova, L. (2018, Aug. 13). *How Czech journalists survive in Babisistan.* mailchi.mp/ecpmf/press-release-media-freedom-in-hungary-is-no-more

The Daily Disruptor. (2018, March 4). *Facebook terminates its experiment with the "Explore" news feed.* www.thedailydisruptorblog.com/post/facebook-terminates-its-experiment-with-the-explore-news-feed

Thurman, N., Dörr, K., & Kunert, J. (2017). When reporters get hands-on with robo-writing: Professionals consider automated journalism's capabilities and consequences. *Digital journalism, 5*(10), 1240–1259.

5

Exploring Journalistic Cultures

Patric Raemy and Lea Hellmueller

Journalism exists around the globe in different social and political contexts. And while journalists worldwide see themselves as journalists who create and maintain journalism, research has documented that journalism cultures tend to vary on a number of dimensions. As we shall see in this chapter, journalism can be understood as a belief system varying according to the distinct ideas and perceptions about how public communication should look like, what journalists are and what role they should play and perform in society. Hence, what journalism is, what it should be and ought to do depends on macro, meso, and micro contexts. And while most comparative research focuses on interpreting journalistic cultures from a macro perspective, primarily focusing on journalistic normative roles, we argue that it is important to include organizational and individual contexts when interpreting perceptions and performances of journalistic cultures.

It is a safe assumption that most journalism scholars share a belief that journalism matters in most countries around the world. In democratic countries, journalistic work is seen as a major contributor to public opinion and political life, whereas in more authoritarian governments journalism has the function to inform citizens—at least within the bounds of what is deemed acceptable in that society. Scholarly interest in journalistic cultures has grown exponentially in the past couple of decades as global markets, borderless information technology and transnational conglomerates are making the world increasingly interconnected. Researchers and educators have been fascinated by questions about how journalism is similar and different across the globe—examining the national level as the unit of analysis and applying the nation-state as the natural organizing principle (Reese, 2001) when comparing journalistic cultures. Challenges of this approach, as we will see later, are first, that we somehow implicitly assume that countries are relatively homogenous internally when comparing on the national level. Second, methodology speaking, processes of globalization seem to undermine the comparative rationale relying on the nation as the unit of analysis, and, new approaches are needed to fit transnational as well as country-internally heterogeneity processes within existing research designs (Hellmueller & Konow-Lund, 2019). Finally, we question how the often heavy focus on normativity can reflect journalism's identity and legitimacy in society as part of journalistic culture.

To date, comparative communication research has documented that journalism cultures across countries tend to vary on a number of dimensions, including the levels of interventionism, power distance, market orientation, objectivism, empiricism, relativism, and idealism (Hanitzsch, 2007). Hence, in a first step, this chapter's goal is to discuss these journalism cultures—defined as a "particular set of ideas and practices by which journalists legitimate their role in society and render their work meaningful" (Hanitzsch, 2007, p. 369). Journalistic culture can manifest in three states (Hellmueller, 2017): as sets of ideas (e.g., values, attitudes, beliefs, professional identities), as practices (e.g., newsgathering), and as artifacts (e.g., news content) (Hanitzsch et al., 2019). Most common to assess journalistic cultures is to examine normative roles of journalists in different countries (e.g., "what role should and do journalists conceive of and perform in various countries?"). The considerable growth of role-related research in recent years (Hanusch & Vos, 2019) related to the exploration of journalistic cultures, reflects the ongoing relevance of this research. However, the literature review and the state of research suggest assuming that the often-used normative approach on the macro level (e.g., role conceptions and role performances) does not capture the full spectrum of journalistic cultures. In other words, from the perspective of journalistic cultures globally, we know much about the normative element of its culture (i.e., how much importance journalists ascribe to certain roles, acting as a watchdog, for example) and how it compares on a macro level (i.e., how the importance of these roles varies based on different political contexts), but less about the context of journalistic practices and professional identities (e.g., how these roles are negotiated within organizational duties and personal aspirations in daily work). Relating this to the definition of journalistic cultures, we know little about its second part, that is about comparing "practices by which journalists legitimate their role in society and render their work meaningful" (Hanitzsch, 2007, p. 369).

We study journalistic cultures to ultimately gain insights into how journalism is shaped and produced. Current approaches suggest that institutional and professional ideals have a weak relationship to journalists' work reality (Raemy et al., 2019). The focus on journalism as a social institution with its service to society, its contribution to public opinion, and ultimately its contribution to democracy sometimes precludes the exploration of other aspects of journalism in a global context, such as the connections among normative demands and journalists' actual work, work realities, and professional identities. The normative lens on journalistic culture leaves out some important aspects of journalistic cultures that could include questions such as: how are interviewing techniques different across cultures (e.g., routinized practices) and how does that impact perception of watchdog performance (normative demands)? What risks are journalists exposed to and how do they respond to uphold certain norms such as keeping government officials accountable?

We address this gap in this chapter by providing (1) an overview of previous studies examining journalistic cultures; and (2) providing an outlook of how future research could address this gap in empirical comparative research examining journalistic cultures.

JOURNALISTIC CULTURE AND JOURNALISTIC IDENTITY AND LEGITIMACY

When we begin to define and compare journalism across countries and social systems, we should consider that many aspects of journalism are the subject of discussion and reflection: What is and should be the performance of journalism? What functions does and should journalism have in a society? How do journalists perceive their roles? At a more macro and sociological perspective, journalism can be understood as an institution in a society, hence, a social system in which certain roles are performed and practices undertaken (Luhmann, 2000). If we look at journalism's identity (i.e., what journalism is) through such a lens, we explore the role of journalism in societies, its functions, and developments and how individual actors coincide with these rather macro structures (Ahva & Steenson, 2020). If we understand journalism as an institution and system, we shed the focus more on normative functions in relation to other social systems (economy, law, health care, education, etc.), discussing what journalism should be and ought to do in society (Christians et al., 2009; Schudson, 2008). Hence, the main purpose of exploring journalistic culture on a macro perspective is to understand what journalism's identity, place, and legitimacy in society is (Hanitzsch & Örnebring, 2020).

Global journalistic cultures have been mostly examined through large international comparative studies (e.g., Hanitzsch et al., 2019; Mellado et al., 2017) that focus on shared sets of ideas and practices through the study of journalistic roles, role enactment, and role performance. For example, journalists' conceptions of their roles constitute the main component of the *Worlds of Journalism* project. That project represents the most comprehensive examination of journalistic cultures around the world consisting of data from more than 27,500 journalists in sixty-seven countries (Hanitzsch et al., 2019). Journalistic conceptions of their roles in society are defined as "discursive resources that journalists deploy as they reflect on their profession, thus rendering their work meaningful" (Hanitzsch et al., 2019, p. 33). The examination of journalists' role conceptions speaks to how normativity is construed by journalists and sets the parameters of what is appropriate and what is not acceptable. Roles function as generalized and aggregated expectations that journalists conceive of in society (Donsbach, 2012). Results of the *Worlds of Journalism* project reveal that role conceptions such as journalists acting as informers, reporters, watchdogs, investigators, and educators dominate the global worldview of journalists across the sixty-seven countries (Hanitzsch et al., 2019). Furthermore, journalists—especially in non-Western countries—emphasized the importance of critical rapportage about those in power, as manifested in the *change agent* role (p. 167). This shows that, from a normative point of view, journalists in most countries strive to contribute to political processes and discussions.

However, despite this rich empirical research exploring journalistic cultures and roles, we should consider that most studies arrive at conclusions about what journalism is out of a normative, structural, and institutional lens by aggregating individual journalists' survey responses (Hanitzsch & Örnebring, 2020). For example, the *Worlds of Journalism* project revealed that in the U.S. context, roles that fit under the "watchdog" function elicit the strongest agreement among journalists. U.S. journalists see classic monitorial roles as most important while rating roles that suggest journalistic advocacy much lower (Vos & Craft, 2016). Chinese journalists, on the other hand, perceive as most important to report things as they are and to provide analysis of current events, but also to support national development and to provide advice and direction for daily life. A majority of journalists in China see importance in providing the kind of news that attracts the largest audience, influencing public opinion, and supporting government policy (Zhou & Zhou, 2016). Similarly, the most important roles for Tanzanian journalists are to provide the kind of news that attracts the largest audience, and also to promote cultural diversity. In summary, they embrace roles that foster tolerance and national development (Kalyango, 2017).

These examples of journalistic cultures around the world reflect journalists' priorities and personal understanding of what good journalism should be. However, these findings tell us little about what journalistic output actually looks like in these countries. Hence, news production processes remain rather "black boxes" and we know little about how such normative ideals matter for how news turns out the way it does: that is by understanding meso levels' influences (e.g., organizational normative ideals, as well as final news output), routine levels (e.g., in the newsgathering process and interaction with sources), and, finally, by understanding micro-level influences (e.g., how norms are individually negotiated, moderated by and integrated into professional identities of journalists).

While the *Worlds of Journalism* project focuses mostly on the set of ideas, that is, role conceptions, recent scholarly work shifts the focus from explaining what journalists think their role consists of (using survey methodology) to analyzing actual practices (Mellado et al., 2017) by conducting content analysis of news stories to explain differences in journalistic cultures. However, we argue that news content and journalistic practices are conceptually distinct and refer to news content as journalistic artifacts rather than practices as many different practices can lead to the same news story. The practice of the performance of journalistic roles (i.e., the study of journalistic roles in news stories) has been conceptualized as "journalistic role performance" (Mellado & Van Dalen, 2014) or "journalistic role enactment" (Tandoc et al., 2013). In other words, there has been a complementary interest toward an examination of journalistic roles in news content as the focus of empirical research in comparative studies on journalistic cultures (Hellmueller & Mellado, 2015). However, there are at least two points to consider when exploring journalistic culture through journalistic role performance:

First, the majority of prior research has interpreted journalistic practices and role performance based on normative expectations of what journalism should be and do, overlooking the role of personal background and other determinants of journalistic performance. For example, Mellado et al. (2017) show that at the national level, some countries like Ireland follow the expectations of a liberal media system with performing the disseminative type of reporting while Greece and Spain perform the watchdog role at a higher level than, for example, the United States. Meanwhile, the United States ranks higher in normative roles not pointed out in the literature before, such as the trend toward more interventionism or interpretative news (Mellado et al., 2017). While these differences are important for understanding journalistic cultures across the world, they do not fully capture the reasons behind such shifts in normative roles. We can only speculate that increasing political polarization and declining revenues have an impact on interpretative news in the United States, for example. Furthermore, what we may treat as similar at the level of the analysis (e.g., normative idea of being a watchdog) can comprise a myriad of differences at a closer look, that is in the way the watchdog is actually integrated in daily journalistic practices. For example, journalists in the Anglo-Saxon countries may share a professional ideology (i.e., objectivity), but may exhibit substantial differences at the individual level (e.g., tendency to value interpretive forms of journalism in particular situations). In other words, although journalists orient themselves on similar institutional norms (objectivity, detachment, etc.), the negotiation and interpretation of these norms might differ between countries, organizations, and individuals (see Hanitzsch & Vos, 2017; Raemy & Vos, 2020) depending on organizational and individual contexts.

Second, there are several analytical and conceptual difficulties when describing journalistic culture based on journalistic role performance. Journalistic performance is the result of a collective outcome of media organizations and less of individual journalists (Mellado, Hellmueller, & Donsbach, 2017). Hence, journalistic performance can indicate a different normative understanding of journalism than one would expect based on journalists' individual perceptions. This is not surprising when we consider that journalistic work is led by journalistic norms but is not a product of individual normative convictions. As we shall see further down in this chapter when we discuss the global orientation on Western journalistic norms, journalistic culture can function even when it differs from a Western normative understanding.

Finally, there might be an encoding–decoding issue with research exploring journalistic culture by examining journalistic performance through quantitative content analysis. It might be difficult to explore journalists' encoding of role performance by quantitatively measuring and decoding news content. Looking at the results of research exploring role performance (see Mellado et al., 2017; Tandoc et al., 2013; Raemy et al., 2019), we hear little about journalists themselves discussing their own role performance and how they decode roles in media output. Hence, the often claimed ideal-practice gap in journalism might be more of an encoding–decoding gap between journalists and researchers. This said, a few studies are attempting to explore journalists' "narration of role performance" (Hanitzsch & Vos, 2017) by describing how journalists' narrate, interpret, and negotiate their roles, performance, profession, and organizational duties (see Siegelbaum & Thomas, 2016; Raemy & Vos, 2020; Ranji, 2020). After reviewing the literature, we could conclude that most studies exploring journalistic culture follow the assumption about the existence of multiple beliefs about what journalism is or should be on a macro (i.e., across countries), meso (across organizations and professional communities), and micro level (across individuals). Again, journalism still is—despite extensive research about its identity—a belief system that depends on different normative expectations (Nerone, 2013). To date, international comparative studies focus primarily on macro-level phenomenon, such as social system (e.g., political system) influences on perceptions and enactments of journalistic roles when studying journalistic cultures. This limits our understanding about journalistic cultures: What do we really know about journalistic cultures when we learn that journalistic roles and role performance differs across countries and political systems? Hence, we attempt to examine and better understand journalistic cultures by discussing a few often-overlooked themes.

DOMINANCE OF WESTERN JOURNALISTIC NORMS

Historically, journalistic roles have been described in the context of a Western understanding of what journalism is and ought to be in an advanced democratic society. Journalism scholarship tends to "celebrate" (Hanitzsch & Örnebring, 2020, p. 118) an understanding of journalism as an institution that is detached from other social institutions and especially from the government. Hence, the freedom of speech, freedom of reporting, objectivity, and power balance seem to be considered iconic roles for journalists in most countries—even those with more restricted political systems (Hanitzsch et al., 2019; Mellado et al., 2017). To be a watchdog or investigative journalist seems to be a motivation that has led many journalists into their profession. However, the daily work in a newsroom might not always allow this type of time-consuming journalistic work. Let us take a closer look at two very different media systems to provide a comparative example: Switzerland and Iran.

The Swiss media system is characterized by high levels of trust in media overall and few constraints on journalistic freedom of reporting. The 2020 World Press Freedom Index of *Reporters Without Borders* ranked Switzerland 8th in the world (see www.rsf.org). However, most journalistic content does not reflect journalists' ideal roles (Raemy et al., 2019). The Swiss case therefore can be seen as a baffling example when it comes to iconic journalistic roles. Even though Swiss journalists identify with normative roles such as investigative or civic-oriented roles, they seem to rarely enact those roles despite their high freedom of reporting (Raemy et al., 2019). This suggests that journalistic roles might not be fixed scripts leading to fixed behavior in news production. Instead, journalistic roles may serve as orientation points that motivate journalists to do their work well (Raemy & Vos, 2020).

Another example is Iranian journalism performed in a more restricted political sphere. It comes as no surprise that studies have found a larger gap on roles related to holding powers accountable between journalists' ideal roles and journalistic performance in more restricted media systems, in which journalists perceive low autonomy (Hanitzsch & Örnebring, 2020; Mellado et al., 2020). However, even in such restricted contexts, journalists' motivation to follow Western journalistic roles seems to be important as they try to provide critical reporting within the bounds of the political system. One example is Ranji's (2020) study that shows that in a restricted media system like Iran, journalists hold on to iconic (Western) journalistic roles and institutional norms. Similar to their Swiss colleagues, Iranian journalists see journalistic roles as motivation and yardstick for solid journalistic work. However, Iranian news content might not always reflect these roles. Hence, Iranian journalists do orient themselves according to iconic journalistic roles and see themselves as performing an important institutional mission with a distinct professional identity, even though they are operating under pressure and are forced to align their practices with the restrictive Iranian media law. Hence, Iranian journalists are creating and maintaining journalism which—albeit not free—represents an important institution in Iranian society. Iconic journalistic roles allow the Iranian journalistic field to function (although differently from Western expectations of a functioning journalistic field) even though the media output does not fully reflect journalistic ideals.

To summarize, while journalists share global normative roles such as watchdog reporting, the negotiation, interpretation, and practical performance might differ between countries, organizations, and individuals.

JOURNALISTIC CULTURE AS AN AGGREGATION OF COUNTRY-SPECIFIC JOURNALISTIC ROLES

The exploration of journalistic culture through journalism's normative function in society underlines the importance of normative theories for journalism as an institution. However, as we can see in previous sections, studies often focus on the description of journalistic cultures while discussion about the specific relationship between journalism and its public gets less attention. Sjøvaag (2010), for example, suggests paying more attention to the specific "social contract" where journalists "promise" to act responsibly in return for trust in media, freedom of reporting, and independence of the press. Since journalistic culture varies across different social systems, it is important to understand the different country-specific social contracts between the media and the public: What are the expectations of journalism? What are the possibilities for journalism to satisfy these expectations? How does journalism actually fulfill the social contract? Hence, the definitions of what good journalism is, what its performance should be, and what roles journalists should fulfill might differ across countries.

Looking back at our initial examples of journalistic culture in the United States, China, and Tanzania, we might expect distinct political, cultural, and societal settings as well as differences in professional autonomy and freedom of reporting, despite the fact that journalists in these three countries seem to embrace similar institutional journalistic roles. As a result, the practice of journalism and journalistic work might differ significantly between these countries. Hence, it is crucial to consider the country-specific context when exploring journalistic roles.

The common values of journalism and journalists' professional role conceptions are not static but further vary in different contexts, depending on influences from the macro, meso, and microlevels, including history, religion, political system, organizational context, freedom of reporting, etc. One reason for the weak relationship between journalists' perceptions of roles related to political life and the practiced role performance found in news content documented in prior research could stem from the conceptualization of journalistic roles. For example, the "worlds of journalism" as well as the "role performance around the globe" research projects use common methods to compare journalistic cultures. Hence, an important aspect of journalistic culture remains overlooked: that researchers should thoroughly explore and carefully consider the specific social contract between journalism and society and its influence on journalists' role perceptions and performances (Sjøvaag, 2010).

Raemy et al. (2018), for example, show that exploring a role conception within a specific political and social system has several advantages and provide some arguments that role-related research differs across social systems. Hence, besides role-related research in a global context, more local research with adapted role-related conceptual approaches is needed. Since Switzerland differs in some crucial ways from other countries, Swiss journalism can illumine what to expect in cases of high journalistic autonomy. What the authors found with a contextualized approach was a tighter connection between journalists' ideal roles and their perceptions of role enactment (Raemy et al., 2018), suggesting that their specific designed role models better fit Swiss journalism. This reveals the importance of understanding the context in which journalistic roles are studied and theorized. In other words, journalistic roles are relational to the social and political system in which they exist, thus legitimizing the political structure and its normative value for the public at large. This shows again that journalism is a belief system linked to a specific social system: society defines what journalism is and journalism defines what its society is (Christians et al., 2009).

JOURNALISTIC CULTURE AS DIFFERENT ROLE NEGOTIATIONS AND PROFESSIONAL IDENTITIES

After discussing different aspects and contexts of journalistic cultures, we conclude this chapter by returning to our initial questions: What is journalistic culture and why does its exploration matter?

The overarching goal of exploring journalistic culture is to find out what journalism's identity and legitimacy (i.e., the perception, function, and performance of journalism among journalists and society in general) are in a specific sociocultural context. This has been accomplished primarily by exploring journalists' role conceptions via survey ratings and by exploring journalistic role performance via content analyses. However, the identification of journalism is a difficult mission because journalism is multifaceted, and its performance is influenced by different levels of determinants. Therefore, we suggest to critically read studies about journalistic cultures and ask what specifically has been examined. As we have shown, it can be questioned if research about journalists' perceptions of journalistic institutional norms truly reflects journalistic culture. And although this issue has been recognized in recent studies, journalistic culture still seems to be decoupled from how journalism operates in a specific organizational and societal setting. Hence, future research should better connect macro, meso, and microcontexts of journalism.

In role-related research, we find terms such as role conceptions, orientations, enactments, performance, institutional norms, professional norms, and professional identity. There seems to be general agreement that these terms are related. However, often, studies provide insufficient explanations about what these terms really mean and what is getting measured when using one of these concepts. This likely stems from different levels of analysis in which journalism and its performance can be studied. Early on, scholars tried to entangle macro, meso, and microcontext that shape journalism's identity and news content. For example, Reese (2001) explored the hierarchy of influences that shape media content and distinguished between several levels of analysis: individual, routines, organizational, extra-media, and ideological levels. Based on these analytical distinctions, many studies strive to focus on a specific level of analysis or to find relationships between levels. For example, Hellmueller and Mellado (2015) suggest shedding more light on the link between role conceptions and role performance by taking into consideration the gatekeeping context, the organizational and societal levels when analyzing journalistic roles. However, this seems to be a difficult attempt when using research methods that either focus on the perceptions of individual journalists (explored mostly via surveys and interviews) or on journalistic performance as the collective output of a media organization (explored mostly via content analysis), or when exploring relationships between these two distinct levels of analysis (Mellado & Hellmueller, 2017).

So, what do we really know about global journalistic cultures based on existing studies? We basically know that journalists' perceptions on professional standards differ across countries. However, these perceptions are framed through what scholars laid out to be the professional standards in journalism. It is difficult to explore in-depth the manifold expressions of journalistic culture via standardized surveys. We suggest therefore for future studies to *explore and compare context-based journalistic cultures*. It makes sense to take a closer look at country-specific journalistic roles and focus less on the question how journalists fit to globally defined journalistic roles but more on what specific roles fit best to journalists working in a specific context. The comparative aspect of such studies then could include the element of *role negotiation* (Raemy & Vos, 2020) rather than the importance of *role conception* or *role performance*, mainly because context-based roles would inherently assume the importance of such roles (see figure 5.1). It should include questions about how normative roles are negotiated differently across contexts, rather than a focus on the actual importance of the norm (e.g., watchdog seems an important role in xy country). This means a shift toward focusing on the *social meaning of roles* (questions could possibly include: what are the most important elements of being a watchdog for you? In what situations have you experienced restrictions to this role?).

An overarching research question for future research could be "how do journalists negotiate institutional roles and organizational roles within their personal identity?" This research outlook goes beyond previous work that integrated some items that control for the practical implementation of journalistic roles: For example, in a German context, Weischenberg et al. (2006) argue that the study of role conceptions is not of relevance as long as it does not have an actual practical consequence for news coverage. Survey items following such an approach in Germany have asked journalists particularly about the distinct dimensions of journalistic roles: journalists are first asked to tell how important certain roles are for themselves personally as part of their profession and they are further asked (only for the items that they agreed on mostly) how successful they are in realizing these goals in their actual reporting. It is recommended to listen to what journalists say and let them narrate their individual negotiations between institutional roles, organizational roles, and personal identity. This might be challenging to accomplish with quantitative methodological approaches.

Future research could also rethink, enhance, and refine our understanding of journalistic culture by considering and connecting professional practice and personal identity with

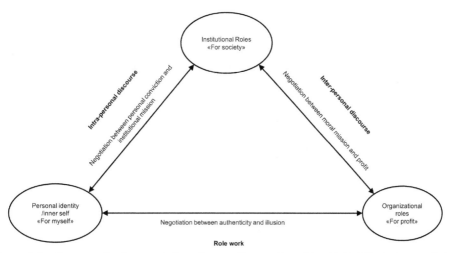

Figure 5.1. **Process of role negotiation. Source: Raemy, P., & Vos, T. P. (2020). A negotiative theory of journalistic roles.** *Communication Theory.* **doi.org/10.1093/ct/qtaa030**

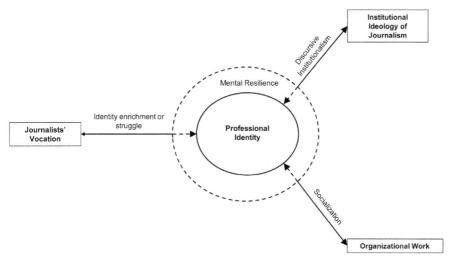

Figure 5.2. **Constitution and formation of professional identity in journalism. Source: Raemy, P. (2020). A theory of professional identity in journalism: Connecting discursive institutionalism, socialization, and psychological resilience theory.** *Communication Theory,* **54(4), 547. doi.org/10.1093/ ct/qtaa019**

institutional normativity. The conflation of the terms "journalistic roles" and "journalists' professional identity" indicates that these distinct concepts are often used synonymously. This is problematic since—as discussed in this chapter—institutional normativity is not the same as work practice. We suggest paying more attention on studying *journalists' professional identity* (Raemy, 2020) as a conceptual approach to better understand and compare journalistic culture (see figure 5.2).

Professional identity in journalism can be understood as journalists' reflection about their vocation, organizational work, and institutional mission (Raemy, 2020). It is formed and adapted due to constant changes in journalists' personality, organizational context, and the journalistic field as a whole. Hence, journalistic identity is a result of the interplay between different processes that lead to professional identity. Therefore, it might be risky to extrapolate journalistic culture based only on the notion of institutionalized journalistic roles and perceptions. Instead, future research should explore journalists' professional identities across countries in order to discover distinct journalistic cultures—embedded in the very day-to-day practice, struggles, and challenges of journalists across the globe.

CHAPTER SUMMARY

Journalistic culture is the result of more than rating of norms or materialization of role performance. Future studies should examine journalists not only as actors who use scripts to perform institutional roles but also as actors with agency to bring a role to life by adapting or rewriting scripts to specific situations in order to perform their institutional roles, which may include both personal and organizational dimensions. Such perspective on journalistic roles could better explain journalistic cultures across countries, as the result of negotiation between macro, meso, and microcontexts as well as personal, organizational, and institutional aspirations, missions, and duties.

DISCUSSION QUESTIONS

1. What is journalistic culture? Please discuss what you would consider to be the most important elements in your definition.
2. What are the micro- and meso-level aspects of journalistic culture and how can they be examined?
3. Why does research on journalistic culture focusing only on macro-level phenomena fall short of providing a full picture of journalism practice within a country?
4. How might institutional journalistic roles differ from journalists' professional identity and work practice?

BIBLIOGRAPHY

Ahva, L., & Steenson, S. (2020). Journalism theory. In K. Wahl-Jorgensen & T. Hanitzsch (Eds.), *International Communication Association (ICA) handbook series. The handbook of journalism studies,* 2nd ed. (pp. 38–54). Routledge.

Christians, C. G., McQuail, D., Nordenstreng, K., White, R. A., & Glasser, T. L. (2009). *Normative theories of the media: Journalism in democratic societies. The history of communication.* University of Illinois Press. doi.org/10.5406/j.ctt1xcjws

Donsbach, W. (2012, June 19). *Journalists' role perception.* Wiley. onlinelibrary.wiley.com/doi/abs/10.1002/9781405186407.wbiecj010.pub2

Hanitzsch, T. (2007). Deconstructing journalism culture: Toward a universal theory. *Communication Theory, 17*(4), 367–385. doi:10.1111/j.1468-2885.2007.00303.x

Hanitzsch, T., Hanusch, F., Ramaprasad, J., & de Beer, A. S. (Eds.) (2019). *Worlds of Journalism: Journalistic cultures around the globe*. Columbia University Press.

Hanitzsch, T., & Örnebring, H. (2020). Professionalism, professional identity, and journalistic roles. In K. Wahl-Jorgensen & T. Hanitzsch (Eds.), *International Communication Association (ICA) handbook series. The handbook of journalism studies* (2nd ed., pp. 105–122). Routledge.

Hanitzsch, T., & Vos, T. P. (2017). Journalistic roles and the struggle over institutional identity: The discursive constitution of journalism. *Communication Theory, 27*(2), 115–135. doi.org/10.1111/comt.12112

Hanusch, F., & Vos, T. P. (2019). Charting the development of a field: A systematic review of comparative studies of journalism. *International Communication Gazette, 46*(4), 174804851882260. doi.org/10.1177/1748048518822606

Hellmueller, L. (2017). Gatekeeping beyond geographical borders: Developing an analytical model of transnational journalism cultures. *International Communication Gazette, 79*(1), 3–25. doi.org/10.1177/1748048516656304

Hellmueller, L., & Konow-Lund, M. (2019): Transnational journalism. *The International Encyclopedia of Journalism Studies*. Wiley. onlinelibrary.wiley.com/doi/abs/10.1002/9781118841570.iejs0179

Hellmueller, L., & Mellado, C. (2015). Professional roles and news construction: A media sociology conceptualization of journalists' role conception and performance. *Communication & Society, 28*(3), 1–11.

Kalyango, Y. (2017, January 4). *Country Report. Journalists in Tanzania*. epub.ub.uni-muenchen.de/31747/1/Country_Report_Tanzania.pdf

Luhmann, N. (2000). *The reality of the mass media. Cultural memory in the present*. Stanford University Press.

Mellado, C., Hellmueller, L., & Donsbach, W. (Eds.). (2017). *Journalistic role performance: Concepts, contexts, and methods*. Routledge.

Mellado, C., Mothes, C., Hallin, D. C., Humanes, M. L., Lauber, M., Mick, J., Silke, H., Sparks, C., Amado, A., Davydov, S., & Olivera, D. (2020). Investigating the gap between newspaper journalists' role conceptions and role performance in nine European, Asian, and Latin American countries. *The International Journal of Press/Politics, 25*(4), 552–575. doi.org/10.1177/1940161220910106

Mellado, C., Hellmueller, L., Marquez-Ramirez, M., Humanes, M. L., Sparks, C., & Wang, H. (2017). The hybridization of journalistic cultures: A comparative study of journalistic role performance. *Journal of Communication, 67*(6), 944–967. doi.org/10.1111/jcom.12339

Mellado, C., & van Dalen, A. (2014). Between rhetoric and practice. *Journalism Studies, 15*(6), 859–878. doi.org/10.1080/1461670X.2013.838046

Nerone, J. (2013). The historical roots of the normative model of journalism. *Journalism: Theory, Practice & Criticism, 14*(4), 446–458. doi.org/10.1177/1464884912464177

Raemy, P. (2020). A theory of professional identity in journalism: Connecting discursive institutionalism, socialization, and psychological resilience theory. *Communication Theory, 54*(4), 547. doi.org/10.1093/ct/qtaa019

Raemy, P., Beck, D., & Hellmueller, L. (2019). Swiss journalists' role performance: The relationship between conceptualized, narrated, and practiced roles. *Journalism Studies, 11*(2), 1–18. doi.org/10.1080/1461670X.2018.1423631

Raemy, P., Hellmueller, L., & Beck, D. (2018). Journalists' contributions to political life in Switzerland: Professional role conceptions and perceptions of role enactment. *Journalism, 15*(5). doi.org/10.1177/1464884918802542

Raemy, P., & Vos, T. P. (2020). A negotiative theory of journalistic roles. *Communication Theory*. doi.org/10.1093/ct/qtaa030

Ranji, B. (2020). Journalistic illusion in a restrictive context: Role conceptions and perceptions of role enactment among Iranian journalists. *Journalism, 10*(23), 146488492092202. doi.org/10.1177/1464884920922026

Reese, S. D. (2001). Understanding the global journalist: A hierarchy-of-influences approach. *Journalism Studies, 2*(2), 173–187. doi.org/10.1080/14616700120042060

Schudson, M. (2008). *Why democracies need an unlovable press*. Polity.

Siegelbaum, S., & Thomas, R. J. (2016). Putting the work (back) into newswork. *Journalism Practice, 10*(3), 387–404. doi.org/10.1080/17512786.2015.1025415

Sjøvaag, H. (2010). The reciprocity of journalism's social contract. *Journalism Studies, 11*(6), 874–888. doi.org/10.1080/14616701003644044

Tandoc, E. C., Hellmueller, L., & Vos, T. P. (2013). Mind the gap: Between journalistic role conception and role enactment. *Journalism Practice, 7*(5), 539–554. doi.org/10.1080/17512786.2012.726503

Vos, T. P., & Craft, S. (2016, July 31). *Country Report. Journalists in the United States.* epub.ub.uni-muenchen.de/34878/1/Country_report_US.pdf

Weischenberg, S., Malik, M., & Scholl, A. (2006). *Die Souffleure der Mediengesellschaft: Report über die Journalisten in Deutschland.* [The prompters of the media society. Report about journalists in Germany]. UVK.

Zhou, B., & Zhou, Y. (2016, October 18). *Country Report. Journalists in China.* epub.ub.uni-muenchen.de/29702/1/Country_report_China.pdf

6

Global Journalism and Mass Communication Education in the Digital Era

Tudor Vlad

The field of communication has dramatically changed in the past 30 years, but what is currently happening in mass communication academic programs is strongly related to the early years of journalism education and cannot be analyzed without a historical perspective. This chapter argues that, in order to anticipate further changes in the digital era, one needs to see journalism and mass communication higher education as a process where the past legitimizes the present and predicts the future.

Journalism as an occupation began in the middle to late nineteenth century as a response to the emergence of a mass press (Barnhurst & Nerone, 2009). Journalism has never been a profession. The sociology literature has classified it as an occupation, defined as a social role that produces social and financial results (Hall, 1994). In order to move to the next step, the status of the profession, journalism would have had its practice controlled and protected through legal regulations, like medicine and law. The other criteria to accede to the professional status—having schools that teach the discipline based on relatively similar curricula, creating members' associations, and, to a certain degree, developing a code of ethics (though this last aspect would require a more complex discussion)—have been at least partially met. However, the essence of the occupation of journalist in the modern era is tightly connected to a right that is stipulated in most of the constitutions around the world: freedom of speech (which includes freedom of the press). Requesting a license or authorization for each individual who wants to perform public communication would have hurt this fundamental principle. In addition, day-by-day practice has shown that people with different backgrounds and educations have the ability to accurately gather information, investigate, report, write, and edit. So, it is no surprise that, in their early years, universities did not teach journalism. It was not taught until 1088 in Bologna, nor at Oxford until 1096 and at Sorbonne until around 1150, although rhetoric and literature were both parts of the preliminary curriculum during the medieval ages.

BEGINNING OF JOURNALISM EDUCATION
AROUND THE WORLD

Journalism education as a higher education discipline does not have a long history since the academic community was reluctant to accept the press as a field of study until the early twentieth century (Zelizer, 2009). Journalism courses at the college level were first offered in the United States, and since then the curricular models have impacted the discipline around the world. The first two American schools to offer printing classes were Washington College in 1869 and Kansas State College in 1873. The University of Missouri offered its first classes of journalism in 1878, and the University of Pennsylvania offered them in. In Europe, l'Ecole supérieure de journalism was established in Paris in 1899.

Initially, journalism programs were mostly established in English departments. Later, many of them decided to be self-standing departments, legitimizing themselves through two main functions of the university: teaching and service. The increasing number of students and the media industry demand for journalism graduates were the strengths of these programs. Only later, at larger and well-funded universities, did journalism programs start focusing on research. These programs grew as colleges of communications collected and preserved resources.

A decision with a strong and long-term impact was the early incorporation of advertising and public relations courses into the journalism curricula. Advertising, defined as the business side of journalism, has been taught at the University of Missouri since 1908, when the first school of journalism in the United States was launched. Other journalism departments followed this strategy, sometimes competing with business or psychology schools. Four other journalism programs in the country included advertising courses in the first decade of the twentieth century. The University of Illinois offered the first public relations course in 1920, and Boston University launched the first-degree program in this field in 1947. Even if some of those public relations courses were not taught within the journalism programs at the beginning, the relationship between the two disciplines became stronger and stronger, as many public relations practitioners had a journalism background. The inclusion of advertising and public relations in the journalism curricula and then the creation of Ad/PR departments within the journalism and mass communication schools attracted more female students, which contributed to the steady growth in enrollments. It also compensated for the decline in the percentage of students enrolled in traditional areas of journalism after the 2007–2008 global financial crisis.

Speech or English departments were the hosts for radio education in the 1930s. Most of the courses initially focused on oral skills. The reluctance of journalism faculty to focus on media other than print postponed the time when broadcast classes were broadly embraced as a part of mass communications programs. It was only in the 1960s when broadcast news courses became a regular part of those curricula.

Mass communication researchers sometimes ignore that the Western media history and business model are not universal. Totalitarian or authoritarian regimes have used newspapers, radio, and television as propaganda tools (Josephi, 2010). The political system transformed many journalists in those countries into activists with their education focused more on their loyalty to the government than on their ability to report and write. The number of journalism schools in those countries was limited, and the content of the courses reflected more government expectations and ideology than professional journalism skills. In those totalitarian systems, the media business principles did not reflect the Western model based on sales and advertising. Totalitarian governments decided in the twentieth century how many media should be established, what the circulation of newspapers should be, how many radio and TV channels should exist, and what the journalists' salary should be. The governments controlled the media content through direct censorship. In the twenty-first century, authoritarian governments have become more sophisticated in dealing with the media, and—in many countries—political or business influences have replaced state control.

Many studies following the classic book *Four Theories of the Press* (1956) have analyzed patterns in the relationship between journalism behaviors, media markets, and policies, and how journalists perceive the role of media. However, those cultural and political differences have had less impact on journalism and mass communication curricula than the early history of journalism education. An examination of 30 years of journalism and mass communication education in the United States, based on two annual surveys of graduates and administrators in U.S.-based programs (Becker & Vlad, 2018), reveals that those trends identified in the pioneering phase still impact journalism education in the digital era.

The United States mass communication model has been prevalent not only because it was the first one, but also because it was legitimized from the beginning by its relationship with the media industry. Many countries, especially in the West, "imported" and adapted that model for economic reasons. Others—because they were encouraged to do so. As an example, journalism education in emerging democracies in East and Central Europe benefited significantly from U.S. financial and logistic support. Mass communication programs were created and modeled through funding from the U.S. government (often through programs administered and implemented by IREX or Internews) or from private organizations, such as the Open Society Foundations (Vlad & Balasescu, 2010).

Academic vs. In-house Training

Although the newspaper and later the broadcast industry were extremely profitable for a long time, media organizations were not willing to appreciate or support the education of the journalists who contributed to their success (Flores & Subervi, 2014; Hansen, Paul, DeFoster, & Moore, 2011). Instead, in-house training and existing labor pipelines were strategies used to supply qualified journalists (Becker, Hollifield, & Vlad, 2016).

At the time when l'Ecole supérieure de journalism was established in Paris in 1899, it was perceived by many as a bizarre idea. French journalists were almost unanimous in thinking that their job could only be learned in the newsroom. As Goulet (2009) showed, the story of the school and its founder, Dick May, was an illustration of that epoch's competition among literature, social sciences, and journalism about who should own social writing ("écriture du social").

Journalism education in Russia started after 1917, with students selected from the working class. The first journalism program was created in 1921 in Moscow, but senior media managers attended special Communist party schools, with the idea that they had an important role as ideological propagandists. Later, language and literature departments incorporated mass communication programs. Currently, the journalism and mass communication curricula in Russia have modernized, and individuals who want to pursue a career in media and related communication areas either study in a higher education institution or get training in newsrooms and mid-career centers (Vartanova & Lukina, 2017).

In China, the University of Missouri School of Journalism created the first journalism department at St. John University in Shanghai in 1920, and two other journalism programs at Yenching University in Beijing in 1924 and Fudan University in 1929 (Guo & Chen, 2017).

American professors taught in those programs and made a case for the need for journalism courses in higher education. After 1949, Chinese journalism schools embraced the Soviet model, with focus on the Communist ideology and on the role of the journalist as a propagandist. After the tragic stagnation of the Cultural Revolution, mass communication education was revived, becoming a combination of Western and Soviet principles.

In the United Kingdom, with its long and vibrant newspaper tradition, journalism training was done almost entirely in the newsrooms much longer than in other European countries. Universities embraced mass communication higher education only in the 1970s, but the number of such programs has grown exponentially, with more than ninety universities and colleges offering such curricula (Frost, 2017). Still, many skeptics argue that the apprenticeship method is more appropriate to produce strong media professionals. In 2016, the presenter of one of the most popular BBC radio programs said that "the idea of three years at university doing journalism is barmy" (Golding, 2019, p. 511).

At the beginning of the twentieth century, local journalists in sub-Saharan African countries ruled by European colonial powers had limited access to higher education. Mass communication is currently taught at many universities in Africa, with the majority following a Western model in the structure of their programs. The most popular curriculum has been based on the vocational U.S. model (Murphy & Scotton, 1987). In the Arab region, journalism schools are typically located in state-owned academic units, and students learn more about how to report the governments' accomplishments rather than to investigate sensitive issues. United States or West European professionals conduct most of the media training across Africa and the Middle East (Mutsvairo & Bebawi, 2019). In recent years, African journalism scholars have argued that mass communication education in their countries should focus and reflect the specifics of their culture and journalism philosophy. An explanation of this dichotomy between the local and the Western journalism discourse is the growing difference in professional backgrounds among faculty (Skjeardal, 2011).

In Latin America, media education has been affected by economic and sociopolitical instability resulting from coups, dictatorships, guerilla wars, and terrorist acts for over half a century (De Oliveira Soares, 2020; Mateus, Andrada, & Quiroz, 2020). Until the 1960s, most of the training was performed in the newsroom. The development of the media industry and its need for professional workers stimulated the emergence of academic education in the field. Starting in the 1980s, many journalism programs adopted the Latin American model that focused more on creating communication abilities than on teaching journalistic skills (Moreira & Lago, 2017). This strategy was promoted by the International Center for Advanced Studies in Communications for Latin America created by UNESCO in Quito (Ecuador) to help the region develop critical schools of communication. Toward the end of the century, this approach lost ground, and the new UNESCO Model Curricula for Journalism Education, developed in 2007, has been embraced by many journalism and mass communication programs in the region.

The evolution of mass communication education in India followed the path of many other states in Asia and Africa that achieved autonomy or independence from their European colonial rulers. In India, currently one of the nations with the highest number of newspaper readers, journalism education started in the 1950s, after the country attained independence from the British Empire in 1947, although some attempts to start a journalism program were made at the Punjab University in 1941 (Muppidi, 2008).

In Japan, another country with extraordinary media industry and newspaper readership, some journalism courses have been taught since 1920. Sophia University had one of the oldest departments of journalism, founded in 1932, but its courses were purely theoretical. In 1948, like other higher education institutions in the country, the university was reorganized and designed following the American model, but the approach of not teaching practical skills has continued. Traditionally, Japanese media organizations trained their employees in the newsroom, but in the 1990s they found that recruiting well-trained graduates would be more advantageous economically. As a result, at the beginning of the twenty-first century, influential newspapers such as *Asahi Shimbun* initiated a dialog with prestigious Japanese universities to create schools of journalism that focus more on vocational training (Valaskivi, 2007). Even today, however, the Journalism School at Waseda University promotes itself as "the first and only journalism school at the graduate level in Japan that promotes both the theory and practice of journalism" (Global Investigative Journalism Network, 2020, p. 1).

All these cases illustrate that when media proliferated in many countries in the last part of the nineteenth century and the first half of the twentieth century, journalists learned their job in the newsroom, based on an apprenticeship model. The United States was the exception, and the main explanations were the strong relationship between journalism education and the media labor market and the early decision by journalism schools to offer instruction for other communication areas, in addition to print. For many decades in the last century—in other countries around the world—journalism education was less open to add to its curricula broader areas of communication, even when the discipline found its place in academia (Deuze, 2006; Weaver & Willnat, 2012).

The advent of the digital era and the 2007 global financial crisis have resurrected and added complexity to the debate about what kind of training a communicator needs. Initially, the journalist's status was legitimized by her or his contribution to a product that was distributed through legacy media organizations: first newspapers, later radio and television. In the modern era, a degree in mass communication or a related field of study has strengthened this status, but the association with traditional media has remained a crucial factor. For a while, the trend toward journalistic professionalization seemed to consolidate even after the Internet opened new and unrestricted channels of communication. However, the economic crisis leads to a drop in advertising following a decline in audiences. Media managers struggled to compete with news aggregators and free online content. This decline occurred in many countries (Medina & Barron, 2013), but the numbers were staggering in the United States. Since 2008, American newspapers have lost almost 50 percent of their employees (Grieco, 2020), and—as a result—they have been unable to provide extended coverage of their communities. Many of those who lost their jobs used their communication skills to identify new occupations. They are the new, non-traditional mass communicators, from citizen journalists to corporate communicators. Since 2014, a slight recovery in communication-related jobs has been attributed to digital news organizations, but the COVID-19 crisis has produced a new wave of layoffs and furloughs in the media industry (Poynter Report, 2020). Globally, schools of journalism have made, and are making, efforts to implement curricular changes to reflect and—in the best-case scenario—to anticipate changes in the broad communication industry and in that labor market.

Curricular Adjustments vs. Radical Innovation

The second important debate in journalism education is what should be the main focus of curricular offerings. Should it prepare students for the practice of journalism or should it be an analysis of that practice? In other words, should it provide practical skills for jobs in professional communication or should it embrace a more scholarly perspective for better conceptual understanding of journalism as a process? With its relationship with the broad communication industry and with the abundance of undergraduate programs, journalism education in the United States seems to heavily opt for the former.

Willard G. Bleyer, who created the journalism program at the University of Wisconsin in 1905, argued that all courses in the journalism curriculum should teach how to think critically about news production and its consequences. In contrast, Walter Williams, the founder of the School of Journalism at the University of Missouri in 1908, modeled the curriculum to teach the students how to perform newspaper work. These two individuals had very different educational and professional backgrounds, which explains the major differences in their approaches: Bleyer had a doctorate in English, while Williams didn't have a college degree (though later served as president of the university), but owned a newspaper. During more than a century of journalism and mass communication education, this distinction between the Missouri Model and the Wisconsin Model has remained relevant. These two models are not mutually exclusive and have both evolved to embrace advertising and public relations and to reflect the dramatic changes in the media industry.

Such differences exist in journalism education in many other countries. In Europe in the twentieth century, the location of journalism training and education reflected this tension. It started with newsroom apprenticeship versus more formal education outside media outlets. It continued through another dilemma: specialized institutes or centers versus academic programs hosted by universities (Goodman & Steyn, 2017).

China chose the Missouri Model in the 1920s, but later developed a Soviet-style curriculum. In Africa, where most of the journalism programs are located in higher education institutions, debates about the prevalence of vocational or academic approaches are common. Josephi (2010) argued that—in spite of huge variations of cultural and political conditions in countries around the world—the curricula are relatively consistent or at least compatible. UNESCO (2007, 2013) has made two attempts to further homogenize mass communication education in developing countries by producing model curricula.

Researchers examined how these UNESCO initiatives have impacted ninety-five journalism programs in thirteen countries of the Middle East (Tahat et al., 2017). They concluded that mass communication education in the region has made steps in aligning to those models, but that the programs were still dominated by theory to the detriment of practice, which was in part the result of hiring faculty with little experience in the media industry and of limited equipment to teach journalistic skills.

The turmoil in the media industry in the digital era has exerted an unprecedented amount of pressure on journalism and mass communication schools. An examination of how these programs reacted to the emergence of new media shows little change. A majority of administrators of 483 journalism programs in the United States surveyed in 2008–2009 reported that their curricula still followed historical, industrial lines. The administrators also said they were teaching some skills that were applicable across media platforms (Becker, Vlad & Simpson, 2014). Changes in departmental structures were also slow. A journalism school usually consisted of three departments: journalism (print), telecommunications (broadcast), and advertising and public relations. It took a while to realize that traditional structures may prevent students from being prepared for the new media world and it took even longer to convince faculty that change was needed. By 2015, many programs had merged their journalism and telecommunications departments, and some of them combined management, marketing, advertising, and public relations courses into a strategic communication curriculum. Revised curricula now included more courses on web layout, design, writing, and editing for the web, using audio/video/photos on the web, social media, entrepreneurial "start-up," and management skills for online publishing, search engine optimization, and web analytics (Becker et al., 2014).

An examination of journalism schools that have had a successful transition in terms of curricular development and the ability to attract students suggests that significant innovations need to be implemented in the curricula. Students are less attracted by traditional media majors and are aware of the new requirements of the communications labor market. The likely explanations are that those graduates tend to perceive communications as a broad industry and that their curricula, with more focus on entrepreneurship than other majors, have given them the mental ability and the tools to adjust to this new reality. In spite of dramatic changes in the media environment, large-scale curricular reform has taken place slowly and with multiple difficulties, but journalism educators today realize that the status quo was not an option.

Besbris and Petre (2019) suggested that journalism schools in the United States continued with structural and curricular changes in an effort to respond to the de-professionalization of the communications industry. Interviews conducted with administrators, faculty, and staff from forty-four journalism programs, identified three main strategies to address the new "contingent" labor market: dismantling boundaries between journalism and other communication occupations, such as public relations; teaching and stimulating entrepreneurship among students to address the challenges of an unpredictable job market; and speeding up the process of incorporating new technological skills.

CHALLENGES FOR GLOBAL JOURNALISM EDUCATION

Journalism education has confronted two related issues in recent years, both connected to the public's trust in media. Gunter and colleagues at the University of Wisconsin studied the "media hostile phenomenon" (Gunther & Liebhart, 2006), originally documented through the social psychology work of Vallone, Ross, and Lepper (1985). Their experiments showed that audiences sometimes tend to identify more bias in a message attributed to a journalist than to the same message if attributed to other, less authoritative, sources (such as a student). The researchers also found that a story associated with a large audience (a newspaper story, as an example) was more likely to produce a contrast reaction, while a message supposedly designed for a low-reach context tended to lead to an assimilation bias.

Trust in media—always low in totalitarian and authoritarian systems—has been one of the main assets of consolidated democracies. A steep decline in media credibility in the West presents a serious problem not only for the mass communication industry but also for the entire society. In recent years, many Western countries have witnessed a polarization of the audiences, While it is not clear if the media has led the public to this division, or if media responded to the audiences' needs and demands, there is no doubt that the media hostile effect undermined media credibility. In facing this challenge, journalists have developed strategies to maintain their authority. Carlson (2017) examined how professional journalists can remain relevant and trustworthy in an era of polarization when many people get their information from social media. In order to legitimize their occupation, journalists should use three main strategies: transparency in their professional work, creating stories that adhere to high journalistic standards, and rewarding media products that reflect criteria of excellence.

Journalism schools and the news industry need to do more to emphasize the role of education, training, and high ethical standards in the complex process of accurately informing the public, in addition to accepting the shifting communication landscape and increasing competition from non-traditional communicators. Audiences tend to ignore the fact that traditional media are still the producers and providers of a vast majority of investigative journalism pieces. Many media organizations do not make public their code of ethics and do not describe their news ideation, source verification, and production routines, but perhaps doing so will increase their credibility.

In authoritarian countries and emerging democracies, journalism schools usually teach the right concepts in terms of media accuracy and accountability. The problem for their graduates is that they often face a different reality in the newsroom, due to political, economic, or legal pressures (Josephi, 2010). In recent years, especially since populist discourse—often under the form of nationalistic fervor—has successfully penetrated the public sphere of consolidated democracies, the risk of a growing discrepancy between journalism education and newsroom constraints and compromises has become very real.

The second challenge in terms of media trust and accountability in the era of post-truth and the "fake news" is defined as information that is fabricated and intentionally misleading (Allcott & Gentzkow, 2017). Social media have been criticized for disseminating fake news, but traditional media has been accused of a similar approach. Politicians in the United States and several European Union countries have questioned the credibility of legacy media, to the satisfaction of those who are unwilling to accept information that does not align with their own political beliefs.

In an effort to combat the "fake news" and "post truth" phenomena, scholars have suggested that journalism programs redesign investigative journalism classes and equip students with skills to enforce fact-based reporting in the digital era (Mutsvairo & Bebawi, 2019). While it may take a while for the new curriculum to have an impact in the industry, journalism schools could develop more outreach initiatives to teach media literacy at the middle school and high school level.

NON-ACADEMIC PARTNERSHIPS

As Berger and Foote (2017) recommend, journalism academic programs should also intensify their collaboration with non-academic organizations that provide valuable professional training. The Poynter Institute in St. Petersburg, Florida, is one example: it started in 1975 with in-person training for journalists and for those who aspired to work in the media; In 2005, it created an "online university" that currently offers 100 interactive courses. The Poynter Institute has responded in a variety of ways to the "fake news" crisis. In 2018, PolitiFact, a full-time fact-checking website with partners in sixteen countries, became a part of Poynter. Another unit, the International Fact-Checking Network, has gathered over sixty fact-checking organizations on six continents to share best practices in identifying fabricated news. Poynter's media literacy project MediaWise is another attempt to teach American teens how to distinguish fact from fiction online (Poynter, 2020).

Many other non-academic organizations have developed media training programs, including the U.S.-based Internews, International Research and Exchanges Board, the International Center for Journalists, the Center for Investigative Reporting, the British BBC Training Programme, the Centre for Investigative Journalism, the Thomson Reuters Foundation, Radio France International Training Division, and the Konrad-Adenauer-Stiftung's Media Programme, among others.

Becker and Vlad (2005) identified seventy organizations and foundations in twenty-five countries outside the United States involved in media assistance programs in developing countries, including NGOs, foundations, and multinational organizations. Hume (2004) found that at least $600 million was spent on media training abroad by the U.S. government and media foundations alone during the 1990s. Becker and Vlad (2005) estimated that U.S. and non-U.S. institutions spent about $1 billion per year in journalism training internationally, although there was little coordination among those programs. Funders, journalism schools, and training organizations should better coordinate their efforts and develop partnerships as well as outcome assessment tools.

RECENT TRENDS

The title of Berger and Foote's chapter, "Taking stock of contemporary journalism education: The end of the classroom as we know it," anticipated the extraordinary challenges that journalism education has faced since the COVID-19 crisis erupted. It is too early to assess the long-term impact of the pandemic on the future of academic education. The shift to online delivery and distance learning for both domestic and international students may lead to further changes in journalism programs that have to better articulate the value of in-person interview interaction skills as well as the ability to distinguish between accurate and fabricated information, especially online. The trend toward deprofessionalization in the communications professions may also need to be reexamined.

In the aftermath of the economic crisis, The Knight Foundation argued that journalism programs must be "willing to destroy and recreate themselves to be part of the future of news" arguing that, in the digital era, the "teaching hospital" model should be applied to journalism (Newton, 2012). Others argue that the field needs more research during this age of major transformations to better understand how new technologies have impacted journalism (Lewis & Molyneux, 2018), ushering new avenues in scholarly research (Carlson et al., 2018).

Like many other issues in journalism education, this controversy is not new. The Missouri approach required practical skills from the teachers and no scholarly record, while the Wisconsin strategy added vocational training to a critical view of the topics (Halpern, 1987). The economic resources of a journalism program can be the decisive factor in the path chosen. Limited resources and equipment may lead to more conceptual classes rather than hands-on training. A resourceful college of journalism that can provide adequate equipment to every student may focus more on the practical components.

The situation is less complicated for universities in transition countries that have little experience in journalism education. They had to hire faculty either from media organizations or from established disciplines, such as literature, sociology, and psychology. With few professors, almost no textbooks, and limited expertise in designing an educational plan, it is understandable why so many universities in emerging democracies adopted U.S. journalism curricula. Even today, programs in many parts of the world struggle to find faculty with solid academic credentials.

Another difference exists in the method of assessment and review of educational institutions in the United States and abroad. There are more than 480 journalism and mass communication programs in the United States in 2020, but only 117 of them are accredited through the Accrediting Council on Education in Journalism and Mass Communication (ACEJMC, 2020). This system is different from a majority of other countries, where the Ministry or

Department of Education coordinates the process, and accreditation and reaccreditation are mandatory for a school to function.

CHAPTER SUMMARY

Journalism and mass communication education will remain relevant as long as it attracts talented students and provides evidence that its graduates are competitive in the job market. To do that, educators need to understand and embrace the field of mass communication in its new complexity and broaden their curricular options, as students will likely pick those specializations that will help them get a job in the fast evolving media industry. Journalism schools should also be more active outside the academy, developing media literacy programs for citizens and collaborating with non-academic organizations to combat fake news. Teaching digital technology skills and analyzing how social media have influenced the media industry are also needed. Challenges to journalism education have stimulated agility and growth in the past, so one can hope for the same evolution in the future.

DISCUSSION QUESTIONS

1. How have new communication technologies impacted journalism as an occupation in the digital era?
2. What are the two main journalism education models mentioned in this chapter? Can you describe their characteristics?
3. What are the major changes in journalism and mass communication curricula in the last decade?
4. How has the "fake news" phenomenon affected media trust among the general public?
5. What has been the role of advertising and public relations in journalism and mass communication education?

BIBLIOGRAPHY

Accrediting Council on Education in Journalism and Mass Communications (2020). History. www.acejmc. org/about/history/

Allcott, H., & Gentzkow, M. (2017). Social media and fake news in the 2016 election. *Journal of Economic Perspectives, 31*, 211–236.

Barnhurst, K., & Nerone, J. (2009). History of journalism. In Wahl-Jorgensen, K. & Hanitzsch, T. (Eds.), *The handbook of journalism studies* (pp. 17–28). Routledge.

Becker, L. B., & Vlad, T. (2005). Non-U.S. funders of media assistance projects. Report prepared for the John S. and James L. Knight Foundation. www.grady.uga.edu/coxcenter/Activities/Act_2005_to_2006/ Materials05-06/Knight_International_Report_December_2005_v16.pdf

Becker, L. B., Vlad, T., & Simpson, H.A. (2014). Annual survey of journalism and mass communication enrollments: Enrollments decline for third consecutive year. *Journalism and Mass Communication Educator, 69*(4), 349–365.

Becker, L. B., Hollifield, A., & Vlad, T. (2016). The labor market for university journalism and mass communication graduates: The role of the media industries. www.grady.uga.edu/coxcenter/ Conference_Papers/Public_TCs/Becker_Hollifield_Vlad_MMEE_AEJMC_2016_8_9_16.pdf

Becker, L. B., & Vlad, T. (2018). *The changing education for journalism and the communication occupations: The impact of labor markets*. Peter Lang.

Berger, G., & Foote, J. (2017). Taking stock of contemporary journalism education: The end of the classroom as we know it. In R.S. Goodman & E. Steyn (Eds.), *Global journalism education in the 21st century: Challenges and innovations*, 245–266. Knight Center for Journalism in the Americas.

Besbris, M., & Petre, C. (2019). Professionalizing contingency: How journalism schools adapt to deprofessionalization. *Social Forces*. DOI: 10.1093/sf/soz094

Carlson, M. 2017. *Journalistic authority*. Columbia University Press.

Carlson, M., Robinson, S., Lewis, S. C., & Berkowitz, D. A. (2018). Journalism studies and its core commitments: The making of a communication field. *Journal of Communication, 68*(1), 6–25.

De Oliveira Soares, I. (2020). Educommunication landmarks in Latin America: what should be considered in the last 50 years. In J. C. Mateus, P. Andrada, P., and M.T. Quiroz (Eds.), *Media Education in Latin America*. Routledge.

Deuze, M. (2006). Global journalism education. *Journalism Studies, 7*(1), 19–34.

Flores, M., & Subervi, F. (2014). Assessing the job satisfaction of U.S. Latino journalists. *Journalism Practice, 8*(4), 454–468.

Frost, C. (2017). The United Kingdom juggles training and education: Squeezed between the newsroom and classroom. In R.S. Goodman & E. Steyn (Eds.), *Global journalism education in the 21st century: Challenges and innovations*, 199–218. Knight Center for Journalism in the Americas.

Global Investigative Journalism Network. 2020. Journalism School of Waseda University, Japan. gijn.org/ member/journalism-school-of-waseda-university-japan/

Goodman, R. S., & Steyn, E. (Eds.) (2017). *Global journalism education in the 21st century: Challenges and innovations*. Knight Center for Journalism in the Americas.

Grieco, E. (2020). *U.S. newspapers have shed half of their newsroom employees since 2008*. Pew Research Center. www.pewresearch.org/fact-tank/2020/04/20/u-s-newsroom-employment-has-dropped-by-a-quarter-since-2008/

Golding, P. (2019). Media studies in the UK. *Publizistik, 64*, 503–515.

Goulet, V. (2009). Dick May et la première école de journalisme en France. Entre réforme sociale et professionnalisation.

Gunther, A. C., & Liebhart, J.L. (2006). Broad reach or biased source? Decomposing the hostile media effect. *Journal of Communication, 56*, 449–466.

Guo, K., & Chen, P. (2017). The changing landscape of journalism education in China. *Journalism & Mass Communication Educator, 72*(3), 297–305.

Hall, R. H. (1994). *Sociology of work*. Pine Forge Press.

Halpern, S. A. (1987). Professional schools in an American university. In B. R. Clark (Ed.), *The academic profession: National, disciplinary, and institutional settings* (pp. 304–330). University of California Press.

Hansen, K. A., Paul, N., DeFoster, R., & Moore, J. E. (2011). Newspaper training program shows gains in social media. *Newspaper Research Journal, 32*(3), 40–51.

Hume, E. (2004). *The media missionaries: American support of journalism excellence1 and press freedom around the globe*. The John S. and James L. Knight Foundation.

Josephi, B. (2010). *Journalism education in countries with limited media freedom*. Peter Lang.

Lewis, S. C., & Molyneux, L. (2018). A decade of research on social media and journalism: Assumptions, blind spots, and a way forward. *Media and Communication, 6*(4), 11–23.

Mateus, J. C., Andrada, P., & Quiroz, M.T. (Eds.) (2020). *Media Education in Latin America*, Routledge.

Medina, M., & Barron, L. (2013). The impact of the recession on the TV industry in Mexico and Spain. *Communication & Society, 26*(2), 27–46.

Moreina, S.V., & Lago, C. (2017). Journalism education in Brazil: Developments and neglected issues. *Journalism & Mass Communication Educator, 72*(3), 263–273.

Muppidi, S. (2008). Journalism education in India. *Media Asia, 35*(2), 67–83.

Murphy, S. M., & Scotton, F. (1987). Education dependency and journalism education in Africa. Are there alternative models. *Africa Media Review 1*(3), 11–35.

Mutsvairo, B., & Bebawi, S. (2019). Journalism educators, regulatory realities, and pedagogical predicaments of the "fake news" era: A comparative perspective on the Middle East and Africa. *Journalism & Mass Communication Educator, 74*(2) 143–157.

Newton, E. (2012). *Journalism schools aren't changing quickly enough.* Nieman Lab. www.niemanlab.org/2012/09/eric-newton-journalism-schools-arent-changing-quickly-enough/

Poynter Institute. (2020). *Ethics and fact-checking.* www.poynter.org/poynter-thought-leader/

Poynter Institute. (2020). *The coronavirus forces furloughs, layoffs and print reductions at newspapers across North America.* www.poynter.org/newsletters/2020/the-coronavirus-forces-furloughs-layoffs-and-print-reductions-at-newspapers-across-north-america/

Siebert, F. S., Peterson, T., & Schramm, W. (1956). *Four theories of the press: The authoritarian, libertarian, social responsibility and Soviet communist concepts of what the press should be and do.* University of Illinois Press.

Skjerdal, T.S. (2011). Teaching journalism or teaching African journalism? Experiences from foreign involvement in a journalism programme in Ethiopia. *Global Media Journal, 5*(1), 24–51.

Tahat, K., Self, C. C., & Tahat, Z. Y. (2017). An examination of curricula in the Middle Eastern journalism schools in light of suggested model curricula. *Journal of Organizational Culture, Communications and Conflict, 21*(1), 1–23.

Valaskivi, K. (2007). *Mapping media and communication research: Japan.* University of Helsinki Department of Communication: Communication Research Center. Retrieved on March 14, 2020, from www.helsinki.fi/crc/Julkaisut/ReportJapan.pdf

Vallone, R.P., Ross, L., & Lepper, M.R. (1985). The hostile media phenomenon: Biased perception and perceptions of media bias in coverage of the Beirut massacre. *Journal of Personality and Social Psychology, 49*, 577–585.

Vartanova, E., & Lukina, M. (2017). Journalism education in Russia: How the academy and media collide, cooperate, and coexist. R.S. Goodman & E. Steyn (Eds.), *Global journalism education in the 21st century: Challenges and innovations*, 155–174. Knight Center for Journalism in the Americas.

Vlad, T., & Balasescu, M. (2010). Few educators, many media and journalism programs: Journalism and mass communication education in Romania after the fall of communism, in B. Josephi (Ed.), *Journalism Education in Challenging Environments.* Peter Lang.

UNESCO. (2007). *Model curricula for journalism education for developing countries and emerging democracies.* UNESCO.

UNESCO. (2013). *Model curricula for journalism education. A compendium of new syllabi.* www.unesco.org/new/en/communication-and-information/resources/publications-and-communication-materials/publications/full-list/model-curricula-for-journalism-education-a-compendium-of-new-syllabi/

Weaver, D., & Willnat, L. (2012). *The global journalist in the 21st century.* Routledge.

Zelizer, B. (2009) Journalism and the academy. In K. Wahl-Jorgensen and T. Hanitzsch (Eds.), *Handbook of journalism studies.* Routledge.

7

Navigating the Uncharted Waters of Journalism Ethics and Responsibilities in a Twenty-first-Century Information Age

Katerina Tsetsura and Dean Kruckeberg

Journalists throughout the world have varying freedoms and rights that have been granted by their governments. However, nation-states' legacy news media also adhere to—or, at the least, are greatly influenced by—values that are espoused by journalists' indigenous professional communities. What are journalism's professional role and function in a twenty-first-century information age and what should be journalists' professional ethics? This chapter argues that ethical news gathering by professional journalists and the dissemination of this news by transparent and unfettered news media remain essential. Nevertheless, the practice of journalism will likely yield a deprofessionalized model.

Journalism's established professional values worldwide often include the fair and unbiased presentation of news that has been conscientiously and impartially gathered by professionally trained journalists and that is disseminated by news media that are intent on providing balanced, accurate, and truthful reportage. News values such as these—as well as assumed transparency of any external influences on this news coverage—have elevated journalism in some societies to that of a perceived essential institution that has professionally adhered and publicly declared ethics.

However, particularly in a marketplace economy in which news is a commodity, journalists must also provide a product that is demanded by—and, therefore, can successfully compete for—consumers. In today's media environment of "fake news," disinformation, and misinformation, journalism's ethical norms may appear to be increasingly amorphous and nonprofessional. As legacy news media ponder new economic models to assure future sustainability, journalists are feeling increasing pressures to reconceptualize their professional identity. Considerable evidence suggests that an elitist professional approach toward journalism may yield a deprofessionalized—ostensibly more democratized—model.

An examination of the future of journalism and its ethics must be predicated on this meta-question: What are the role and function of journalism, specifically what purpose does journalism serve in a twenty-first-century information age that has witnessed increasing media distrust and non-transparency? Defining journalism as a professionalized occupation and defending its societal role as an institution becomes especially problematic when considered on a global scale. From a global perspective, we can be no more precise than to say that *journalism* is what *journalists do*—a tautology that illustrates the difficulty of defining this occupation that historically has achieved varying levels of professionalism and that has fulfilled multiple roles and agendas worldwide.

Prognoses of the future of journalism and its declared ethics and responsibilities must begin with an understanding of these concepts: society, global society, and society-at-large; ideology and values; profession, professionalism, and de-professionalization; truth, incomplete truth, and a lie; trust, transparency, opacity, and pseudo-transparency; and culture, community, and professional community.

SOCIETY, GLOBAL SOCIETY, AND SOCIETY-AT-LARGE

Hardt (1979), in his mandate for the study of mass communication in industrialized Western societies, emphasized that such examination must begin within the context of a theory of society that defines the position of that society's individual members. Hardt (1979) noted that this examination must address freedom and control of expression, of private and public spheres of communication, and whether a democratic system of mass communication exists.

Sociologists define a society as a large complex of human relationships, "referring to a system of interaction" (Berger, 1963, p. 26). Luhmann (1982; 1995; 1997) conceptualized society as consisting of various social systems, for example, law, politics, economics, and mass media. These social systems interact and influence one another to sustain a functioning organism. Their elements control their reproduction, while autonomously defining their boundaries. Although no external system can connect directly to them, these social systems maintain communication with the outside. Restricting society to human populations, Hobbes and Blank (1975) noted a common societal culture and a comprehensive social system: "A large-scale human grouping that shares a common culture and that possesses a comprehensive social system including all of those social institutions required to meet basic human needs" (p. 506).

Such definitions would appear to preclude a *global society* that shares a common culture and a comprehensive social system. Although Vujnovic and Kruckeberg (2015) predicted that a *global culture* is emerging, not only in people's adoption of universally available consumer products, but also—at varying levels—in the melding of their social, political, economic, and cultural values, Nevertheless, it must be acknowledged that a global society does not presently exist in its social, political, economic, and cultural dimensions; except for perhaps a few core values, the world's societies do not share universal ideologies, worldviews, or a comprehensive social system. Thus, to greater or lesser extents, societies remain discrete, if not unique. Nevertheless, although a *global society* and *society-at-large* may remain invalid variants of the term society, these descriptors are commonly used to refer to the world's collective human population.

Despite today's global information age in which communication is not bound by time or space, journalism's role and function are usually examined within the context of indigenous societies in individual nation-states. Likewise, journalism's ethics and responsibilities are often perceived primarily within those parameters.

IDEOLOGY AND VALUES

Merrill, Bryan, and Alisky (1970) observed that each nation's press system is usually in close step with that nation's ideology. Historically, the practice of journalism has been grounded in indigenous ideologies (Hardt, 1979). Bell (1988) observed that ideology has come to mean a creed that is held with the will to believe, that is, with dogmatism and stridency. He described ideology as the interplay of culture and politics.

Journalism is likewise grounded in indigenous values. Goodstein, Nolan, and Pfeiffer (1993) adopted Rokeach's definition of values as enduring beliefs that a specific mode of conduct or existence is personally or socially preferable. Similarly, a value system is defined as an enduring organization of beliefs about preferable modes of conduct or behavior. Lambeth (1992) observed that values, both moral and immoral, define what is considered good and what is considered bad, in a society.

Kruckeberg (1998) observed that a specialized occupation develops its values, ethical standards, and professional parameters. Although journalism as a professionalized occupation must exist within the context of its society's ideology and values, journalists as a professional community have the responsibility, albeit not always the freedom and opportunity, to identify and articulate their professional ideology and values. Importantly, these professional ideologies and values need not be restricted to journalists' indigenous societies but are often contingent upon the level to which journalism is practiced as a professionalized occupation within a society and the professional journalism education that exists in that society. Tsetsura and Valentini (2016) conceptualized a normative model to understand media ethics decision-making on a global level. This "Holy" Triad is represented by an isosceles triangle that illustrates the equal importance of personal, professional, and environmental values as the main influencing forces in the ethical decision-making process.

Journalism's literature has documented the existence of professional values such as objectivity, non-bias, truth-seeking, and service to the public (Schudson, 2008; Zelizer, 2004). The Ethical Journalism Network found that most journalism values statements worldwide focus on these core principles: (1) Truth and Accuracy; (2) Independence; (3) Fairness and Impartiality; (4) Humanity; and (5) Accountability. The Ethical Journalism Network advocates that journalists must be accountable to correct errors, express sincere regret for these errors, listen to the concerns of audiences, and provide remedies when journalists are unfair (Ethical Journalism Network, n.d.).

Of course, such values are not universally—nor equally—shared among journalists' indigenous professional communities; furthermore, in some societies, attempts to adhere to these principles may be fraught with danger (e.g., "These Are the 10 'Most Urgent' Cases of Threats to Press Freedom Around the World in July 2020," *Time* Staff, 2020, July 1). It is instructive to contrast ethical variances in the practice of journalism with that of the historically recognized profession of medicine. Physicians share with their counterparts in other societies worldwide, not only the science of that profession's body of knowledge but also largely universal ethical values in their perception of their role and function.

PROFESSION, PROFESSIONALISM, AND DEPROFESSIONALIZATION

Of course, articulation of a professional ideology and values begs definitions of a profession and professionalism. Although acceptance of the need for journalism as an institution in some form may be assumed in most societies, defending journalism as a profession becomes more daunting. For example, in the United States, journalism in the legacy news media is a highly professionalized occupation, but—in the strictest sense—cannot be a profession.

The traditional professions are law, medicine, and the clergy. Those practicing in these professions are said to have answered a calling to practice an occupation that is deemed essential to society. A member of a profession ostensibly does not respond to the marketplace, but primarily practices that profession to serve humankind. In modern, complex society, one could argue that many professions exist. However, some scholars maintain that no professions exist today (Macdonald, 1995). This is because virtually all occupations that seek the class, status, and power of a profession respond to—and must compete in—the marketplace to earn their livelihoods.

Certainly, journalists may feel a calling to journalism, which they regard as a service that is essential to society. However, a profession has further criteria that can be collapsed to include: (1) a body of knowledge of some consequence; (2) prescribed formalized education that teaches the knowledge, skills, and abilities that are deemed requisite by the professional community, which achievement is externally validated through licensing that creates barriers-to-entry for aspirants who do not meet benchmark proficiencies; (3) a professional community that is often manifested in professional associations; and (4) a code of ethics that defines that professional community's agreed-upon and adhered-to relationship to society.

Of course, a considerable body of knowledge exists of the craft of journalism, and unquestionably the requisite knowledge, skills, and abilities of professional journalists are considerable. Nevertheless, despite being a highly professionalized occupation for which a journalist may well feel a calling, has been given professional education, and to which professional ethics the journalist adheres, journalism cannot be a profession in the United States. This is because every citizen has First Amendment rights to practice journalism, requiring no prescribed education and external validation such as are requisite for bona fide professions. Neither is there a requirement to adhere to the ethics that are agreed upon and adhered to by journalism's professional community.

JOURNALISM ETHICS AND EXAMPLES OF ETHICS CODES WORLDWIDE

Consideration of ethics is needed when examining journalism as a professionalized occupation, which illustrates the likelihood of journalism's increasing deprofessionalization. A profession defines its relationship to society through its ethics, which, in fact, can be anything that this professional community wants them to be as long as those ethics are within the confines of its government's laws and within the parameters of its society's social norms.

In journalism, ethics focus largely on objectivity and non-bias, truth-seeking, and other standards that help to assure the ideal of service to the public and democracy (Schudson, 2008; Zelizer, 2004). For example, the National Union of Journalists Malaysia (n.d.) includes in its objectives to "defend the freedom of the Press, to deal with the professional conduct of its members and to maintain high ethical standards in journalism." Its NUJ Code of Ethics declares that the first duty of journalists is to respect truth and the public's right to truth. The journalist will defend the principle of freedom in the honest collection and publication of news as well as the right of fair comment and criticism. The code declares that journalists will not suppress essential information or falsify documents and the journalist will rectify harmful inaccuracies. Anonymity of sources must be protected to the extent possible. Grave professional offenses listed in the code include plagiarism, slander, libel and unfounded accusations, and the acceptance of bribes in consideration of publication or suppression (National Union of Journalists Malaysia, n.d.).

The Code of Ethics of the National Federation of Brazilian Journalists, describing the proper conduct of a professional journalist, includes duties to reveal facts of public interest, fight for freedom of thought and expression, and oppose corruption, especially that which intends to manipulate information. A journalist should not prevent the expression of opposed opinions or free debate (Accountable Journalism, n.d.).

Noting that freedom of speech is the foundation of a democratic society, the "guidelines for journalists" of the Union of Journalists in Finland emphasizes that good journalist practice is based on the public's right to access information. The journalist has the obligation to resist outside pressures that attempt to prevent or limit communications. Facts must be distinguished from opinions and fictitious materials, and clear demarcation must exist between advertising and editorial content. Hidden advertising must be avoided (Union of Journalists in Finland, n.d.).

As these examples illustrate, ethics codes give considerable attention to the appropriate use of journalism's tactics and techniques. To varying extents, recognition and acceptance of these ethics transcend cross-culturally—perhaps to some extent universally—among those who consider themselves to be professional journalists. Recent studies (Yang, Taylor, & Saffer, 2016) suggest that commonly held values and ethics include professionalism, moral standards, expertise, society, social justice, and human rights.

In summary, despite journalism's failure to meet the criteria of a profession in countries having First Amendment-type rights (because everyone has a right to freedom of expression), journalists and society-at-large might reasonably consider journalism as practiced in the legacy news media to be a professionalized occupation that can and should be practiced accordingly, that is, as a bona fide profession. Furthermore, through formalized professional education that teaches the knowledge, skills, and abilities of the craft of journalism, journalists in multiple societies have come to adopt a particular way of identifying and solving professional issues and problems, as well as sharing similar professional worldviews.

Thus, although the practice of journalism may not be controlled through external validation and formal regulation in some countries, and thereby barriers-to-entry cannot protect practitioners' control of who practices journalism in these societies, the criteria of a profession are sufficiently satisfied in many nation-states to allow their journalists to have a professional identity and to encourage a discrete professional community that has its literature, prescribed education, and code of ethics. Such journalists recognize and accept an obligation to act professionally, that is, to practice journalism as a professionalized occupation.

TRUTH, INCOMPLETE TRUTH, AND A LIE

Truth is foundational to the practice of professional journalism. Tsetsura and Kruckeberg (2017) defined truth as factual, complete, and unbiased information, which has been collected and verified, and that is presented accurately, thus attempting to achieve the ideal of objectivity with transparency about the process of information gathering, presentation, and analysis. They defined incomplete truth as news and other information that may be by-and-large accurate, but in which the news gatherer or disseminator has intentionally omitted contextualizing information or has purposely failed to identify influences that have altered the presentation of this information. They say a lie is information that the communicator knows to be false and that is presented with the intent to deceive or mislead. These three definitions lay a foundation for further understanding of the importance of trust and transparency in relation to media as a societal institution.

TRUST, TRANSPARENCY, OPACITY, AND PSEUDO-TRANSPARENCY

Journalists earn trust in the presentation of news when these journalists are known to adhere to traditional news values of fairness in the pursuit of objectivity. Public trust and media credibility are rooted in the belief that the communicator's message is truthful and accurate. News media transparency means that no hidden influences exist in the process of gathering and disseminating news or other information that is presented as truth (Tsetsura & Kruckeberg, 2017). News media opacity occurs when hidden influences exist in the process of gathering/disseminating news that is presented as truth, for example, any form of undisclosed payment for news coverage or any influence on journalists and news media's decisions that is not clearly stated in the finished journalistic product. Vujnovic and Kruckeberg (2016) defined pseudo-transparency as a set of strategic actions through which organizations attempt to appear transparent by creating a sense or experience of transparency, rather than actually being transparent to their publics. Pseudo-transparency can impede efforts to establish and maintain trust among various people and organizations. It can also be used as a term to describe non-genuine efforts to be transparent by those who claim to be journalists or media representatives who might have a hidden agenda because they, in fact, work for a particular organization, company, or government.

CULTURE, COMMUNITY, AND PROFESSIONAL COMMUNITY

Culture, in its anthropological sense, is a blend of traits that differentiate individuals from another culture based on beliefs, attitudes, practices, and identities. Johannesen, Valde, and Whedbee (2008) observed that U.S. culture has emphasized dual concerns for freedom of communication and the responsible exercise thereof. Professional communities develop unique cultures that reflect the ideology, values and value systems, and the ethics of their professionalized occupations. Bauman (1995) observed, "Communities are theorized as first and foremost *cultural* formations" (p. 151). Thus, understanding culture and cultural traits is essential to investigate and comprehend how a professional community, particularly a journalistic community, forms.

NAVIGATING UNCHARTED WATERS

Because the practice of journalism worldwide has been grounded in indigenous ideologies and values as well as in varying levels of professional education, defining journalism and identifying its societal function is, indeed, problematic when being considered on a global scale. However, such frame of reference is essential at a time in which communication is transmitted immediately throughout geo-political space, in which news consumers have multiple—oftentimes conflicting—worldviews, and in which individuals can belong to multiple virtual communities, some of which may be dysfunctional to themselves as well as to others. The trajectory of communication technology has proven disruptive, exacerbating the tensions of multiculturalism within a globalized world in which increasing uncertainties of social, political, economic, and cultural sustainability exist. Most certainly, communication technology has significantly affected the practice and reception of journalism, as noted here.

MONOPOLY OF KNOWLEDGE

The role and function of journalism have been contingent upon a monopoly of knowledge that was only shared by those who had access to printing presses and radio and television stations, that is, the mass media. At least, such was the case until the advent of new global communication technology, that is, the Internet, the World Wide Web, and, in particular, social media that have allowed anyone with a Facebook, Twitter, or YouTube account to challenge and effectively destroy this monopoly. Anyone and everyone—known or unknown, credible or not—now has the power and influence to compete head-on with the pre-existing monopoly of knowledge of journalists and their legacy news media that had been uniquely empowered by printing presses and radio and television stations. Also challenged was the economic viability of these legacy news media as advertisers soon recognized the reach and influence of those using the platforms of social media that were not bound by traditional marketplace geography and restraints, financial and otherwise, of a mass media oligarchy.

Those discovering their newly found voices did not possess journalists' body of knowledge, nor did they have validated and uniform journalism education, nor were they bound by professional communities to adhere to a mutually agreed-upon code of ethics. In what quickly had become a global cacophony, messages—often sent anonymously—traveled unabated beyond the borders of nation-states, without restriction or effective censure by even the most authoritarian and oppressive governments. And these messages oftentimes were consumed and appreciated with less concern about their perceived credibility than for consumers' confirmation bias and entertainment value. Rubin (1978) once observed that no ethical standards are *built into* the mass media. This certainly holds true for the Internet, the World Wide Web, and social media.

Thus, in a relatively short span of time, journalism as an institution and as a professionalized occupation has been—and will likely continue to be—eroded, perhaps irretrievably so. This erosion often takes place through technological or social media channels by individuals without the educational background or adhered to codes of journalism ethics of those professionals who previously had enjoyed a monopoly of knowledge and access to expensive presses and radio and television stations. Furthermore, these disrupters have effectively encroached upon advertising revenue, which in the past had represented a sustainable and lucrative income source that previously had seemed immune to threat.

A PROFESSION OF JOURNALISM?

Journalism, both as an institution and as a professionalized occupation, will likely continue to be eroded. In liberal democracies, this specialized occupation is under immense threat of becoming unsustainable in the forms in which it had evolved throughout much of its history. Ironically, journalism's traditional values and ethics are needed now more than ever before in a complex global society that is rapidly changing.

As an institution, journalism in some form exists in modern societies, although dominant ideologies as well as other sociopolitical, economic, and cultural factors have significantly influenced its practice and have impacted what is deemed to be newsworthy. Certainly in democratic societies, journalists are expected to disseminate comprehensively gathered and carefully vetted news of significance and interest that is expected to be presented fairly and objectively, that is, without bias. However, the distinctions between what may be called strategic mass communicators and journalists are often blurred today. This may be especially true when PR professionals design campaigns, advocating through media channels on behalf of political causes, parties, or candidates—which may be compared to the way journalists under authoritarian press systems promote government propaganda messages.

WILL JOURNALISM BE RELEVANT TO FUTURE SOCIETIES?

Will journalism be critical, indeed even relevant, to future societies? Optimists predict that the role of the professional journalist would be secure and the press would not be in jeopardy as an institution. However, the future role of journalists might be changing from merely recording events as they happen to digesting, condensing, and evaluating overwhelming amounts of information that is widely available to consumers in raw form. The roles of journalists and journalism as an institution and legacy news media will be challenged in significant ways, with accompanying ethical ramifications in a global communication system that will be virtually impossible to regulate and in which historical professional standards cannot be applied.

A printing press or a radio or television station is no longer needed to practice journalism and provide information to a large audience, thus undermining the gatekeeping function of legacy media. The era of globally pervasive digital media allows everyone to broadcast their worldviews and disseminate information that may be perceived as "facts." Journalism will likely be deprofessionalized when citizens become their own journalists, both in their dissemination of "news" and as consumers of information from an immense number of sources that they can re-frame for themselves and to others as "news." However, can the value of journalism and journalists in the digital era lie in accurate, balanced, and reliable information-gathering and fact-checking? Perhaps the dramatic digital transformation will be a call for re-examination of existing paradigms of what journalism is and how it operates.

THE FUTURE OF JOURNALISM AND ITS ETHICS

In contemplating the future of journalism and its ethics, it is important to distinguish between journalism as an institution and as a professionalized occupation. Indeed, the future of journalism may not be the future of those who nevertheless consider themselves to be journalists and who, indeed, may possess journalism professional knowledge, skills, and abilities. Molla (2019, para. 4) reported: "New data . . . shows that the plight of journalists may not be that bad—if you're willing to consider a broader definition of what constitutes 'journalism' and its para-industries." She observed:

> Many journalism and PR jobs didn't go away so much as change their names. People who once worked in journalism or PR have commonly transitioned into job titles like "content writer" and "social media manager" . . . They're not working for newspapers or TV, but they are still applying the same skills . . . These are jobs where you are fact-finding and interviewing—pretty much a journalist.

Others have also noted the merging between some aspect of journalistic work with public relations functions. This is true not only for online publications, but also for mainstream journalism.

A recent analysis of journalism and public relations codes of ethics from thirty-three countries demonstrated that these two occupations now share these convergent values: professionalism, moral standards, and expertise (Yang, Taylor, & Saffer, 2016). There are also trends toward increasing deprofessionalization in both journalism and public relations, prioritizing skills that focus on technical and tactical knowledge and abilities.

Journalism's continuing sustainability as an institution and a professionalized occupation is in jeopardy in a confusing era of "fake news" and post-truth, in which its professional values and ethics are needed more than ever before. Journalism's monopoly of knowledge has been eroded by the Internet and social media, eviscerating the advertising revenue that historically had sustained journalism in the legacy news media. Furthermore, media credibility and public trust in the presentation of news by professional journalists who historically have striven to adhere to the traditional news values of fairness, objectivity, and transparency have not safeguarded journalism as an institution or as a professionalized occupation.

Scholars and practitioners have pondered the obsolescence of the legacy news media and have questioned whether the concept of news will continue to have meaning in the digital era. Some have even further questioned the agenda-setting role of traditional media as individuals around the world are surrounded by information from myriad electronic channels. This raises the question whether professional journalism will continue to exist in its current form and how it might evolve—from simply as a handy descriptor for current events to a reliable and legitimate source of news that has been screened and verified by human experts.

Finally, will professional journalism schools and the professional practices and ethical values they espouse become passé? This remains an open question, considering the fact that many citizens throughout the world have chosen to become their own journalists, disseminating information that they deem as news and consuming information from other individuals that these sources may present as news. Today, every person can be his or her journalist within a global milieu of interactive multimedia and may even select to access only those information channels that they find consistent with personal beliefs.

CHAPTER SUMMARY

Despite existing concerns, the role of professional journalists might not be in jeopardy. Their role in the digital era may be to digest, condense, and evaluate overwhelming amounts of information that is readily available to consumers in raw form. This, of course, suggests that journalism and the role of journalists will change in significant ways, with accompanying ethical ramifications. One certainty is that journalism will remain community-based because of people's opportunity to join multiple communities, whether these are physical or virtual. However, this community journalism will likely be deprofessionalized and ideologically based, perhaps practiced by those who would be better described as *strategic communicators* rather than as *journalists*.

If such reality is deemed unacceptable, it is up to the scholarly and practitioner communities of journalism to discover alternative paradigms to assure the continued existence of the traditional role and function of journalism as an institution and a professionalized occupation. Disseminating factual information from reliable news sources must remain the cornerstone of journalistic inquiry; however, an elitist approach toward journalism that is restricted to "professional journalists" will likely evolve into a deprofessionalized and more democratizing model that may prove more amenable to the digital information age.

DISCUSSION QUESTIONS

1. What should be the role and function of journalism? Should this role and function be universal in all societies worldwide?
2. Is it likely to expect that the roles of journalists and strategic communicators will become increasingly blurred? Would this be desirable or harmful to democratic societies?
3. How can professional journalism and the legacy news media remain sustainable in the digital information age?
4. Do you agree that journalism's traditional values and ethics are needed now more than ever? Why or why not?

BIBLIOGRAPHY

Accountable Journalism. (n.d.). *Code of ethics of the National Federation of Brazilian Journalists.* accountablejournalism.org/ethics-codes/Brazil-Journalist

Bauman, Z. (1995). Searching for a centre that holds. In M. Featherstone, S. Lash, & R. Robertson (Eds.), *Global modernities* (pp. 140–154). Sage.

Bell, D. (1988). *The end of ideology.* Harvard University Press.

Berger, P. L. (1963). *Invitation to sociology: A humanistic perspective.* Anchor Books.

Ethical Journalism Network. (n.d.). *The 5 principles of ethical journalism.* ethicaljournalismnetwork.org/who-we-are/5-principles-of-journalism

Goodstein, L., Nolan, T., & Pfeiffer, J. W. (1993) *Applied strategic planning: How to develop a plan that really works.* McGraw-Hill.

Hardt, H. (1979). *Social theories of the press.* Sage.

Hobbes, D. A., & Blank, S. J. (1975). *Sociology and the human experience.* John Wiley & Sons.

Johannesen, R. L., Valde, K. S., & Whedbee, K. E. (2008). *Ethics in human communication.* Waveland Press.

Kruckeberg, D. (1998). Future reconciliation of multicultural perspectives in public relations ethics. *Public Relations Quarterly, 43,* 45–48.

Lambeth, E. B. (1992). *Committed journalism: An ethic for the profession* (2nd ed.). Indiana University Press.

Luhmann, N. (1982). *The differentiation of society.* Columbia University Press (Original work published 1971).

Luhmann, N. (1995). *Social systems.* Stanford University Press.

Luhmann, N. (1997). *Die gesellschaft der gesellschaft.* Suhrkamp.

Macdonald, K. M. (1995). *The sociology of the professions.* Sage.

Merrill, J. C., Bryan, C. R., & Alisky, M. (1970). *The foreign press: A survey of the world's journalism.* Louisiana State University Press.

Molla, A. (2019, Feb. 25). Chart: How the definition of "journalist" is changing. *Record.net.* www.recode.net/2019/2/25/18224696/chart-transition-journalism-public-relations-content-social-media-jobs?fbclid=IwAR0bjHOkq67tInrzm25jB7-rQXa-NZQqWXQFPOmrilE-xBIS-OY_HenGMg

National Union of Journalists Malaysia (n.d.). *National Union of Journalists Peninsular Malaysia.* www.nujm.org/nuj/about.php

Rubin, B. (1978). The search for media ethics. In B. Rubin (Ed.), *Questioning media ethics.* Praeger.

Schudson, M. (2008). *Why democracies need an unlovable press.* Polity Press.

Time Staff. (2020, July 1). These are the 10 'most urgent' cases of threats to press freedom around the world in July 2020. *Time.* time.com/5861990/most-urgent-threats-press-freedom-july-2020/?utm_source=newsletter&utm_medium=email&utm_campaign=the-brief&utm_content=20200701&et_rid=31906584

Tsetsura, K., & Kruckeberg, D. (2017). *Transparency, public relations and the mass media: Combating media bribery worldwide.* Taylor and Francis/Routledge.

Tsetsura, K., & Valentini, C. (2016, November). The "holy" triad in media ethics: A conceptual model for understanding global media ethics. *Public Relations Review, 42*(4), 573–581.

Union of Journalists in Finland. (n.d.). *Guidelines for journalists.* journalistiliitto.fi/en/ground-rules/guidelines/

Vujnovic, M., & Kruckeberg, D. (2015). Conceptualization, examination, and recommendations for a normative model of community-building for organizations managing change using new media. In E-J. Ki, J-N. Kim, & J. Ledingham (Eds.). *Public relations as relationship management: A relational approach to the study and practice of public relations* (2nd Ed.). Routledge.

Vujnovic, M., & Kruckeberg, D. (2016). Pitfalls and promises of transparency in the digital age. *Public Relations Inquiry, 5,* 121–143.

Yang, A., Taylor, M., & Saffer, A. (2016). Ethical convergence, divergence or communitas? An examination of public relations and journalism codes of ethics. *Public Relations Review, 42,* 146–160.

Zelizer, B. (2004). *Taking journalism seriously.* Sage.

II

WORLD REGIONS

8

Media in Sub-Saharan Africa

Yusuf Kalyango, Jr.

This chapter examines and highlights the state of media in sub-Saharan Africa as it relates to the practice of journalism, as well as political cultures that dictate media performance, policies, and developments. It is important right from this onset to first clarify the disjunction of the African continent into the geopolitical cultural space of sub-Saharan Africa from mostly the rest of the continent's north. As this chapter focuses on countries located south of the Sahara on the continent, the analysis draws from a representative sample of fifteen out of those forty-six African countries that make up sub-Saharan Africa (see figure 8.1). Meanwhile, this cluster of countries also has some considerable economic, social, political, and nationalistic variants that cannot be overlooked. In examining journalism and the media in all their forms, a few analytical cases from the fifteen countries will highlight some of these variations, reflecting a broader scope of the subcontinent.

Just as there is not a unison homogeneous *Africa*, likewise, *media* on this vast subcontinent is understood as a plural noun. Media here are defined as encompassing a myriad means of mass communication with various forms of content and messages produced and disseminated through different channels by individuals, groups, communities, agencies, or professional entities including print, digital or LAN, broadcast, static or mobile electronic, and via different forms of products used to display, access, interact, experience, consume, and regenerate (such as viral). One of these key professional entities is journalism. The chapter begins with the legacy platforms (traditional terrestrial television, radio, newspaper, and magazines) to contemporary digital media and social media platforms.

The principal arguments here allow students and educators of media and journalism to understand the development of this field and industry from the subcontinent's colonial era to date. In discussing the underlying issues and developments, some specific cases are presented to highlight some innovations and entrepreneurial approaches in the use of new media forms and journalism practices to engage citizens in sociopolitical awareness including health-related pandemics. While there are significant progress and expansion of media channels to access information by the masses on the continent, traditional FM and community radios continue to play a pivotal role in informing and *educating* citizens because of limitations from low general literacy, particularly in rural African communities, and low media literacy in the use and applications of new communication technologies. Despite media literacy challenges, there is a

AFRICA

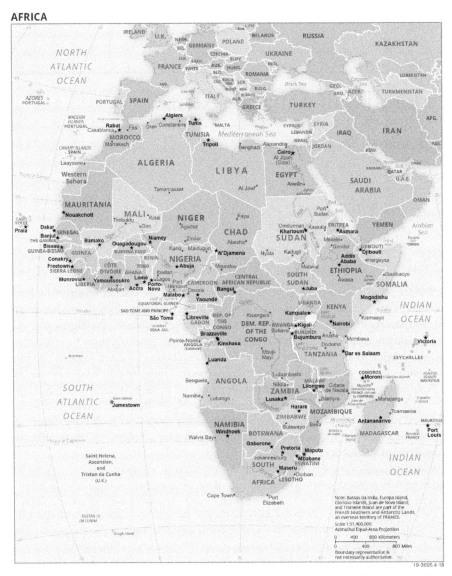

Figure 8.1. Map of continental Africa encompassing Sub-Saharan Africa. Sub-Saharan Africa is a vast geopolitical cultural region on this map covering three quarters of the continent, except the northern region, northwest, and parts of the northeast. Source: CIA World Factbook.

steady increase in media accessibility due to information sharing for both print and electronic media, and the growth of the mobile digital readership and use, plus the expansion of various media channels that foster effective delivery of information.

For contextual purposes to underscore media performance in the region, a case study is presented at the end of this chapter related to media use, media exposure, perception of government efficacy, and access to health-related services in the Afrobarometer datasets from the following countries: Benin, Cape Verde, Sierra Leone, Ghana, and Liberia (for Western

African countries) as well as Botswana, Kenya, Tanzania, Uganda, and Zimbabwe (for Eastern and Southern Africa), as well as Rwanda, Ethiopia, Zambia, South Africa, Nigeria, and Burundi. In closing this exploration of media in sub-Saharan Africa, a brief empirical case of media performance on the frontlines of a major public health pandemic is chosen here to illuminate media development and innovations.

This contemporaneous empirical public opinion data on media use and performance tracks the coverage of the Ebola health pandemic—amid the HIV/AIDS health scourge—in 2015, using the Afrobarometer Round 6 data of 2014/15 (Afrobarometer, 2017) public opinion surveys. The chapter briefly illuminates all the important advancements in the digital mobile and social media revolution in the region as it relates to mass empowerment, expanded media freedoms, and the rule of law in this era of social media.

HISTORICAL ROOTS: PERFORMANCE AND SYSTEMS

Running a media organization that produces and delivers news and current affairs across the continent and especially in sub-Saharan Africa was never an easy enterprise. Since colonial and postcolonial times—from the 1950s to 1960s—most media organizations, namely the printing press, newspapers, magazines, national radio, and television, were government parastatals. Yet, despite being owned and run by public servants who also doubled as professional journalists, they faced political regimes that imposed self-censorship with the justification that it serves in the national interest as part of development journalism (Faringer, 1991; Kalyango & Eckler, 2010). The practice of muzzling the press to tow state propaganda by the state-owned news media in most of Africa was widespread, as news editors and journalists were subjected to censorship and direct political control for decades, spiraling into this century (Faringer, 1991; Ocitti, 2006).

From the 1960s to mid-2000s, political actors still targeted the media as enemies of progress, while journalists became increasingly critical of the activities of corrupt politicians and incompetent leaders (Kalyango, 2011; Spurk et al., 2010). For instance, in 1964, senior journalists formed the Press Union of Liberia specifically to defend the journalists' rights (Spurk et al., 2010). In Ghana, the press and radio broadcasting date back to the colonial period when colonizers used those media as a political strategy to ensure that peripheral regions were linked to the urbanized people of the Gold Coast (Anokwa, 1997). Later, when ownership of the media shifted into the hands of nationalist Ghanaians, the focus of media changed to advocate for national sovereignty from British rule and independence. The use of media to advance nationalism, independence, and political development was common across the region.

According to Anokwa (1997), media roles changed again after independence in order to build nationalism and patriotism in postcolonial African nations, such as Ghana. For instance, in postcolonial Sierra Leone, the media faced several challenges from both civilian and military dictatorships (Bau, 2010). The Sierra Leone government controlled the broadcast media before the outbreak of war in 1991, while newspapers were dominated by private ownership (Tam-Baryoh, 2006). This was the same media set up in other countries such as Kenya, Tanzania, and South Africa. Sierra Leone's capital city, Freetown, was the central location for the national television and radio broadcasts, with a few regional radio outlets and gutter press serving the remaining parts of the country.

In remote countrysides of Benin, Cape Verde, Sierra Leone, Ghana, and Liberia, Botswana, Kenya, Tanzania, Uganda, and Zimbabwe, newspapers suffered low readership from the 1960s to the mid-1990s due to high illiteracy and lower circulation. Meanwhile, in Benin, there were other major problems during the media's infancy after independence. A time of political strife marked post-independent Benin, experiencing strings of military takeovers (Adoun & Awoudo, 2013). According to Adoun and Awoudo (2013), the East German government started Benin's first media outlet, Radio Cotonou, in 1953, and in cooperation with France, led to the first television station in 1972. In countries like Benin, Cape Verde, Botswana, Burundi, Rwanda, and Mali, the governments permitted only the State-run broadcast media from the 1950s through the 1990s. Benin's media landscape rapidly became one of the most vibrant in sub-Saharan West Africa at the start of this millennium, and independent media outlets continued to grow and thrive.

In Cape Verde, the government still operates a radio station, television station, and the major national newspaper—and that is similar to other countries like Burundi, Uganda, Ethiopia, Rwanda, Zambia, and others. Cape Verde is an important case to explore because, just like Burundi and Congo-Brazzaville, it is one of the most understudied African nations. Yet, Reporters without Borders (2018) ranked Cape Verde as the most respectful protector of press freedoms among Lusophone countries. Since 2000, journalists in Cape Verde have consistently described the country as having an enviable press freedom environment in Africa due to enforceable laws, pragmatic media, and watchdog voices that are respected (BBC, 2018). From 2000 to 2010 in Cape Verde, there were neither reports of journalists' arrests nor media harassment despite the advocacy media rights groups' concern over a defamation clause (Freedom House, 2013). No other country among those examined here has a similar record of media autonomy in that same period in this millennium.

Comparable to countries in Western Africa, all news media in precolonial and postcolonial East Africa—Kenya, Uganda, and Tanzania—were owned and controlled by their respective governments. However, Kenya had permitted independent newspapers by mid-1970s. For many decades since the 1960s, the performance of the traditional (legacy) media in these three countries was grounded on promoting the national presidential agenda. The news media did not have an independent voice of reporting about any civil issues of public interest. For instance, from the 1960s through the 1990s, Ugandan, Kenyan, and Tanzanian leaders appointed some politicians to manage the national broadcasting media and even newspapers in order to effectively control the ideological mass appeal and suppress any accountability over corruption, nepotism, misuse of public funds, and public health matters (Rubongoya, 2007). In some countries such as Nigeria, Rwanda, Burundi, and Ethiopia, both radio and television's current affairs programming and newscasts were sometimes used by political leaders to produce inflammatory messages calling on citizens to rise in arms against certain groups to protect national sovereignty at all costs based on ethnicity or religious beliefs (Nyamnjoh, 2005).

For all the sub-Saharan African countries examined here, the twentieth century was marred by political instability due to authoritarian militaristic non-democratic governance, nepotism, high rate of illiteracy, poor reading culture, and ethnic divisiveness (Kagwanja, 2006; Kaiser, 2000). Most of these governments in the region exploited these volatile circumstances to control both the media and citizens. However, throughout sub-Saharan Africa, things dramatically changed following the liberalization of the economy and state-owned enterprises, including the national media starting in the early 1990s. This economic liberalization and attractive investment incentives triggered the proliferation of media outlets and journalistic freedom and media independence across the region.

MEDIA OWNERSHIP AND ECONOMICS
FOR LEGACY MEDIA

The media landscape across the region is gradually expanding. Monrovia, the capital of Liberia, has more than fifteen independent radio stations, with two that broadcast nationwide. Community radio, known for its developmental role, has expanded to more than fifty stations in Liberia, while the number of television stations stands at six, but many journalists affiliated with these news media outlets often face intimidation and occasional physical attacks (Freedom House, 2019a,b). The media sector in Liberia includes fully funded state-owned and private media outlets. According to the Freedom House report, privately owned media in Sierra Leone are not financially self-sustaining and have to rely on funds from politicians and international donors. Due to this financial dependence, the press in Sierra Leone does not have enough potency to carry out its duties as a watchdog and faces pressures to tow the government line. This challenge for the press is not exclusive to Sierra Leone but also for other countries in the region including Benin, Cape Verde, Liberia, Botswana, Rwanda, Tanzania, Uganda, and Zimbabwe.

In spite of these challenges, journalists in Sierra Leone continue to monitor and hold the government, institutions, and politicians accountable. Although radio, television, and newspapers are all popular forms of media in Sierra Leone, the immense reach and appeal of radio over other types of media are indisputable. One major problem is that state-owned media and journalists were still under-funded at the start of this millennium and most of the broadcasting equipment and publishing machinery had become obsolete (Tam-Baryoh, 2006). The civil war in Sierra Leone took a toll on human capital and infrastructure. So, this pushed the traditional media sector into the hands of untrained media practitioners; about 70 percent of trained media practitioners had fled the country by the early 2000s (Malan et al., 2003). Even the post-civil war developmental programs that attempted to build capacity for journalists and media practitioners to replace those who had initially fled and then returned home were temporary and underfunded.

In Ghana, a large number of media outlets provide quality information, including engaging citizens to freely express their views on radio talk shows and phone-in programs on television, but their main topic of discourse is power and political partisanship, not public health issues (Sikanku, 2014). Besides Nigeria, Ghana has one of the most diverse and vibrant media environments in West Africa, but according to Freedom House (2019), "government agencies occasionally limit press freedom through harassment and arrests of journalists, especially those reporting on politically sensitive issues." The state-owned *Ghana Broadcasting Corporation* operates two national radio stations and one station in each region. Also, the major newspapers in Ghana primarily provide news coverage that favors the government and politicians in power or the presidency. Currently, the Ghanaian government still controls and owns the major national newspapers but a few privately owned newspapers are growing, which is also the same case in several other countries examined here, such as Benin, Cape Verde, Liberia, Botswana, Uganda, and Zimbabwe. Independent newspapers in Ghana that conduct investigative journalism are branded as opposition media and those journalists are denied equal access to public records.

In Benin, there are privatized print media and joint-ownership of the broadcast media between the government and private individuals (Adoun & Awoudo, 2013), which is similar to other media ownership systems examined here. Liberalization of the newspaper industry in

Benin also opened up opportunities for politicians to use newspapers to pursue their own political agenda. This is not a new trend, as politicians own media outlets as commercial business ventures in many other African countries (Kalyango, 2011). By 2015, there were about 120 newspapers, magazines, and periodicals circulating in Benin (Grätz, 2017). Most of these newspapers and magazines are not profitable, and more than half of the dailies that circulated in 2010 were off the market by 2018. In Benin, "most media outlets receive direct financial support from politicians and few are considered genuinely independent" (Freedom House, 2019a,b); although the government provides both electronic and print media to report news freely without fear of persecution, and independent journalists provide plurality of opinion and viewpoints.

MEDIA POLICIES AND REGULATORY SYSTEMS

The divestiture of state-owned media in the 1990s led to privatized print media and joint-ownerships of the electronic media between the government and private individuals. Yet for legacy media in some of the countries examined here, media struggles continued to stymie their development primarily due to intervening factors stemming from media policies, restrictive laws, corruption, and presidential hegemony (Kalyango, 2011; Mwenda, 2007). As the governments of Benin, Botswana, Uganda, Zimbabwe, and elsewhere restructured and privatized the national media, they also established institutional monitoring centers to scrutinize the burgeoning independent media. For example, the *Supreme Media Board* in Benin and the *Uganda Media Centre* as well as other entities in other countries were established to "ensure that the government is fairly and objectively represented in the media" or to "foster a positive communication environment between government and the media" (Kalyango, 2011, p. 93). Generally, the relationship between private media and those media monitoring centers remains confrontational.

Some of these government-run monitoring centers have enforced some unwelcome 'standards' for journalists and private media, while at the same time channeling development aid to state-owned media and leaving out privately owned media (Grätz, 2017). These centers are also mandated to issue professional credentialing identity/press cards. Although these government-run monitoring centers are mandated to facilitate further professional training for journalists on a regular or annual basis, many of these media surveillance facilities do not provide such policy-mandated opportunities to young mid-career professionals from the privately own media establishments. Instead, these centers in some countries such as Uganda, Zambia, Tanzania, Cape Verde, and Ethiopia flex their muscles by confronting media managers with what they believe are abuses of media autonomy, accusing media practitioners of defamation or publication of false or unverified information, especially during national elections campaign period (Skjerdal & Ngugi, 2007). The private media in most of the sub-Saharan African countries endure these threats and continue to thrive despite the harsh environment.

Besides the establishment of the media monitoring centers in some countries, some governments also passed draconian laws disguised under the banner of democracy, but which were intended to suffocate any independent media that are deemed adversarial. The laws typically have legal controls and constraints on media autonomy engrained in penal codes. Statutory provisions for sedition and criminal libel are still used in many sub-Saharan African countries to hamper the free functioning of the independent investigative media. For instance, stringent media laws in the Eastern African countries of Uganda, Rwanda, Tanzania, and even Ethiopia can land journalists and their editors or news producers in prison on charges of terrorism using the *Penal Code* for reporting on the presidency (Limpitlaw, 2016; Mwenda, 2007;

Wanta & Kalyango, 2007). Similar to Western and Central Africa, the countries in Eastern and Southern Africa also have legislation that prohibits a myriad type of mass communication and journalistic reporting, including but not limited to the following.

Sub-Saharan African governments' *prohibitions* include the following: dissemination of information, publications, and images that undermine the authority of a public officer; anything that would constitute treason; information that is contrary to the interests of public order; anything that contains certain election-related information; information that would be construed contrary to the interests of public health; or constituting the boosting or elevation of terrorists or terrorism agendas; mass communication that contains alarming information, or incitement to boycott or lead to protests; and or any media publications that may constitute any criminal defamation (Limpitlaw, 2016). In Rwanda, for instance, there are the *Rwanda High Council* and its subsidiary, the *Rwanda Media Commission*, which are established to enforce similar prohibitions, and the Rwanda Journalists and Media Practitioners' Code of Ethics (RMC Code of Ethics) also enacted as an enforceable law to ensure that journalists can self-regulate, while being monitored.

Politicians in Kenya passed the following controversial media laws in early 2014, which effectively silenced independent critical voices of media by imposing hefty fines coupled with a ban or imprisonment. The two laws were the *Kenya Information and Communication Act*—which was an amendment in 2014—and the *Media Council Act*. However, the Kenyan government is not as harsh on independent media and news reporters as its Burundian or Rwandan counterparts. The Uganda penal code laws included the *Press and Journalists Act* of 2000 and the *Access to Information Act* of 2005. They regulate the ability of the adversarial press to report on state institutions that violate human rights and the constitution.

> *The Prevention of Terrorism Act, No. 30 of 2012*: The 2014 Amendments to the Prevention of Terrorism Act provides for a new section 36A(1) which empowers the National Security Organs (the Kenya Defence Forces, the National Intelligence Service and the National Police Service) to intercept communication for the purposes of detecting, deterring and disrupting terrorism. This has obvious implications for a journalist's need to protect his or her sources.
>
> (Limpitlaw, 2016, pp. 376–377)

When these surveillance regulatory centers to monitor media activities and publications are established, their mandate is typically broad, vague, overreaching, and sometimes present this allure of a guardian. Take, for instance, the Rwanda Media Commission (RMC), which was established as a regulatory monitoring body particularly responsible for enforcing the journalistic code of ethics called the RMC Code of Ethics. The RMC acts as the primary and highest adjudicator of complaints against the electronic and print media, "representing the broader interests of journalists, and defending media freedom, and media consumers in general" (Limpitlaw, 2016, p. 477). There are similar surveillance agencies that enforce some of the stringent media laws in most of the countries highlighted in this chapter: Benin, Cape Verde, Sierra Leone, Ghana, Liberia, Botswana, Nigeria, Kenya, Tanzania, Uganda, Rwanda, Ethiopia, South Africa, and Zimbabwe.

LEAPFROGGING INTO THE FUTURE

Since 2010, the rapid growth and spread of smart mobile communication technology across Africa and the cheap access to data on mobile cellular phones have rapidly impacted how journalism is practiced and many other aspects of social interactions, cultural engagements, political communication, and economic life in sub-Saharan Africa (Kalyango, 2019; Mare, 2013). It is not simply a phenomenon of Africans holding mobile phones and smartphones to engage in social networking. It is now more advanced than that and intertwined with journalism practices. Due to social media platforms, African journalists can follow and track breaking news in real-time and cover major crises as they develop, including national elections by monitoring public engagements on platforms such as *Facebook, Twitter,* or *YouTube,* and *WhatsApp* (Benson, 2013; Kalyango, 2019; Paulussen & Harder, 2014).

Digital Revolution and Social Media

While continental Africa still lags behind most of the world's Internet reach, there has been slow but steady Internet penetration in most of the rural sub-Saharan Africa. The proliferation of digital media and mobile communication has allowed the subcontinent to leapfrog into the twenty-first media century. Before smart mobile phones, city or municipal residents in countries like Cape Verde, Benin, Zimbabwe, or Ethiopia were more politically active than people residing in rural areas; and whereas older people were more sociopolitically active and engaged in community leadership than younger people—between ages 21 and 35—that changed at the turn of this millennium (Joiner & Okeleke, 2020). This changed with the advent, rise, and adoption of mobile phones and smart devices with relatively inexpensive access to Internet data. The affluent youth and mid-career working adults are now more politically engaged, actively advocating for their rights and connected globally.

The rapid growth of independent media channels through social media and the spread of smart mobile communication technology across Africa, coupled with the cheap availability of data on mobile cellular phones has rapidly impacted many aspects of social, cultural, political, and economic life. By 2019, sub-Saharan Africa with a population of close to 1.1 billion, exceeded 450 million unique mobile subscribers—or about 45 percent of the population who also could potentially have access to both television content (and *YouTube*) on their smartphones (Joiner & Okeleke, 2020). Across sub-Saharan Africa, the number of mobile users has increased by about 18 percent annually from 2010 to 2015. According to Joiner and Okeleke (2020), since 2010, sub-Saharan Africa continues to be the world's fastest-growing region in the world for mobile phone subscribers. The region is emerging as a hyperactive hub for economic innovation using information communication technologies and sociopolitical changes, using social media as a backdrop for marketing, mobilizing, or mediating these developments.

The most popular social media outlets in sub-Saharan Africa continue to be *Facebook, WhatsApp,* and *YouTube* in that order, while *Twitter* is used primarily by the working class, educated elites, and government officials. Some regions have developed unique Africa-based networking sites that have recorded on average about half a million users. The countries examined here comprise French-speaking (Francophone) and English-speaking (Anglophone) nations as their international language of business and official business discourse, social networking interactions, and international relations. Social media are now considered the new communication frontiers in local and professional-foreign languages for current affairs and news dissemination among a substantial proportion of the working population, including student populations at the high school senior level, university, and tertiary institutions. That comes with new governmental regulatory oversights all across the region, as in Sierra Leone:

> Private discussion remains largely open. Authorities reportedly monitor discussions on social media platforms, including WhatsApp, although few arrests have been made for online discussions or

comments. On election day in 2018, the police briefly shut down the internet, preventing people from communicating about the polls and the results.

(Freedom House, 2019)

The growing popularity of social media outlets on smart mobile phones in this region has noticeably changed the political behavior of how some African leaders in Benin, Cape Verde, Ghana, Liberia, Sierra Leone, Botswana, South Africa, Zambia, Zimbabwe, Burundi, Ethiopia, Kenya, Rwanda, Tanzania, and Uganda interact with and engage citizens. A majority of the working class and middle-class city dwellers in all those countries—particularly in Nigeria, South Africa, and Kenya—spend more time visiting websites and apps on their mobile phones than watching television, radio, or using laptops and desktops. Some reports about mobile use estimate that about 95 percent of the affluent Africans on the subcontinent now own a smartphone.

Alternative Journalism?

Broadcast and print journalists from the mainstream legacy media in sub-Saharan Africa have also embraced the social media phenomenon, not just as competing platforms for the mainstream channels, but as a way to broaden their reach, breadth, and engagement. There are many instances where citizen eyewitnesses and journalists have converged on social media outlets such as *Facebook*, *Twitter*, or *YouTube* for breaking news and live updates on *WhatsApp* during major accidents, social conflicts, political rallies, and protests. This form of convergence has necessitated the advent of alternative journalism and collaborative reporting arrangements between mainstream journalists and some eyewitness content producers. This has reformed and broadened the media coverage, reduced the costs of reporting breaking news, and provided the voices of previously silenced and marginalized groups.

Consequently, journalists and news editors who were previously harassed and intimidated have been empowered by this new digital revolution and the proliferation of smart mobile phones. Journalists and social media influencers in various countries on the continent are now generally free to express their views on politics and political leaders without direct intimidation, crackdown, and fear of state surveillance. This newfound mass appeal of social media apps has increased public engagement and empowerment as well as created perceived threats to authoritarian leaders on the subcontinent. Consequently, many of these concerned governments have resorted to amending the laws to control the use of social media for political use.

Another important development in this context is the emergence of numerous innovative independent mobile news platforms all over sub-Saharan Africa, which provide news and current affairs through digital media platforms. These include *AfricaNews* (www.africanews.com) covering major news events across Africa, *African Independent* (www.africanindy.com) rewriting Africa's narrative, and *AllAfrica* (allafrica.com) publishing around 600 reports a day from more than 140 news organizations and over 500 other institutions on every topic. There are also a multitude of country-specific prominent independent mobile news platforms, such as IOL (www.iol.co.za) from South Africa and *TheCable* (www.thecable.ng) from Nigeria, among other country-specific examples.

Also, many young African entrepreneurs are developing and launching innovative mobile apps for news, current affairs, trade, marketing, investments, banking, and social networking. These include *Baidoo* (badoo.com) a social discovery network all across sub-Saharan Africa; *OurHood* (ourhood.co.za/splash) connecting communities in Southern Africa; and *EastAfricanTube* (eastafricantube.com) a video sourcing and networking site for Eastern Africa and beyond, among many others.

MEDIA IN ACTION—PUBLIC HEALTH PANDEMICS

When nearly 23,000 people were infected and more than 9,000 people died from the Ebola virus in three West African countries—Guinea, Liberia, and Sierra Leone—between August 2014 and February 2015, many journalists covering that major health outbreak faced challenges from their local governments. For example, police arrested newspaper publishers in Senegal in an attempt to stifle news dissemination regarding the epidemic (Borowski, 2014). Consequently, due to the legacy media blackout in Guinea, Liberia, and Sierra Leone, many citizens in remote areas of the affected countries lacked an understanding of the virus and conspiracy theories that were being spread around. But does this intimidation of the media, and the resulting fear of exposing bad governance on the sub-continent, relate to how the public perceives media performance on matters as important as a public health crisis?

In 2016, empirical data based on the Afrobarometer public opinion surveys were analyzed—by this author—to determine the relationship between the citizens' perceptions of media's effectiveness in revealing corruption and perceptions of government effectiveness in addressing health-related concerns. Results in Benin, Cape Verde, Sierra Leone, Ghana, and Liberia showed a small but significant positive correlation between the perceived effectiveness of the news media at revealing corruption and the composite variable of how well/badly the government is perceived to be handling health-related issues. This indicates that the more effective respondents saw the news media at revealing corruption, the higher they rated the government's performance regarding health-related issues.

Another question in that analysis examined how well the governments, individually and collectively, were handling health-related issues depending on how often individuals had to go without health-related necessities. The public opinion data analysis in Benin, Cape Verde, Sierra Leone, Ghana, and Liberia showed that the more often respondents had to go without food, water, and medical treatment, the worse their perception of how the government was handling health-related issues. Also, interestingly, the more effective the respondents in some of these countries (Benin, Liberia, and Sierra Leone) saw the news media doing a better job at revealing corruption, then the more effective those respondents saw the government at handling health-related issues and that also correlated with more satisfaction they had with the government. Overall, these results underscore the importance of free and independent media in sub-Saharan Africa.

Analysis from the same dataset also found a majority of respondents in Benin, Cape Verde, Sierra Leone, Ghana, and Liberia stated that their government was handling "fairly well" or "very well" the job of combatting HIV/AIDS in spite of the high rates of HIV/AIDS; despite the lack of proper medical care in many clinics and hospitals. Most governments in Africa have collaborated with some non-governmental organizations in rolling out programs to stop the spread of HIV/AIDS. Therefore, even though HIV/AIDS is still very much a problem in some African countries, respondents in Benin, Cape Verde, Ghana, Liberia, and Sierra Leone in the 2014/15 surveys seem to believe the government was working hard to fix this issue.

Balancing Exploitation

In light of the vibrant social media growth and alternative journalism in the region, governments in sub-Saharan Africa are increasingly creating new media regulations and licensing procedures, essentially exploiting the autonomy of independent voices—curbing social media influence—while at the same time increasing state revenues. That, conceptually, is a balancing exploitation. For instance, many governments in sub-Saharan Africa enacted unpopular prohibitive social media tax laws between 2017 and 2019, which they imposed on the use of platforms such as *Facebook*, *WhatsApp*, *Twitter,* and other African networking sites. These are monthly levies imposed on citizens who own and use a smartphone to access social media platforms. However, following a public outcry against these balancing exploits in countries such as Benin, Sierra Leone, Nigeria, and others against these measures, political leaders in some of these countries were forced to repeal some of the social media monthly levies. Yet, in countries such as Uganda, Zambia, Zimbabwe, and Ethiopia, levies on social media are still enforced.

However, these laws have neither deterred nor suppressed online political discourse in these countries. On the contrary, these measures triggered more social media political activism and mass mobilization against the repressive actions of those governments, forcing many positive changes in terms of expanding the media landscape and empowering journalists all across sub-Saharan Africa. Additionally, social media are increasingly leveling the playing field for the previously exploited and disadvantaged opposition politicians.

As mobile technology and social media use is steadily growing across the continent, rural dwellers are slowly taking advantage of their smartphones to stay connected and get more active in the virtual community. However, there is still inadequate access to Internet resources in most of the rural sub-Saharan Africa due to low literacy rates and low media literacy, particularly because of the lack of awareness of how to use, search, and utilize relevant applications of new technologies. For this region, there are no known funded governmental or institutional structures in place for rural dwellers to promote technological and media literacy. Consequently, the idea of enabling ordinary Africans to be active communicators with competencies and understandings of political and legal rights, and to become critically engaged citizens in a democratic society is seen as too emancipatory and counterproductive to some of the politicians' authoritarian rule.

Since colonial days from the early 1950s to 1960s, traditional mainstream media—namely radio, television, magazines, and newspapers—played a significant role in the people's struggles for liberation against colonialism and exploitation. However, when the European colonizers, particularly from Great Britain, France, Belgium, Germany, Portugal, Spain, and the Netherlands granted independence to most of the sub-Saharan African countries, many African leaders then used these same media outlets as propaganda tools to promote their own political agendas without any media oversight and accountability. These African political leaders also used radio, terrestrial television, and state-owned newspapers to advance the spirit of consolidating nationalism, while also enforcing presidential and political patronage.

Meanwhile, over the course of three decades—from the 1980s to 2000s—the traditional mainstream media also altered many African cultures and values among the youths who were exposed to the Western pop-culture through television news and documentaries, movies, music, television sitcoms, comics, and fashion magazines. Overall, traditional mainstream media were used as instruments of political power. The role of state-owned media was to serve national political-ideological agenda of the major ruling political parties in favor of the presidency; while at the same time using media outlets to promote agricultural productivity, government-sanctioned social welfare programs, and health campaigns among the African populations.

In the early part of the twenty-first century, women in sub-Saharan Africa remained much less likely than African men to engage in collective actions or contact politicians, regardless of their socioeconomic status or attitudes (Coffe & Bolzendahl, 2011). Social media engagement and mobile media interactions are changing that phenomenon. Indeed, smartphones and digital media play an increasingly important role in promoting political participation, especially among women—in the fifteen countries examined here—and have contributed to the necessity for political leaders to also use social media to reach and actively engage with their constituencies.

It appears that many citizens of sub-Saharan Africa may still need targeted information campaigns and news from the media to provide them with information about healthcare needs and emergencies like the Ebola outbreaks or HIV/AIDS—among other critical issues, including the COVID-19 global pandemic. Access to correct and timely information will ensure that citizens on the subcontinent can make informed choices—about public health concerns, governance, economics, and education, to name but a few—that affect their lives, often through the use of mobile phones and online portals accessible even to those living in remote areas.

CHAPTER SUMMARY

This chapter reviewed media development in sub-Saharan Africa from the colonial era to date. It traced the evolution of journalism and media from strictly state-controlled institutions to more liberalized, market-driven enterprises. While traditional political and economic factors remain critical for media development in the region, technological growth has been a critical component of the media transition in sub-Saharan Africa, enabling innovative and entrepreneurial approaches to overcome structural disadvantages. Overall, there is a concerted effort to keep digital devices such as smart mobile handsets and Internet data pricing affordable, despite the heavy reliance on mobile data because of the lack of fixed-line broadband availability in some parts of sub-Saharan Africa. Remarkably, the region as a whole is making steady progress with acceleration of the digital communications infrastructure development and media performance.

DISCUSSION QUESTIONS

1. How would you describe the evolution of the media in sub-Saharan Africa?
2. What is the state of journalism in sub-Saharan Africa in terms of press freedom and rule of law?
3. Can you identify the main factors at plays as local media systems transitioned from fully state-controlled to liberal, market-driven enterprises across the region?
4. Considering the growth of media in sub-Saharan Africa to date, what is the utility of social (and legacy) media in advancing the human capacity development of Africans?

BIBLIOGRAPHY

Adoun, W. R. H., & Awoudo, F. K. (2013). *Report on public broadcasting in Africa: Benin.* Open Society Initiative for West Africa.

Afrobarometer. (2017). *A pan-African series of national public attitude surveys on democracy, governance, and society.* Dataset retrieved for statistical analysis. afrobarometer.org/

Anokwa, K. (1997). Press performance under civilian and military regimes in Ghana: A reassessment of past and present knowledge. In F. Erbio & F. W. Jong-Edot (Eds.), *Press freedom and communication in Africa* (pp. 3–28). Africa World Press.

BBC. (2018). *Cape Verde country profile.* www.bbc.com/news/world-africa-13148486

Bau, V. (2010). Media and conflict in Sierra Leone: National and international perspectives of the civil war. *Global Media Journal-African Edition, 4*(1), 1–27.

Benson, T. (2013). Media convergence: Networked digital media in everyday life, *Ecquid Novi: African Journalism Studies, 34*(3), 172–174, DOI: 10.1080/02560054.2013.853363

Borowski, M. (2014). West African media on Ebola: Sensationalist or promoting public health? www.dw.de/west-african-media-on-ebola-sensationalist-or-promoting-public-health/a-17852856

Coffe, H., & Bolzendahl, C. (2011). Gender gaps in political participation across Sub-Saharan African nations. *Social indicators research, 102*(2), 245–264. doi.org/10.1007/s11205-010-9676-6

Faringer, G. L. (1991). *Press freedom in Africa.* Praeger.

Freedom House. (2013). *Cape Verde, Country Report 2013.* freedomhouse.org/country/cape-verde/freedom-world/2013

Freedom House. (2019a). *Sierra Leone, Country Report 2019.* freedomhouse.org/country/sierra-leone/freedom-world/2019

Freedom House. (2019b). *Ghana, Country Report 2019.* freedomhouse.org/country/ghana/freedom-world/2019

Grätz, T. (2017). Media development, censorship and working conditions of journalists in the Republic of Benin (West Africa). In Bussotti, L., de Barros, M., & Grätz, E. (Eds). *Media freedom and right to information in Africa.* Centro de Estudos Internacionais.

Joiner, J., & Okeleke, K. (2020). Definitive data and analysis for the mobile industry: Sub-Saharan Africa, Q3 2019. *GSMA Intelligence,* London, U.K. data.gsmaintelligence.com/research/research/research-2020/region-in-focus-sub-saharan-africa-q3-2019

Kagwanja, P. M. (2006). Power to Uhuru: Youth identity and generational politics in Kenya's 2002 elections. *African Affairs,* 105, 51–75.

Kaiser, P. (2000). Postmodern insurgencies: Political violence, identity formation and peacemaking in comparative perspective. *The Journal of Modern African Studies, 38*(3), 511–549.

Kalyango, Y. Jr. (2011). *African media and democratization: Public opinion, ownership, & rule of law.* Peter Lang Publishing.

Kalyango, Y. Jr. (2019). African journalism. *The International Encyclopedia of Journalism Studies.* Wiley. doi.org/10.1002/9781118841570.iejs0168

Kalyango, Y. Jr., & Eckler, P. (2010). Media performance, agenda building, and democratization in East Africa. *Communication Yearbook,* 34, 355–389.

Limpitlaw, J. (2016). *Media law handbook for Eastern Africa.* Konrad-Adenauer-Stiftung Regional Media Programme: Sub-Saharan Africa.

Malan, M., Meek, S., Thusi, T., Ginifer, J., & Coker, J. (2003, March 1). *Monograph 80: Sierra Leone, building the road to recovery.* www.issafrica.org/publications/monographs/monograph-80-sierra-leone-building-the-road-to-recovery-mark-malan-sarah-meek-thokozani-thusi-jeremy-ginifer-patrick-coker.

Mare, A. (2013). A complicated but symbiotic affair: The relationship between mainstream media and social media in the coverage of social protests in southern Africa. *Ecquid Novi: African Journalism Studies, 34*(1), 83–98, DOI: 10.1080/02560054.2013.767426

Mwenda, A. (2007). Personalizing power in Uganda. *Journal of Democracy, 18*(3), 23–37.

Nyamnjoh, F. (2005). *Africa's media, democracy and the politics of belonging.* Zed Books.

Ocitti, J. (2006). *Press politics and public policy in Uganda: The role of journalism in democratization.* Edwin Mellen Press.

Paulussen, S. & Harder, R. A. (2014). Social media references in newspapers. *Journalism Practice,* 8(5), 542–551. DOI: 10.1080/17512786.2014.894327

Rubongoya, J. (2007). *Regime hegemony in Museveni's Uganda: Pax Musevenica.* Palgrave MacMillan.

Sikanku, G. E. (2014). Consolidating inter-media agenda-setting research in Ghana: A study of associational relationships among wire, online, and print news media. *Journal of Black Studies,* 45(5), 396–414.

Skjerdal, T., & Ngugi, C. M (2007). Institutional and governmental challenges for journalism education in East Africa. *African Journalism Studies,* 28(1), 176–189.

Spurk, C., Lopata, S., & Keel, G. (2010). Measuring the democratic quality of radio news: Experiences from Liberia. *Journal of African Media Studies,* 2(2), 173–192.

Tam-Baryoh, D. (2006). *Sierra Leone: Research findings and conclusions.* BBC World Trust. downloads. bbc.co.uk/worldservice/trust/pdf/AMDI/sierra_leone/amdi_sl_full_report.pdf

Wanta, W., & Kalyango, Y. Jr. (2007). Terrorism and Africa: A study of agenda building in the United States. *International Journal of Public Opinion Research,* 19(4), 434–450.

9

Media in the Middle East and North Africa

Claudia Kozman

Perhaps no region in the world has witnessed as many transformative changes in such a short period of time as the Middle East and North Africa (MENA). Decades before the recent conflicts began, the countries experienced a significant transformation that largely altered their societies. Whether uniting scattered tribes under one state or changing the rule of law in another, the region brings together countries that share as many differences as they do similarities. Whereas some countries took their present shape only a few decades ago, others have inhabited the region for dozens of centuries. Foreign occupation from the Romans, the Ottomans, and World War I (WWI) allies France and Great Britain has changed the boundaries of the countries, destroying old ones and creating new ones. Regardless of to whom territories belonged at a specific point in time, the MENA region is home to some of the oldest and culturally richest countries in the world. Ancient civilizations, such as the Sumerian, Assyrian, Akkadian, Hittites, and Babylonian civilizations, occupied the Asian side of the region more than 12,000 years BC, while the African side was the land of Egyptian dynasties starting the sixth millennium BC. The civilizations that inhabited Mesopotamia and the Fertile Crescent, an area referred to as the cradle of civilization, provided us with models of early city-states and empires. Mesopotamia—present-day Iraq, Kuwait, Syria, and Turkey—is also the birthplace of mathematics, concept of time, agriculture, written scripts, and maps. Adding to these contributions, thriving ancient Egyptian dynasties provided the modern world with a plethora of inventions, the most significant of which are papyrus sheets, mummification, irrigation, and the pyramids.

Today, the MENA stands as a hotbed of conflict, an area boiling with turmoil and unrest. Known for its repressive regimes and dictatorial styles of leadership, the region comprises countries that share characteristics based on culture, language, and history. At the same time, it recognizes several sub-groups that occupy the extremes of the spectrum in terms of their economies, political systems, and societies. Although Arabic is the dominant language in the region, the MENA encompasses three non-Arab countries: Iran, Israel, and Turkey. Irrespective of language, the MENA is divided into sub-regions that are bound by their geographic location and historical trajectories (figure 9.1). In the west of Asia, the Levant or *Mashreq* comprises Iraq, Iran, Israel, Lebanon, Palestine, and Syria. The other countries in the Asian

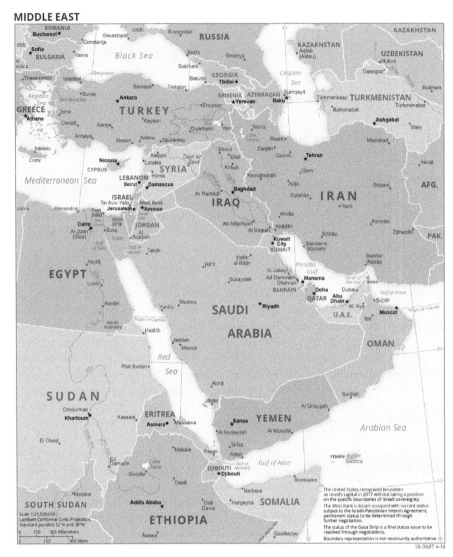

Figure 9.1. Map of the MENA region. Source: CIA World Factbook

part of the region—Bahrain, Kuwait, Oman, Saudi Arabia, United Arab Emirates, Qatar, and Yemen—belong to the Arabian Peninsula and oversee the Persian Gulf. On the African side, Egypt, Libya, and Tunisia are joined by the *Maghreb* countries Algeria and Morocco.

Far from being a homogenous region, the MENA combines differing styles of government as well as different perceptions of personal freedoms and views on media roles. Where extreme wealth renders one country prosperous, poverty strips another of basic living conditions. While hereditary monarchies appoint leaders by default, political chaos rules elsewhere. Although the MENA primarily consists of Arab nations, belonging to one did not always foster a sense of Arab identity. Throughout the years, the region experienced sporadic periods of stability due to the oil boom in the Gulf and the Arab-Israeli conflict that united many

Arab countries against Israel. The civil war in Syria and ongoing conflict in Iraq and Yemen have also significantly affected the region in recent years.

Mapping the political scene in the region is crucial for understanding how journalism and the media operate. This chapter provides an overview of political developments, technological advancements, and societal norms, and highlights the roles that governments, technology, economy, culture, and journalistic norms play to shape the media in the MENA.

POLITICAL SYSTEM

The MENA has recently captured world attention due to political turmoil and the ensuing conflict that has toppled governments or shaken up political elites in unprecedented ways (El-Issawi, 2016). These conflicts are a direct result of decades of oppression local governments have exercised on the people, with varying degrees of control. Although the countries differ in the type of political systems they have, the region as a whole is characterized by an omnipresent, controlling political style of rule that shows little respect for human rights and individual liberties. The political systems that govern the countries in the MENA have taken the forms of monarchies and republics with variations within the systems as well. Jordan, for instance, is a constitutional monarchy with a parliament that enjoys legislative power. It differs from the Saudi Arabian absolute monarchy where the king holds absolute power. Lebanon and Syria are neighboring republics with massively divergent styles that pit the dictatorship of the Assad family in Syria against the absence of any state power in Lebanon. Political pluralism exists in the region, but is not as common. Among the countries whose laws allow opposition parties are Lebanon and post-war Iraq, in addition to Israel and Jordan, among others.

The political systems in the region have influence that extends beyond politics. With their ability to create laws, governments can shape the media landscape through regulation of the economy, technology, and public life. In his attempt to classify Arab media, William Rugh (2004) divided the Arab media systems into three main types: *loyalist*, *mobilization*, and *diverse*, in addition to a hybrid one he called *transitional* for the countries that have moved between systems. According to Rugh, loyalist systems are those whose media pledge loyalty to the governments, such as the Gulf countries, except Kuwait. In mobilization systems, media take a revolutionary and active role in supporting the government, such as in pre-war Syria and Iraq, whereas in diverse systems, such as Lebanon and Kuwait, media pluralism rules. Rugh's models were used widely until 2011 when a wave of protests, known as the Arab uprisings, hit several countries and changed the political and media systems. Regardless of how the political system is set up, however, clear trends emerge from the similar ways governments exercise their power.

CONSTITUTION AND MEDIA LAWS

The level of media control in a country manifests itself through various laws and policies that governing bodies put in place to regulate the media. In the MENA, governments do not accept free speech in the pure sense of the term and have more or less similar regulations across the region. Most national constitutions and legal documents guarantee freedom of expression. The problem, however, rests with the application of these policies that remain promises on paper. The Syrian constitution, for instance, permits free speech but it was put on hold between

1963 and 2011, during the state of emergency the Baath Party placed the country under. One major way governments have continuously used to curb media freedom and get away with unconstitutional moves against the media has been relying on generic statements that offer no clear mode of interpretation. Vague concepts, such as threats against national security, harming national feelings, protecting public morals, and offending public decency are common in many constitutions. Without explicitly stating what constitutes a threat, or how does one measure harm against nationhood, governments apply these concepts in any manner they wish, which, in most cases, is to punish any violations. In 2020, Amnesty International raised concerns about a new vague law in Qatar, which criminalizes different types of speech and expression. The amendment to the Qatari Penal Code includes imprisonment for any form of expression whose intent is to "harm national interests, stir up public opinion, or infringe on the social system or the public system of the state" (Amnesty International, 2020, para. 2).

To supplement the vague concepts outlined in their constitutions, rulers in the MENA exercise their control over the media in four distinct manners. In almost all countries, the media sector is under the purview of the Ministry of Information and, in most cases, appoints editors or approves editorial changes. Explicit forms of control come in the shape of direct censorship of media content and financial support. Media censorship shares many similarities across the region, especially in the sub-regions. All countries in the MENA have laws that punish blasphemy and/or insulting religion, usually under penal codes, with varying sentences that include fines and imprisonment. One of the harshest penalties is in Kuwait where blasphemy is considered a crime punishable by law through fines that range between $36,000 and $720,000 and a prison sentence of a maximum of seven years. Saudi Arabia has no penal code because the Islamic law (Shari'a) is the only law that governs the country, with royal decrees and fatwas also taken into consideration (Library of Congress, 2017). In the Saudi court system, blasphemous acts could be punished by fines, imprisonment, whipping, and even death. Sexually explicit material, such as pornography, is another content type that is forbidden in most countries. In the Gulf, criticism of Islam, the ruling family, government, friendly countries, defense, and the military are not allowed. Some countries, like Oman and UAE, also forbid content that incites violence and disrupts public order. To these, Bahrain adds inciting sectarianism and offending public morals. In Saddam Hussein's Iraq, the death penalty was used for anyone insulting the president. Such laws are more relaxed in Lebanon, considered to be one of the freest countries in the region, where freedom of expression is guaranteed but defamation of public officials is criminalized. Iran and Turkey also include freedom of expression in their constitutions, but with several restrictions, such as anti-terror laws in the case of Turkey.

From a financial standpoint, explicit control is also exercised through governmental support that takes the form of direct subsidies and advertisements. In loyalist media systems, such as the Gulf and Jordan, the government officially advertises in media outlets, in addition to government employee subscriptions. In parts of North Africa, economic pressure from the government is translated into access to printing facilities, advertising revenues, and financial qualifications for startups. In pre-revolution Tunisia, the government withheld advertising to a magazine for being negative about the country, while the Algerian authorities have exercised monopoly of news imports and printing.

Implicit media control comes in two main forms: licensing and guidance channels. It is not uncommon for governments to grant licenses to media requests from cronies that support them and decline the rest, as in the case of pre-2011 Syria and Iraq under Saddam Hussein. In Lebanon, licensing regulations exist but similar to other rules, they are not enforced. The situation is loose to the extent that television channel *Télé Lumière* broadcasts without a license, while *NBN* received a license before it even existed. In the Gulf, where the media were dubbed loyalist by Rugh (2004), most requests for licenses are usually granted since media loyalty to the royal family is guaranteed. This is the case in all Gulf countries, except Kuwait whose landscape resembles the Lebanese one in its diversity. In addition to Kuwait and Lebanon, Jordan is more tolerant of the opposition than other countries, allowing opposition parties access to the media. The situation in Palestine is somewhat complicated due to the shared power between the Palestinian Authority in the West Bank, Hamas in the Gaza Strip, and Israel. In the case of the latter, licenses are granted by the Ministry of Communication with few restrictions.

Lastly, authorities control the media through guidance channels that take the form of public broadcasting, national news agencies, and pro-government personnel. The official news agencies speak on behalf of the ruling elites and act as a public diplomacy tool that projects a positive image of those in power. Some of the most prominent and tightly controlled news agencies are MENA (Egypt), SANA (Syria), IRNA (Iran), Petra (Jordan), and SNA (Saudi Arabia). Guidance is also passed on through unofficial personnel or editors appointed by the government, creating an atmosphere of both direct censorship and indirect self-censorship.

Perhaps the most daring infringement of media freedom in the MENA is trying journalists who criticize the government in criminal courts. Harassment, arbitrary detention, torture, and death are some of the many outcomes journalists face in the region. Jail sentences are common for violations of all sorts that threaten, directly or indirectly, ruling elites' status. In the twenty-first century alone, the numbers have surpassed the 600th mark, 377 of whom have died, according to the latest reports from Committee to Protect Journalists. Of the 611 journalists, 483 were detained in Turkey, Saudi Arabia, Iran, and Egypt. The majority of these incidents, 407 to be exact, took place after 2011. Recently, authorities in Egypt intensified their crackdown on journalists, causing Amnesty International to call Egyptian prisons the journalists' newsrooms in 2020. A 2019 CPJ report placed Turkey, Saudi Arabia, and Egypt, respectively, as the world's worst jailers, after China. Turkey and Iran have been declared the world's largest prison for journalists in at least two years in the new millennium. Turkey's crackdown on dissenting journalists worsened after Erdogan claimed the presidency in 2014, and intensified after the failed coup attempt in 2016. For the two years that followed, more than 180 media outlets were closed down (Hong, 2018). Since 2010, the country's anti-terrorism laws have allowed the government to arrest and detain journalists, mostly Kurds, who criticize it and even hand down sentences of 166 years (Amnesty International, n.d.). One of the most recent violations against the media comes from Iran where authorities imprisoned journalist Pouyan Khoshhal in 2019 for using the word "death" instead of "martyrdom" to describe a Shiite saint in a newspaper article he wrote. He was later fired and forced into exile. In Palestine, the PA, Hamas, and Israel engage with various types of violations of press freedom, mainly against Palestinian journalists. In addition to raiding media offices and shutting them down, Israeli forces arrest, harass, detain, and interrogate Palestinian media workers (Freedom House, 2017). Media watch groups, such as Reporters Without Borders, continuously condemn the injuring and obstruction of journalists from covering protests by Israeli security forces.

DIGITAL AND SOCIAL MEDIA

Digital platforms, in general, and social media, in particular, have opened new avenues for the public to voice their opinion. Such freedom was unimagined in the pre-Internet era and has come with a price. The ability of people to say what they wish has also made them targets for governments that crackdown on freedom of expression (Richter, & Kozman, 2021). In most cases, cybercrime laws regulate the Internet and all digital media, therefore any anti-government or anti-religion statements are considered crimes. Arbitrary detentions and charges are made against citizens who dare defy these laws. In general, topics that are off-limits in the overwhelming majority of Arab countries are politics and religion. A recent example comes from Jordan where the Jordanian Cybercrime Unit tried a 17-year-old female in 2020 after charging her with blasphemous thoughts that insult religious feelings. A similar incident took place in 2010 in Saudi Arabia when a student was sentenced to 10 years in prison and 1,000 lashes for his atheist posts. In 2018, UAE human rights activist Ahmed Mansoor was sentenced to 10 years in prison and fined $270,000 for his social media posts. In Turkey, a doctor was found guilty of insulting Erdogan after depicting him as *The Lord of the Rings'* Gollum in photos he posted on Facebook in 2014. And in Egypt, a student was jailed for three years for adding Mickey Mouse ears on President Al-Sisi's photo.

THE ARAB SPRING

Sparked by the act of a local street vendor, a wave of protests known as the "Arab Spring" hit the Arab countries and lead to unprecedented political changes across the region. The Tunisian fruit vendor Mohamed Bouazizi set himself on fire in December 2010 to protest corruption in the country, inadvertently becoming the catalyst to many protests that engulfed the region. Following Bouazizi's incident, street protests named the Jasmine Revolution erupted across the country, eventually leading to the end of the 25-year dictatorship of Tunisian President Zine El-Abidine Ben Ali. In January 2011, thousands of people gathered in Egypt's Tahrir Square to demand the resignation of another Arab dictator, President Hosni Mubarak, who was soon ousted. In the same month, crowds in Yemen gathered to protest against the 30-year rule of President Ali Abdullah Saleh, who stepped down in 2012. In neighboring Libya, national demonstrations led to the end of President Muammar Gaddafi's reign after 42 years at the helm. Weeks later, Syrian citizens stood against President Bashar Al-Assad's regime—whose family has been in power since 1971—marking the beginning of a civil war that is yet to end. About the same time, mostly Shiite activists in Bahrain protested the oppression of the Sunni government but were soon subjected to a crackdown and persecution by the authorities. Although some of the changes have placed the countries in complete chaos, to many, the Arab Spring remains a symbol of the power of the people. The overthrow of Ben Ali, Mubarak, and Gaddafi, and the weakening of Al-Assad have given young Arabs the impetus to fight for their rights. To do so, they turned to social media to organize themselves, voice their opinions, and support one another, away from the prying eyes of their governments. Although research findings have not reached a consensus on the exact role social media played in the Arab Spring, what is clear is that protestors harnessed the power of social media to amplify their message and broadcast in real-time what was happening on the ground to the rest of the world (Aday et al., 2012). A later study about protests in the Arab world found that Internet use for political reasons has a positive influence on citizens, increasing the likelihood of participation in protests, while also deepening socioeconomic divides (Ahmed & Cho, 2019).

Reporters Without Borders' 2020 *list of* "digital predators" includes several MENA countries that have intimidated journalists through harassment, state censorship, spying, and surveillance. The report reveals Algerian government trolls use personal attacks and shaming tactics against journalists, whereas pro-regime bots in Saudi Arabia spread false information through thousands of tweets per day. In Israel, a cyber technology company's spyware used WhatsApp to target specific individuals, while elsewhere, an international company's spyware that is sold only to governments was used to target Moroccan journalists (Reporters Without Borders, 2020).

To sum up, both the traditional and social media landscape in the region needs to be examined in light of recent political developments. Ongoing conflict and instability as well as the rise of new political actors have put the media in a vulnerable position, facing repressive measures, such as fines and arrests, as well as cyberattacks against journalists.

ECONOMY

The economies of the MENA countries vary greatly, cramming into a small region some of the wealthiest and poorest countries in the world. On one extreme lie the Gulf Cooperation Council (GCC) countries, led by Qatar, UAE, and Kuwait—who are among the richest countries in the world—while on the other extreme, worn-torn countries like Yemen, Iraq, and Syria live in poverty. The economy of the GCC is highly dependent on oil revenues, which have helped fuel the non-oil sector, and thus diversify their economies to reduce oil dependency (Saif, 2009). As a whole, the region enjoys abundant natural, mineral and non-mineral resources, such as phosphate, iron ore, and coal. The leading natural resource is crude oil with one-third of the world's reserves lying in the region. The MENA also contains the world's largest natural gas reserves in Iran, followed by Qatar in third place.

One visible outcome of a country's economy is found in the media sector's adoption of new technologies. As detailed in the next section, wealthy countries in the MENA enjoy state-of-the-art facilities and media cities. Beside the luxuries they afford their employees, these technologically advanced facilities also allow the media a bigger share of the market, due to their ability to engage in more advanced marketing, thus attracting more consumers and offering them enticing communication platforms (Mellor et al., 2011). The two global leaders of MENA television news, *Al-Jazeera* and *Al-Arabiya* provide dozens of services to their audiences. In the case of *Al-Jazeera*, its products include main channels in Arabic and English, in addition to the specialized platform for the youth, AJ+.

Media ownership in the region is both public and private with more community media starting to mushroom in several countries. Historically, most media in the region started as government owned before privatization took place as a result of political and social reform. In some countries where the government does not necessarily own all media, such as in the Gulf, Syria, and Jordan, it controls the sector through extended family members and its cronies. From a political economy perspective, the concentration of ownership in the MENA is mostly horizontal with a conglomerate owning several media outlets. The leading examples in the region are three broadcast companies from Saudi Arabia: MBC group, Rotana, and OSN that individually own dozens of specialized media outlets. Media ownership is a significant element of media systems, especially when the media are not regulated properly, leading to their use as a political tool (Della Ratta et al., 2015). For a long time, Arab media moguls like Saudi Arabia's Prince al Waleed bin Talal and Waleed Al-Ibrahim, Egypt's Naguib Sawiris, and Lebanon's Pierre el Daher and al Hariri family dominated the media scene in the region due to the massive successes of their media companies (Della Ratta et al., 2015). In 2020, Arab media ownership has changed faces somewhat, with governments consolidating their power through media ownership and takeovers, such as in Egypt, Morocco, and Saudi Arabia.

Wealth in the region is concentrated not only in a few areas but also in a few individuals. Business conglomerates are prevalent in the MENA, of which the media form a significant part. Due to the historical importance of the media, it is not surprising to find the wealthiest people in the region owning investments in the media as well. Among Forbes' 2020 list of world billionaires, those from the MENA are concentrated in Egypt, Israel, Lebanon, and the UAE. Several of these billionaires—such as Egypt's Naguib Sawiris, Lebanese brothers Taha and Najib Mikati, Turkey's Murat Vargi, and Israel's Arnon Milchan and Shaul Shani—have made their fortunes in the telecommunications sector.

TECHNOLOGY AND INFRASTRUCTURE

One of the biggest disparities we see in the MENA region is in technological infrastructure. Physical structures, technology software, and soft skills present a serious barrier to media development, exacerbating the existing digital divide between age groups and literacy levels. The topography of the region with its vast deserts and rough terrain, combined with the existence of some tribal ethnicities and the concentration of wealth in specific areas, has led to major differences in the impact of technology on the media and their audiences. Geographic barriers and the concentration of life in the big cities leave those living on the outskirts deprived of advanced communication. Where urban areas enjoy the most recent technological products—whether it is low-cost Internet, fast connections, or the availability of satellite television—rural areas lack everyday basics. Expectedly, these issues affect larger and poorer countries—such as Libya, Iraq, and Egypt—more than smaller, wealthier ones, like most of the Gulf countries. The gaps in broadband infrastructure across the region and within the countries themselves worsen the digital divide between the urban and rural areas (Gelvanovska et al., 2014). Although authorities in the MENA acknowledge the critical role broadband Internet plays in their efforts of "nation building and the transition to a knowledge-based economy"—roughly translated into creating job opportunities and reducing poverty (Gelvanovska et al., 2014, p. 18)—other factors come into play. The instability in the region has rendered issues of Internet connectivity more of a luxury than a necessity. The failing Lebanese economy, the devastation in Syria, and the continuous conflict that plagues Iraq and Palestine have put technological advancement on the back burner.

In their assessment of the state of broadband networks in the MENA, Gelvanovska et al. (2014) identified the critical role broadband Internet plays as "an enabler of democracy and social transformation" (p. 23). While digital connectivity facilitated networking among anti-government protesters—whether in 2011 in Egypt and Tunisia or in 2019 in Iran, Iraq, and Lebanon—governments did not sit back and watch the situation unfold. They were quick to find measures to curb freedom of expression and in many cases prosecute opinion leaders. In the 2019 nationwide demonstrations that hit Iran, Iraq, and Lebanon, Internet shutdowns and media blackout were the authorities' response to protests. In Lebanon, cable providers briefly banned opposition television channel *Al Jadeed* in areas of the southern Beirut suburbs, known to be strongholds of the pro-government party Hezbollah. The entire country also experienced what the protestors dubbed "a media blackout" for not getting media coverage of their protests, even from opposition media. In Iraq, following the protestors' declaration of the beginning of the revolution on October 25, 2019, the government shut down the Internet intermittently for two months and social media sites completely until the protests ended. In Iran, the government pulled down the Internet connectivity lever for one week in the entire country to deflate the protests. From a technological perspective, this could only have been possible with the centralized intranet service that Iran had been building to have more control over the content and limit content from abroad, an article in *Wired* reported (Newman, 2019).

As one facet of technology, social media are increasingly becoming a staple of daily life, especially for younger generations. Online platforms provide members of the MENA public with a space to share their opinions and discuss public affairs away from the strict government control that characterizes traditional media. Citizens' use of social media, however, is not only for political reasons. A 2019 survey of seven Arab nations by the Northwestern University in Qatar revealed politics and entertainment rank first as news topics Arab audiences engage in. The survey also showed WhatsApp and Facebook lead other social media in their usage, 75 and 71 percent, respectively. Television, which has traditionally been the most used platform for news, declined in popularity in these countries and is almost on par with interpersonal communication, the Internet, and messaging apps in providing news. The phenomenon of influencers is present in the MENA as well. About a quarter of those surveyed view influencers' social media posts more than those from traditional media (Northwestern University in Qatar, 2019).

Within the technology sector, mobile telephony is an area worthy of attention. The steady growth of mobile connections in the region, with contributions projected to reach $225 billion in 2025, makes the MENA host to some of the most saturated mobile markets globally (GSMA, 2019). Special low rates cater to members of the public who cannot afford pre-paid cards, thus making use of post-paid deals that include Internet access—and at times only WhatsApp access as in the case of Lebanon. Besides WhatsApp, VoIP such as Skype and Viber is highly popular across the region due to its low cost compared to calling or text messaging via mobile phones.

Technological advancements can also be measured by examining media infrastructure. In the MENA, this varies not only across the region but also within a country itself. Pan-Arab media, such as *Al-Jazeera* and *Al-Arabiya*, occupy large spaces, whereas small local ones do not exceed a floor in a building. Naturally, the wealthy countries lead in innovative thinking as well, devising business models that take into consideration news and entertainment consumption habits in the region. Jordan and the UAE were at the forefront of media innovations, creating in 2001 the Jordan Media City and the Dubai Media City. The latter claims to be the MENA's largest integrated media hub with more than 1,500 companies that bring together local and global brands in all sectors of media life. Beside state-of-the-art infrastructure that houses media outlets, the City also encompasses entertainment venues, a hotel, healthcare, and fitness facilities. Since then, several areas have started planning their own media cities, including Qatar Media City initiated in 2017 and Saudi Media City in 2020.

CULTURE AND SOCIETY

Throughout the decades, Arab governments have kept a tight grip on the media as a means to foster national unity and define cultural relevance. This was most pronounced in the 1950s through the socialist policies of Egypt's president Gamal Abdel Nasser who advocated for the idea of one Arab nation—the *umma*. His ideologies, dubbed Nasserism, saw the media as a powerful tool and positioned radio (*Sawt Al Arab*) at the core of his goals. Arab nationalism also encompassed other countries that used films (such as *Djamilah* and *Salaheddin*) and children's media (*Captain Majed* and *Al Arabi Al Sagheer*) to spread the ideologies of the *umma*. Much has changed, however, since then. Globalization has altered Arab societies, diluting Arab traditions and norms due to the infiltration of international cultural values. The media imperialism of the West—traditionally exhibited through *CNN*, Hollywood, and *MTV*, and more recently YouTube and Netflix—have affected MENA societies as well, leading some critics to strongly oppose globalization, contending that it leads to a loss of cultural identity and corrupts Arab youth.

The transitions in Arab societies are largely affected by the economies of the region as well as a growing youth cohort that stands at 16 percent of the population, according to 2019 United Nations data. Besides the fundamental role they played in the Arab uprisings, youth are considered a key to the development of the region, according to a joint report by the Issam Fares Institute and UNICEF (Khouri & Lopez, 2011). The report noted that youth activism and political/civic participation have been low, mainly constricted to participating in NGOs and political parties. Among the youth population, the report states, women are becoming increasingly active, leading social movements in Lebanon, Jordan, Egypt, Morocco, and Kuwait. Due to ongoing conflict in several countries, the future of Arab youth is murky. Blockades, civil war, and restrictions on movement in Palestine, Syria, Yemen, among others, deny young Arabs basic education and raise the levels of illiteracy in the region.

MENA's diversity is reflected in many religions, languages, and ethnicities that make up the population of the region. In the Arab countries, besides Arabic, indigenous languages such as Kurdish and Tamazight are used in some areas including Iraq, Syria, Turkey, Morocco, and Algeria. Outside the Arab countries, Farsi is the main spoken language in Iran, while Turkish and Hebrew dominate in Turkey and Israel, respectively. North Africa alone is home to several ethnicities, including the Berber and the Tuareg who have their own languages. The Gulf region as well hosts various nationalities that form large expat communities of labor workers from Southeast Asia and Westerners holding white-collar jobs. The dominant religion in the MENA is Islam, which is practiced in all the countries comprising the region. Besides Islam, Christianity is central to political and public life in Lebanon, home to the largest Christian community in the region, after Egypt. The remaining Christian minorities in the region are mostly found in Syria and Iraq, with numbers have been gradually decreasing. Although the overwhelming majority in Israel are Jews who recognize Judaism as their religion, Muslims and Christians form a small minority.

As mostly Islamic societies, the Arab countries are bound by religious rules, which vary across the region. In general, the majority of the Gulf states force strict adherence to Islamic laws, especially as they concern women. The only exception among the Arab countries is Lebanon whose constitution does not list a state religion. The strictest forms of control are found in Saudi Arabia, whose male guardianship system strips women of their rights. For a long time, women in the kingdom were not allowed to marry, travel, vote, or access education and healthcare. Until 2018, women were forbidden to drive or sit next to males in restaurants. The dissolution of gender segregation in restaurants and the opening of cinemas for the first time in 35 years are some of the reformist acts commissioned by Crown Prince Mohammed bin Salman, who aims to introduce social reform and modernization to the country through his project "Vision 2030."

Religious restrictions on media content, based on Islamic laws, also extend to visuals that could pose threats to the preservation of Islamic values. Many pan-Arab television shows blur out alcoholic beverages in foreign productions. In the Arabic subtitles, mentions of alcohol are usually referred to as "juice" instead of "wine" or "beer," for example. Print advertisements are also modified for the sub-region where they will be disseminated. An advertisement that shows a woman's skin beyond what is allowed (generally only hands and the face are allowed in some countries) is not available in some sub-regions. Large agencies tend to provide region-sensitive variations of the advertisement during the photo shoot where the same product ad is shot in at least two versions: one for the Gulf and one for the rest. As a cheaper option, the image can be altered electronically, by coloring out the arms, neck, and cleavage.

JOURNALISTIC PERCEPTIONS

Journalists in the MENA region face some of the harshest challenges in conducting their work. Although they differ from one another in their perceptions of their roles, as a group they encounter many difficulties that constantly put their lives at risk. Pressure from authorities, physical danger in conflict zones, and the absence of financial and professional support are a few of the issues journalists in the region struggle with. Whether due to lack of funding or unawareness of the importance of professional training and support, few media outlets provide their journalists with opportunities to advance in their work or protect themselves from physical and psychological harm.

Overall, political parallelism is high in the region due to the affiliations of media outlets with their governments and political parties, or due to censorship and other control mechanisms. As such, autonomy exists only in rare instances. Although journalists can perceive themselves as autonomous, they are subject to pressure from high-ranking personnel at their institutions, who yield their power to ensure journalists' products align with the values of the specific media outlet (Hafez, 2008). The histories of autocratic regimes across the region have led journalists to assume the role of government supporters whether by choice or force. The idea of activism and dissent has only recently started to gain traction. One reason could be the changes that the Arab region experienced after the uprisings in 2011. Far from being the norm, dissenting journalists face serious repercussions, as detailed earlier in the chapter. The most significant incident that grabbed world attention is the assassination of Saudi journalist and strong government critic Jamal Khashoggi at the Saudi consulate in Istanbul in 2018. Although the Saudi court handed out five death sentences, it dismissed charges against others and cleared two high-ranking officials, one of whom was the former top adviser of the Crown Prince, from their involvement in the case.

In the presence of high political parallelism and control over the media, those wishing to engage in investigative journalism do so with the awareness of the risks involved. Arab Reporters for Investigative Journalism (ARIJ) is one organization in the region that stresses the importance of investigative reporting and trains journalists in proper procedures. Since its inception in 2006, ARIJ has helped launch national centers in Iraq, Morocco, Palestine, Syria, Tunisia, and Yemen.

Regarding journalistic perceptions and role performances, a few reliable data about MENA journalists exist. Surveys from Lawrence Pintak and colleagues reveal Arab journalists hold national identities and personal values as important. Although some journalists reported democracy to be important for a free press, they also believed they should balance the needs of the government with those of the public (Pintak, 2010). The second survey, which was published in *The Global Journalist*, indicated journalists play two mains roles: activists with a focus on political and social reform and guardians of the government, the region, Islam, and Arab culture (Pintak & Ginges, 2012). A survey of Israeli journalists showed they practice self-censorship when the topic poses a threat to national security and perceive fact-checking as a central journalistic value (Tsfati & Meyers, 2012).

CHAPTER SUMMARY

The MENA region has been going through tumultuous changes since the Arab uprisings in 2010, which resulted in a massive transformation of the countries' political and media systems. Civic engagement and freedom of expression have expanded, especially online, but with the ubiquity of the Internet came more constraints from authoritative governments that rushed to control all forms of digital media. Violations against journalists continue to rise, especially in Egypt, Iran, Saudi Arabia, and Turkey. The region's various economies also play a role in their media system, particularly with regard to technology and infrastructure. Wealthy countries in the Gulf provide more advanced technologies to their media and audiences, compared to the Levant and North Africa. Overall, the media in the MENA are subject to the laws imposed by national governments that seek to regulate content and consolidate power. This has resulted in high political parallelism where media outlets become mouthpieces of the ruling elite, either by choice or force.

DISCUSSION QUESTIONS

1. What are some of the main issues that media in the MENA region face? Can you suggest possible ways to address some of these issues?
2. Where do you see the youth playing a significant role in effecting change in the region?
3. In what ways do the cultures and traditions of the countries in the MENA affect the public's acceptance of how the media function in its country?
4. Considering all the elements that exert pressure on journalists, is journalistic autonomy possible? If no, how can it be achieved? If yes, in which area would it be most impactful?

BIBLIOGRAPHY

Aday, S., Farrell, H., Lynch, M., Sides, J., & Freelon, D. (2012). *Blogs and bullets II: New media and conflict after the Arab Spring*. Peaceworks: United States Institute for Peace.

Ahmed, S., & Cho, J. (2019). The Internet and political (in)equality in the Arab world: A multi-country study of the relationship between Internet news use, press freedom, and protest participation. *New Media & Society, 21*(5), 1065–1084.

Amnesty International (n.d.). *Turkish troubles: Freedom of expression endangered in Turkey*. www.amnestyusa.org/turkish-troubles-freedom-of-expression-endangered-in-turkey/

Amnesty International (2020, January 20). *Qatar: Repressive new law further curbs freedom of expression*. www.amnesty.org/en/latest/news/2020/01/qatar-repressive-new-law-further-curbs-freedom-of-expression/

Della Ratta, D., Sakr, N., & Skovgaard-Petersen, J. (eds.). (2015) *Arab media moguls*. I.B. Tauris.

El-Issawi, F. (2016). *Arab national media and political change*. Palgrave.

Freedom House (2017). *Freedom of the press 2017 — West Bank and Gaza Strip*. www.refworld.org/docid/59fc67afa.html

Gelvanovska, N., Rogy, M., & Rossotto, C. M. (2014). *Broadband networks in the Middle East and North Africa: Accelerating high-speed internet access*. The World Bank.

GSMA. (2019). *The mobile economy 2019*. data.gsmaintelligence.com/api-web/v2/research-file-download?id=39256194&file=2712-250219-ME-Global.pdf

Hafez, K. (Ed.). (2008). *Arab media: Power and weakness*. Continuum.

Hong, J. (2018, September 18). *Erdogan's Turkey: The world's biggest prison for journalists*. Newsweek. www.newsweek.com/erdogans-turkey-worlds-biggest-prison-journalists-opinion-1125718

Khouri, R. G., & Lopez, V. M. (2011). *A generation on the move: Insights into the conditions, aspirations and activism of Arab youth*. Issam Fares Institute for Public Policy and International Affairs, American University of Beirut, Lebanon.

Library of Congress (2017, March 3). *Blasphemy and related laws*. www.loc.gov/law/help/blasphemy/index.php#skip_menu

Newman, L. H. (2019, November 17). *How the Iranian government shut off the Internet*. Wired. www.wired.com/story/iran-internet-shutoff/

Northwestern University in Qatar (2019). *Media use in the Middle East: A seven-nation survey*. www.mideastmedia.org/survey/2019/

Mellor, N., Ayish, M., Dajani, N., & Rinnawi, K. (2011). *Arab media: Globalizing and emerging media industries*. Polity Press.

Pintak, L. (2010). *The new Arab journalist: Mission and identity in a time of turmoil* (Vol. 85). IB Tauris.

Pintak, L., & Ginges, J. (2012). Arab journalists. In D. H. Weaver and L. Willnat (Eds.), *The global journalist in the 21st century* (pp. 429–442). Routledge.

Reporters Without Borders (RSF). (2020, March 12). RSF *unveils 20/2020 list of press freedom's digital predators*. rsf.org/en/news/rsf-unveils-202020-list-press-freedoms-digital-predators

Richter, C., & Kozman, C. (Eds.). (2021). *Arab media systems*. OpenBook Publishers.

Rugh, W. A. (2004). *Arab mass media*. Praeger.

Saif, I. (2009). The oil boom in the GCC countries, 2002–2008: Old challenges, changing dynamics. *Carnegie Papers*, 15, 1–29.

Tsfati, Y., & Meyers, O. (2012). Journalists in Israel. In D. H. Weaver and L. Willnat (Eds.), *The global journalist in the 21st century* (pp. 443–4457). Routledge.

10

Media in Central and Eastern Europe and Russia

Ioana A. Coman and Christopher Karadjov

By all accounts, 1989 was a remarkable year for Eastern Europe, when newly found media freedoms went hand in hand with a whirlwind transition toward political and economic liberation. In the decades since then, the transformation is all but accomplished. Many of the facets of Eastern European and Russian societies could not be imagined at the time, and certainly among them is the state of their media. From the Baltic to the Adriatic and from Prague to Vladivostok these vastly diverse countries, nations and cultures have produced a plethora of media systems that share as many common traits as they differ from each other.

On November 11, 1989, a dozen handwritten pages appeared on the walls of Sofia University in the capital of Bulgaria. Someone had posted a disjointed narrative of a life story, interspersed with political rants and poetry. Two days had passed since the Berlin Wall had effectively disappeared and barely 24 hours since Bulgaria's ruler of 35 years Todor Zhivkov had been sacked. Within a week, hundreds more pages were glued to the university's grey granite walls with people adding handwritten or typed-up stories with gripes and complaints. Some were anonymous, some were signed—sight unseen in a part of the world, where mere graffiti could land you in jail.

In Bucharest, the capital of Romania, dictator Nicolae Ceausescu was still able to order the government television to broadcast his last public appearance as of December 21, 1989, in front of some 100,000 people. Much to his astonishment, he was booed on live television and four days later he was shot by means of a quick military tribunal. After a few bloody skirmishes, Romania was also set on the path of transformation.

In fact, the fall of the Berlin Wall on November 9, 1989, was the result of the political momentum helped in no small measure by a media occurrence. Günter Schabowski, a spokesperson for the East German Politburo, mistakenly said in front of the cameras that the citizens of his communist country would be able to travel abroad without any impediments, starting immediately. Within minutes of his statement crowds started venturing across the checkpoints into East Berlin and the much-feared barrier between the two systems was no more.

Such observational vignettes illustrate the disjointed start of a remarkable transformation in Eastern Europe after the end of communism, a major political change for the countries in the regions as well as their media systems.

EUROPE

Figure 10.1. Map of Central and Eastern Europe. Source CIA World Factbook

WHAT IS EASTERN EUROPE?

For the purposes of this chapter, Central and Eastern European (CEE) countries in alphabetical order include Albania, Belarus, Bosnia and Herzegovina, Bulgaria, Croatia, the Czech Republic, Estonia, Hungary, Kosovo, Latvia, Lithuania, Moldova, Montenegro, North Macedonia, Poland, Romania, Russia, Serbia, Slovakia, Slovenia, and Ukraine. Of those, Yugoslavia comprised constituent republics of Bosnia and Herzegovina, Croatia, Montenegro,

Macedonia, and Serbia until 1991; Kosovo was legally a part of Serbia until 2008 and is presently a partially recognized state (see figure 10.1).

Russia is habitually classified as "Eastern Europe" because its political and economic center of gravity is decidedly European, even though three-quarters of its territory stretches beyond the Ural Mountains and all the way to the Bering Sea on the border between Asia and North America. This chapter groups Russia with Central and Eastern Europe because of historical similarities as part of the Soviet bloc, while noting the distinctions that this country has. The three Baltic states—Estonia, Latvia, Lithuania—along with Belarus, Moldova, Russia, and Ukraine were inside the 15-republic USSR (also known as the Soviet Union) until 1991. Czechoslovakia comprised the present-day Czech Republic and Slovakia until 1993. After the unification of Germany in 1991, Eastern Germany has been considered part of Western Europe and thus has "left" the ranks of CEE. Several CEE countries are members of both the European Union and NATO: Bulgaria, Croatia, Czech Republic, Estonia, Hungary, Latvia, Lithuania, Poland, Romania, Slovakia, and Slovenia. Albania, Montenegro, and North Macedonia are NATO members.

POLITICAL SYSTEM

After the end of the Cold War, all countries of Central and Eastern Europe along with Russia transitioned and can be classified formally as democracies, albeit with significant distinctions insofar as their relative freedoms are concerned. There is also a wide diversity in terms of their media systems. Reporters Without Borders maintains the most widely cited index of media freedoms, which in its 2020 edition shows a range between Estonia in the respectable 14th place, Latvia in the 22nd, and Russia and Belarus in 149th and 153rd, respectively. The rest of the CEE countries are spread in between these extremes.

The media transition behind what Churchill infamously dubbed in 1946 "The Iron Curtain" began in 1985 with the start of Mikhail Gorbachev's dual policy of *glasnost* (openness or transparency) and *perestroika* (restructuring or reforming the economic and political system). Of those, *glasnost* enjoyed the most immediate success because it resulted in the eruption of media outlets across the Soviet Union although little changed in the rest of the countries. Yugoslavia was already enjoying by comparison fairly free media, while Albania remained a closed totalitarian country. Yet the chatter that originated from the Soviet media was sufficiently subversive because what started as a discussion of Stalin's repressions and their renunciations morphed by the end of *perestroika* into open questioning of the basic ideological principles upon which the Soviet Union and its allies had built their societies.

Until the end of the Cold War, the media across all countries in the region fell under the Soviet Press Model where the basic function of journalism was to promote socialist/communist ideology. In the post-1989 transition, several media models emerged some of which resembling the Liberal Media Model while others containing remnants of the Soviet Press Model. According to Dobek-Ostrowska (2015) who merged the classic Four Theories of the Press with the Hallin and Mancini (2004) categorization, four media models exemplify the region today: Liberal Hybrid Model typical in countries such as Estonia, Czech Republic and Slovenia; Politicized Model reflecting Bulgarian, Hungarian and Romania media; Media in Transition Model for countries such as Albania, Kosovo, Moldova and Montenegro; and Authoritarian Model for Belarus and Russia. While the transition of media systems in the region continues, it is important to acknowledge its diversity as well as shared historical roots.

From a classical typology perspective, most of the post-communist media would fall under the Liberal Media Model. The specific ways in which this model was applied and developed in the post-communist countries aroused numerous analyzes and comments—in essence, many argue that it is more of a "libertarian" model than a liberal one, due to the obvious elements of violating the principles of the market economy, non-regulation, blind pursuit of quick profit and abdication from the elementary responsibilities of the press (Gross, 2002; Jakubowicz, 1995). Hallin and Mancini (2014), commenting on the typologies proposed by them in their reference work, consider that the Polarized Pluralist model is most likely to be dominant in Central and Eastern Europe. Others, however, argue that it would be more accurate not to apply one of these initial models but to "rethink" and extend the proposed framework to adapt to the specific conditions in the region (Voltmer, 2013).

Of course, there are unique characteristics in different countries. There are also additional factors such as clientelism that may need to be taken into account. In Romania, for example,

> the political system, unclear in its nature and still shifting in line with a still evolving democracy, does not explain the mass media system. It is the vessel in which Romanian cultural predilections find full expression, and in turn explain both the relationship between the political and mass media system and the nature and functioning of the latter. (. . .) Clientelism and the political parallelism of the media are often expressions of the powers of the manager-journalist or star journalists and not only of owners of the mass media, of the political system and its culture, and of the politicians.
>
> (Coman & Gross, 2012, p. 472)

Press Freedom, Privacy Laws, and Censorship

In all post-communist countries, the newly formed constitutions guaranteed freedom and pluralism of the press. In some countries, laws for the media or communication appeared very quickly: Poland by the 1990 law amended in 1996, Lithuania (1990), Estonia, Latvia, Russia with the 1990 law replaced by the 1992 law; Ukraine (1993) and Belarus with the 1994 law (Giorgi, 1995, Gross, 2002; Hiebert, 1999, pp. 90–93). In other countries (Bulgaria, Hungary, Romania), after many confrontations and debates, politicians and journalists seemed to agree on a "status quo" based on the conclusion that no law can serve all interests, and that the current balance, created through a series of tacit negotiations and agreements, creates a convenient balance for all stakeholders.

The laws of audio–visual have raised many controversies. Careful analysis of these laws shows that they have not eliminated the influence of politics on the media. In the public system, the members of the Audiovisual Councils are appointed and revoked by the Parliament, sometimes by the Government, and the same applies to the Boards of Directors and the presidents of radio and public television. In addition, "even more dangerous are: (a) terminological inaccuracy, the use of partial terms defined and subject to interpretation by control and judicial agencies, which are not yet politically independent; and (b) the considerable power attributed to national audiovisual councils—councils susceptible to manipulation and control by the government, dominant political parties in parliament and/or the presidency" (Gross, Hiebert, 1996, p. 54; also see the recent legislative changes for the governmental control over audiovisual in Poland and Hungary).

In all Eastern European countries, various laws protect privacy (especially after integration into and under the influence of European Union directives). However, there are numerous violations of these rights, violations favored by the generalization and success of the tabloid press, on the one hand, and the ineffectiveness of sanctions (small fines, infinitely lower than the advertising profit gained due to large audiences) applied by the Audiovisual Councils, or by the courts. Through the Constitutions and the various laws mentioned above, censorship has been abolished and should no longer exist. However, various professional associations and NGOs report numerous cases of censorship of journalists, not by political or military institutions, but by employers and editors.

A characteristic of post-communist media is the alignment between media institutions with different political and economic interest groups and endemic corruption in the media outlet (Coman, 2010). Eastern European journalists did not identify self-regulating mechanisms as an efficient solution for professional issues (summary in Eberwein et al., 2017). Under these conditions, the editorial and management groups exercise strict control over news topics and approaches, eliminating any investigation that could affect the interests of their sponsors. Since there are multiple interests and external pressures from stakeholders, individuals can get a balanced picture of controversial issues or political news by browsing various media outlets and cross-referencing their information sources with what is circulating on social media.

ECONOMY AND MEDIA OWNERSHIP

Political reforms were only half the job of this region's remarkable transformation since 1989. All countries in Central and Eastern Europe and Russia have progressed from planned economies to free markets; they have traded Marxism-Leninism for capitalism as the dominant ideology that guides their means of production, labor, and finances. Significant disparities remain within this classification, though (Bohrmann et al., 2007). Similar to the case of politics, some countries have their economies incorporated into the European Union, some are aspiring EU members, while others like Russia are maintaining a careful distance from the EU based on mutual dependencies.

Media Pluralism, Commercialization and Concentration of Ownership

Starting from the idea of the homogeneity across the region and of the similarities in the post-communist transition from the communist to the democratic press, Jakubowicz (1995, p. 40–42) notes that the following steps are necessary when it comes to successfully democratize mass media:

- Liquidating the control system by abolishing the state monopoly over the press, the means of production in the press, and the distribution system;
- Creating an adequate legal framework, through constitutional guarantees and special laws, for freedom of expression and free access to information;
- Developing laws and regulation that limit political influence over media;
- The professionalization of journalism to ensure professional autonomy through professional norms, codes of ethics, university programs, and the creation of media accountability and media monitoring systems by civil society representatives.

Mass media evolved from being a part of the propaganda system of the party-state to an institution in its own right, thanks to a gradual replacement of the state with the market. The privatization of the press took place in the absence of an adequate legal or normative framework. Governments and various agencies, businessmen, and journalists have been forced to face a rapid transition to a tough and uncompromising market economy. In the print media, privatization materialized by withdrawing institutions (titles of publications, offices, equipment, distribution networks) from state control and placing them under the control of local or international companies, professional associations of journalists, or other investors such as banks. There were two distinct processes in the print media: (a) spontaneous privatization, which took place immediately after the collapse of the communist system and provided for the direct takeover of publications by journalists working there; and (b) state-mediated privatization (through transfer bodies whose mission was to liquidate state-owned enterprises in the print media). In the audiovisual sphere, the state has retained its influence (and control) over public service media, privatization refers to the leasing to local or foreign groups of one of the national television channels (as in Hungary or the Czech Republic), to the splitting of public service in various companies (in some states it owns shares—as in Russia) or in the transformation of public office into a public foundation (the case of Hungary). Nevertheless, the state retains control over the national news agency. It should be noted though that private radio and television stations are popular across the region.

From an economic standpoint, the media markets in the countries of Central and Eastern Europe are characterized by incomplete development and fragmentation. Despite the success and expansion of some media groups, the ownership structure in the media in these countries is quite diverse. The print media includes both independent publications and publications subsidized by the state, political parties, NGOs, or churches. The independent media exist through joint venture companies with local and foreign capital or can be owned by local groups or cultural, educational, or civic organizations. Crossbreeding is common, with many publications having both state capital (directly or mediated by other state institutions) and private capital. In the audiovisual sector, the landscape seems simpler: public service institutions are clearly separated from commercial institutions. There are no obvious signs of monopolistic control in the Central and Eastern European media market; at the same time, the constant merging process through which large trusts are expanding their influence is concerning, as evidenced by the declining number of independent publications and positions.

The mass media transition in post-communist countries was initially marked not by the flow, often aggressive, of foreign capital and by a flow Western audiovisual programs. For example, the structure of television programs in countries such as Bulgaria, Lithuania, Romania, Russia, and Slovakia shows that foreign programs represent more than 40 percent of total broadcasts. Films, series, music, and documentaries are dominant. Moreover, the programs in the original language of the respective country are modeled after concepts and programs from the West, as well as the foreign programs received through satellite dishes or cable distributors.

JOURNALISTIC FACTORS

The post-communist media were, and remain, the most eloquent, palpable, and active proof of the freedom of expression gained after the collapse of the Soviet bloc. However, freedom of expression is not synonymous with gaining professional maturity, nor with responsibly exercising the mission of a fourth estate, nor with equalizing the rights and opportunities of access to media for all citizens (Czepek et al., 2009).

Drawing on existing research (see Dobek-Ostrowska, 2019; Eberwein et al., 2017; Gross & Jakubowicz, 2013; Radu, 2016) some general features can be identified across the region. The first is the entry of a new generation of journalists into the profession after 1989. Young people integrated in the media and then came to control the profession, occupying leadership positions in newsrooms. In most cases, they come from different professional fields and do not have a university degree in journalism. They imposed themselves through opposition to former employees of the communist press, which gave them a sense of superiority, based on the idea that those who did not work in the communist media and were not affected by communist ideology are ab initio good professionals. Their discourse was dominated by certain professional self-sufficiency, based on the idea of a "mission" in whose name they chose the press, a mission that does not require any kind of critical self-assessment, no kind of journalistic readings, no distorted training and improvement. According to distinguished Polish researcher Valery Pisarek, they are "the Pampers generation—confident, convinced that they are better than everyone else, but completely ignorant from a professional point of view" (1998, p. 206).

Another characteristic is the professional heterogeneity that is also reflected by the dispersion of professional organizations. In each of these countries, there were at least two politically oriented and often competing professional associations. Journalists across the region consider themselves an "elite" of society, but their perception of the role of the media is somewhat confusing. Most local journalists see themselves as "representatives of the fourth estate."

However, they cannot define precisely what their influence entails. The adversarial perspective usually dominates, with journalists considering that their role is to oppose those in power (regardless of the party or group in power), to criticize it and uncover their abuses (Gross, 2002). Journalists failed to impose their control over this professional field and did not impose the sanctioning of those who do not respect the professional rules. In these countries, several codes of ethics have been adopted, some belonging to professional associations, others to large media outlets, but that there are no signs that these codes are strictly observed or that those who do not follow them are sanctioned by the journalistic community. This reality, correlated with the absence of a coherent system of media accountability reflects the lack of strong professional culture, a set of common values, and norms of behavior (Eberwein et al., 2017, Fengler et al., 2014, Radu, 2016).

When examining the journalistic profession across the region it is important to zoom in on two main components, namely (a) the conception of the role of the journalist and (b) their social position. According to the first criterion, the roles identified by Pisarek (1998) for Polish journalists can be generalized: the *militant* (concerned with defining an opinion and influencing the public); the *disc jockey* (focused on entertainment and/or information mixed with entertainment) and the *craftsman* (attentive to respect for professional values). From the perspective of the second criterion, it should be noted that the profession has become increasingly divided between "barons" and those who do daily journalism. The initial excitement that marked the first moments after the fall of communism disappeared and was replaced by the struggles to impose a "dominant coalition" and tensions stemming from the daily wear and tear of maintaining or disputing control. The great mass of journalists is not protected from the abuses of their bosses—neither by law, nor by clear conventions, strong unions, or professional tradition. Moreover, a significant number of "media moguls" have appeared in the Eastern European landscape. These former journalists, now strong businessmen, are a force in the media (and sometimes in politics) in their countries.

Under these conditions, those who work in the media find themselves in a situation characterized by ambivalence: as representatives of the media, they have gained a certain social prestige, but have simultaneously become targets of political pressure and market economy forces (they feel threatened by the possibility of salary cuts and even unemployment). Journalists across Eastern and Central Europe enjoy a certain elite status while at the same time suffer from the lack of trust of the audience; they claim to have a "mission," but their actions are stigmatized by professional errors. The loss of public trust can be explained by the intersection of several series of facts:

- Inability of journalists to provide a convincing picture of their mission and failure to defend the public interest;
- Tabloidization of the press and journalistic style, which led to journalists being identified as entertainment providers and to the decrease of the public dimension of their role;
- Widespread corruption, which also affected the media, although a pact of silence was instituted over the business of the media, the fortunes of employers and media leaders, the numerous leaks that ensued speak of the fabulous fortunes of such moguls.

Education

The ambiguity that is specific to the field of journalism accounts for the fact that journalism education was characterized and by the ambiguity of goals, and, consequently, by diverse patterns across the region, fitting Gerd Kopper's (2005, p. 309) formula: "Journalism education is a very special sort of construct, with its goal of educating people to enter into a job of rather imprecise requirements that has become one of particular visibility among some pivotal professional segments in modern societies." The various training paths—free access without required academic training; access through formal training in the newsroom; access conditioned by getting a university degree—compared to professions such as law, engineering, medicine, account for the ambiguous relations between the educational system in journalism and the profession, on the one hand, and the academy, on the other hand. This unique professional configuration leads toward a hybrid pattern, characterized by a combination of practical activities that simulate real-world newsrooms and that aim at developing practical skills and some rather theoretical courses that are meant to build a conceptual understanding of the profession (Frolich & Holtz-Bacha, 2003; Terzis, 2009).

Throughout post-communist Europe, the journalism faculties, schools, and departments have seen a spectacular increase in numbers. The combination of the social prestige of a job in journalism and the social prestige of a university degree led to attracting many, and higher education degrees are becoming important guarantees for career success. On the other hand, the universities profited from the chance to obtain extra income from increasing the number of registered students in journalism: picturing potential candidate cohorts who pay tuition fees sparkled for some universities, either state or private ones (Hiebert & Gross, 2003).

And, as in other fields, *imitation* and *restoration* processes took place (Gross, 2002; Sparks & Reading, 1998). At the beginning, such processes were the result of the promotion campaigns coming from or modeled after Western structures. These campaigns were mainly focused on:

- Creating branches of educational institutions, such as the American University in Bulgaria or the Central-European University in Hungary, BBC schools in almost all of the post-communist countries, many training centers according to the vocational center model from France, Germany, or Holland;
- Supporting local faculties by bringing in professors, professional trainers, or journalists from Western countries to teach various topics (usually for a short period of time) or to counsel the new;
- In-service training for the permanent faculty staff (by means of teaching observation activities or updating content and class materials, or encouraging them to register in Master's or Doctoral degree programs, at universities or vocational schools);

- Resource transfer such as book and equipment donations, access to information systems, and financial donations;
- Creating and financing inter-university exchange programs (Tempus, Erasmus, Socrates in Europe, USIA, Fulbright, Knight Foundation in the United States);
- Supporting the integration process of these organizations into international professional organizations, including the European Journalism Training Association (EJTA), Association of Education in Journalism and Mass Communication (AEJMC), Reseau des ecoles francophones de journalisme (Theophraste), and Journet-UNESCO, as well as participating in international conferences on specific topics.

Overall, these efforts were aimed at synchronizing journalism training to Western standards and, by extension, supporting the process of creating professional, fair, and ethical media. The second trend (restoration) was brought forth by the defensive reactions of the existing faculty who, with few exceptions, tried to maintain and legitimate the teaching content and methods that they were used to—in order to secure their academic status, which was threatened by the new professional vocabulary, new curricula, new teaching methods and by the "invaders" who were penetrating into the system.

Many of the newly founded university programs did not have resources to develop new curricula so they "recycled" along the way. Courses that were supposed to follow a new curriculum did not change their content much. Instead developing more hands-on activities, many tried to "sell" their old courses in linguistics, rhetoric, history, sociology, and philosophy under the "label" of journalism courses.

Second, the journalism core courses are frequently shadowed by a bunch of courses that, by Western standards, would be considered complementary. Unfortunately, local interests create a legitimating discourse to justify a large number of non-journalism courses based on the notion that they are essential for the developing cultural awareness of future communicators. Moreover, journalism departments became the victims of their own success: The journalism and communication departments became the "milking cows" for other depopulated colleges: as a consequence, they were joined by force to the sociology, philosophy, liberal arts colleges.

THE DIGITAL LANDSCAPE

Similar to other world regions, new and social media have become common channels for media producers as well as media consumers across Central and Eastern Europe and Russia as Internet access has become ubiquitous in most of the region (Reuters Institute, 2020). Online news sources continue to increase in popularity not only for the younger generation but among the general public, with Facebook being the most popular social media platform.

On the one hand, the rise in online news consumption has led to new media ventures and coalitions (digital only/digital first) with different focal areas (e.g., investigative, fashion, or lifestyle journalism.) to open. For example, in Romania, *The Rise Project* is an NGO of investigative journalists as well as activists and computer programmers whose mission is to investigate local and cross-border organized crime and uncover corruption networks through cutting-edge investigative techniques and technology (www.riseproject.ro/investigation/). Another example is *Press One*—an online magazine publishing investigations, feature stories, and interviews (pressone.ro).

More cross-border investigative collaborations are also taking place. For example, a team of Bulgarian and Romanian journalists led by the investigative journalism websites *Bivol* and

RISE Project Romania exposed the misuse of European Union funds in Bulgaria and Romania in what became known as the #GPGate scandal. The investigative team was funded by the European Commission through the European Centre for Press and Media Freedom (ECPMF), which is a common way to finance such digital-only journalistic ventures.

On the other hand, media and audiences have had to face increasing misinformation and disinformation often distributed via social media—a serious concern in other parts of the world as well. The 2020 Reuters Institute *Digital News Report* showed that while the COVID-19 pandemic reinforced the need for reliable, accurate journalism, it also showcased the often futile fight against conspiracies and online misinformation (Newman, 2020), a worrying trend considering the fact that trust in the news has been declining, especially in countries such as Bulgaria and Romania. Low trust is especially concerning in the case of Hungary where government criticism of "fake-news" media and their favoritism toward certain state-supported channels have made the general public less trusting and more aware of media bias.

RUSSIA'S TROLL FACTORIES: DISINFORMATION CAMPAIGNS ON SOCIAL MEDIA

The Mueller Report, published by the U.S. Department of Justice in March 2019, discussed Russia's attempts to influence elections in the United States via Internet troll factories producing "fake news" and targeted disinformation campaigns. The main culprit was named as *Internet Research Agency*, known in Russian as *Glavset'*. It is based in Saint Petersburg, but its offshoots operate from as far as African countries and certainly from locations in Northern Macedonia, Romania and Bulgaria. IRA's task has been to exert influence on behalf of Russia's political and economic interests via social media (mainly Facebook, Twitter, YouTube and WhatsApp). *The Mueller Report* explains how such troll factories have been operating. For instance, they have propagated Facebook groups with purported conservative bias (e.g., Tea Party News), or fake Black social justice groups (e.g., Blacktivist), pseudo-LGBTQ groups (e.g., LGBT United), or religious groups (e.g., United Muslims of America). U.S. intelligence agencies have long posited that hackers related to Russian intelligence services try to outdo each other in attempts to spread disinformation abroad. The end goal has been to affect the democratic routines, including the ability to have open discussions, free elections and reliable media. Some researchers have labeled these processes as the "weaponization of social media." Their assertion is that in the battle of veracity vs. virality, truth loses ground. Disinformation campaigns have gained tremendous attention in the West and are certainly not unique to Russia. The main concern has been social media channels are used to manipulate foreign publics. EU and NATO have identified cyber warfare as a major threat coming from Russia. They have created several channels, e.g. the newsletter and website called *Disinformation Review* to counter Kremlin's influence on social media on subjects ranging from the Crimea annexation and the downing of MH17 to military conflict in Ukraine and the migration crisis. European allies have also expressed concern about attempts to influence recent elections in Germany, the United Kingdom, as well as those for the European Parliament. In most cases the issue is spreading disinformation, encouraging discord and amplifying distrust in centrist parties. Despite the fact that the Cold War ended decades ago, shades of it have re-emerged via social media, amplified by modern technology and Internet culture.

CHAPTER SUMMARY

The media systems in the transitional democracies of Central and Eastern Europe and Russia have undergone tremendous change after the end of the Cold War, ushering away from the Soviet press model that dominated the region for decades. While some of the countries in the region feature open and free commercial media others have followed authoritarian trends. Threats against journalists have remained a challenge. Communication technologies and social media have deeply affected media operations and journalism practice across the entire region. Global challenges such as the spread of disinformation and "fake news" are also relevant in the region.

DISCUSSION QUESTIONS

1. How have the countries of Central and Eastern Europe transformed their media from a Soviet Press Model to a predominantly Liberal Media Model?
2. What are some of the challenges in transforming journalism education in the region?
3. Choose two countries from Central or Eastern Europe and compare their levels of media freedom. How can you explain the observed differences or similarities?
4. Can you find an example of a disinformation campaign on social media that is attributed to Russia or another country in the region?

BIBLIOGRAPHY

Bohrmann, H., Klaus, E., & Machill, M. (2007). *Media industry, journalism culture and communication policies in Europe.* Von Halem.

Coman, I., & Gross, P. (2012). Uncommonly common or truly exceptional? An alternative to the political system-based explanation of the Romanian mass media. *The International Journal of Press/Politics,* 17(4), 457–479.

Coman, M. (2010). Journalistic elites in post-communist Romania: From heroes of Revolution to media moguls. *Journalism Studies, 11*(4), 587–595.

Czepek, A., Hellwig M., & Nowak E. (eds). (2009). *Press freedom and pluralism in Europe.* Intellect.

Dobek-Ostrowska, B. (2019). *Polish media system in a comparative perspective.* Peter Lang.

Eberwein, T., Fengler, S., & Karmasin, M. (eds). (2017). *The European handbook of media accountability.* Routledge.

Fengler, S., Eberwein, T., Mazzoleni, G., Porlezza, C., & Russ-Mohl, S. (eds.) (2014). *Journalists and media accountability. An international study of news people in the digital age.* Peter Lang.

Frolich, R., & Holtz-Bacha, C. (2003). *Journalism education in Europe and North America.* Hampton Press.

Giorgi, L. (1995). *The Post-Socialist media: What power the West?: The changing media landscape in Poland, Hungary, and the Czech Republic.* Avebury.

Gross, P. (2002). *Entangled evolutions: Media and democratization in Eastern Europe.* Woodrow Wilson Center Press.

Gross, P., & Jakubowicz, K. (Eds.). (2013). *Media transformations in the post-communist world: Eastern Europe's tortured path to change.* Lexington Books.

Hiebert, R., & Gross, P. (2003). Remedial education: The remaking of Eastern European journalists. In Frolich, R., & Holtz-Bacha, C. (Eds.), *Journalism education in Europe and North America* (pp. 257–282). Hampton Press.

Jakubowicz, K. (1995). Media as agents of change. In Paletz, D., Jakubowicz, K., & Novosel, P. (Eds.), *Glasnost and after: Media and change in Central and Eastern Europe*. Hampton Press.

Kopper, G. 2005. Journalism education and practice. In Rothenbuhler, E. & Coman, M. (Eds.), *Media Anthropology* (pp. 309–317). Sage.

Pisarek, W. (1998). A la recherche des journalists polonaise. In Feigelson, K., & Pelissier, N. (Ed.), *Tele-revolutions culturelles: Chine, Europe Centrale, Russie*, Paris: L'Harmattan.

Radu, R. N. (2016). Sanctioning journalistic misconduct: An application of cumulative prospect theory to journalistic self-regulation issues. *Journalism, 17*(8), 1095–1112.

Reuters Institute. (2020). *Reuters Institute digital news report 2020*. reutersinstitute.politics.ox.ac.uk/sites/default/files/2020-06/DNR_2020_FINAL.pdf

Sparks, C., & Reading, A. (1998). *Communism, capitalism and the mass media*. Sage.

Terzis, G. (Ed.). (2009). *European journalism education*. Intellect.

Voltmer, K. (2013). *The media in transitional democracies*. Polity Press.

11

Media in Western and Northern Europe

Elisabeth Fondren

This chapter offers an introduction to the media systems of Western Europe (Germany, Austria, Switzerland, France, Belgium, Luxembourg, and the Netherlands) and Northern Europe (Denmark, Norway, Sweden, Finland, the United Kingdom, and Ireland) (see figure 11.1). In particular, the entry describes the historical evolution of the political system, the role of technology, economic and cultural frameworks, professional norms, and working conditions, including newsroom diversity, in relation to the European media landscape.

Journalism in this region is characterized by high levels of political freedom, a public service mindset, and state-supported public broadcasting. Although Western and Northern Europe is culturally diverse and quite heterogeneous as a region, there are broad commonalities in terms of media structures and governance, absence of government interference and censorship, a long-standing tradition of partisan press outlets, and journalistic professionalization and education.

The chapter begins with a discussion of the political press in Europe, state regulations and support of public broadcasting, and the rise of the Internet age. Next, it traces the impact of technological developments, economic policies and frameworks, the cultural history and notions of a European public sphere, journalistic professionalism, and diversity in newsrooms and news coverage. Throughout the chapter, some key features and characteristics of European journalism will be highlighted and contrasted with the variation of other parts of the region.

POLITICAL SYSTEM

A free and independent press plays an important role in the region, and together with strong national journalism cultures is seen as a cornerstone of European democracies. Since the end of World War II in 1945, European journalism and media are characterized by high rankings of press freedom, political stability, and investments into public service communications.

Different Media Models

Using Hallin and Mancini's analysis of Western press systems, there are at least three models visible in the region: the Mediterranean or Polarized Pluralist Model for Spain, Italy, and

EUROPE

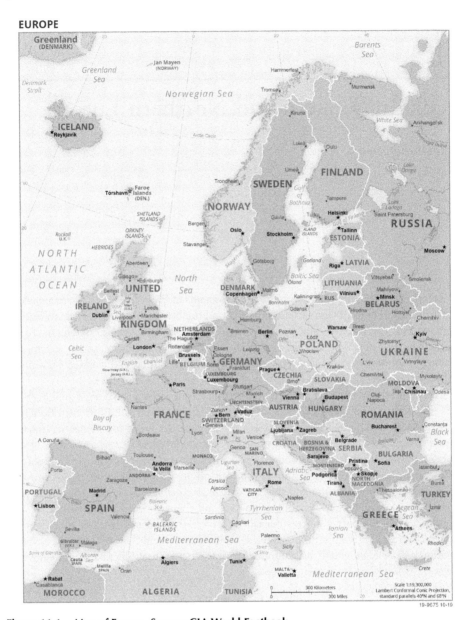

Figure 11.1.   Map of Europe. Source: CIA World Factbook

France; the North/Central Europe or Democratic Corporatist Model, including countries such as Belgium, Denmark, Finland, and the North Atlantic or Liberal Model that encompasses Britain and Ireland (Hallin & Mancini, 2004). An important distinction is that some Western European countries have mixed media system, for instance, the United Kingdom is a mixed case as its press shares traits of both the Liberal and Democratic Corporatist models, and France shares characteristics of the Polarized Pluralist and Democratic Corporatist models (Hallin & Mancini, 2004). Much of the Western and Northern European countries discussed in this chapter can be described as Democratic Corporatist media systems. Hallin and Mancini's (2004) comparative—and largely conceptual—typology suggests that political systems strongly affect the media and specifically politics-media parallelism, to a varying degree depending on the specific nation.

Political Stability and State-Media Relations

Historically, Western European media has featured strong ideological ties between the press and political parties, which means newspapers have often favored a partisan style of reporting (Van Dalen, De Vreese, & Albæk, 2012). Newspapers, and indeed partisan media, played an important role in educating citizens and advancing political liberties. In the Scandinavian countries, a distinct socialist press developed in the early twentieth century. In mid-century Denmark, for instance, national as well as regional and local newspapers represented a wide range of partisan perspectives, but also social and religious ones. A depoliticization of the news did not take place in many European countries until the 1970s and 1980s. But even today, European journalism is characterized by its wide range of political and partisan opinions, which audiences expect and rely on in their decision-making processes.

Most Western European countries enjoy a high level of political stability, which is rooted in strong institutions and political parties with longstanding traditions. Political parties in the region are aligned on the left-to-right political spectrum and cater to different voter segments. In Switzerland, for instance, parties have traditionally sought compromise and formed a coalition government. The rule of law and the authority of the legislative and parliamentary bodies are respected, and the state is not seen as an enemy of the press. Typically, established national European governments safeguard political order, hold democratic elections, and manage their vast welfare state and social policies. In recent years, electoral majorities in some major countries, for instance in France, have changed, and several countries, including Germany, the Netherlands, and the United Kingdom have seen the rise and resurgence of right-wing and EU skeptical parties. The 2020 Brexit decision, following the United Kingdom's 2016 referendum to leave the European Union, was one of the most controversial political stories of the decade. The decline of public trust in government and the rise of cynicism against public institutions is a trend that journalists all over Europe report and highlight (Newman et al., 2020).

Press Freedom, Privacy Laws, and Absence of Censorship

In terms of the media's role, journalism across the European continent is instrumental in people's ability to stay informed and forming political opinions. The mandate and expectation of journalism in democracies are to provide citizens with balanced, accurate, timely, and complete information while shying away from the term "objectivity" (Hallin & Mancini, 2004). Press criticism of government institutions, political leaders, or policy goals remains an important cornerstone of European journalism.

Democratic systems of government were established in the early twentieth century, with Austria and Germany being the exception. Germany became a representative democracy in 1949, after two world wars and the rule of the Nazi regime, which included the strict censorship and control of the press. After the Second World War, the partisan nature of the press was reestablished. Today, Germany's constitution (Grundgesetz, Art. 5) protects freedom of expression and press freedom and Germany continually ranks in the top twenty of international rankings on press freedom by Reporters without Borders and the Freedom House.

Since 2018, Germany's social media law (Network Enforcement Act or NetzDG) compels social media companies to delete information that may be illegal or contains hate speech. Observers have criticized this media regulation, arguing it would incentivize *over-blocking* by social media platforms—including content posted by politicians or extremist views—to avoid fines.

The Nordic countries (Norway, Finland, Sweden, and Denmark) rank highest in terms of press freedom not only in the region, but around the world. While there is no formal media censorship, governments have instituted some rules for the media. In Sweden, for instance, a press law prohibits officials from pressuring journalists to disclose their sources. In the same vein, journalists are not allowed to disclose information about a source without the permission of that source. The system of ombudsmen—dating back to the 1960s in Sweden and then taking shape in other countries including the United States—and press councils are widespread and particular features of how journalists operate in Scandinavian countries. Laws guaranteeing freedom of press reach back more than 200 years and were established in Sweden in 1766 (and finalized in 1812), in Norway (1814), in the Netherlands (1815), in Belgium (1831), and Denmark (1848).

Media Regulation and Legislation

In terms of protecting people's rights from government interference and individual's reputational rights, including libel and privacy laws, there is no Europe-wide set of laws or guidelines and each country sets its particular standards. In France, for instance, libel and privacy laws are highly complex and rigid. Compared to its EU neighbor countries, France has some of the toughest laws on hate speech, allowing citizens to take legal action in cases of hate speech online, including blog posts, tweets, and Facebook comments. The Nordic countries also have strong protection against libel and complaints are handled by the press councils and argued outside of the courts. Sweden, Norway, the Netherlands, Ireland, and France have legislation that safeguards freedom of information and the public's right to know. In other countries, such as the United Kingdom, this type of legislation has not been enacted, although the country has a longstanding tradition of granting reporters access to parliamentary debates and government information.

TECHNOLOGY AND INFRASTRUCTURE

Most of the countries of Northern and Western Europe are urbanized with highly industrialized centers and are technologically advanced. Citizens of this region generally enjoy a high standard of living, free public education, and excellent social security systems. Online media outlets have quickly become an important news source for people, and most if not all major newspapers operate a fully digital version that is updated with news and stories throughout the day, sometimes several times per hour. While most online and Internet media started as free versions, publishers are increasingly moving toward a digital subscription model. The ongoing globalization and commercialization of mass media have produced broad convergence between print and audio–visual material used by journalists.

Technological Advancements and Investments

The European Union—the governing body of twenty-seven member states with headquarters in Brussels—has outlined economic plans for investing in digital infrastructure and technologies. The European Union has vowed to invest large sums in smart grid infrastructure by 2027, stressing that improvements in e-infrastructure are critical for networked products, services, and digitization efforts of member states, also coined as the "digital single market" (EU Commission, 2020).

While large questions about governance and political sovereignty among member countries remain, the discussions of widespread 5G and digital infrastructures are on top of the political agenda in Germany, Netherlands, and Sweden, among others. The small country of Belgium (11.4 million inhabitants)—with Brussels as the capital of the European Union and seat of NATO—is often seen as a forerunner in digital infrastructure. In 2007, Google chose Wallonia, the country's French-speaking part, to build its European data centers, the backbone of Internet technologies. In 2018, Google announced €250 million additional investments as well as the building of training, education, and entrepreneurship program at its St. Ghislain facility (Calvert, 2019).

The advent of high-speed Internet and investments in broadband connectivity have significantly impacted the mode of delivery across European newsrooms, namely from electronic communications to wireless and digital communications. In Germany, for example, both ARD and ZDF, the two state-supported public broadcast channels, use digital video broadcasting through several online platforms. Experts agree that in the future, the participation of public service broadcasters in developing and getting new media formats and digital technologies off the ground will be crucial. The expectation is rooted in the spirit of public service news and providing innovative content, but also platforms that can be widely accessed free of charge.

Data Journalism and Digital-Born Media

One of the most promising recent trends has been the ability to utilize new technologies to actively support and enable better journalism across Europe. Two recent initiatives stand out: The *Bureau Local* is a collaborative, investigative journalism network in the United Kingdom and *CORRECTIV*, a pioneering nonprofit newsroom in the German-speaking region. Both outlets use a technology-based, data-driven, and collaborative approach to investigate political and social injustices or abuse of power. The United Kingdom's *Bureau Local*, for example, has broken a number of high-profile stories including local finance scandals and tax evasion.

Digital-born news is especially popular in Southern European countries, such as Spain and France, which in Hallin and Mancini's terminology have a Mediterranean or *Polarized Pluralist Model* media system. New journalistic venues and innovative start-ups in these countries are particularly successful as older and more legacy media are becoming less influential and less profitable (Borelli, 2019). And while the new data-driven style of reporting and visualization adds to readers' understanding and produces quality journalism online, reporters are increasingly under pressure in understaffed newsrooms where journalists have to multitask and work faster than ever.

In the spring of 2020, the global coronavirus crisis accelerated the shift to digital news and online journalism, as newspaper consumption has fallen and due to lockdowns, people did not have access to print publications. Research indicates that during the COVID-19 onset, people relied mostly on television news and online news sources (Newman et al., 2020, p. 9). According to the Reuters Digital Report, for example, the traffic to BBC News' website doubled between January 2020 and April 2020 (Newman et al., 2020, p. 11). Journalists at all major European outlets covered the global health pandemic using large data visualization, interactive stories, multimedia reporting, and utilized various digital platforms to reach their audiences.

Digital Sphere and Digital Divide

Across Europe, the digital divide has been reduced, but only slowly, as the well-educated and well-connected Western and Northern European countries tend to have better infrastructure and digital skills relative to neighboring countries in the South and East. The European Union's push toward a digital single market, critics point out, could exacerbate the chasm between the geographic regions and new member states such as Malta, and further deepen the digital divide in these countries. According to the EU, the majority of EU member states either have underdeveloped media literacy policies, or no media literacy policy at all (EU Commission, 2020).

In terms of online access, however, it is important to point out that Internet penetration rates in Western and Northern Europe are among the world's highest: for instance, Belgium's Internet penetration rate as of 2020 is 94 percent; the Netherlands—96 percent; Sweden—96 percent; Switzerland—94 percent; and Denmark—98 percent. The average European Internet penetration rate is equally high (87.2 percent) according to recent data (Internetworldstats, 2020). The Nordic countries top the European index for Internet connectivity, integration of digital technology, as well as the willingness to pay for news. For instance, 26 percent of people in Nordic countries pay for news (with 42 percent in Norway), compared to 20 percent in the United States and only 14 percent in Australia and 10 percent in Germany (Newman et al., 2020). The popularity of social media as people's main source for news is growing across the region. This places pressure on both regulatory bodies and tech giants to implement policies that are in line with the region's high expectation of independent, fair, and truthful online news content.

Digital Disinformation Campaigns

In the current media environment, digital media literacy is seen as a core element in safeguarding democracy and pluralist society. As part of the digital transformation, European audiences are wary of the growth of disinformation hubs, fake news, and troll farms, which are seen as a threat to democratic debate and quality of information (Martens, Aguiar, Gomez-Herrera, & Mueller-Langer, 2018). While access to digital news is growing across Western and Northern Europe, people are increasingly concerned about dis- and misinformation campaigns online (Newman et al., 2020). Since 2020, the European University Institute leads the EU-wide efforts and directs the European Digital Media Observatory (EDMO), which aims to promote broad digital literacy and fight disinformation.

ECONOMY

The European Union, with its 450 million citizens, is home to the third-largest economy in the world. The economies of Germany, the United Kingdom, France, and Italy, respectively, top the member bloc's ranks in terms of strongest national markets and GDP. All of the Western and Northern European countries are classified as high income, which enables both media consumers and producers. London is considered the news capital of Europe although each country's capital tends to be a national media center. There are also several international media corporations, for example, Bertelsmann or Bauer Media Group, which are headquartered in this region and operate around the world.

Media Pluralism

Ideally, a pluralist media economy would include a wide number of operators and owners in order to minimize market concentration and further consolidation of media channels and content. On the other hand, when the media is highly concentrated, potential bias might spread. Large conglomerates are not always transparent about what media they own or control, and the quality and diversity of news, critical information, and a democratic debate might be threatened.

In the recent decade, the EU has launched some initiatives to identify and analyze threats to media pluralism—both digital and traditional—that are tied to economic models, technological developments, global changes in Internet advertising, and increased market capitalization. While political conditions in Western and Northern Europe are stable, media in Eastern Europe may be subject to political interference, especially during the ongoing economic decline and merger of media companies. The EU co-funded *Media Pluralism Monitor* (MPM), an organization that consists of academic and expert teams in each EU country, observes developments and risks to media pluralism across these areas: basic protection, market plurality, political independence, and social inclusiveness. In 2017, the MPM report found that no European country analyzed was completely free from risks to media pluralism.

Moreover, the technological evolution of digital news, services, and information has had significant consequences for the strength of news media ecologies. Since traditional media, in particular newspapers and magazines, are continuing to decline—due to changes in consumer and funding models—advertisers have taken to the Internet and mobile phones to advertise more widely and for a fraction of the cost. Changes in how news is gathered, produced, shared, and consumed have had ripple effects on how owners and companies use and expand their use of online media, by bypassing journalism and traditional gatekeepers. In 2014, online advertising (often through digital giants such as Facebook, Google, and Amazon) surpassed TV campaigns across the European Union. In markets such as the United Kingdom, Sweden, and Denmark, online advertising makes up the largest share of all media advertising.

Media Audiences and Commercialization

The level of news consumption in Europe remains high and citizens increasingly access—and pay for—journalism online. Media companies have increasingly moved toward consolidation and commercialization of media outlets and content. As in other parts of the world, experts observe that European media companies are segmenting audiences into several channels. In the Scandinavian countries, however, the newspaper market is still stronger than in the rest of Europe. In Norway, for example, newspapers are doing well, but large newspaper owners have heavily invested in electronic media. The public service broadcaster NRK, financed by a public service license, remains the most widely watched and listened to channel in the country.

The case of Norway is interesting to highlight because most people are willing to pay for news through online subscriptions. This means they have access to paid news from national, regional, and local newspapers, which in turn has enabled these brands to diversify their journalism offerings for an online environment (Reuters Digital News, 2020). The Netherlands, Germany, Austria, and Switzerland too have high numbers of newspaper readers, although media outlets are following the lead from U.S.- and U.K.-based news organizations and increasingly diversifying their digital and online subscriptions. Another noteworthy trend in the region is the establishment of niche journalism venues and startups across Europe that have found ways to successfully market *slow news* and thoughtful, in-depth reporting as opposed to commercialized and ad-heavy content. Examples include the London-based *Delayed Gratification* magazine and the U.K.-wide *Tortoise Media*.

Concentration of Ownership

France, as one of Europe's largest media economies, offers a good example of existing laws on transparency in media ownership and freedom of communication. These regulations stipulate that editors of a broadcasting station or a publication must publicize information about that media's ownership patterns and funding. In terms of media concentration, France's Competition Authority works to bolster pluralism and diversity of media channels and outlets by enforcing strict licensing that prohibits individuals, groups, or conglomerates to own, control, or edit media shares that exceed 30 percent nationally. This is especially important with regard to political publications and programs. The Nordic countries Finland, Sweden, and Denmark have no legislation that might restrict the consolidation of media companies and thus a high degree of media ownership concentration. In Austria, the ownership patterns are equally concentrated in a few media groups with excessive power. One of the key players is the public service broadcaster ORF, which is neither politically nor financially independent from the state government. The country's media policy is marked by strong regulatory elements and little self-regulation (Doyle, 2002).

CULTURE

Although the population ranges from densely populated states such as Germany (83 million inhabitants) to smaller countries such as Finland (5.5. million inhabitants) and tiny nations such as Luxembourg (600,000 inhabitants), the region shares a common cultural and historic heritage. In addition to political, technological, and economic factors, media production and consumption in Europe are heavily influenced by common cultural and historical trends.

Media scholars argue that Western and Northern European journalists do not operate in identical press traditions and that external media and political structures in place shape the news content. Despite such diversity, observers point out that there are "more similarities than differences across western European news systems," including a consensus over fundamental journalistic duties (Esser & Pfetsch, 2004, p. 16). At the same time, comparative studies suggest that national borders in terms of journalism still matter, for instance in how much preference journalists give to news, opinions, or both; how journalists perceive their roles (Hanitzsch, Hanusch, Ramaprasad, & De Beer, 2019) and how newsrooms are organized (Esser, 1998). The dominant view among communication scholars is that there is no one uniform journalism culture in the EU member states (Van Dalen et al., 2012). German journalism, for instance, follows the traditional political character, which tends to place more value on opinion and less value on news compared to other countries in the region. British journalists, in contrast, see their role as transmitters of facts, as neutral reporters of current affairs, and there is a large sector of tabloid and entertainment news.

Trans-European Media Culture

There is no indication that a model of 'European journalism' will develop anytime soon, even though critics argue that a European-wide audience is present. It is unlikely to see a distinctly European journalism model emerge; instead, European media are expected to continue to follow global and in particular U.S. journalism trends. This Americanization of European news is often confined to news format, but not necessarily news content.

Over the past decade, scholarly discussions have investigated the lack of EU-wide media, the fact that Europe is often reported as a *foreign story*, and British media's (tabloid) reporting on EU politics, which culminated in the Brexit coverage. "When Europe does get news coverage, it is largely structured to fit with national concerns and national stereotypes" (Örnebring, 2009, p. 6). European journalists, just like their counterparts in other countries, can be described as *localists* since they write and frame news according to their country-specific contexts.

In the United Kingdom, for example, the democratic deficit and the agnostic approach toward the European Union have been one of the major trends in reporting about EU affairs. In Germany, on the other hand, economic issues, the plurality of cultures, and the complexity of the political process shape the EU coverage. National correspondents are reporting EU news through national frames throughout the region. Another trend is that traditional foreign correspondents are substituted by new types of reporters, including freelancers and amateurs who *parachute* in to join the Brussels press corps to cover EU politics but have generally limited experience in covering policy issues (Fondren, Hamilton, & McCune, 2019). It is also important to note the popularity of some pan-European programming such as the *Eurovision Song Contest*, which is an annual pop music TV contest that is among the world's longest-running public broadcast programs. Millions of Europeans gather in front of their televisions or online streaming devices to see the musicians compete.

Journalistic Perceptions

Reporters, editors, and producers in Western and Northern Europe are influenced by their professional norms, practical and/or academic training, and their work is guided by strong notions of autonomy and independence from the state or governing bodies. The history and development of the principles of press freedom across European states are closely tied to the ideal of the press functioning as a "Fourth Estate" in Western democratic societies.

Professional Norms and Roles

Researchers have shown how different professional norms and perceptions of journalistic roles are reflected in news coverage. The origins and consequences of different journalistic cultures and therefore different news content in European journalism can be measured across this spectrum: pragmatic-sacerdotal, impartial-partisan, and information-entertainment. Journalists' professionalism and news content are directly and inherently related. In Germany, for example, researchers have found a correlation between individual journalists' perception of their professional roles and the news or commentary they produce (Esser & Umbricht, 2013). Hanitzsch et al. (2019) have argued that both intrinsic and extrinsic forces make up the social institutions that influence how journalists across the world perceive editorial autonomy and professional independence. Research has also found that strong reporting, editing, and networking skills are seen as crucial at the Austrian universities of Salzburg or in various EU-journalism cultures (Örnebring & Mellado, 2018).

DANISH CARTOONS 2005 AND *CHARLIE HEBDO* 2015

In 2005, the Danish cartoon controversy underscored the growing cultural polarization between Islamic and Western societies across Europe whose Muslim population has increased over time. This case also highlighted the need for sensitivity in editorial decision making and different perceptions about the limits of media freedom (Strömbäck et al., 2008). The Danish newspaper *Jyllands Posten*—among the country's top media outlets—published twelve cartoons of the Prophet Mohammed. The editor argued that the cartoons were meant to stimulate debate and discussion around issues of Islamist extremism as well as journalistic self-censorship. Some of the cartoons were considered to be particularly offensive to people of Muslim faith, for instance, the image of Mohammed with a turban shaped like a bomb that was about to explode. These cartoons caused a global furor and were labeled by some as hate speech. Anti-Danish protests and boycotts began to boil across the Muslim world. A few months later, several European newspapers decided to re-publish the cartoons as a statement of support for freedom of expression. Reactions against this editorial decision ranged from individual disapproval and peaceful protests to death threats and violent attacks on several Danish embassies, consulates, and journalists.

On January 7, 2015, two brothers who were part of a radical Islamist terrorist group stormed the building of the French satirical magazine *Charlie Hebdo*. They killed twelve people, including the editor, and injured eleven others. In the aftermath of the attacks, EU media chose to report differently about the event; some papers immediately published the magazine's offensive cartoons, arguing they were vital to the news value of the story, but others were more reluctant. European public opinion as well as editorial stances seemed to be in favor of printing the cover of the first *Charlie Hebdo* issue after the attacks. This issue showed a caricature of Mohammed saying, "All is forgiven." The small French satirical magazine *Charlie Hebdo* was well known for featuring offensive cartoons since French media has a tradition of political and religious satire that may seem extreme to other liberal democracies. After the violent attack on the magazine, many media organizations around the world chose to re-publish their cartoons in a show of solidarity. In Europe, large crowds gathered in big cities and in front of French embassies with the slogan "Je suis Charlie" to show their support for free speech. Both cases illustrate the challenges with finding a balance between media freedom and media responsibility.

Press Associations

In the early twentieth century, European newspaper editors and publishers organized in professional organizations such as Press Councils or membership associations that were nonpartisan and promoted high standards of journalism. Many of these national organizations became quite influential, since they had high membership, were independent from politics, and dealt directly with readers' complaints. Over time, these associations developed more formal principles of self-regulation and journalism ethics. They promoted journalistic autonomy in reporting, the right to know for media organizations, high standards of the profession, and they established editorial statues. Today we call this process professionalization. The Swedish Press Council, for instance, dates back to 1916. In Norway, Germany, and the Netherlands, editorial statues and a formal system of complaints were also instituted and continue to be an important part of how the press operates in these countries.

Codes of Ethics and Value Systems

Although the professional journalistic codes across Western and Northern European nations vary, the ethical frameworks of these associations share similarities, namely the objective to report the truth and lobby for increased press freedom. National guidelines often pose the questions "what can media do?" and "what should media do?" at the forefront of discussion. In the German case, the German *Presserat*, a press council, and the German *Pressecodex*, a code of media ethics, are instruments of self-regulation as members regulate and oversee professionals' work ethics and also deal with wrongdoings. In Germany, as in many other European countries, media ethics, concerns for quality journalism, and media accountability go hand in hand.

In the British media code, the National Union of Journalists' maxims are derived from a tradition of liberal philosophy and a long history of press freedom. However, a clear market-oriented approach and a debate after the 2011 *News of The World Scandal* prompted harsh criticism and discussions about media ethics. The British Press Complaint's Commission serves a similar function as the German Press Council. The European Federation of Journalists (EFJ) is the largest professional organization for members of the press in Europe. Established in 1994, the EFJ advocates for journalists' rights and independence across all media sectors and promotes free expression as a fundamental right (Article 10, European Convention on Human Rights).

Journalism Education

European universities, media organizations, and industry leaders are trying to respond to the ongoing changes in the media landscape by leveraging and re-thinking their teaching of what modern journalism is and should be. University courses in journalism (radio, TV, online, and print journalism) exist in most countries of Western Europe and the Nordic countries. Some European media and journalism programs are among the top-ranked globally. For example, the programs at the Austrian universities of Salzburg or Vienna; the programs at the Danish universities of Aarhus and Roskilde; the University of Tampere in Finland; the Dutch University of Amsterdam, and the Swiss universities in Zurich, Basel, and St. Gallen. In Germany, prestigious journalism schools include the German School of Journalism in Munich (Deutsche Journalistenschule) and the Henri-Nannen-Schule in Hamburg. While traditionally, aspiring reporters apprenticed or completed traineeships at publishing houses, today most entry-level journalists have university degrees in communication or media studies.

DIVERSITY

Media play an important role in the social and cultural construction of how audiences perceive their country, their neighbors, and minority groups. Journalists are tasked with sourcing a multitude of perspectives and viewpoints to accurately portray people's opinions, reactions, and differences. Supporting media pluralism across the European continent, as mentioned earlier, is a distinct goal of EU political and academic institutions. Through increased analysis and hands-on training, members of the press are reminded of their social responsibility, which includes providing more representative content across all media forms, promoting the expression of diversity in gender, race, and ethnicities, and making sure that their media content is non-discriminatory or biased toward certain groups of people or views.

Race, Class, and Gender in the Profession

There is an ongoing debate about the role and quality of journalism as it relates to minorities and the coverage of diverse populations in EU journalism. Data show that European newsrooms are less diverse than their populations, and feature few women in leading editorial positions. In some countries, newsrooms are also marked by class, allowing only highly educated people from privileged cultural backgrounds to assume advanced managerial roles and responsibilities in creating content. This absence of working-class perspectives is recognized as a problem as it relates to the question of how media brands can build trust and sensitively cover rural or provincial topics and trends. Outside of big cities, media organizations may face a talent shortage for regional and local newspapers, especially in Germany and the United Kingdom, but less so in Sweden (Borchardt et al., 2019). Research on representation in newsrooms has also found that European media are not doing enough and that there is a distinct lack of gender equality in managerial and content creation roles. Women are also underrepresented when media quotes experts on economic, scientific, or political news. The gender pay gap is also a reality for many European media organizations.

Supporting Media Diversity

Research on media diversity suggests that issues of immigration, migration, race and ethnicity, sexual orientation, gender, disability, and age often fall short of being fairly represented in the media and that, on occasion, media reports perpetuate negative stereotypes. In the Netherlands, media diversity is actively supported by the Dutch Press Fund, an independent authority that supports print publications with loans and research grants, and works to improve minorities' representation and access to journalism. EU institutions support the program *Media in Europe for Diversity and Inclusiveness* (MEDIANE), which provides industry training, journalism education, and workshops on inclusivity and producing intercultural media content across Europe. Across the region, media and diversity experts stress that diverse newsrooms are seen as key to building trust among different audiences, however, with the economic decline in journalism jobs available, the pool of applicants might shrink, leading to diverse candidates 'opting out' from the profession altogether (Borchardt et al., 2019, p. 11).

CHAPTER SUMMARY

Media structures and governance in Western and Northern Europe share broad commonalities, including a tradition of public service media and partisan press, absence of government interference, and strong journalistic professionalization and education. Despite these similarities, there is also a diverse heritage in terms of language, culture, and history. The interplay between these macro-level factors affects media development and journalism growth across the region, which consistently ranks at the top of the world in terms of media freedom and journalistic autonomy. Journalists in Western and Northern Europe, however, have not been immune to outside pressures, direct threats, and disinformation campaigns, especially in the age of social media.

DISCUSSION QUESTIONS

1. From what you have read in this chapter, how are the media systems across Western and Northern Europe similar or different? List your five key findings.
2. Journalists covering European Union politics and public affairs often have problems reaching audiences that go beyond the highly educated and media literate population living in urban centers. What are your suggestions for how journalists could 'localize' and/or 'universalize' stories about the European Union and its impact on all people in the region?
3. In the summer of 2015, the German government allowed more than one million asylum seekers from the Middle East and beyond to stay. Research how different media across Europe covered this political and humanitarian decision and note the main differences in media framing of the migration issue that you observe.
4. How has social media affected journalism across the region? Find current examples from a specific country to illustrate your answer.
5. In your opinion, what is the right balance between media freedom and media responsibility when it comes to covering sensitive topics such as religion?

BIBLIOGRAPHY

Borchardt, A., Lück, J., Kieslich, S., Schultz, T., & Simon, F. (2019). *Reuters Report, Talent and Diversity in the Media 2019*. Reuters Institute for the Study of Journalism.

Borelli, J. (2019). *Rebooting journalism: How media startups overcame the business model crisis?* Reuters Institute for the Study of Journalism.

Calvert, W. (2019, June 03). Google plans fourth Belgian data center for €600 million. *Data Centre Dynamics* www.datacenterdynamics.com/en/news/google-plans-600-million-on-fourth-belgian-data-center/

Doyle, G. (2002). *Media ownership: The economics and politics of convergence and concentration in the UK and European media*. SAGE.

Esser, F., & Umbricht, A. (2013). Competing models of journalism? Political affairs coverage in US, British, German, Swiss, French and Italian newspapers. *Journalism, 14*(8), 989–1007.

Esser, F., & Pfetsch, B. (Eds.). (2004). *Comparing political communication: Theories, cases, and challenges*. Cambridge University Press.

Esser, F. (1998). Editorial structures and work principles in British and German newsrooms. *European Journal of Communication, 13*(3), 375–405.

EU Commission. (2020). *Innovation and networks*. ec.europa.eu/inea/en/connecting-europe-facility

Fondren, E, Hamilton, J. M., & McCune, M. (2019). Parachute Journalism. In Vos, T. P. & Hanusch, F. (Eds.), *International Encyclopedia of Journalism Studies* (pp.1–5). Wiley Blackwell.

Hallin, D. C., & Mancini, P. (2004). *Comparing media systems: Three models of media and politics*. Cambridge University Press.

Hanitzsch, T., Hanusch, F., Ramaprasad, J., & De Beer, A. S. (Eds.). (2019). *Worlds of journalism: Journalistic cultures around the globe.* Columbia University Press.

Hanitzsch, T., Hanusch, F., Mellado, C., Anikina, M., Berganza, R., Cangoz, I., . . . & Virginia Moreira, S. (2011). Mapping journalism cultures across nations: A comparative study of 18 countries. *Journalism Studies, 12*(3), 273–293.

Internetworldstats. (2020). *Internet in Europe Stats.* www.internetworldstats.com/stats4.htm

Martens, B., Aguiar, L., Gomez-Herrera, E., & Mueller-Langer, F. (2018). *The digital transformation of news media and the rise of disinformation and fake news.* RC Digital Economy Working Paper, No. 2018–02. Joint Research Centre Technical Reports.

Newman, N., Fletcher, R., Schulz, A., Andı S., & Nielsen, R. (2020). *Reuters Institute Digital News Report 2020.* Reuters Institute for the Study of Journalism.

Örnebring, H., & Mellado, C. (2018). Valued skills among journalists: An exploratory comparison of six European nations. *Journalism, 19*(4), 445–463.

Örnebring, H. (2009). *Comparative European journalism: The state of current research.* University of Oxford, Reuters Institute for the Study of Journalism.

Preston, P. (2009). *Making the news. Journalism and news cultures in Europe.* Routledge.

Strömbäck, J., Shehata, A., & Dimitrova, D. V. (2008). Framing the Mohammad cartoons issue: A cross-cultural comparison of Swedish and US press, *Global Media and Communication, 4*(2), 117–138.

Van Dalen, A., De Vreese, C. H., & Albæk, E. (2012). Different roles, different content? A four-country comparison of the role conceptions and reporting style of political journalists. *Journalism, 13*(7), 903–922.

12

Media in Asia and the Pacific

Nakho Kim

While it is not easy to draw an all-encompassing picture for journalism in the Asia-Pacific region, due to its sheer size and diversity, it can be argued that many practices in Asian journalism are rooted in *postcolonial* experiences. As such, discussions about Asian journalism have typically involved the notion of *development journalism*, which extends into debates about unique Asian values that are sometimes used to justify different forms of state control over journalistic practices. The ideas that journalism should be used to actively help national development and that journalists should act as activists for democratization are common for the region. The Internet era also boosted investigative journalism trends and ushered the proliferation of citizen-driven alternative journalism.

JOURNALISM IN THE ASIA-PACIFIC REGION

When doing a quick Internet search for "journalism in Asia" in the English language, the top results usually center around one overarching theme, which is journalists under attack. It may be about censorship in China or the downright oppression by the Laotian government, painting a dire picture of an exotic region that, by and large, lacks vibrant free press systems. If we wish to encounter information on how journalism work gets done in Asia, more specific search terms are needed. These include keywords such as how the news media industry is structured; what kinds of policies other than "government censorship" are in place; and most of all, how journalism work impacts those societies.

This may give the Asia-Pacific Region an unexpectedly marginalized status, considering that almost two-thirds of the world's total population lives in Asia and that the continent includes some of the most industrially and economically advanced nations in the world. Even when we narrow down the focus to the news industry, several of the most read news outlets in the world operate from Asia. With its high-density population, it is no surprise that India boasts some big numbers in the news industry, publishing four of the top ten highest circulated newspapers in the world as of 2019. But even with a smaller population of 126 million and amid global trends of shrinking newspaper circulation, Japan's two largest newspapers, the

Yomiuri Shimbun and the *Asahi Shimbun* had a noteworthy daily circulation of 8.1 million and 5.6 million each in 2018 (Newman et al., 2019).

Much of the news we get about that region is based on coverage produced by local journalism organizations or at least heavily influenced by the local practices of journalistic work. If we want to make better sense of news in the Asia-Pacific region, it is necessary to explore their news media systems as an essential context, just like it would be quite hard to understand political news in the United States, if we are not aware of the highly partisan cable news channels and talk radio.

This chapter offers an overview of basic trends and characteristics of journalism practice in the Asia-Pacific region. First, it provides an overview of Asia and reasons why we can categorize it as a region, touching upon postcolonial background. Second, it explores how such historical experiences gave rise to a development journalism trend and a debate around what unique Asian values that journalism should follow. We will trace how these developments led to systems of government and journalism relationships unfolding in more diverse ways than pure censorship. Third, we will touch on the other side of the same coin, which is the role of journalists as agents of democratization in society. Instead of acting as detached observers, the argument goes that journalists should be active advocates resisting authoritarian powerholders and advancing social progress and development. Fourth, the chapter outlines how fertile ground for alternative journalism grew in the mix, ranging from community media to online citizen journalism; and how online channels have been countered or even repurposed by local governments, as exemplified by the so-called public diplomacy initiatives.

DEFINING "ASIA-PACIFIC"

How do we define the Asia-Pacific region in terms of a dominant media system? Ideally, we will need to think in terms of regional commonalities that lead to patterns of journalistic practices, policies, and industry. This approach, namely first analyzing the journalism media environment of each nation, categorizing common patterns, and then finding clusters of such in regional areas, was used to develop a categorization in Hallin and Mancini's (2004) seminal work *Comparing Media Systems*. They used variables such as the structure of media markets, political parallelism, professionalization, and the role of the state, to yield three distinct news system models. However, their media models apply only to the geographical regions of Europe and North America.

Although this chapter aims to explain the Asia-Pacific as a whole, it is essential to note that common patterns in media systems for this region are less bound by geographic proximities, but more so by the social progression of each nation (see Figures 12.1 and 12.2). For example, let us take a look at East Asia, which roughly encompasses countries such as China, South Korea, North Korea, and Japan. In China, we can discover what would approximate the classic communist media model combined with commercialism. At the same time, in Japan, there is a highly industrialized and privatized system with a culturally authoritarian twist. South Korea can be seen as a dynamic media environment with conflicting pulls between development journalism ideas and democratization. At the same time, North Korea boasts a pure state-controlled system.

Other sub-regions are not any simpler. Southeast Asia offers an excellent example of how diverse political situations and economic conditions influence the news, even when it looks like they are similarly putting onerous regulations on journalism. The taboos of what may be

ASIA

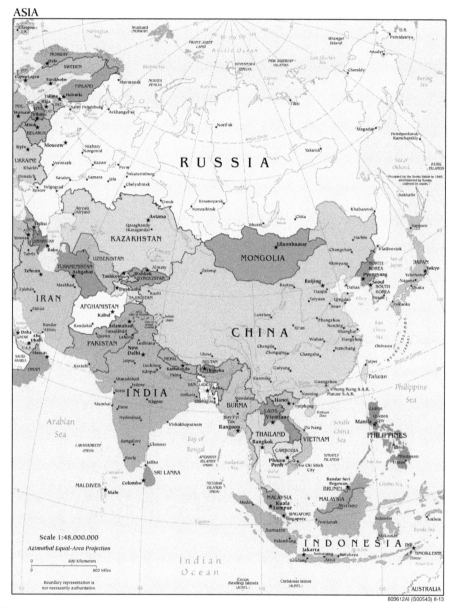

Figure 12.1.   Map of Asia. Source: CIA World Factbook

permitted in news coverage differ between the absolute monarchy in Brunei and the strict communist rule in Laos; resources for reporting differ between the poverty-ridden Timor and the highly developed Singapore. Within this diversity, more ambitious nations such as Thailand and Malaysia are actively trying to become network hubs for regional news production by bolstering their media infrastructure.

Sharing historical background does not necessarily result in similar media systems. The difference between Chinese culture-based societies such as authoritarian mainland China,

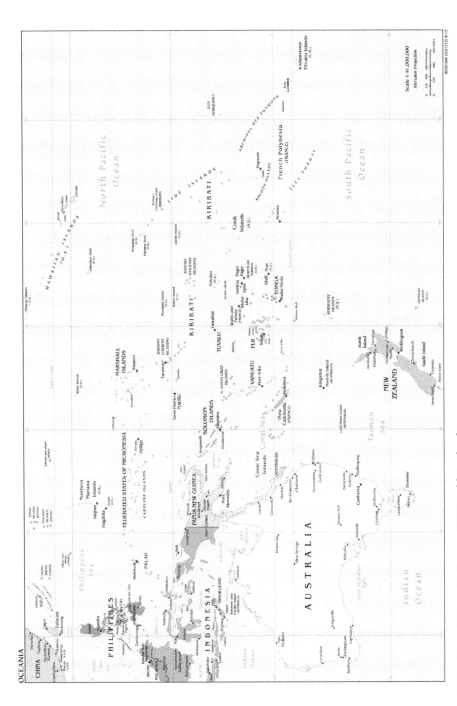

Figure 12.2. Map of Oceania. Source: CIA World Factbook

westernized Hong Kong, and Japan-influenced Taiwan could not be any starker. Sometimes language-based ethnicities can form their media sub-systems within a single nation, as exemplified by the Tamil-language media in India. Having made this disclaimer, let us proceed with the historical background that binds the Asia-Pacific region together, although, as we have shown above, the same seed led in different directions and, by extension, different conceptions of journalism across the region.

POSTCOLONIALISM: BRIEF HISTORICAL CONTEXT

It would be impractical to lay out several thousand years of history for every nation-state in the Asia-Pacific region that has developed stable and sophisticated social systems with strong cultural traditions. Instead, let us start from the point when many to most of those legacies were suddenly upended. In the late nineteenth to mid-twentieth centuries, many Western imperialist powers went forth taking control over Asian countries, motivated by the need for economic growth and propelled by modernized military prowess. As such, many to most nations in that region experienced formal or de facto colonialization or had to spend a considerable effort to thwart it. For example, India was colonized by the British, the Philippines by Spain and the United States, and Vietnam by the French. Though China was not formally colonized, it was still heavily exploited by the British. Japan, while attempting to avoid colonialization by Western powers, mimicked their imperialist philosophy. It became a colonizer by annexing Korea and trying to colonize parts of China as well by establishing a puppet regime in Manchuria. When Japan lost World War II it fell under semi-colonial rule by the United States for seven years. Only after the establishment of the United Nations in 1945, many nations became independent (United Nations, 2016).

This is where the concept of *postcolonialism* comes in. It is the idea that a liberated social entity is strongly influenced by the experience of having been colonized by others. It includes issues such as how the periods of exploitation skewed the social structure with lasting impact; how much of the advanced social institutions and processes planted by the colonial powers need to be reused or eliminated; and especially, how people should take action to overcome the historical pain and attempt to regain their sense of agency.

For many newly liberated nations in the region, the postcolonial project involved reconnecting with the rich cultural past of pre-colonialization while establishing a modernized system within the postwar world. While the specific approaches differed, a couple of common themes were there with varying levels of consensus. One is a strong desire for economic growth, and the other is pursuing national integration as part of rediscovering social identity. Unsurprisingly, the ways to achieve those goals took several different pathways. China chose to adopt a Leninist communism model with a pre-industrial tweak known as Maoism, radically severing ties with the historical past as exemplified in the populist movement "cultural revolution." India opted for a more open embrace of the British systems they were left with, while smaller countries such as South Korea and Singapore choosing a strongman-led rapid economic development.

The development of the journalistic environment in the region, such as professional norms, relationships with power holders, and industry structure, reflects this larger historical context. The countries in the region were propelled to devise new journalistic infrastructures in a relatively short period to become competitive with the rest of the world. These include the incorporation of universal (more often than not Western) journalistic norms, legal protection of press freedom, and business models that do not sacrifice independence. At the same time, the expectation was put on journalism that it should contribute to the larger social need for economic and political success, thus making it fit under the umbrella of development journalism.

DEVELOPMENT JOURNALISM

In postcolonial Asia, economic growth was often seen as a priority task for nation-building as prominently exemplified by Japan, South Korea, Singapore, and others. Once a society achieves some stability, the logical step would be to pursue initiatives to foster economic development and other social campaigns designed to increase national prosperity. The role of the media, especially journalism, in this sense would be to support the urgent common goal of the whole society by acting as a close partner to the state in those initiatives. Its function includes directly informing people about state initiatives as well as garnering popular support for them.

As such, several countries installed state-owned news outlets, especially in the form of TV channels with large news components. They were mostly not in the independent public service style as the BBC, but rather more directly under the influence of the current government. For example, Japan's NHK and South Korea's KBS are public channels that appear independent by being governed by a dedicated board, which is not a government agency. However, the majority of the board members are appointed by the government, making their independence dependent on the will of political actors. Other cases are more straightforward, with Hong Kong's RTHK being formally a government department, making it hard to oppose the official views on political matters.

Similarly, the IBC in the Philippines operates under the Presidential Communications Operations Office. It can go beyond a single channel, as is the case in Singapore, where free over-the-air TV is monopolized by MediaCorp, which is owned by a state investment agency. Though there are many cases where those public media outlets attempt to gain independence from political power in recent years by introducing new governance structures and legal protection, the progress is rather slow, as exemplified by Indonesia's TVRI and Thailand's TPBS.

The concept of development journalism reaches deep into the history of modernization theories. But in the Asian context, it was first openly promoted early on by organizations such as the Press Foundation of Asia (PFA) in 1967. To paraphrase their proclamation, it rested on the idea that journalism's role in a developing society is to inform people about the development processes that make their lives better. In this initial version, it was not advocating for authoritarian push. On the contrary, the PFA had several members who were proponents of press freedom and wanted to keep their organization funded by regional agencies and international foundations instead of the state government and built the independent news service *Depthnews* in 1968 to serve as a development news hub.

However, development journalism became an international focus in the West through the New World Information and Communication Order (NWICO) debate in the 1970s, which was spearheaded by the UNESCO and culminated in publishing the MacBride commission report in 1980 (see chapter 5 for more details). The report concluded that we need to build capacity in media and communication in developing countries through both infrastructure and human resource development and should put less focus on negative international news and instead focus on media communication for the development and preservation of cultural identity.

Many Western countries did not agree with those ideas since they were strong proponents of the "free flow of information" paradigm and opposed state-led models. However, it struck a chord in several Asian governments as a means to justify their current operations. It provided legitimacy to using state-governed news outlets to serve news that corresponds to nation-building priorities, such as the semi-planned economy and authoritarian political stability. Whereas the origin of Asian development journalism was about educating the people for development, this approach was more about the role of the state (Burrett & Kingston, 2019).

The justification made good use of the "preservation of cultural identity" argument in particular. To distinguish themselves from the Western journalism role model where journalists were supposed to hold powers to account by criticizing them, Asian journalism ethics needed to be defined as something else. As such, the argument was that the relationship between state and journalism should be more harmonious and collective-oriented because those are supposed to be the unique cultural characteristics of Asia (Mehra, 1989).

Defining Asian culture around harmony and collective-oriented conformity could raise some serious questions on a closer examination. Still, at its time, it was a practical solution to carve out a path for how a modern Asian society could reconcile development and democracy. The easiest way to maintain a strong focus on state-led development, which results in a tight grip on people without being considered as a dictatorship, is to argue that it is a unique Asian version of democratic culture, after all. Theorized by Singapore's Prime Minister Lee Kwan Yew and propelled by Malaysia's former Prime Minister Mahathir Mohamad, the idea was that there are unique Asian values that prioritize patriarchal family, community, and harmony, as a form of collective good. Such values would naturally affect the relationship between the press and government. Journalists would need to respect and yield the authority of political leaders; establishing media policies that minimize societal friction and unorderly criticism of the state would be desirable. Calling such practices undemocratic was positioned as an intrusion into Asian culture from a Western viewpoint. With this logic, regulation of media content, including censorship and other laws favoring political power holders, became justified. The newly established media system reflected this notion of journalism's role in society and also affected the public's expectation of the news media, especially public channels. It may be one of the reasons why international comparison surveys such as the annual *Reuters Digital News Report* consistently rank Asian countries low in terms of trust in news.

The most straightforward type of media control comes through direct governance of state enterprises, as is the case in communist countries such as Vietnam, Laos, and China. But in other cases, it takes more subtle forms. In Singapore, government regulation comes in the form of high-pressure policy guidelines. Even the Internet is censored through laws controlling political use. In 1996 when the Internet was still at an early stage of becoming a household service, Singapore was quick to legislate the Internet Code of Practice, a content guideline to prohibit online material that is "objectionable on the grounds of public interest, public morality, public order, public security, national harmony, or is otherwise prohibited by applicable Singapore laws." When it comes to monitoring online content, Asia countries also learn from one another. As described in a 2018 article in *Time* magazine, "most Southeast Asian states have steadily sacrificed freedoms in the name of stability, looking to China as a guiding model for information control" in the recent decade (Quackenbush et al., 2018).

Sometimes the pressure comes from cultural practices, as exemplified by Japan's notorious "Kisha club." Translated as the reporter's club, it is a long-standing tradition that a reporter can access official sources only by becoming a member in a highly restrictive pool. Due to its closed-circle characteristics, it is prone to promote self-censorship and exclude critical viewpoints against their partners. Although many Japanese journalists and editors have criticized this system, the government made efforts to keep it in place by restricting officials from direct contact with individual reporters.

CULTURAL IMPERIALISM AND MANGA

According to Encyclopedia Britannica, imperialism refers to the notion of a nation extending power over another nation and gaining political and economic control. Cultural imperialism is the idea that this pattern occurs also at the cultural level when a colonizer imposes its cultural values onto the colonized. This does not require political colonialization, but rather the dominance of and dependency on foreign media or cultural products, which can undermine local social norms and values. As such, recognizing the elements of cultural imperialism and overcoming them is considered an essential task in a postcolonial society.

The global influence of Manga, a Japanese style of comics, can be a good example to explore this concept. Comics have been recognized as symbols of cultural infiltration and ideological export, partly due to their seemingly low-brow popularity (*How to Read Donald Duck* by Dorfman & Mattelart [1975] is a good classic text to start with). But in the case of Manga, the progression was more layered.

The modern manga style was invented by Tezuka Osamu in post–World War II Japan, which was under a quasi-colonial rule by U.S. military forces. With a visual style strongly influenced by Disney and other American comics, he created immensely popular works such as *Tetsuwan Atom* that encouraged people to imagine a highly developed future Japan. Partly due to their active role in helping people to work toward rebuilding a war-torn country, Manga evolved into the quintessential Japanese popular culture and a huge entertainment media industry (as of 2018, around $3.96 billion in the domestic market).

For some Asian countries, however, Japan's growing influence was met with caution due to the history of colonialization. By extension, Manga was perceived as a vanguard of Japan's renewed imperialist motives, this time in the form of culture. A prominent example would be South Korea, a former colony of Japan, where legally licensed publishing of Manga started only in 1991. Manga had already influenced generations of local comics artists and had been popular following through pirated copies long before that. Still, it took time to work around the fear of cultural imperialism. Similarly, China prohibited import of Manga in 1995 to "protect domestic culture" (Wang, 2005) as a backlash to its growing popularity.

Another stage unfolded in the 2000s when Manga reached a breakthrough in North America and Europe in terms of market and cultural influence. The genre diversity, character development styles, and animation tie-in approach that the manga industry had perfected over the years finally gained a firm position in Western youth culture. Furthermore, Western manga fandom was quick to globalize through online spaces. This success promoted a vast expansion of manga publications in South and Southeast Asia, igniting another round of debates regarding cultural imperialism. Much focus was given to how to cultivate a domestic industry where local comics artists can find success against the globalized blockbuster manga franchises.

In all, the manga phenomenon demonstrates how postcolonial efforts can be more complex than simply cutting all ties with what previous colonizers, especially when it comes to cultural influences.

Rapid shifts in how the media function can happen as well, as the case of Hong Kong demonstrates. Hong Kong's news media had long been operating under the liberal British model while it was still under the colonial jurisdiction. Still, when their political status changed in 1997, they had to adapt to the pressure from mainland China. Over time, local officials and regulators were filled with stronger pro-China stances, who expanded on the regulatory ban, attack on alternative media, and ad removals. This trend took a more drastic turn, such as physical violence against news media personalities in connection with the democratic movement against Chinese governance. The annual press freedom ranking by Reporters Without Borders (RSF) for Hong Kong went from 18th in the world in 2002 to 61st in 2018, reflecting this trend.

In all, development journalism was initially intended to play a nation-building role in promoting rapid development, and maybe even constructing a unique cultural model of modernity. Later, however, it was also repurposed for government control and turn an authoritarian turn. So was development journalism a doomed concept, bound for undemocratic practices? Maybe not, as the next section shows.

JOURNALISTS AS AGENTS OF DEMOCRATIZATION

As the concept of an "Asian" value system remained hotly debated, the then-retired South Korean politician Kim Dae-Jung penned a lengthy essay in the magazine *Foreign Policy* titled "Is Culture Destiny? The Myth of Asia's Anti-Democratic Values" (Kim, 1994). Referencing Confucianism and other core Asian philosophies, he argued that Asian values are primarily about the moral obligation of the ruling class to a peaceful world. He added that, in traditional Asian societies, legitimacy comes from the bottom-up through the consent of the people, and that the Asian political systems are full of checks and balances.

If Asian values are centered around caring about the collective, and at the same time, keeping those in power accountable, it can be argued that journalists have a role to play as agents of democratization (Loo, 2019). Especially in societies that are perceived to have a more authoritarian political system, journalists can embrace the mandate to become social activists instead of detached observers, as is often the case in Western European news. Indeed, researchers have applied the media systems framework by Hallin and Mancini (2004) to analyze the South Korean journalism model and concluded that a "democratization model" needs to be introduced as a new category. After all, the political parallelism in that society is not simply about the news reflecting the messages of their preferred political parties; instead, mainstream news media have actively influenced parties and civil society.

Unsurprisingly, pursuing such a democratization role is met with oppression in various nations. In the annual RSF reports on press freedom, several Asian nations rank quite low on the scale, with North Korea landing in 180th place, which is the lowest ranking possible, due to the ironclad state monopoly of all information. China fared only slightly better in 176th place, with its large-scale censorship of adversarial political content and imprisonment of professional and citizen journalists. Even worse, half of the sixty-two deaths of journalists worldwide in 2018 happened in Asia.

Some authoritarian Asian regimes adopted an even more fundamental approach, which was to delegitimize the democratization work of journalists. In Cambodia, the democracy-leaning newspaper *The Cambodia Daily* was shut down in 2016 under the government's claim that they owed $6.3 million in unpaid taxes, while another independent newspaper was sold off to people with government ties. Myanmar, which was under international criticism due to its oppressive treatment of the Rohingya people, utilized the Unlawful Association Act, which prohibits communication with the "rebels" to penalize reporting from the conflict zone.

Another striking example is the media environment in the Philippines under the Duterte administration. With a fair amount of popular support, the government took a proactive approach, such as hiring networks of social media influencers to fill the social discourse with favorable opinions and delegitimizing journalists criticizing the government (Ong & Cabañes, 2018). The same team was also tasked with mobilizing online trolls to mock and threaten journalists. In 2016, the news site *Rappler* undertook an investigation into this government-sponsored online disinformation campaign. In return, *Rappler* was sued with ownership irregularity and tax evasion, to dissolve the organization. Also, the government sued the editor-in-chief, Maria Ressa, on the grounds of criminal "cyberlibel" for a news article published in 2012 and ruled her guilty in 2020.

On the other hand, success cases of the role of Asian journalism in democratization exist as well, as evidenced in the Presidential impeachment in South Korea in 2016. Impeaching the highest executive official through an institutional process is typically only possible with an overwhelming public consensus, which is rarely reached in a relatively stable society with high levels of political polarization and low trust in journalism. South Korea was already a highly divided society with a stable, conservative base, and then-president Park's approval never sunk below 30 percent during the first three years despite policy missteps. Public trust in news media was only in the lower range of 20 percent. Despite such conditions, the cable TV news station JTBC provided an impactful expose of government corruption, in a series of back-and-forth with the government's attempted countermeasures. The prolonged public debate ignited massive protests, which led to regime change.

Championing for the people is not only about fighting government powers, but also about giving a voice to minorities. New Zealand is a model case in this regard, with its attention on the indigenous people. The news media landscape of New Zealand is largely similar to the British model, in that the regulations are liberal, and there is a BBC-like public network managed by the government. However, a significant number of news outlets have been established to serve the Maori population over time, with the first Maori-language radio station had started in 1988 and TV in 2004. Moreover, government-led projects such as the *Maori media Sector Shift* are in place to improve indigenous media.

Journalism acting as a champion of democracy can appear in a rather populist position, but it can also be an unapologetically elitist one. In a way, this position is still connected to the idea of development, but in terms of achieving more developed democratic rights beyond mere economic wealth. For this reason, some scholars consider the democratization norm in Asian journalism as yet another category of development journalism (see Bromley & Romano, 2012; Richstad, 2000).

Such elitist elements can become a weakness in an Internet-based hyperconnected media environment where people feel empowered to champion themselves as part of "direct" democracy. Traditional functions of journalists such as agenda-setting and framing can be perceived as an intrusion by the self-serving elites. This mechanism, when combined with popular development-oriented nationalistic sentiments and government initiatives, can manifest in trends such as China's public diplomacy efforts globally. Public diplomacy is an umbrella term used to describe communication by government, non-government organizations, and individuals that aims to achieve diplomatic effects, most notably constructing a favorable image of the country's actions (see Chapters 14 and 15 for more details). Although the Chinese government created a public diplomacy department in 2004 and managed several initiatives, much of the actual work in the information campaigns is primarily done by ordinary people connected on social media wishing to express nationalistic sentiments. In this activism, there is not a lot of room for traditional investigative reporting with a democratization norm, which may dig out uncomfortable truths about one's society. This clash between autocratic and democratic values raises the question of how to conduct public-interest journalism by actively incorporating the voices of the people and still doing good journalistic work, building on the strong tradition of alternative journalism in the region.

ALTERNATIVE JOURNALISM IN ASIA

For many Asian postcolonial countries, establishing a news media environment was a development project that needed to be done efficiently (Anand, 2018). Whether they were state-led public outlets or large commercial media companies, often the task was to apply modern Western media models as fast as possible while enabling state regulations. Developing ethical traditions and solidifying them into stable practices was not an option. If the government chose to take an authoritarian approach toward traditional media, critical voices were also muffled.

Moreover, such a catch-up approach was not favorable to the representation of marginalized geographic and demographic groups. For example, despite having a huge media industry, non-Hindi-speaking ethnicities tend to have less news coverage. Regional journalism in South Korea remains underdeveloped, with most industry resources concentrated on national media.

The situation did change with the advent of more affordable networking capabilities and equipment, first through local community radio, which is easy to set up and produce highly localized content. In India, *Namma Dhwani* and *Radio Ujjas* were launched around 2000 by NGOs, carrying radio news with topics of local development and rural female empowerment. The *Tambuli Project* in the Philippines in the 1990s combined community radio with printed material and even public blackboards to provide better access to news for rural communities. Community radio, such as *Koori Radio,* helped represent indigenous people in Australia. Even today, low-power local radio news plays an important role in rural parts of Indonesia and Thailand.

The Internet and mobile phones followed. The Internet user population in Asia is large, though access is far from being equally distributed among countries. Countries like South Korea and Singapore ran state-level initiatives to provide affordable broadband early on. Latecomers like China caught up quickly, reaching 850 million users as of 2019. Other technology industry centers such as India and Taiwan were also quick to establish national policies to expand their online and mobile user base. However, some countries in the region have a much lower penetration rate due to political regulations such as in Myanmar and North Korea, or simply due to the prohibitively high cost relative to household income.

As technology use increased, many news organizations in the region were quick to start posting articles produced for mainstream media on their websites. Opportunities for alternative journalism emerged shortly after as online producers could circumvent government control in countries with tight regulations. Singapore's *Sintercom,* for example, was an online news community launched in 1994 that attempted to bypass government interference to provide free-flowing news until it eventually was sued by the government and shut down in 2001. Another prominent example is *Ohmynews*, a South Korean news site launched in 2000 that mostly publishes articles written by outside contributors (per its catchphrase, "every citizen is a reporter"). It is regarded as a pioneering case of citizen journalism that quickly became hugely influential. Its success was partly based on the high broadband penetration and the growth of online user culture in that country at that time, but also because it was a liberal-leaning alternative to the conservative newspapers that comprised the majority of the market. A similar case with immense popularity among the South Korean public was the political news podcasts like *Nakkomsu* in the latter half of the 2010s.

However, it is difficult to copy a successful model from one country to another. In 2006, the Japanese firm *Softbank* invested heavily in launching *Ohmynews Japan* in hopes of filling a similar demand. Japan at the time was also dominated by conservative giants in the newspaper market so a platform for fresh voices was largely missing while the younger generation was heavily connected online. However, the new site struggled from the start. Within a year, the citizen journalism aspect was scrapped, and the site shut down after two years. Another homegrown project was the citizen journalism site *JanJan*, which had a smaller operation and focused more narrowly on social issues, which lasted significantly longer until 2010. *Buzzfeed Japan* was launched in 2015 as a collaboration between *Buzzfeed* and *Yahoo! Japan*. Another prominent project is the *Waseda Chronicle*, claiming itself to be a "journalism NGO." It was founded by the journalists behind the Fukushima meltdown special coverage at the mainstream newspaper *Asahi Shimbun*.

NGO funding often provides revenue for online news outlets. Taiwan, for instance, has grown a vibrant news media market ever since martial law ended in 1987. The online news site *The Reporter* was launched with the goal of independent investigative journalism in 2015, but they opted to operate with a decidedly not newsroom-like structure. Instead, they have issue-based teams, as a project-oriented NGO would operate. Their revenues come from the publication of books based on their articles and support from the Reporter Cultural Foundation NGO.

The format and approach of alternative journalism can differ to meet the unique needs of the country they operate in. *Rappler* was launched in the Philippines in 2011 as a general news site with a focus on social media engagement. However, when the populist authoritarian Duterte government stepped into power, the media began specializing in exposing state-sponsored disinformation campaigns and fact-checking, despite political pressure.

Pursuing alternative news in online spaces happens even when specific media outlets do not exist as is the case in China. Because all news media fall under the regulatory jurisdiction of the Propaganda Department, it is impossible to have an outlet that has critical views of the government. If media operates from overseas to circumvent the control, it is met with the infamous "Great Firewall of China," an umbrella term for a set of legislative and technological measures to block access to outside content. As such, sometimes messages on social media and other online forums become news outlets in a quasi-citizen journalism manner. This happened during the Wenchuan earthquake in 2008, for example, when official media did not have access to the disaster site, and people had to rely on live footage posted by Chinese citizens on social media instead. With the growing influence of social media, government control has sharpened. During the early days of the COVID-19 outbreak in Wuhan, a citizen journalist posted videos of temporary workers transporting deceased patients, claiming to the world that the situation is dire. Soon after, he suddenly disappeared from public view for two months, and afterward uploaded a new video saying that he was put on a "forced quarantine" (Kuo, 2020).

Although the Asia-Pacific region is too big and too diverse to allow easy generalizations, journalism practice by and large started from each nation's postcolonial experiences and their attempts to modernize and grow. That is why discussions about Asian journalism involve the notion of development journalism, which included the notion of unique Asian values. Unfortunately, the concept has also been used by powerholders to justify state regulation and control of the press in the name of collective-oriented harmony.

At the same time, Asian values and the goals of social development involve strengthening of democratic governance, which gives journalists the rationale for becoming active agents of democratization. In this environment, citizen journalism and other forms of alternative media offering diverse political viewpoints and serving marginalized communities have emerged. As technology use in the region grows, the role of online and social media journalism is expected to increase over time.

CHAPTER SUMMARY

The media in the Asian region can best be understood through a developmental journalism perspective. The region has been strongly influenced by the process of globalization and ongoing technological change, which has made the flow of information hard to control. Alternative news sites and investigative journalism enterprises continue to increase in numbers and popularity, especially among the younger generation. Concerns about cultural imperialism, Western influence, and the preservation of national identity remain pertinent across Asia and the Pacific.

DISCUSSION QUESTIONS

1. The "Asian values" argument has been used as a justification for authoritarian control over the press. Does it mean that there are no unique cultural differences that shape journalism work in the region?
2. If you are working in a Western news outlet and your job is to select news from media across the Asia-Pacific region, what should you consider when selecting your news sources?
3. What differences do you notice between an Asian news site and U.S.-based news site in the coverage of a certain issue—for example, COVID-19 or K-pop? After comparing them side-by-side, what can you tell about the state-media relationship?
4. Examine the trends in press freedom in the Asia-Pacific region over the past ten years. Which countries gained and lost ranking? Which political and economic events happened during that time that may have influenced such fluctuation?
5. How do the headlines and layout differ between an Asian-language news site and its English version? Discuss what may have led to those differences.

BIBLIOGRAPHY

Anand, V. E. (2018). Partner in Development: Development Journalism. In Anand, V. E., & Jayanthi, K. (Eds.), *A handbook of journalism: Media in the information age.* SAGE.

Bromley, M., & Romano, A. (Eds). (2012). *Journalism and democracy in Asia.* Taylor & Francis.

Burrett, T., & Kingston, J. (Eds.). (2019). *Press freedom in contemporary Asia.* Routledge.

Dorfman, A., & Mattelart, A. (1975). *How to read Donald Duck.* International General.

Hallin, D. C., & Mancini, P. (2004). *Comparing media systems: Three models of media and politics.* Cambridge University Press.

Kim, D. J. (1994). Is culture destiny?. *Foreign Affairs, 73*(6), 189.

Kuo, L. (2020, April 22). Missing Wuhan citizen journalist reappears after two months. *The Guardian.*

Loo, E. (2019). Reading "Asian Values" into Journalism Practices in Asia. In *Oxford research encyclopedia of communication.* Oxford University Press. doi.org/10.1093/acrefore/9780190228613.013.781

Mehra, A. (Ed.). (1989). *Press systems in ASEAN states.* Asian Mass Communication Research and Information Centre.

Newman, N., Fletcher, R., Kalogeropoulos, A., & Nielsen, R. (2019). *Reuters Institute Digital News Report 2019.* Reuters Institute for the Study of Journalism. reutersinstitute.politics.ox.ac.uk/sites/default/files/inline-files/DNR_2019_FINAL_27_08_2019.pdf

Ong, J. C., & Cabañes, J. V. A. (2018). *Architects of networked disinformation: Behind the scenes of troll accounts and fake news production in the Philippines.* The Newton Tech4dev Network.

Quackenbush, C., Meixler, E., Solomon, F., Regan, H., Hincks, J., Barron, L, & Haynes, S. (2018, June 21). Press freedom is under attack across Southeast Asia. Meet the journalists fighting back. *Time.* time.com/longform/press-freedom-southeast-asia/

Richstad, J. (2000). Asian journalism in the twentieth century, *Journalism Studies, 1*(2), 273–284.

United Nations. (2016). *Decolonization.* Welcome to the United Nations. www.un.org/en/sections/issues-depth/decolonization/index.html

Wang, Y. (2005). *The dissemination of Japanese manga in China: The interplay of culture and social transformation in post reform period.* (Master's thesis). Lund University, Lund, Sweden.

13

Media in Latin America

Manuel Alejandro Guerrero

Latin America is a land of strong contrasts, not only because of its rich geographical diversity, but also because of stark inequalities. In the region, one can find some of the largest modern urban centers alongside inaccessible rural communities that lack the most essential public services, as well as some of the largest income disparities in the world, with functioning democracies alongside authoritarian rule.

Latin America stretches from the U.S.-Mexican border in the north to Tierra del Fuego in the Chilean and Argentinian Antarctic in the South, and comprises twenty countries without considering the Anglophone and Dutch-speaking nations, but only those whose predominant languages are Spanish, Portuguese, and French (Mignolo, 2005). In general, the region shares common historical and cultural traits, having been part of the Spanish and Portuguese empires and achieving independence after the Napoleonic wars in Europe (See Figure 13.1 and Figure 13.2). By the second half of the twentieth century, most countries in the region lean toward liberal democracy. However, democratic practice has been uneven, since during the second part of the twentieth century most countries experienced different forms of authoritarianism, and one of them, Cuba, a Communist regime still in place. Moreover, between the 1960s and the late 1980s, harsh military dictatorships were established in some of these countries, including Brazil, Argentina, Chile, Peru, Guatemala, and Uruguay. By the 1980s, a wave of transitions away from authoritarian rule hit the region. These trends re-inaugurated electoral competition, party politics, voting rights, and—most relevant to this chapter—pluralistic arenas of political debate in which media and journalism played important roles.

Democratic consolidation has been uneven in the region. In most countries, political competition, regular elections, and relatively pluralistic access to power are observed. Nevertheless, the effectiveness of the rule of law, accountability, and transparency in government are still evolving. Consequently, human rights abuses, political and corporate corruption, and different forms of violence are still common across the region.

Latin America has experienced economic growth in the twenty-first century, although it has slowed down due to lack of investment, low productivity growth, and weak infrastructure, coupled with uncertainty in the business climate (Werner, 2020). In general, the region has not been able to offer solid and sustained solutions to its most evident problem: inequality.

CENTRAL AMERICA AND THE CARIBBEAN

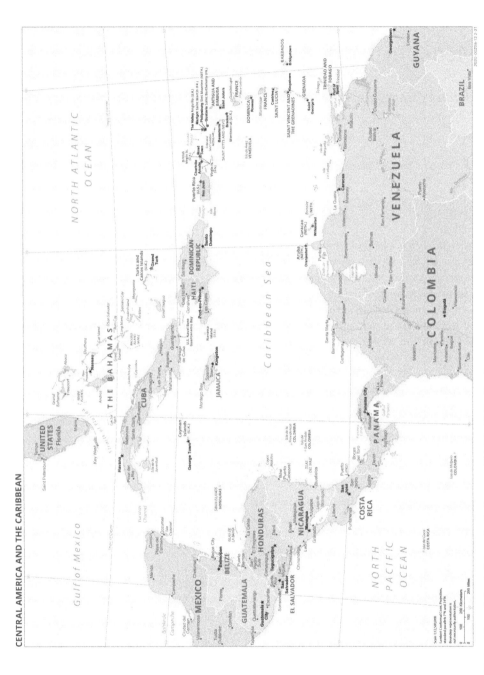

Figure 13.1.   Map of Central America*. Source: CIA World Factbook

*Even though geographically Mexico is part of North America, it is included here based on historical and cultural similarities across the Latin American region.

SOUTH AMERICA

Figure 13.2. Map of South America. Source: CIA World Factbook

In strict economic terms, about 30 percent of the population lives under the poverty line and the top 10 percent have income levels that are seventy times larger than those of the bottom 10 percent (CEPAL, 2019). Such disparities are also reflected in racial terms in several countries, and in gender terms in most of them, which helps to preserve existing cultural and social inequalities.

Social unrest and mobilization have also increased over time, fostered by more participatory younger generations and facilitated by the widening reach of digital technologies. As in many parts of the world, dissatisfaction with the establishment and traditional politics has been on the rise, but this is not necessarily good news for democracy in Latin America. In this respect, the level of "satisfaction with democracy" has been steadily declining from 44 percent in 2008 to only 24 percent in 2018 (Informe Latinobarómetro, 2018, 2019). At the same time, populism has added stronger pressures on democracy, offering short-term solutions based on personal leadership and contributing to increased polarization. These trends pose important challenges to the media, especially when adding to the equation high levels of anti-press violence coming both from politics and organized crime.

THE IMPACT OF THE POLITICAL SYSTEM ON MEDIA AND JOURNALISM

Following Hallin and Mancini's (2004) assertion that political systems broadly shape the media landscape, their impact in Latin America can be assessed according to the following criteria: media freedom, access to information, and journalistic independence and performance.

Media Freedom

In the constitutional texts of all Latin American countries—including Cuba—freedom of speech is recognized, as in most Western countries, not as an absolute right, but subject to certain restrictions regarding time, place, and manner, though not regarding political content. Nevertheless, in countries that experienced authoritarian rule, secondary regulations, executive ordinances, and criminal codes exist to censor freedom of speech and the press. Although some of these regulations have been abolished or are in the process of being replaced, there are still some gray areas that, coupled with the ineffective application of new laws, end up challenging the scope of media freedom and journalistic performance.

For the printed press, there are no licenses for publishing, though some countries require registration in public offices and ministries. In the case of broadcasting, according to a UNESCO's report on freedom of expression, Latin America has moved into the adoption of more transparent and clearer criteria for allocating licenses (UNESCO, 2018). Also, most countries have established independent broadcast regulators that are usually part of broader telecommunications authorities. However, the region's contrasts are evident in these aspects as well. For instance, in spite of the general trends to openness and transparency, there are still some countries, like Venezuela, Nicaragua, and to a lesser degree Bolivia, where the process of issuing licenses and the criteria for revoking them are dependent more on the government's will to silence critical voices than on objective and technical aspects. But if in these countries, governments have used regulation to exert pressures on their critics, in other countries like Brazil or Mexico, the broadcast and telecommunications regulatory agencies have been under strong influence not from politics, but from the corporations they are supposed to oversee.

With the implicit acceptance of local governments, these agencies have applied the law—or exempted its application—in ways opportune to the corporations and not necessarily to the public interest.

Besides licensing, another resource used by governments to favor or punish the media for their editorial stance has been through state subsidies and official advertising. In most countries, there are no specific limits to the amount of public money that could be destined to this sort of support, nor on how to allocate such resources to the media. In Colombia, the Fundación para la Libertad de Prensa (Foundation for Freedom of the Press, FLIP) has established that this kind of advertising serves as an indirect mechanism for censorship (La FLIP, 2018). In Brazil, President Jair Bolsonaro has threatened critical media with a ban on public funding (Veiga, 2020). Even in countries where there are criteria to limit the political use of state funding, like Argentina and recently Mexico, these public resources are allocated to only a handful media organizations without clear explanations. In Uruguay, a more comprehensive legislation to reduce discretion in public resource allocation was approved by the Chamber of Deputies, but not by the Senate, showing that, in the end, political interests do not want to lose their leverage on the media. Chile seems to be an exception, since early in 2020 it approved measures to increase transparency for allocating public funds (Henríquez & Wolfersdorff, 2019).

Another aspect where the political system has affected media freedom has to do with the legal status of community media, especially community radio stations. Latin America has been a pioneer in the development of community radio, so it is no surprise that the World Association for Community Radios was founded there in 1990. These are not-for-profit stations whose programming aims to benefit the development of a specific community. In Latin America, many community radios are rural and, in countries like Mexico, Guatemala, Peru, or Bolivia an important number of them also transmit in different local native languages. Although there have been reforms to acknowledge the legal existence of these types of radios, for years they operated not only without legal recognition, but with the explicit opposition of commercial private broadcasters who defined them as "pirate stations" since they lacked licenses. These stations have played an important role in areas where access to other media has been difficult and use their content to promote local traditions and identity and uncover local abuse of power, exploitation of natural resources, and the expansion of organized crime. In countries where the rule of law is weak, community radio collaborators—usually unpaid members of the community they serve—are still harassed, threatened, and even murdered when reporting on those issues, as has occurred in Brazil, Guatemala, and Mexico.

Another legal tool used to curtail media freedom has been the use of criminal codes for defamation lawsuits. Until recently, defamation was punishable by prison in most Latin American countries and was used effectively by authoritarian rulers. In the past decade, Mexico, Argentina, and El Salvador have decriminalized cases regarding freedom of speech, putting them under civil law. Other countries are now in the process of decriminalizing defamation, and only four countries—Brazil, Cuba, Venezuela, and Ecuador—still keep the criminalization of defamation. In Ecuador, for example, any information that may be considered offensive, even cartoons, is open to sanction and the government has the legal prerogative order to stop the publication of any information in the name of public interest.

Access to Information

According to the Global Open Data Index (2018), more than half of the countries in the region provide effective access to public information, as measured by fifteen criteria including government budget, government spending, procurement, company registration, electoral results, and national statistics. Cuba, Venezuela, and Nicaragua are at the extreme of opacity, providing almost no information to the public, as compared to Brazil, Chile, Mexico, Uruguay, Colombia, and Argentina that provide most of the information considered by the index. Also, most of the countries have passed public information and transparency laws, except Cuba, Costa Rica, Bolivia, and Venezuela. Moreover, according to the Global Right to Information Center Index, Latin America has some of the best rights to information laws, Mexico's being number one, after analyzing more than one hundred laws of the kind around the world (Nalvarte, 2017).

In spite of this progress, in some countries, the problem lies not only in the laws themselves, but in specific actions that governments take to obstruct effective access to information through indirect means. Though Latin American is not the region whose governments lead the requests of content removal from Internet and social digital networks, their number has been on the rise. While the number of removal requests on Twitter amounted to forty-nine in 2014, it rose to ninety-seven in 2017, 101 in 2018, and sixty-four in the period between January and July 2019, according to Twitter's Transparency Report (Twitter Transparency Report, 2020). These sorts of requests for Google typically amount to one digit figures per year in most countries, except for Argentina (1055 in 2017; 1239 in 2018; and 1679 in 2019) and Brazil (2384 in 2017; 3720 in 2018; and 6348 in 2019), whose figures have increased year by year (Google Transparency Report, 2020). Recently, important debates have emerged regarding the "Right To Be Forgotten" (RTBF), which while based on human rights, the UNESCO's Report on Freedom of Expression and Media Development underlines two aspects of concern with enacting RTBF regulation: "firstly, the application of the principle of non-intermediary liability for online content that they have not produced; secondly, to deal with the tensions between the right to protect personal data, privacy and reputation of Internet users, while also protecting freedom of expression and the right to access information" (UNESCO, 2018, 9). This second preoccupation becomes relevant in the preservation of history regarding human rights abuses under past military dictatorships that have, in many cases, been given amnesty.

Journalistic Independence and Performance

Latin America's contrasting realities also define the conditions of journalistic performance. On one extreme, countries like Uruguay and Costa Rica provide a context in which independent and professional journalism flourishes. On the other, countries like Venezuela openly prosecute and imprison journalists critical to the regime. Another country in the region—Mexico—was labeled as one of the most dangerous countries in the world for journalists due to the number of unsolved murders. In a recent report, Reporters Without Borders underlines the increasing hostility in Latin America, where journalists constantly experience different forms of intimidation (RSF Index, 2020). This situation can be explained, in part, by the ineffective rule of law. Other reasons include discrediting critical journalism by governmental officials, unchecked police violence, digital attacks such as hacking and trolling, and the collusion between political actors and organized crime.

In countries like Venezuela, Brazil, Nicaragua, Mexico, El Salvador, and until recently, Bolivia, it has been an increasingly common practice that the heads of government themselves discredit the work of critical journalism, and even refer to specific journalists by name. President Bolsonaro of Brazil has frequently insulted and humiliated journalists, especially female journalists, who have been critical of his administration. In Mexico, President López Obrador has repeated that critical journalism is serving obscure interests and has referred to specific journalists by name as members of "a conservative mafia" (*Mafia del Poder*) that opposes his political project in favor of the poor. In El Salvador, President Bukele, an intense Twitter user, mocks and attacks his critics through this platform almost daily. These sorts of criticisms have been feeding an atmosphere of hate, polarization, and mistrust, and have enabled these presidents' followers to use social media to orchestrate attacks on journalists and critical media outlets (Rogers, 2020). Furthermore, in the case of Venezuela and Nicaragua, critical journalists have not only been fired from their jobs, but many have been put under surveillance by the state intelligence services and some have even been arbitrarily detained. In Nicaragua, the directorate of the news organization Confidential—one of the most prestigious in Central America—had to flee into exile in 2018 after the media's offices were raided by government security forces. Additionally, foreign correspondents have been expelled from Venezuela, and it is not uncommon for critical media outlets in this country to experience Internet shutdowns and blocking of their web services.

Also, episodic violence against journalists covering demonstrations and rallies has gone unchecked and has not been properly investigated. Recent cases where journalists covering public demonstrations of different sorts—against price increase of public transportation in Chile, against gender violence in Mexico, and in the cases of contested elections in Argentina and Bolivia—have suffered from police aggression, without such cases being properly sanctioned by the authorities.

Cyber-bullying and online hacking have also become more frequent in some countries in the region as independent journalism has started using digital platforms as publishing alternatives to their stories, especially those related to corruption, abuse of power, and organized crime. In countries where most conventional media have been closely tied to political power or where media property concentration is higher, alternative media organizations have emerged, most of them digitally based, focused on investigative reporting, and mostly lead by journalists. Brazil, Colombia, Peru, Guatemala, Mexico, El Salvador, Argentina, and Honduras offer interesting examples of these sorts of media organizations, which are usually dependent on subscriptions and/or support from national and international donor organizations. A number of investigative journalists have faced online harassment and hacking.

This situation is especially worrying in a region considered to be the deadliest for journalists, where an average of ninety journalist per year have been murdered, according to the Observatory of Killed Journalists (2020). The Observatory concludes that most of the cases in which journalists have been harassed, threatened, attacked, and murdered relate to the coverage of local affairs regarding political power abuse, corruption, and crime, as some other studies have already shown (Rafsky, 2014). The high rate of journalists' murders in the region results mostly from impunity, since the authorities fail to carry on an adequate investigation (Article 19, 2019; Asmman, 2018). According to some estimates, only 11 percent of these cases are resolved (UNESCO, 2018). The Committee to Protect Journalists (CPJ) establishes that the worsts cases in the region occur in Mexico, Brazil, and Colombia (Witchel, 2018). Besides high murder rates, non-fatal attacks on journalists have also increased over time, including online harassment, death threats, abductions, beatings and torture, illegal detention, and theft and destruction of equipment and infrastructure (UNESCO, 2018). Reasons for this impunity include corruption of law enforcement agencies, deficient justice systems, and, most of all, the collusion between politics and organized crime (RSF Report on Journalists, 2018). The regions where journalists are most vulnerable are those located in drug trafficking corridors as well as borderline zones (Witchel, 2018).

In summary, media freedom in the region is curtailed through direct government action and indirect legal measures, in spite of constitutional precepts granting freedom of the press. Some governments in Latin America have also hindered access to information in spite of the laws. All of these, combined with ineffective protections for journalists in many countries, lead to tolerating anti-press violence, either from organized crime, political actors, or their collusion. This limits the watchdog role of journalism and media independence in the region.

THE EFFECTS OF THE ECONOMY ON MEDIA AND JOURNALISM

The twentieth century brought about the expansion of mass media that accompanied mass industrialized culture and facilitated media concentration. Authors like Bagdikian (2004) have shown how property concentration in international media markets has been expanding at an impressive speed, transforming large corporations into gigantic multinationals difficult to oversee and tax, with serious risks to democratic societies (Baker, 2007). Latin America—with a predominantly private and commercial media business model—has not been alien to such processes, where its own large corporations have developed a strong relationship with political power. An important factor that has preserved this relationship is the use of discretionary state funds, which allows government officials to control the media through discretionary control of public finances—a significant source of media revenue, especially in countries with small economies.

Historically, in most countries, the most important role of printed press has been the inter-mediation of interests among different groups of the economic and political elites. This is a reason why newspapers play an important role in shaping public debates and discussion may affect public opinion. Broadcast media, while also close to political groups, have been mostly oriented toward mass consumption of entertainment, though newscasts have always been present. Studies show that TV newscasts are the most popular source for news and informa-tion in the region (Alcántara, Buquet, & Tagina, 2018), though in general, radio is still the medium with the highest penetration and consumption (UNESCO, 2018). The ties between media organizations and political interests have ended up distorting the watchdog function of news media in several cases (Guerrero, 2014). However, it is not that watchdog journalism is absent, but that the unveiling of corruption and scandals in conventional media responds more to their realignment with certain political interests than to editorial decisions taken in favor of the public interest. Recently, Observacom (2019), a leading NGO reporting on media concentration and freedom of expression in Latin America, published a report about nine cases (from Colombia, Argentina, Brazil, Chile, Guatemala, Mexico, Nicaragua, Peru, and Uruguay) where media concentration and the interests of media owners negatively affected the performance of professional and independent journalism.

During the 1980s and 1990s, as a result of the Western neoliberal wave, Latin America entered into a stage of strong economic liberalization coupled by deregulation and privatiza-tion policies. These trends did not promote more plural and competitive media markets, but larger concentration of ownership (Mastrini, 2019). The changes in policy benefited the largest traditional media groups, since they were able to take an important technological leap and consolidated their market positions, as in Peru, Argentina, Brazil, or Chile. Moreover, the arrival of new political elites in the new competitive electoral arenas as a consequence of the transitions from authoritarian rule did not change the old property structures and, instead, forged new alliances between different political groups and the traditional media elites, as in Mexico, Colombia, and Central America.

Recently, many countries have adopted new regulations that try to limit media and tele-communications concentration. In Argentina, Uruguay, Brazil, and Ecuador, these regulations prevent or limit cross-ownership, since they equate media and content diversity with owner-ship plurality, while in Mexico, the regulation focuses on anti-trust principles and the promo-tion of market competition (UNESCO, 2018).

Conventional news media in Latin America are experiencing difficult times—as is the news industry around the world—due to the changes in economic structures and business models. The explosive growth of a wide variety of platforms and sites providing all sorts of content—including information—has proved deeply challenging to most traditional media organiza-tions in the region, especially in those countries where commercial advertising markets have not been strong enough to sustain a large variety of outlets without state aid. The consequent fragmentation of content consumption brought about by digital technologies has also proved challenging to subscription-based models that some outlets have put to test with ambigu-ous results. What has become evident is the reduction of the traditional news hole and the favoring of more "attractive" formats and soft-news at the expense of investigative reporting. There have also been significant reductions in newsroom personnel and deteriorating work-ing conditions for many journalists. The fewer job opportunities keep wages low and many journalists end up working for different employers at the same time or fulfilling multiple roles in the same organization.

In summary, both historical trends and recent transformations of the economic structure have affected media and journalistic performance in Latin America. Ownership concentration has become higher in the region since the market liberalization and deregulatory reforms of the late 1980s and 1990s. Moreover, the close relations between traditional media elites and political actors have affected the watchdog role of the media, either by not properly covering certain issues or by being silent when the commercial and political interests of the owners are at risk. However, some countries have approved legislation to limit media concentration. Also, the transformation of the global economy has affected the financial viability of traditional media, since the advertising markets have moved into the digital world. The consequences for the news media include reduction of spaces dedicated to certain journalistic genres, increase in soft-news publications, reduction of newsroom personnel, and deterioration of the journalists' working conditions. The situation poses challenges for conventional media and journalists. For the media, the options are either making stronger efforts to improve their journalistic coverage so prestige may consolidate their bases for advertisers and subscriptions, or become more dependent on state aid at the cost of losing further independence. For journalists, the options are either staying within media organizations in increasingly fragile conditions, or continuing to explore the possibilities brought by the digital revolution for publishing their work and communicating directly with their publics.

CULTURE AND TECHNOLOGY

Internet penetration in Latin America has been growing steadily, although it is still below the average of countries in English-speaking North America and Western Europe. In Latin America, Brazil is the country with most Internet users, about 150 million as of 2020, fol-lowed by Mexico with 89 million, and Argentina and Colombia with 35 million each, and the country with the largest Internet penetration in the region is Chile with a rate of 83.4 percent, followed by Argentina with 78.6 percent and Peru with 75.2 percent (Clement, 2020a). Latin America also has some of the largest number of social media users. As for Twitter, Brazil ranks fourth in the world—behind the United States, Japan, and India—and Mexico occupies ninth place (Clement, 2020b). In the case of Facebook, Brazil ranks fourth in the world—behind India, the United States, and Indonesia—and Mexico fifth (Clement, 2020c). Regarding Instagram, Brazil ranks third—behind only the United States and India—and Mexico is in eighth rank (Clement, 2020d). Finally, as for the number of YouTube subscribers, Brazil is third and Mexico fourth in the recent world ranking (ChannelMeter, 2019).

In spite of these figures, and congruent with the sharp contrasts that characterize the region, the digital divide is still large. The difference in access between rural and urban Latin America averages 27 percent, with more than 40 percent of the population with no access to digital technologies and the services they carry (Cerrar la Brecha Digital, 2019). Needless to say, the poorest areas have the worst infrastructure, though governments are implementing different strategies to reduce the gap and, in some areas, the growth of mobile telephones has been compensating for the lack of fixed telephony and infrastructure (Bridging the Gender Gap, 2015).

The digital revolution has posed challenges for media organizations, specifically the pressure from mushrooming new sites and platforms on their financial health and the reallocation of advertising resources into the myriad of new digital players. Another challenge comes from the transition to the digitization of TV, which is occurring in the region. So far, Mexico is the only country that has successfully completed this transition. Though many other countries have issued policies to complete the switchover by 2025, which include plans to ensure access for low-income audiences. In general, they seem to fall short of broadening pluralism and diversity, since in most cases such plans grant the spectrum use to current broadcast operators (UNESCO, 2018). UNESCO (2018, 18) also notes:

> Traditional broadcasting groups of the region (Televisa, Clarin, Globo) have managed to capture relevant positions through the uploading of television content online, maintaining their presence in the online world. Video streaming is dominated by Netflix, but there are growing local initiatives that arise mainly from [regional] telecom operators (Telefónica, América Móvil, Telecom Argentina, Claro) and cable television companies (Cablevisión). A multi-platform model forms a clear regional trend for native media companies.

The challenges posed by technology may also present new opportunities for redefining journalistic practice, improving professionalism, and strengthening its independence. On the one hand, it is true that journalists' working conditions in media organizations have become more precarious, as previously discussed. But on the other, digital platforms present journalists new opportunities for performance. For instance, many investigative journalists who have not found spaces to publish their stories in conventional media—either because of news hole limitations or political reasons—are uploading them in the digital sphere. Moreover, new forms of association and collective work have developed among journalists from different countries in order to investigate and publish online on sensitive topics where single-journalist actions may be risky, such as corruption, power abuse, and organized crime. The digital world has enabled journalists who are committed to investigation and professional practice to found or strengthen organizations referred to as "alternative" media, covering stories that traditional media usually do not or at least not fully. Some of these alternative media include the Empresa Brasil de Comunicaçao (Brazil), the Red Nacional de Medios Alternativos (Argentina), La Nueva Prensa (Colombia), Prensa Ambulante (Peru), and Pié de Página (Mexico). Also, the digital landscape has enabled seasoned journalists and investigative journalistic ventures to reach wider audiences and consolidate their presence in the public eye, like Quinto Elemento Lab (Mexico) and El Faro (El Salvador). In many cases, these journalistic efforts require financing from a wide array of sources, including international foundations such as the Open Society, the Ford Foundation, or the Fojo Media Institute. In this way, digital technologies pose challenges and opportunities for a renewed journalism.

Although specific urban sectors compose the main audience for these journalistic organizations, one clear barrier for the expansion of their readership has probably to do with media literacy. While it is true that social media and these alternative journalistic organizations have provided new channels for civic participation, deliberation, and eventual action regarding topics, like women's rights, sexual diversity rights, and environmental issues (Peña, Rodríguez, & Sáez, 2016), media literacy is still uneven among the general population. Most definitions of media literacy highlight the importance of critical thinking skills regarding the ways media content is created, read, distributed, and shared (Mihailidis, 2012; Potter, 2004), going beyond the problems of access and connectivity. There are few governmental efforts to adequately insert media literacy instruction into the formal curriculum of elementary education and teaching practices.

In spite of these limitations, it is true that the digital landscape has favored the emergence of external pluralism in terms of contents, both regarding information and entertainment. Increasingly, the digital world brings forward debates on topics where inequalities have preserved in Latin America, like racism, indigenous people's rights, access to public services and natural resources. In Mexico, more than a decade ago Trejo Delarbre (2006) intuited that the then "new" digital media would serve precisely as an alternative way for deliberation and debate of those many topics that did not find enough space in conventional media. Eventually, this assumption became true in time in most Latin American countries, and digital spaces became places for protest and resistance as well. In this regard, many countries witnessed the ways digital social media were used to arrange, organize, and coordinate civic protests on the streets of Latin American cities in Argentina, Chile, Brazil, Colombia, Ecuador, and Mexico. Year 2011 was particularly a hot year. In Chile, the students protested in massive concentrations against the continuous privatizing of education. In Colombia, students rallied in the past months of the year against the passing of a new education reform that did not grant the right to education. In Mexico, students created the specific hashtag #Masde132 (more than 132) to protests against the front-runner candidate to the presidency and the way most conventional media were manipulating the information in his favor. Here, the students were able to organize, through social media, rallies of more than one million people and, with the support of Google, a debate among the presidential candidates, except, of course the front-runner who declined to participate. All these movements fostered the idea that the digital sphere was the new space for civic participation, which was true, though it has also become a space for polarization, as has been discussed.

A crucial issue regarding changes in culture and the media is gender equality, which crosses all topics discussed so far. According to the Global Gender Gap Report 2018, Latin America and the Caribbean is the third-highest ranked region in the world with an average remaining gender gap of 29.2 percent. This places the region behind Western Europe and North America and slightly ahead of Eastern Europe and Central Asia (Global Gender Gap Report, 2018). Regarding access to information and communication technologies (ICT), though the gap has reduced in recent years, women still face different barriers compared to men: education, employment, and discrimination still play a role in explaining gender differences in ICT use (Barrantes, Aguero, & Matos, 2018). Even among the youth, there are still seven women online for every ten men.

The same gender disparities are still visible both in terms of the labor market and media content and representation. According to the Global Media Monitoring Project (2015), the majority of people who work in the media in Latin America are males, especially in positions of decision-making, top administration jobs, and leading roles in newsrooms, though the number of female reporters and news presenters has increased from 38 to 43 percent between 2005 and 2015. Although women's overall presence in the news as compared to men's remains highly unequal, the gap is decreasing. However, the percentage of news stories specifically about gender equality or gender stereotyping amount to only 7 and 5 percent, respectively, figures behind those of English-speaking North America, but above Europe's (Who Makes the News, 2015: 82 and 87). Still, in Latin American media, women are represented in relation to housekeeping activities thrice as much as men; the proportion is almost eight males for each two females in stories related to politics and government.

In summary, technology and cultural practices affect recent developments in media and journalism. The digital revolution has altered the economic structures and the traditional business models upon which media were based. More online platforms and wider range of contents, including news and information have undermined traditional media sources of revenue. That has led to the increase of soft news, reduction of investigative journalism, and more precariousness in journalistic working conditions. At the same time, online channels have opened up opportunities for journalists to seek new publishing spaces and reach wider audiences. The latter is also dependent on media literacy. The digital gap between rural and urban Latin America as well as between males and females remains. Gender equity must also be improved in the media and journalistic culture in terms of issues, representation, and labor roles played by women in media organizations.

CHAPTER SUMMARY

Many challenges for media and journalism in Latin America remain. Waisbord (2019) affirms that today's news media are vulnerable as a result of four trends: major transformations in the economic foundation of the commercial news industry; the precariousness of labor conditions; the upsurge of anti-democratic forces; and anti-press violence. In Latin America, a region full of contrasts, these problems have been exacerbated and underscore the challenges that the region's media and journalists face.

While political interference is still common in traditional media organizations, new digital information sites have proved to be important alternatives for professional and investigative journalism. Collective and journalistic group work published online has also become a way to circumvent organized crime pressures on local news organizations and single-journalist reports. The digital landscape has offered alternatives for reducing the historic dependence of journalists in traditional media outlets (and their owner's interests), publishing on sensitive topics, and connecting with certain audiences, especially the educated urban youth.

Crucial problems, above all anti-press violence, governments' undue pressures, gender inequality, labor precariousness, and media literacy, need to be addressed more effectively, although positive changes are visible. These include efforts made by new journalistic associations to publish on topics that were uncommon before the digital revolution. Lots of work remains to be done, but new connections between quality journalism and society are already established in the majority of countries, and this is good news for professional journalism and can be good news for democracy as well.

DISCUSSION QUESTIONS

1. What are some of the most pressing challenges in terms of gender equity in the Latin American media landscape?
2. Is there a relationship between the difficulties in establishing effective media laws and transparency rules in the region and the risks to media freedom and journalistic independence?
3. How would you assess the role of technology in media development as well as in providing a digital public sphere in Latin America?

BIBLIOGRAPHY

Alcántara, M., Buquet, D., & Tagina, M. (2018). *Elecciones y partidos en America Latina en el cambio de ciclo.* Centro de Investigaciones Sociológicas.

Article 19. (2019, February). Protocolo de la Impunidad en Delitos contra Periodistas. *Article 19.* articulo19.org/informeimpunidad/

Asmann, P. (2018, October). Impunity persists in LatAm cases of murdered journalists. *InSight Crime.* www.insightcrime.org/news/brief/impunity-persists-latam-murdered-journalists/

Bagdikian, B. H. (2004). *The new media monopoly.* Beacon Press.

Baker, C. E. (2006). *Media concentration and democracy: Why ownership matters.* Cambridge University Press.

Barrantes, R., Aguero, A., & Matos, P. (2018, March 16). Understanding the ICT use gender gap in Latin America. The 46th Research Conference on Communication, Information and Internet Policy. papers.ssrn.com/sol3/papers.cfm?abstract_id=3142380#

Bridging the gender gap: Mobile access and usage in low and middle income countries. (2020, February). *Groupe Spéciale Mobile.* www.gsma.com/mobilefordevelopment/resources/bridging-gender-gap-mobile-access-usage-low-middle-income-countries/

CEPAL. (2019, September). Panorama Social de América Latina. *Comisión Económica para América Latina.* www.cepal.org/es/publicaciones/44969-panorama-social-america-latina-2019

Cerrar la brecha digital en AL y el caribe depende de la transformación de Fondos de Servicio universal. (2019, July). *CAF-Banco de Desarrollo de América Latina.* www.caf.com/es/actualidad/noticias/2019/07/cerrar-la-brecha-digital-en-america-latina-y-el-caribe-depende-criticamente-de-la-transformacion-de-los-fondos-de-servicio-universal/

ChannelMeter. (2019, March). YouTube's top countries. *Medium.* medium.com/@ChannelMeter/youtubes-top-countries-47b0d26dded

Clement, J. (2020a, January). Global regional internet penetration rate. *Statista.* www.statista.com/statistics/265149/internet-penetration-rate-by-region/

Clement, J. (2020b, July). Twitter: Most users by country. *Statista.* www.statista.com/statistics/242606/number-of-active-twitter-users-in-selected-countries/

Clement, J. (2020c, July). Facebook: Most users by country *Statista.* www.statista.com/statistics/268136/top-15-countries-based-on-number-of-facebook-users/

Clement, J. (2020d, July). Instagram: Users by country. *Statista.* www.statista.com/statistics/578364/countries-with-most-instagram-users/

Global Gender Gap Report (2018). *World Economic Forum.* reports.weforum.org/global-gender-gap-report-2018/

Global Media Monitoring Project (2015). *Who makes the news?* cdn.agilitycms.com/who-makes-the-news/Imported/reports_2015/global/gmmp_global_report_en.pdf

Global Open Data Index. (2018). *Open Knowledge Foundation.* index.okfn.org/place/

Google (2020). *Google Transparency Report*. transparencyreport.google.com/

Guerrero, M. A. (2014). The 'Captured Liberal' model of media systems in Latin America. In Guerrero, M. A. & Márquez-Ramírez, M. (Eds.), *Media systems and communication policies in Latin America* (pp. 43–65). Palgrave-McMillan.

Hallin, D. C., & Mancini, P. (2004). *Comparing media systems: Three models of media and politics.* Cambridge University Press.

Henríquez, M., & Wolfersdorff, J. W. (2019, December). Iluminando el opaco gasto en publicidad del gobierno. *CIPER Chile—Centro de Investigación e Información Periodística.* www.ciperchile.cl/2019/12/09/iluminando-el-opaco-gasto-en-publicidad-del-gobierno/

Informe Latinobarómetro 2018. (2019). *Corporación Latinobarómetro.* www.latinobarometro.org/lat.jsp

La FLIP inicia una serie de investigaciones sobre la pauta oficial en Colombia. (2018, September). *Fundación para la Libertad de Prensa.* flip.org.co/index.php/es/informacion/noticias/item/2276-la-flip-inicia-una-serie-de-investigaciones-sobre-la-pauta-oficial-en-colombia

Mastrini, G. (2019). More owners than ever. Concentration in the Latin American communication landscape of the 21st century. *Global Media Journal, 17*(32), 1–9.

Mignolo, W. (2005). *The idea of Latin America.* Wiley-Blackwell.

Mihailidis, P. (2012). *News literacy: Global perspectives for the newsroom and the classroom.* Peter Lang.

Nalvarte, P. (2017, June). Leyes latinoamericanas de acceso a la información entre las mejores del Mundo. *Sociedad Interamericana de Prensa.* www.sipiapa.org/notas/1211522-leyes-latinoamericanas-acceso-la-informacion-las-mejores-del-mundo

Observacom (2019, July). ¿Quién es el guardián del perro guardián? *OBSERVACOM.* www.observacom.org/quien-es-el-guardian-del-perro-guardian/

Observatory of Killed Journalists. (2020). *UNESCO.* en.unesco.org/themes/safety-journalists/observatory

Peña, P., Rodríguez, R., & Sáez, C. (2016). Movimiento estudiantil en Chile, aprendizaje situado y activismo digital. *OBETS Revista de Ciencias Sociales,* 11(1), 287–310.

Potter, W. J. (2004). *Theory of media literacy: A cognitive approach.* SAGE.

Rafsky, S. (2014, September). Who is killing Central America's journalists? *Committee to Protect Journalists.* cpj.org/reports/2014/09/who-is-killing-central-americas-journalists-impunity-violence-murders-unsolved/

Rogers, T. (2020, February). How independent journalists in Latin America are finding new ways to hold power to account. *Nieman Reports.* niemanreports.org/articles/how-independent-journalists-in-latin-america-are-finding-new-ways-to-hold-power-to-account/

RSF. (2020). RSF 2020 index: Latin America's dark horizon for press freedom. (2020, April). *Reporters Without Borders.* rsf.org/en/rsf-2020-index-latin-americas-dark-horizon-press-freedom R

SF. (2018, November). RSF report on journalists who are targeted by organized crime. rsf.org/en/reports/rsf-report-journalists-who-are-targeted-organized-crime

Trejo Delarbre, R. (2006). *Viviendo en el aleph: La sociedad de la información y sus laberintos.* Gedisa.

Twitter Transparency Report. (2020). *Twitter.* transparency.twitter.com/en/removal-requests.html#removal-requests-jan-jun-2019

UNESCO. (2018). *World trends in freedom of expression and media development.* www.unesco.org/new/fileadmin/MULTIMEDIA/FIELD/Kingston/pdf/world_trends_freedom.pdf

Veiga, G. (2020, June). Bolsonaro dio otro paso para controlar las malas noticias de su gobierno. *PAGINA12.* www.pagina12.com.ar/272274-bolsonaro-dio-otro-paso-para-controlar-las-malas-noticias-de

Waisbord, S. (2019). The vulnerabilities of journalism. *Journalism, 20*(1), 210–213.

Werner, A. (2020, January). Outlook for Latin America and the Caribbean: New challenges to growth [Web Blog] *International Monetary Fund.* blogs.imf.org/2020/01/29/outlook-for-latin-america-and-the-caribbean-new-challenges-to-growth/

Witchel, E. (2018, October). Getting away with murder. CPJ's 2018 Global Impunity Index spotlights where journalists are slain and their killers go free. *Committee for the Protection of Journalists.* cpj.org/reports/2018/10/impunity-index-getting-away-with-murder-killed-justice-3/

14

Media in North America

Zac Gershberg and D. Jasun Carr

For over a century, the media systems of the United States and Canada resembled what Hallin and Mancini (2004) considered a Liberal Model, "characterized by a relative dominance of market mechanisms and of commercial media" (p. 11). A strong legal tradition of freedom of the press—marked by a lack of government interference—facilitated the rise of an independent but profit-oriented cultural environment of media. This history privileged technological innovation in communications as well as news-reporting on facts to objectively present the truth in service of an informed democratic public. But any survey of North American media must also account for concentrated ownership in journalism and a legacy of fierce, even vituperative, advocacy and partisanship. As the twenty-first century enters its third decade, the United States and Canadian systems find themselves destabilized by corporate priorities, technological convergence, and public distrust—so much so that Necushtai (2018) argues that the American model can now be understood as "Polarized Liberal."

While there has, in some ways, never been more news offered to the public than the present time, never has journalism been so threatened as a profession. Allegations of fake news abound, and cutting positions and reduced competition have resulted in over 2,000 American newspapers shuttered between 2004 and 2020, including seventy daily publications (Abernathy, 2020). In Canada, over half of households subscribed to a newspaper in 1995; now that number is less than 20 percent (Public Policy Forum, 2017, p. 15). If a free press is vital to democracy, how is it to fulfill such duties amid so much political cynicism and structural limitations that encroach on the ability of journalists to do their jobs? Recognizing the economic, political, and technological hindrances to news media is a necessary first step, and what this chapter aims to layout.

MEDIA CULTURE: PRACTICES, ETHICS, LAW

Both the United States and Canada enjoy a legacy of free press rights and media innovation. In the nineteenth century, Canadian forests supplied the paper mills for Northern state newspapers in America, and the two worked together in laying the first transatlantic cable for the telegraph to connect information with Europe. In the twentieth century, the Toronto School of media—led by Harold Innis and Marshall McLuhan—transformed how we think of communication technologies. McLuhan, who coined the famous adage, "the medium is the message," became something of an American celebrity by appearing in films and television talk shows. Most professional sports leagues, save for gridiron football, include teams from each country, and it is common for Hollywood films to be shot in Canada. Since Canada is bilingual, speaking both English and French, its media have evolved in a more centralized manner. With respect to radio and television, the Canadian Broadcasting Corporation (CBC), which was and continues to be government funded, began in the 1930s. While the United States has the Public Broadcasting Station (PBS) and National Public Radio (NPR) as subsidized broadcast networks, they did not emerge until decades later and heavily rely on citizen contributions. The Federal Communications Commission (FCC) was created in the 1930s to ensure a decentralized media model that sought to facilitate programming in the public interest. An example of this was the Fairness Doctrine, which demanded a reasonable exchange of balanced views on political information. When the Fairness Doctrine was repealed in the 1980s by the administration of President Ronald Reagan, the result was more partisan and polarizing media discourses on broadcast media.

But the democratic strength of American media has always been print journalism, which, thanks to the First Amendment, has no such federal or state agency overseeing it. Some of the top cultural and literary voices in American history have hailed from print journalism, including, but not limited to, Margaret Fuller, Frederick Douglass, Mark Twain, and Ernest Hemingway. Although Canada still has criminal libel laws and prosecutions (Taylor & Pritchard, 2018), a series of twentieth-century American Supreme Court cases—*Near v. Minnesota* (1931), *New York Times v. Sullivan* (1964), and *New York Times v. United States* (1971)—ensured print journalists were free from prior restraint, libel, and censorship from the government and public officials, respectively. The legal strength of American press freedom appears to be cracking just a bit, however. In 2016, a Florida jury declared Gawker, an online media consortium of sites like Deadspin, liable for invasion of privacy in posting a sex tape involving the famous wrestler Hulk Hogan. The case had been initially dismissed from federal court, but Hogan's legal team—bankrolled by the billionaire tech investor Peter Thiel, who was angered by the site's unethical outing of him as a gay man years before—refiled in state court. It was argued that Terry Bollea, Hogan's real name, had his rights infringed. This was in spite of the fact that Bollea, as Hogan, extolled his own sexual prowess in various media appearances. The damages awarded with the verdict exceeded $100 million, and the judge, having denied a stay for appeal, forced Gawker into bankruptcy. More recently, a former vice presidential candidate, Sarah Palin, has filed a libel suit against the *New York Times* over an editorial and is seeking to overturn the precedent set forth in the *Sullivan* case.

These emerging legal encroachments on freedom of the press clash with the idea of media as the Fourth Estate, which is embedded in the American journalism tradition. The press had the power to uncover serious wrongdoing that led to the resignation of President Richard Nixon, yet future Republican presidents like film star Ronald Reagan and television reality host Donald Trump would leverage their media celebrity to win public support. For a long time, American journalism was led by gatekeepers, which included top producers from the three television networks—ABC, CBS, NBC—as well as top editors and reporters from the nation's leading newspapers and magazines. The limited spectrum of television and the serious style of national print news inspired a great deal of trust in the American public. That legacy, however, has largely been eroded due to economic, technological, and political factors in the twenty-first century. So while the cultural traditions of American journalism remain consistent, its standing and impact on society now ebbs.

This loss of credibility also owes to ethical scandals plaguing American journalism over the past few decades. The press has often prided itself on practicing the values of accuracy, transparency, and truth. Whereas in the past it would take historians years to uncover malfeasance, instances of fabrication, the greatest sin in American journalism ethics, have not been uncommon. A 1992 episode of NBC's Dateline rigged a General Motors truck with incendiary devices to have such vehicles explode on air. In the late 1990s, news emerged that Stephen Glass, a magazine journalist with the *New Republic*, had falsified sources and their quotes for his feature articles. Jayson Blair resigned from the *New York Times* in 2003 for plagiarizing the work of other reporters as well as fabricating quotations. During the presidential campaign of 2004, a CBS News program, *60 Minutes II*, went to air with phony source documents that purported to demonstrate President George W. Bush's abdication of military service. The network's lead news anchor, Dan Rather, attempted to defend the documents, but they had not been verified internally and were exposed by political blogs that analyzed the typeface. Rather resigned soon after, and the incident crystallized for many Americans a mainstream bias against conservative politicians like Bush. In 2014, *Rolling Stone* magazine published a story about a sexual assault on the campus of the University of Virginia. The account of the single source alleging the assault turned out not to be true, and though the story was retracted, *Rolling Stone* lost a defamation case against a campus administrator and settled with the accused fraternity in question.

These examples of fabrication are errors of commission, but the American media has also been beset by other ethical challenges. The tabloid style of television news, in particular, has increasingly played up racially charged sensationalism as well as polarizing debates of political spin. Cases like the O.J. Simpson murder trial, sexual assault allegations concerning the Duke Lacrosse team, and images of a confrontation between white Kentucky high school students and a Native American elder have demonstrated a penchant for divisive news that exacerbates racial conflict. Cable television news and news-talk radio, meanwhile, often feature a pundit-driven format where actual journalistic reporting has been displaced by commentary on horse-race politics. That is, rampant speculation about how news affects politicians and their parties, accompanied by spin to frame such coverage, often dominates the content of broadcast media. In the absence of committed reporting, important stories like faulty claims of weapons of mass destruction, the *casus belli* of the Iraq War in 2003; the excess of mortgage-backed securities leading to the 2008 financial crisis; and the Russian hacking of Americans during the 2016 presidential election, went unchecked until it was too late.

Despite these errors of commission and omission, the legacy and power of North American journalism lives on in the reporting of newspapers like the *New York Times* and the *Washington Post* as well as magazines like *Harper's* and the *New Yorker*. There are also broad explanatory journalism news sites such as *Vox*, and emerging niche online verticals like *The 19th*, which devotes journalistic coverage to women's issues. A fully online and nonprofit model has risen, too, with ProPublica as a well-respected investigative media outlet. In 2019, the *Salt Lake Tribune* became the first daily newspaper to declare nonprofit status. Other organizations have sought a hybrid approach spanning print and digital media, such as *Vice*. It started in Montreal as a magazine, provide hard-hitting coverage of culture and news, and now enjoys its own cable television channel and online news site, in addition to a large presence on social networking and a previous show, "Vice News Tonight," which aired on HBO. To succeed in this media environment, more journalists have had to brand themselves through their presence on social media and chart a path through their own blogs or as freelancers for different news outlets. Shireen Ahmed, a Canadian journalist, covers sport through the prisms of gender and race on various media platforms. She has published in *Sports Illustrated*, *Vice*, *Huffington Post*, the *CBC*, on her blog *FootyBedSheets*, and in a podcast, she co-founded with other women sports journalists, "Burn It All Down." Ahmed's career reflects how establishing and impacting an audience in contemporary media can be done across various communications platforms. Other high-profile journalists have taken to Substack to monetize their work with blog-style newsletters. To cite just two examples from 2020, Anne Helen Petersen left *Buzzfeed* and Glenn Greenwald stepped down from *The Intercept* to become fully independent through Substack. The media isn't one singular entity but a multiplicity of forms and perspectives that facilitate diverse content as a result of convergence.

ECONOMIC AND TECHNOLOGICAL CONVERGENCE

Media convergence runs in two directions, both structurally in financial terms of ownership and blended in terms of communications technologies. One contributing factor to the demise of so many North American media outlets in the past few decades has been the economic consolidation of journalism. This dates back to the deregulatory emphasis of President Ronald Reagan's administration and was accelerated with the Telecommunications Act of 1996, signed by President Bill Clinton. The law relaxed rules governing the concentration of media ownership among newspapers, radio stations, and television networks. Newspaper chains such as Gannett, Tribune, and Hollinger—this last owned by the Canadian Conrad Black—transformed the private ownership model of family-run newspapers. Newspaper chains had existed, of course, but they used to be regional, like McClatchy in California's Central Valley. But the new chains drew investors with the goals of efficiency and profit through synergy, which meant less resources for reporting. This financial media convergence did not translate into journalistic success, however, as cutting positions and reduced competition resulted in the rise of news deserts in North America—communities with no access to journalistic reporting. Although national newspapers such as the *New York Times*, the *Washington Post*, and the *Wall Street Journal* have sustained some financial success in this environment, economic convergence has imperiled smaller publications with grave consequences. As Sullivan (2020) has concluded, "When local news fails, the foundations of democracy weaken. The public, which depends on accurate, factual information in order to make good decisions, suffers" (p. 20).

Broadcast media were also affected as local radio stations and network affiliates were consolidated by larger entities. Prior to the Telecommunications Act of 1996, broadcasters could own no more than thirty-six radio stations and twelve television stations nationwide and were prohibited from amassing more than 25 percent reach in any one medium. Soon after the legislation passed, Clear Channel acquired over a thousand AM and FM radio stations spanning conservative news-talk and various musical genres. Sinclair, which owns television network affiliates, ran eight stations in 1994; by 2020, they owned close to three hundred stations. More broadly, we also find large, horizontally integrated media corporations such as Comcast, which combines telecommunications services such as broadband and cable television along with NBC's television holdings and Universal's film studio and theme parks. Disney owns ABC and ESPN on television as well as Pixar, Marvel, and Star Wars universes of intellectual property. This is in addition to its profitable theme parks, retail merchandise chain, and cruise line.

In 2019, Disney acquired the rights to the Twenty-First Century Fox movie and television archive, which they can draw from in facilitating streaming services they run such as Disney+ and Hulu. The telecommunications provider AT&T, broken up in the early 1980s due to its monopolistic practices, has recently expanded its portfolio from a mobile phone carrier to controlling DirecTV, a satellite television service, as well as Warner Media, which combines a film studio along with television channels such as CNN and HBO.

Traditional journalism also had to compete within a larger, more fragmented media environment marked by technological media convergence. The 1980s brought 24-hour cable news while the rise of the Internet in the 1990s brought blogs filled with opinion-based commentary. Websites like Craigslist resembled classified advertising, long a major source of revenue for newspapers. The rise of social networking in the aughts then encroached on local advertising even more, as did the geopositional opportunities of mobile phone advertising. The financial consolidation facing journalism was challenging enough, but reporters also confronted a culture caught within a polarized political dynamic. With the rise of blogs and then Facebook, Twitter, and Reddit, there was even more and more information and opinion but, continually, less and less relevant reporting on important matters of education, international affairs, and economics. As a Canadian government-subsidized report wrote, "The digital revolution has made a far more open and diverse news ecosystem—and a meaner and less trustworthy one" (Public Policy Forum, 2017, p. 3).

It should be noted that this digital revolution has not been waged on a level playing field. Within both the United States and Canada, the general populace is still divided in terms of access to technology, quality of accessible technology, and digital skills in using these technologies. This multifaceted digital divide exists on multiple fronts. In Canada, rural Internet speeds are roughly twelve times slower than those in urban communities (Canadian Internet Registration Authority, 2020), and within the United States, only 65 percent of rural homes have access to broadband, as opposed to roughly 97 percent of those in urban areas (Federal Communications Commission, 2020). Beyond mere access, the second-level digital divide— the gap in online skills—persists across age, gender, racial, and educational groups. Older citizens are less comfortable with, and less likely to use, the Internet; the less educated use it less frequently; and minority groups are a minority among regular users (Pew Research Center, 2020). This divide is evident not only in general Internet use, but also in the use of social media and mobile applications. And for these low-use groups, the shift to online-centered news and engagement carries a real risk of increased exclusion from the information and cultural capital attainable through the Internet (Büchi, Just, & Latzer, 2016).

Levels of news media trust have been steadily declining in the United States and Canada since the 1970s, and frequent attacks against the press have characterized the modern era. These attacks have contributed to the current lack of trust in the media as a whole, with only 52 percent of Canadians trusting the news overall. However, this number, while problematic, looks positively rosy when compared to the situation in the United States—where only 32 percent of the population trusts the news as a whole (Newman, Fletcher, Kalogeropoulos, & Nielsen, 2019). As media trust is crucial to the role that journalism plays in democracies, the current levels of trust indicate a fundamental weakness in North American media systems. A free and insightful press enables informed political participation by citizens, and represents the foundation of a deliberative democracy as no true deliberation can occur without information to warrant decisions. But in a space where the very facts are up for debate, obfuscated, and buried in an avalanche of spin, the foundations of journalism begin to crumble.

The low level of journalism credibility has been exacerbated by the rise of social media, which has emerged as a major source of news in a rapidly shifting media landscape. With the evolution of online sites, mobile apps, and social networking channels, online news sources have surpassed television, radio, and print as the primary news source for nearly 72 percent of Americans and 75 percent of Canadians (Newman, Fletcher, Kalogeropoulos, & Nielsen, 2019). As nine out of ten North Americans use the Internet regularly, citizens engage in news consumption from online offerings like traditional news sources as well as information channeled through their social networking feeds, which are driven by algorithms trained to cater to their interests. This use of social media as a source of news is, perhaps, paradoxical. For, while people are more likely to use media they find credible (McCracken, 2011), social networking content continues to have lower credibility ratings than any other category (Johnson & Kaye, 2015). Yet social media continues to gobble up audience share—with disastrous consequences for traditional sources of journalism. Digital ads generate a fraction of traditional print ad revenue. Headlines and clips are increasingly shared through social media sites which retain their own advertising revenue while benefiting from the product of the news outlet. And within these social media spaces, the cache and hard-fought trust earned by established news outlets become increasingly difficult to differentiate from those which are intentionally misleading, false, or clickbait. The phenomenon of misinformation is only accelerated by an extremely polarized political environment.

Despite these drops in the level of trust, there are some indicators that journalism is still a valued and integral part of the fabric of both countries. The increasing reliance on mobile devices as a key platform from which to access news media—57 percent of Americans and 51 percent of Canadians indicating that smartphones are their primary device for news (Newman, Fletcher, Kalogeropoulos, & Nielsen, 2019)—demonstrates a continued desire to be informed and engaged at all times. The rise of podcasts as a mediated form of news, which represents a return to both long-form journalism and the heyday of radio programming, has been witnessed in both countries. While the top podcasts include a large amount of true crime and entertainment programming, it is worth noting that offerings from the *New York Times*, NPR, CBC, and BBC are ranked in the Top 100 podcasts for both countries. These mainstream, legacy media outlets are joined by a host of other news programs from newer sources, including *Pod Save America*, WNYC Studios *RadioLab*, and *The Daily Show With Trevor Noah* (Ears Edition) (Chartable, 2020; Winn, 2020). With millions of listeners in both countries, these programs and others like them represent a burgeoning source of information and engagement, as well as a space for new voices to gain trust and enter the conversation.

POLITICAL FACTORS

Allegations of media bias have been made in the United States by conservative politicians since the Nixon administration. Yet trust in journalism reached a peak in the 1970s with the Watergate scandal that led to President Nixon's resignation. Perceptions of credibility have slowly degraded ever since. At first, it was radio personalities like Rush Limbaugh and pundits at FOX News who charged the mainstream media with bias. With the 2016 presidential campaign featuring Donald Trump, however, the Republican Party has assumed a critical stance toward legacy media. The Trump era has been characterized by dismissing any reporting critical of President Trump as "fake news." The term initially referred to digital misinformation shared during the 2016 election cycle which helped propel Trump's victory, but now the moniker is weaponized as a term to dismiss inconvenient facts. Journalists, Trump has said and tweeted, constitute the enemy of the people. Facts, for their part, are no longer considered as grounded in reality, but as expressions of political, moral, religious, and ideological stances. They can be rejected and reframed to suit the needs or preferences of publics that are already politicized. As a result, media professionals are caught in a dangerous crossfire of influence.

POLITICS, POPULISM, AND THE MEDIA

The rise of social media as an information source, free from oversight and with a reach far exceeding any traditional media channel, has proven to be one of the greatest challenges to the Fourth Estate in North America. Freed from the shackles of journalistic and editorial oversight, individuals, companies, and politicians quickly adopted these platforms as opportunities to disseminate their own narratives, views, and "facts" directly to the public at large. And as they did so, journalists and journalistic organizations across North America struggled to adapt to their role within the new attention economy. This struggle is particularly highlighted in the shift in politics and the rise of the populist platforms promoted by Maxime Bernier and Donald Trump—both of whom rely on Twitter for a "scream-until-someone-pays-attention" (Warnica, 2019) barrage of information targeting their own base and promoting their own message. This approach has proven particularly problematic for journalists on both sides of the border to cover. Reporters are faced with the choice of either ignoring their traditional role of providing context for the words of the powerful, or of promoting and restating the often bombastic, biased, or baseless information through their reporting of what are admittedly important events. Challenging the statements made by Trump or Bernier results in immediate claims of bias and plays directly into their framing of "fake news." Failing to do so places the journalist in a position of complicity.

Throughout the entirety of the Trump presidency, and particularly the 2020 U.S. Presidential Election, journalists struggled to balance their duty to report on the statements made by Trump regarding claims of voter fraud and their duty to convey factual and truthful information to the public. Only after the 2020 election, have news outlets directly challenged such power, evident in the decision of several U.S. television networks to refuse broadcasting Trump's post-election speeches. Utilizing editorial oversight to retake their position as gatekeepers and journalists may continue to feed distrust, however. Similar challenges have been faced by social media outlets such as Facebook and Twitter, which have struggled with how to handle misinformation on their platforms and only recently have begun labeling posts by government officials as "disputed content" and even deactivating some accounts. This, in turn, led to more fervent criticism of social media and of the media in general from Trump and his supporters.

Trust in the news media, already under duress from the proliferation of voices and failure of older models of journalistic gatekeeping, is further threatened by unprecedented messages and attacks from the White House itself (Davis & Rosenberg, 2017). Barthel, Jeffrey, and Mitchell (2017) found that the majority of Americans say that the relationship between the president and press is problematic, and that the resulting tension is detrimental to the public sphere. These threats compound each other to create a problematic trend, as media trust is crucial to the role that journalism plays in democracies. While the United States now features politicians regularly running against the media, a similar phenomenon was apparent in Canada during the 2010 mayoral race in Toronto. Rob Ford won a heated election amid allegations of impropriety leveled by the *Toronto Star* newspaper. Ford and his brother, Doug, a city councilman, had hosted a weekly radio show that frequently attacked the press. The animosity only increased when the *Star* reported that Rob Ford, as mayor, was caught on video smoking crack-cocaine. Subsequently, he would not stand for re-election. Though the news media has exposed questionable behavior from political figures like Mayor Ford and President Trump, some consider their priorities misguided. "The North American press has a pathological inability to grasp how much damage they have done to their own brand with their biases, distortions, gullibility, deceptions, and most of all, hubris," writes Kitty (2018). "They have been reduced to shrill mudslinging as they gang up to decimate a target, but then are genuinely surprised they are viewed with disgust by the public" (pp. 99–100).

Other journalism scholars see things differently. "Despite the economic woes of journalism . . . and in the face of declining levels of public trust in 'the media,'" writes Schudson (2020), "professionally produced journalism is very likely better than it has ever been" (p. 39). The question is how to find such strong work and remunerate it. The problems that face North American media largely stem from the continual drive of easy-access consumerism over well-informed citizenship in an increasingly fragmented marketplace. Constant coverage, both celebrating and vilifying the status quo, provides an inoculation effect wherein the conduct once considered shocking becomes mundane. Attacks on journalists with threats of libel have become a common occurrence in the new cultural landscape. And the ensuing media circus provides a very lucrative revenue stream for partisan media free to promulgate and promote their messages.

Nowhere is this media circus more evident than within the battles over access to important figures. Whereas access was one of the defining characteristics of trustworthy and legitimate news sources, the Trump administration subverted this approach by restricting the access of what they view as an opposition press deemed "the enemy of the people." This undermines the ability of journalists to report the news, which is the intended goal. Meanwhile, the president elevated fringe outlets who supported the administration through increased access to official press events and official and unofficial social media channels. Take, for example, the rise of One America News (OAN) network—a far-right news outlet that was born during the Obama administration with the explicit purpose of reaching a far-right audience. Despite numerous claims of overt racism and bigotry, OAN was granted a permanent seat in the White House briefing room and has become one of the top-five most called upon organizations. At the same time, OAN has been depreciated within the Wikipedia community due to their continued publication of conspiracy theories and falsehoods. As OAN and other outlets across the political spectrum have risen to prominence, the public has increasingly become divided and fragmented, drawing upon and sharing only those outlets that fit their ideological bent and degrading trust in the institution of journalism as a whole.

Even those sites separate from traditional journalism, such as Reddit, exist within this partisan media space and act accordingly. When Reddit announced that the popular message board r/TheDonald was to be quarantined (and subsequently removed from the site), users reestablished bases in other media spaces and services, continuing to share articles and information which supports their own view of events. Much like early journalists had to navigate the political landscape of their editors, benefactors, and readers, so too do modern journalists have to navigate the same space writ larger by the vast array of media outlets and social media sources. And, within this space, the same battles will continue to be fought. Journalists and news outlets are likely to continue struggling to maintain viability, yet we know democracy in North America requires an informed public. Journalists operate in an industry beset by the pressures of financial and technological convergence within a hostile public sphere inundated by political skepticism and deliberately planted misinformation. The modern media landscape may move faster now, with more participants, but the rights of a free press, and the confrontations between its practices and those in power, remain in constant vigilance and tension.

CHAPTER SUMMARY

The media in Canada and the United States have faced a number of challenges in the twenty-first century. Technological change, economic consolidation, and political pressures, in addition to decreasing journalistic credibility and increasing political polarization among the public, have significantly impacted media development. As both countries continue to grapple with the influence of social media on the dissemination of information, the role of journalism as neutral mediator remains a fragile one within the Liberal Model, and a potential flashpoint for future movements and populists from both sides of the political aisle.

Populist politicians and corporate consolidation continue their assault on established media practices, and citizens search for voices they trust in a fragmented online media landscape. The rise of social media and the constant connectivity provided by the ubiquity of mobile technology and Internet access have, admittedly, brought these concerns to the fore—but they are not new. The North American media sphere has been grappling with the realities of partisan news and fragmented audiences since its inception, an inherent byproduct of the commitment to a free press. And, as a counterpoint to these threats, the ready access to technology, stable national infrastructures, and relative wealth of both countries has allowed the citizenry and media to, for the most part, adapt to these changes. For, while the media in North America are subject to the pressures of corporate and national interests, the freedom provided to distribute content in a nearly unregulated manner has allowed the media to continuously adapt in their mission to connect with and inform the public sphere.

DISCUSSION QUESTIONS

1. What can news media organizations do to regain trust as the main source of news in North America?
2. Do you think that philanthropy, public subsidies, and/or nonprofit status are effective options for local news organizations in North America to remain viable?
3. Identify an example of a "news desert" in the United States or Canada and report on what, if any, ramifications this has had for the community.
4. How should journalists cover populist politicians who attack the media with allegations of "fake news" and post misinformation through their social media channels?

BIBLIOGRAPHY

Abernathy, P. M. (2020). *News deserts and ghost newspapers: Will local news survive?* University of North Carolina Press.

Barthel, M., Jeffrey, G., & Mitchell, A. (2017). *Most say tensions between Trump administration and news media hinder access to political news.* www.journalism.org/2017/04/04/most-say-tensions-between-trump-administration-andnews-media-hinder-access-to-political-news/.

Büchi, M., Just, N., & Latzer, M. (2016). Modeling the second-level digital divide: A five-country study of social differences in Internet use. *New Media & Society, 18*(11), 2703–2722.

Canadian Internet Registration Authority. (2020). *New internet performance data shows the staggering scale of Canada's urban-rural digital divide.* www.cira.ca/newsroom/new-internet-performance-data-shows-staggering-scale-canadas-urban-rural-digital-divide

Chartable. (2020). *Apple Podcasts—Canada—All Podcasts.* Chartable. chartable.com/charts/itunes/ca-all-podcasts-podcasts

Davis, J. H. & Rosenberg M. (2017). With false claims, Trump attacks media on turnout and intelligence rift. *The New York Times*, January 21. www.nytimes.com/2017/01/21/us/politics/trump-white-house-briefing-inauguration-crowd-size.html?mcubz=0.

Federal Communications Commission. (2020). *2020 Broadband deployment report.* docs.fcc.gov/public/attachments/FCC-20-50A1.pdf

Hallin, D., & Mancini, P. (2004). *Comparing media systems: Three models of media and politics.* Cambridge University Press.

Johnson, T. J., & Kaye, B. K. (2015). Reasons to believe: Influence of credibility on motivations for using social networks. *Computers in Human Behavior, 50*, 544–555.

Kitty, A. (2018). *When journalism was a thing.* Zero Books.

McCracken, B. (2011). *Are new media credible? A multidimensional approach to measuring news consumers' credibility and bias perceptions and the frequency of news consumption.* Unpublished doctoral dissertation, Rochester Institute of Technology, Rochester, NY.

Nechushtai, E. (2018). From liberal to polarized liberal? Contemporary U.S. News in Hallin and Mancini's typology of news systems. *The International Journal of Press/Politics, 23*(2), 183–201.

Newman, N., Fletcher, R., Kalogeropoulos, A., & Nielsen, R. K. (2019). *Reuters Institute digital news report 2019.* Reuters Institute for the Study of Journalism. reutersinstitute.politics.ox.ac.uk/sites/default/files/inline-files/DNR_2019_FINAL_27_08_2019.pdf

Pew Research Center. (2020). *Internet/Broadband fact sheet.* www.pewresearch.org/internet/fact-sheet/internet-broadband/

Public Policy Forum. (2017). *The shattered mirror: News, democracy and trust in the digital age.* shattered-mirror.ca/wp-content/uploads/theShatteredMirror.pdf

Schudson, M. (2020). *Journalism: Why it matters.* Polity.

Sullivan, M. (2020). *Ghosting the news: Local journalism and the crisis of American democracy.* Columbia Global Reports.

Taylor, L., & Pritchard, D. (2018). The process is the punishment: Criminal libel and political speech in Canada. *Communication Law and Policy, 23*(3), 243–266.

Warnica, R. (2019). Can Canada ward off a populist surge? *Politico*, October 2. www.politico.com/magazine/story/2019/10/02/can-canada-ward-off-a-populist-surge-228874

Winn, R. (2020, March 11). Top 100 US podcasts (Apple Podcasts Top Charts). *Podcast Insights.* www.podcastinsights.com/top-us-podcasts/

III

CURRENT ISSUES

15

The Digital Transformation of International and National News Agencies: Challenges Facing AFP, AP, and TASS

Terhi Rantanen and Anthony Kelly

The existence and continuity of news agencies or press associations—the oldest electronic media organizations, which date back to the first part of the nineteenth century—has been taken for granted for a long time. There is still a news agency in almost every country, and they continue to play a significant role as intermediary organizations that provide their services to most media in the country, and also—through their own networks—beyond it. However, digitalization has challenged news agencies to such an extent that some of them have been forced to cease their operations. The Australian News Association (AAP), for example, announced that it would officially shut down its operations after 85 years on June 26, 2020, but was rescued by an 11th-hour bid by a philanthropic investment consortium that now has been given a government grant (Meade, 2020; Wahlqvist, 2020; McQuirk, 2020). In short, many news agencies are struggling financially in the age of digitalization and even the most profitable ones are no longer among the biggest media companies.

The monopoly of speed was for a very long time the domain of news agencies. As Charles Havas, the founder of one of the oldest agencies in the world, once put it, "*vite et bien* [quickly and well]" (Tungate, 2007, p. 180). News agencies exemplified *institutional journalism* (Picard, 2014, p. 504), providing what Carlson (2007, p. 1015) calls the "presentational authority of journalism." Nechushtai and Lewis (2019, p. 299) write that institutional journalism has the ability to "generate cultural meaning through the purposeful ordering, arranging, and highlighting of some news items relative to others." Its coverage often focused on "selected institutions, such as government agencies, educational institutions and financial institutions" (Picard, 2014, p. 504), which further emphasized the semi-official character of news-agency operations even when the agencies were privately or cooperatively owned. News agencies played the role of major gatekeepers, establishing and maintaining a news agenda. Their past may have been glorious, but what about their future?

This chapter explores how news agencies, across different geographical and organizational contexts, have responded to the challenges of digitalization. We outline how digitalization has challenged news agencies in three key areas: (1) the deprofessionalization and deinstitutionalization of journalism; (2) the emergence and development of digital platforms; and (3) the need for diversification. We examine how various news agencies representing different owner-ship forms in France (AFP), the United States (AP), and Russia (TASS) have responded to these challenges by diversifying their operations. While we show that news agencies' diverse responses and strategies have met with varying degrees of success, we argue that the struggle for dominance in which news agencies are currently engaged challenges the notion of what constitutes a news agency at the same time as demanding a reappraisal of how diversification should be defined.

From "Big Five" to "Big Seven"

Our three case studies are Agence France-Presse (AFP) in France, The Associated Press (AP) in the United States, and TASS in Russia, all once described as members of the "Big Five" international news agencies along with Reuters (at the time in the United Kingdom) and United Press International (UPI) in the United States (Alleyne & Wagner, 1993) that once dominated the world's news flows. The majority of international news originated from these five agencies, especially from the four Western agencies. They were once seen as so powerful that UNESCO instructed developing countries to limit their reliance on these major agencies as a source of international news content (Rafeeq & Jiang, 2018, p. 98). Much has changed since the 1970s and 1980s. Reuters is now in Canadian ownership, and UPI is no longer an international agency. Nowadays, there are also new international agencies such as EFE in Spain, Xinhua in China, and Anadolu in Turkey (Surm, 2019).

Since they were founded, AFP, AP, and TASS have had no change of ownership or owner-ship form. AFP was founded in 1944, defined itself then and still defines itself now as a pub-licly owned organization (Surm, 2019; Juntunen & Nieminen, 2019). The AP was founded in 1846 as a not-for-profit news cooperative and continues to define itself as such. Its owners are U.S. newspapers and broadcasters. TASS was founded in 1925. Although it has undergone a number of changes since 1991 (Ob utverzhdenii ustava Informatsionnogo Telegrafnogo Agentstva Rossii, 2014), it has remained in state ownership. The legal status of TASS as a fed-eral state-unitary enterprise has remained unchanged (Vartanova & Vyrkovsky, 2020). Based on the number of offices abroad and the languages in which their news is delivered, AFP, AP and TASS have maintained their positions among what could now be called the "Big Seven" of AFP, Anadolu, AP, EFE, Reuters, TASS, and Xinhua.

Digitalization

Digitalization or digital transformation can be defined as the application of digital technol-ogy to all aspects of human society, including business and trade (Yeganeh, 2019, p. 259). In the digital transformation of news, new media and especially social media play a central role. Digitalization has hit news agencies hard and called into question their viability. News agencies have traditionally operated as business-to-business companies, as wholesalers of news, rather than on a business-to-consumers basis (Vartanova & Vyrkovsky, 2020, p. 2). Their clients—the media, and especially newspapers—have been confronted by major changes to their main income stream. These clients have had to contend with rapidly reducing numbers of subscribers who now look for free news from other sources, as well as with a collapse in revenue from advertisers (Rantanen et al., 2019a). The changes have in turn deeply impacted news-agency business models.

THE DEPROFESSIONALIZATION AND
DEINSTITUTIONALIZATION OF NEWS PRODUCTION

The digital collection and distribution of news by consumers have challenged journalists' role as the sole producers of news, contributing to a *deprofessionalization* (Haug, 1975; Blankenship, 2016) and *deinstitutionalization* (Picard, 2014) of news production. The deinstitutionalization of journalism plays a central role in what Picard (2014, p. 504) calls the "shifting ecology of news provision." It likewise features crucially in what Reese (2016) calls the *"new geography of journalism,"* which is characterized by the unpredictable extension of journalism beyond its traditional organizational confines. This new geography challenges institutional journalism by integrating non-institutional producers, such as YouTubers and citizen journalists, who disrupt the traditional boundaries between the production and consumption of news.

The concept of the *digital circulation of news* (Carlson, 2020) is now often used to describe how news production and consumption have become more closely connected. According to Carlson (2020, p. 234), "[c]irculation includes reception while going further to encompass the institutionalized message flows that shape media reception and practices of message recirculation or commentary that result." When news is exchanged and re-used without charge in the new geography of news, it cannot be controlled in the same way as news wires were in the past. When news circulates in all directions, it thus becomes a good that almost instantaneously loses its value. In this way, while digital circulation exponentially multiplies the production and use of news, it simultaneously makes it more difficult to protect its exclusivity and monetary value.

Even as the democratizing potential of so-called participatory news was being widely lauded, Deuze, Bruns, and Neuburger (2007) wrote about attempts by news organizations to integrate forms of citizen journalism and user-generated content production. Indeed, a number of examples of attempts to create agencies based around the distribution of participatory content demonstrate varied degrees of success, with Citizenside in France and Scoopt in the United Kingdom being integrated to various degrees into AFP and Getty, respectively (Cameron, 2008). The subsumption of these services within the existing structures of dominant media institutions, including news agencies, should serve as a potent reminder of the ongoing imbalance between users and media institutions, even in the context of so-called hybrid media. The fact that Getty shuttered Scoopt within two years of acquiring the service underlines this tension (Cameron, 2008).

THE EMERGENCE AND DEVELOPMENT
OF DIGITAL PLATFORMS

Many digital platforms, especially social media platforms, now serve as important mechanisms through which news is generated and disseminated. Digital news circulation relies on an extensive technical infrastructure in order to make content flows possible. It uses digital platforms that consist of technical components at different levels, such as devices, operating systems, and applications that are dependent on each other but also serve as control mechanisms for their owners (de Reuver, Sørensen, & Basole, 2017, p. 131). Digital platforms associated with Apple, Google, Facebook, and Twitter now assume an important gatekeeping role previously played by news agencies (Hanusch, 2017). Google News, for example, combines news content from many different news providers and displays it to users on a single digital platform (News Media Alliance, 2019, p. 7).

Van Couvering (2017) argues that digital platforms enable the continuing separation of media content from media distribution methods through the use of algorithms for finding and displaying content, based on simple functions like filtering, listing, categorizing, highlighting, sharing, and ranking. Such technologies play a crucial role in the algorithmically driven *digital gatekeeping* of digital intermediaries such as Google and Facebook (Hermida, 2020). For example, News Media Alliance (2019) reported that news content makes up roughly 39 percent of trending queries and 16 percent of high-volume queries in Google Search, while Google and Facebook together have been estimated to drive roughly 60 percent of the traffic to news sites in recent years (Nechushtai & Lewis, 2019). On average, in 2016, 69 percent of all recommendations led to five news organizations (Nechushtai & Lewis, 2019), with only one news agency—Reuters—among these. Algorithms have thus become the invisible hand of a digital gatekeeper, which is no longer necessarily a traditional news agency.

The emergence of digital platforms has created significant challenges for news agencies with regard to the viability of their business models. Jääskeläinen and Yanatma (2019), for instance, describe the disruption caused by the relation between social media platforms and news customers, which indirectly affects the ability of news agencies to monetize their services. The Board of the European Alliance of News Agencies (EANA) has argued that search engines are exploiters of content, benefiting from distribution they have neither created nor paid for (Statement on copyright by the Board of EANA, 2017). When the European Parliament adopted the new EU Copyright Directive in 2019, it was asserted that the Directive would empower creatives and news publishers to "negotiate with internet giants" (European Parliament, 2019). While the Directive was supported by EANA, larger platforms like Google opposed it (Tyner, 2019). This highlights the tensions that exist between new digital platforms and news agencies, particularly where this pertains to the monetization of intellectual property.

It is important to note that, although the circuit of news potentially democratizes news production, it also makes possible new ways of controlling news flows. In a way, Facebook and Google have also become digital gatekeepers of news through the ownership and control of their platforms (Bro & Wallberg, 2014). These platforms not only provide most of the audience for online news: their dominance may potentially *capture* (Nechushtai, 2018) the infrastructures that underpin attempts to legally protect the copyright of news.

Relations between digital platforms and news agencies, however, are not characterized solely by tensions. While AFP has been a vocal campaigner against Google's purported abuse of its search-engine dominance in France (EANA, 2019), the AP has been involved in collaborative efforts with Google to build a tool for sharing more local news more quickly (Schmidt, 2019). Thus, although digital platforms are significant sources of potential growth in usership (Nechushtai, 2018), the tensions they engender have been one of the key forces driving the diversification of news agency product offerings.

DIVERSIFICATION AND THE DEVELOPMENT
OF PROPRIETARY PLATFORMS

News agencies have widely used diversification as their main strategic response to the challenges of digitalization. As Jääskeläinen and Yanatma (2019) note, business diversification relates to transformations in news-agency operations as a direct response to digitalization, which has seen many new digital platforms challenge news agencies' role as the near-exclusive provider of news to their clients. This has not been an easy process, but it has led to significant institutional transformations, particularly in terms of the possibilities opened up for news agencies to deal directly with audiences (Vartanova & Vyrkovsky, 2020). It has challenged news agencies' traditional role as intermediary organizations, potentially bringing them into direct competition with their owners and customers. Most European agencies now see their own clients as their main competitors for the domestic market (Rantanen et al., 2019b).

In 2010, Freedman (2010) described diversification as the response by traditional news organizations to the Internet's disruption of their territory. He outlines a number of prominent approaches, including acquisitions and partnerships, but also most significantly the move to provide online in addition to offline news (Freedman, 2010). Since that time, however, the concept of diversification has been greatly expanded. According to Sükösd (2015), for instance, media diversification may create new forms of competitive media spaces, including new media institutions, ownership patterns and types, channels and platforms, and dispersed geographic designs. Revers (2017) describes journalistic responses to digital platforms as a *diversification of professionalism*, highlighting the differences that exist between journalistic cultures in different places. In our view, diversification should also include increasing the diversity of gender, ethnicity, and languages in terms of management and news reporting staff. Forms of media diversification also vary according to local conditions, as demonstrated by Sükösd (2016).

News agencies, at least in Europe, have used some of the forms of diversification described above, but not all. They have not radically changed their own ownership patterns, although some forms of acquisitions and partnerships have taken place, for example, in the Baltic countries (Lauk & Einmann, 2019) and in Austria (SDA und Keystone Fusionieren, NZZ, 2018). Diversification of content has been widely implemented. This is because a text news service has become largely unprofitable (Rantanen et al., 2019a). Most news agencies in Europe now see picture and video services as among their most important services (Rantanen et al., 2019b). The agencies that do well in Europe now offer not only a news wire, but an edited news service for online publication, a picture and video service, ready-made pages for newspapers, IT services, press releases, and media-monitoring services (Jääskeläinen & Yanatma, 2020).

NEWS AGENCY DIVERSIFICATION

In this section, we zoom in on three news agencies in different countries in order to examine how they have used diversification when responding to the challenges of digitalization: AFP in France, the AP in the United States, and TASS in Russia. Although the long-established distinctions between ownership forms of news agencies have become increasingly blurred in recent decades (Rantanen et al., 2019a), we here select examples with different ownership structures: co-operative (AP), public (AFP), and state (TASS), in order to show how news agencies in different parts of the world have or have not diversified their operations.

These are by no means average national agencies; rather, they all have a strong presence outside their home countries. While AFP, AP, and TASS all define themselves as national news agencies with respect to their own domestic markets, they present themselves as international agencies for global markets (Surm, 2019; Vartanova & Vyrkovsky, 2020). AFP, indeed, is legally required to function as a worldwide service (Loi n° 57–32, 2015). In 2018, AFP had a global presence in 151 countries or territories, with services offered in six languages: French, English, German, Portuguese, Spanish, and Arabic. The AP news report is distributed to its members and customers in English, Spanish, and Arabic, and it has over 100 offices abroad. TASS's reports are in Russian and English, and it has sixty-eight offices outside Russia. Its obligation is, by law, to cover "state policy and public life of the Russian Federation, as well as the most important events taking place abroad" (Ob utverzhdenii ustava Informatsionnogo Telegrafnogo Agentstva Rossii, 2014).

OWNERSHIP AND GOVERNANCE

One of the ways in which media organizations could potentially diversify themselves, when trying to develop new products or expanding into new markets, is through acquisitions and mergers. News agencies are often constrained in their attempts to bring in changes, either because of their relationship to their national governments or their ownership. For example, even if AFP and TASS have not changed their ownership forms, there have been some changes to their statutes. AFP is legally defined as "an autonomous organization with a civil personality and whose functioning is ensured in accordance with the commercial rules" (Loi n° 57–32, 2015). Although there were a number of key reforms to the agency's statutes in 2015, the 1957 law already encoded an important consultative role for two representatives of the French government (AFP, personal communication, May 25, 2020). Between 1991 and 2014, ten legislative changes concerning TASS were introduced by the Russian government, but there have been none since (Ob utverzhdenii Ustava Informatsionnogo telegrafnogo Agentstva Rossii, 2014).

Changes in governance can be seen as part of a diversification process, even if this is often only seen in relation to new products. A more frequently discussed issue is how company governance reflects changes in gender and ethnicity in society at large. For Carter, Simkins, and Simpson (2003, p. 34), the gender, racial, and cultural composition of the board of directors is now one of the most significant issues of governance within a modern corporation. However, as representatives of institutional journalism both national and internationally, news agencies have been rather slow in reacting to these broader social changes.

All three agencies have either a President (AP), a CEO (AFP), or a Director (TASS) as their chief executive. AFP is administered by a Board of Governors that appoints the CEO for a renewable five-year term (Loi n° 57–32, 2015). Over the past 40 years, ten presidents have been appointed (Surm, 2019, p. 8), all of whom have been men. The Board consists of nineteen members (including the CEO, who is elected by the eighteen others), eight of whom are women.

AP's by-laws are corporate documents and are not open for research. It is governed by an elected Board of Directors, currently consisting of sixteen members, four of whom are women. They are elected by members or appointed to the Board by the other Directors. AP has had five General Managers/Presidents since the 1960s (AP, personal communication, May 28, 2020), and they have all been men. Its Press Management Committee, which oversees AP's essential operations, consists of four women and four men.

The Russian government appoints the Director of TASS, who appoints the Editor-in-Chief. The collegial governing body of TASS is the Collegium, which consists of fourteen members (the Director's deputies (ex officio) and the heads of the Agency's major divisions)—currently, two of them are women. TASS has had nine Directors since 1960. The present Director was appointed in 2012, and they have all been men.

NEW PLATFORMS AND AUTOMATION

The three agencies have approached the development of new platforms and the integration of technologies of automation in a variety of ways. All three offer news, both on their platforms and on mobile phones, directly to their users. AFP has been active since 2000 in offering web- and mobile-based news (Rampal, 2019, p. 161). The AP News app on iPhone was launched in 2018 and had 653k downloads and 2.2 million users in 2019. TASS's website was relaunched on a new platform in 2018, boosting site traffic to 19 million unique monthly visitors in that same year and increasing the number again to 23 million by early in 2019 and to 30 million in 2020 but still well behind the other state-owned agency RIA (LiveInternet, n.d.; Vartanova & Vyrkovsky, 2020, p. 11). The TASS mobile news app on iPhone *TASS Seychas* (TASS Now) has offered news in Russian and in English without charge since 2015.

In the earlier years of the past decade, efforts at AFP targeted toward digitalization focused on the development of a new platform for the distribution of the agency's intellectual property. The digital system 4XML was presented as a mechanism that would permit "agents to produce multimedia 'content' intended for customers" (Laville, 2010). A new system was due to be launched in June 2020 (AFP, personal communication, May 25, 2020). Today, alongside developments in image and fact-checking, AFP's Medialab continues this push toward digitalization, with its group of engineers and journalists moving beyond the earlier focus on multimedia to examine new ways of creating interactive content. Among other projects, Medialab has been participating since 2016 in the development of the web video verification tool InVID (Teyssou et al., 2017).

The AP's deployment of automation began in 2014, with a focus on reporting the financial results of U.S.-listed companies, followed by a movement in 2015 toward sports reporting. They estimate that automation has freed up 20 percent of journalists' time, allowing reporters to engage in more complex and qualitative work (Marconi, Siegman, & Machine Journalist, 2017, p. 4). Their approach relies on the datafication of event-driven narratives to produce content using Natural Language Generation. The AP aimed to have produced 40,000 automated stories by the end of 2019, mainly in the domain of business news and sports, with a further goal of deploying image-recognition tools in order to facilitate image labeling in the newsroom. However, the use of NLG also raises ethical issues around the production of errors. The AP, for example, no longer monitors all automatically generated outputs because this is too time-consuming.

Vartanova and Vyrkovsky (2020) write that TASS management views artificial intelligence and virtual and augmented reality as the most important technologies for media entities. However, viewing AI as a strategic step in developing the news sector, the agency is also working on ways of robotizing the collection of routine data, for example, stock exchange quotations and automating the production of financial news coverage (Vartanova & Vyrkovsky, 2020). TASS and Chinese news agency Xinhua jointly launched the world's first Russian-speaking AI news anchor in June 2019.

USE OF SOCIAL MEDIA

Although some news agencies have been frequent critics of social-media platforms, all three of our case-study agencies now use these, including Twitter and Facebook, as a means of reaching their news consumers directly. This represents a shift in the traditional role of news agencies as B2B rather than B2C organizations. The AP was one of the first to use social-media platforms, with one AP executive interviewed by Griessner (2012, p. 17) arguing that to do so had important implications in terms of credibility, brand presence, and developing relations with news consumers, demonstrating the strategic importance of social media for gaining visibility and brand-building (Lauk & Einmann, 2019, p. 9).

Levels of consumer engagement vary across our cases. AFP has a multilingual presence on Twitter, with 3.4 million followers in French and 1.8 million followers in English. AFP has more than 510,000 Facebook followers in English. The AP's Twitter following is more substantial, with 14 million followers in English. The AP also has more than 766,000 Facebook followers and 1.2 million YouTube subscribers. TASS also has a multilingual presence on Twitter: the agency's Twitter account in Russian has 480,000 followers and it has 60,400 followers in English. TASS Facebook in Russian has 615,809 followers. TASS also uses other social platforms such as VKontakte, with 688,988 followers, Instagram with 230,000 followers, TikTok with 17,300, and YouTube with 72,500 subscribers, all in Russian. All figures are accurate as of May 2020.

TASS thus delivers news on all the major mobile platforms. However, as Vartanova and Vyrkovsky (2020, p. 11) write, "the agency's shift towards a B2C market has been seen as a difficult and slow process." This is also shown in its domestic market position. Today, TASS narrowly maintains its leading position as the most cited agency, with the other state-owned agency RIA-Novosti ranked second, and also competing with the privately owned Interfax agency, which is ranked third (Top-3 samykh tsitiruyemykh informatsionnykh agentstv—mart, 2020).

The diversification of products shows similarities across the three agencies. Each emphasizes the important role that images play in terms of their income and visibility. In contrast to text, the copyright on images is easier to protect and thus they maintain their exclusivity. All three agencies have also increased their visibility on social media, although their success is overshadowed by digital gatekeepers such as Google. The era that started after World War II, when news agencies were the main and often only gatekeepers for news flows, has been over for some time. So international and national news agencies have had to adapt and continue to transform as they move toward a B2C market. It is of crucial importance that these agencies maintain and further develop their presence and brand on social media. At the same time, this puts them in direct competition with their media clients, who are trying to do the very same thing.

FINANCING AND NEW SOURCES OF REVENUE

Digitalization has challenged the business models of many news agencies. If the agencies make losses, where do they find new sources of revenue? Given their distinct ownership structures, the forms and scales of revenue for our case-study agencies are all different. The most recent year for which detailed financial information on the AP's operations is publicly available is 2017 (AP, personal communication, May 28, 2020). Annual revenue at the AP peaked in 2008 at $748 million (Rampal, 2019, p. 155) and since then has mostly fallen. In 2017 AP's revenue fell by 8 percent to $510.1 million from $556.3 million in 2016.

While AP receives no subsidies from the state, both AFP and TASS do. AFP had an annual turnover of $325 million (300 million euros) in 2018. However, AFP receives subsidies accounting for 42 percent of its revenue (AFP, personal communication, May 25, 2020).

AFP received $123 million (113.3 million euros) in state subsidies in 2018 as a contribution to the funding of its general interest missions. This figure increased in 2019, with a subsidy totaling $135 million (124.4 million euros). In 2018, AFP saw growth for the first time in four years, with profits in 2019 totaling $5.6 (5.2 million euros), an increase of 19.4 percent on the previous year.

The Russian draft federal budget in 2019 for the next three years provided TASS with 2.9 billion rubles annually ($44.8 million, 40.1 million Euros) (Finansirovaniye SMI iz byudzheta predlozheno uvelichit' na tret', 2019), compared with 1.8 billion in 2016 (Minfin rekomendoval sokratit' finansirovaniye gosudarstvennykh SMI, 2016). It has been estimated that the turnover of TASS is about $60–70 million annually. In 2018, the total share of state financing on the agency's balance sheet was about 65 percent, which has allowed it to obtain direct financing without any obligation to make a profit, enabling the agency to function without commercial pressures (Vartanova & Vyrkovsky, 2020).

The focus on the diversification of products and offerings has arguably been borne out by AFP's revenue streams. In 2018, for example, fully 41 percent of AFP's turnover was generated by sales of images, that is, photo and video (AFP, 2019). As noted by Surm (2019, p. 12), AFP currently generates about 80 percent of its video turnover outside France. Indeed, AFP's Sales Director for Europe has asserted that video is AFP's most internationalized product (Surm, 2019), with AFP's video services growing by 30 percent in 2017.

Insofar as TASS operates without commercial pressure (Vartanova & Vyrkovsky, 2020, p. 8), the agency possesses creative and economic independence to develop its plans around the diversification of its products and production mechanisms (Ob utverzhdenii ustava Informatsionnogo Telegrafnogo Agentstva Rossii, 2014). Speaking in 2019, TASS Director General Sergei Mikhailov argued that state support will "gradually decrease," prompting the agency to generate its own income at a rate that increased "sevenfold in the past seven years."

Since 2017, the AP has no longer published its financial information, making it exceedingly difficult to assess how revenues are being diversified. We only know that in 2017 customer revenues by segment were 48 percent from TV, 23 percent from newspapers, and 9 percent from the Internet. Content licensing was 81 percent by business line in 2019. The AP says that it has worked to make up the shortfall in the newspaper business by investing more in video products and by cutting expenses. In summary, responses to digitalization demonstrate how the very notion of what constitutes a news agency is currently being transformed at the same time as news agencies are redefining the work that they do.

CHAPTER SUMMARY

This chapter explored how digitalization has challenged three news agencies, AFP, the AP, and TASS, once members of the Big Five global news agencies, in a new era where their core role as intermediary news organizations has been challenged. We have provided concepts for and empirical evidence of the challenges they face, but we have also given examples of the ways in which they have diversified their operations in terms of organizational change, technological adaptation, and product development.

The evidence we have is that none of these organizations has radically changed their ownership or governance—they have largely remained as they were originally founded and mainly defined by their ownership forms. Although different in ownership and context, the challenges they face are very similar and show how universal the concept of a news agency once was. It is surprising to see the similarities between TASS and the AP, traditionally seen as antithetical agencies (Alleyne & Wagner, 1993), but now facing the same problems of decreasing customer loyalty and increasing uncertainty of their new role in the digital world.

Our overview of diversification strategies within the three news agencies demonstrates diversification in some areas but not in others. At the same time, some agencies are diversifying their operations and offerings at a faster rate. All may need to draw on their status and reputation as powerful intermediary news organizations, yet they are also burdened by the traditions on which that status rests and resistant to change. This is the dilemma they face as representatives of institutional journalism: change is slow and does not necessarily reflect the changes in the profession of journalism and in societies at large.

DISCUSSION QUESTIONS

1. To what extent are news agencies still needed in the digital age?
2. How successful have global news agencies been in their attempts to respond to the challenges of digitalization?
3. Should the concept of a news agency be redefined in the digital era? If so, how?
4. Considering a news agency of your choice, what steps are they currently taking to diversify their operations?

BIBLIOGRAPHY[1]

AFP. (2019). *Services.* www.afp.com/en/products

Alleyne, M. D., & Wagner, J. (1993). Stability and change at the "Big Five" news agencies. *Journalism Quarterly, 70*(1), 40–50. doi.org/10.1177/107769909307000105

Blankenship, J. C. (2016). Losing their "mojo"? Mobile journalism and the deprofessionalization of television news work. *Journalism Practice, 10*(8), 1055–1071. doi.org/10.1080/17512786.2015.1063080

Bro, P., & Wallberg, F. (2014) Digital gatekeeping. *Digital Journalism, 2*(3), 446–454. doi.org/10.1080/21670811.2014.895507

Cameron, D. (2008). *Mobile journalism: A snapshot of current research and practice.* End of Journalism? Technology, Education and Ethics Conference 2008, University of Bedfordshire, Luton, UK. researchoutput.csu.edu.au/ws/portalfiles/portal/9676405/DavidCameron.pdf

Carlson, M. (2007). Order versus access: News search engines and the challenge to traditional journalistic roles. *Media, Culture & Society, 29*(6), 1014–1030. doi.org/10.1177/0163443707084346

Carlson, M. (2020). Journalistic epistemology and digital news circulation: Infrastructure, circulation practices, and epistemic contests. *New Media & Society, 22*(2), 230–246. doi.org/10.1177/1461444819856921

Carter, D. A, Simkins, B, J., & Simpson, G. W. (2003). Corporate governance, board diversity, and firm value. *The Financial Review, 38*(1), 33–53. doi.org/10.1111/1540-6288.00034

de Reuver, M., Sørensen, C., & Basole, R. C. (2017). The digital platform: A research agenda. *Journal of Information Technology, 33*(2), 124–135. doi.org/10.1057/s41265-016-0033-3

Deuze, M., Bruns, A., & Neuberger, C. (2007). Preparing for an age of participatory news. *Journalism practice, 1*(3), 322–338. doi.org/10.1080/17512780701504864

EANA. (2019). *EANA considers Google is trying to abuse its search-engine.* www.newsalliance.org/news/eana-considers-google-is-trying-to-abuse-its-search-engine-dominance-in-france

European Parliament. (2019). *European Parliament approves new copyright rules for the internet.* www.europarl.europa.eu/news/en/press-room/20190321IPR32110/european-parliament-approves-new-copyright-rules-for-the-internet

Freedman, D. (2010). The political economy of the 'new' news environment. In N. Fenton (Ed.), *New media, old news: Journalism and democracy in the digital age* (pp. 35–50.). Sage Publications.

Griessner, C. (2012). *News agencies and social media: A relationship with a future?* Reuters Institute for the Study of Journalism, University of Oxford. reutersinstitute.politics.ox.ac.uk/sites/default/files/research/files/NEWS%2520AGENCIES%2520AND%2520SOCIAL%2520MEDIA%2520-%2520A%2520RELATIONSHIP%2520WITH%2520A%2520FUTURE.pdf

Hanusch, F. (2017). Web analytics and the functional differentiation of journalism cultures: Individual, organizational and platform-specific influences on newswork. *Information, Communication & Society, 20*(10), 1571–1586. doi.org/10.1080/1369118X.2016.1241294

Haug, M. R. (1975). The deprofessionalization of everyone? *Sociological Focus, 8*(3), 197–213. doi.org/10.1080/00380237.1975.10570899

Hermida, A. (2020). Post-publication gatekeeping: The interplay of publics, platforms, paraphernalia, and practices in the circulation of news. *Journalism & Mass Communication Quarterly*. Advance online publication. doi.org/10.1177/1077699020911882

Interfax. (2019). *Finansirovaniye SMI iz byudzheta predlozheno uvelichit' na tret'* [Proposition to increase media financing from the budget by a third]. (2019, September 26). www.interfax.ru/russia/678102

Juntunen, L., & Nieminen, H. (2019). *The future of national news agencies in Europe—Case Study 3: The Changing Relation Between News Agencies and the State.* London School of Economics and Political Science. doi.org/10.21953/lse.oc95dmr2xy5y

Jääskeläinen, A., & Yanatma, S. (2019). *The future of national news agencies in Europe—Case study 4: Business model innovation in media-owned national news agencies.* London School of Economics and Political Science. doi.org/10.21953/lse.1oelxlquslqm

Jääskeläinen, A., & Yanatma, S. (2020). How do media-owned national news agencies survive in the digital age? Business diversification in Austria Presse Agentur, Press Association and Tidningarnas Telegrambyrå. *Journalism, 21*(12). doi.org/10.1177/1464884919883492

Lauk, E., & Einmann, M. (2019). *The future of national news agencies in Europe—Case study 2: The survival challenges for news agencies in a small market: News agencies in the Baltic countries.* London School of Economics and Political Science. doi.org/10.21953/lse.0160wua5rvg6

Laville, C. (2010). L'AFP: Une agence d'avenir? [AFP: an agency of the future?]. *La revue des médias.* larevuedesmedias.ina.fr/lafp-une-agence-davenir

LiveInternet. (n.d.). All categories: Russia. www.liveinternet.ru/rating/ru/#period=month;geo=ru

Loi n° 57–32 du 10 janvier 1957 portant statut de l'agence France-Presse [Law n° 57–32 of 10 January 1957 on the Statute of AFP]. (2015). www.legifrance.gouv.fr/affichTexte.do?cidTexte=JORFTEXT000000315388

Marconi, M., Siegman, A., & Machine Journalist (2017). *The future of augmented journalism: A guide for newsrooms in the age of smart machines.* Associated Press. insights.ap.org/uploads/images/the-future-of-augmented-journalism_ap-report.pdf

McQuirk, R. (2020, September 18). *Australia pays $3.7 M to help news agency though pandemic.* apnews.com/article/virus-outbreak-australia-media-journalism-19d6e96ec668128c461676ad23c84967

Meade, A. (2020, March 3). AAP to close after wire service tells staff it is no longer viable. *The Guardian.* www.theguardian.com/media/2020/mar/03/aap-to-close-after-wire-service-tells-staff-it-is-no-longer-viable

Minfin rekomendoval sokratit' finansirovaniye gosudarstvennykh SMI [Ministry of Finance recommended reducing funding for state-owned media]. (2016, September 13). Vedomosti. www.vedomosti.ru/technology/articles/2016/09/13/656812-sokratit-finansirovanie-gosudarstvennih-smi

Nechushtai, E. (2018). Could digital platforms capture the media through infrastructure? *Journalism, 19*(8), 1043–1058. doi.org/10.1177/1464884917725163

Nechushtai, E., & Lewis. S. (2019). What kind of news gatekeepers do we want machines to be? Filter bubbles, fragmentation, and the normative dimensions of algorithmic recommendations. *Computers in Human Behavior, 90*, 298–307. doi.org/10.1016/j.chb.2018.07.043

News Media Alliance. (2019). *Google benefit from news content.* www.newsmediaalliance.org/wp-content/uploads/2019/06/Google-Benefit-from-News-Content.pdf

Ob utverzhdenii ustava Informatsionnogo Telegrafnogo Agentstva Rossii (s izmeneniyami na 10 noyabrya 2014 goda) [On approval of the Charter of the Information Telegraph Agency of Russia (as amended on November 10, 2014)]. (2014). Government of the Russian Federation Resolution, May 4, 1994, No 426. docs.cntd.ru/document/9005834

Picard, R. G. (2014). Twilight or new dawn of journalism? *Journalism Studies, 15*(5), 500–510. doi.org/10.1080/1461670X.2014.895530

Rafeeq, A., & Jiang, S. (2018). From the Big Three to elite news sources: A shift in international news flow in three online newspapers TheNational.ae, Nst.com.my, and Nzherald.co.nz. *The Journal of International Communication, 24*(1), 96–114. doi.org/10.1080/13216597.2018.1444663

Rampal, K. R. (2019). Global news and information flow in the digital age. In Kamalipour, Y. R. (Ed.), *Global communication: A multicultural perspective* (pp. 149–178). Rowman & Littlefield.

Rantanen, T., Jääskeläinen, A., Bhat, R., Stupart, R., & Kelly, A. (2019a). *The future of national news agencies in Europe: Executive summary.* London School of Economics and Political Science. doi.org/10.21953/lse.aeginold23jj

Rantanen, T., Jääskeläinen, A., Bhat, R., Stupart, R., & Kelly, A. (2019b). *The future of national news agencies in Europe: Data & visualisations.* London School of Economics and Political Science. www.lse.ac.uk/media-and-communications/assets/documents/research/projects/news-agencies/news-agencies-visualisations.pdf

Reese, S. D. (2016). The new geography of journalism research. *Digital Journalism, 4*(7), 816–826. doi.org/10.1080/21670811.2016.1152903

Revers M. (2017). *Contemporary journalism in the US and Germany.* Palgrave Macmillan.

SDA und Keystone fusionieren [SDA and Keystone merge]. (2018, April 27). Neue Zürcher Zeitung. www.nzz.ch/schweiz/sda-und-keystone-fusionieren-ld.1381420

Schmidt, C. (2019, June 27). *The Associated Press and Google are building a tool for sharing more local news—more quickly.* The Nieman Lab. www.niemanlab.org/2019/06/the-associated-press-and-google-are-building-a-tool-for-sharing-more-local-news-more-quickly/

Statement on copyright by the Board of the European Alliance of News Agencies. (2017). EANA. www.newsalliance.org/news/statement-on-copyright-by-the-board-of-the-european-alliance-of-news-agencies

Sükösd, M. (2015). How to conceptualize media pluralization in China? In P. Valcke, M. Sükösd, & R. Picard (Eds.), *Media pluralism and diversity: Concepts, risks and global trends* (pp. 152–170). Palgrave Macmillan.

Surm, J. (2019). AFP, EFE and dpa as international news agencies. *Journalism, 21*(12). doi.org/10.1177/1464884919883491

Teyssou, D., Leung, J. M., Apostolidis, E., Apostolidis, K., Papadopoulos, S., Zampoglou, M., & Mezaris, V. (2017, October 27). *The InVID plug-in: web video verification on the browser.* MuVer'17: First International Workshop on Multimedia Verification, Mountain View, CA. dl.acm.org/doi/proceedings/10.1145/3132384

Top-3 samykh tsitiruyemykh informatsionnykh agentstv—mart [Top three most cited information agencies in March]. (2020). Medialogiya. www.mlg.ru/ratings/media/federal/7383/

Tungate, M. (2007). *Adland: A global history of advertising.* Kogan Page.

Tyner, A. (2019). The EU Copyright Directive: Fit for the digital age or finishing it. *Journal of Intellectual Property Law, 26*(2), 275–288. https://digitalcommons.law.uga.edu/cgi/viewcontent.cgi?article=1445&context=jipl

Vartanova, E., & Vyrkovsky, A. (2020). Between the state and the market: An analysis of TASS' fall and rise. *Journalism, 21*(12). doi.org/10.1177/1464884919883490

Wahlqvist, C. (2020, June 29). Australian Associated Press sold to consortium of investors and philanthropists at 11th hour. *The Guardian.* www.theguardian.com/media/2020/jun/29/australian-associated-press-sold-to-consortium-of-investors-and-philanthropists-at-11th-hour

Yeganeh, H. (2019). An analysis of emerging patterns of consumption in the age of globalization and digitalization. *FIIB Business Review, 8*(4), 259–270. doi.org/10.1177/2319714519873748

16

Covering International Conflicts and Crises

Raluca Cozma

While the proliferation of mobile technologies and social media has allowed us to be connected to the most remote corners of the world, a tweet generated by a protester in Hong Kong, for instance, does not constitute foreign correspondence. What the journalism profession understands by foreign correspondence is the coverage of people, events, and places abroad by *our* press corps. This press corps is an elite (and ever-shrinking) group of professionals who are well trained and have a strategic overview of world affairs that allows them to roam large swaths of the planet in search of stories of interest to their home base (Hamilton, 2009). These professionals have long-term experience, news judgment, and foresight as they relate to the locations they are stationed in, and they enjoy quite a bit of trust and esteem among their editors at home, who have a hard time overseeing their every movement due to geographic distance. Foreign correspondents see the world from the perspective of the country they are sending their dispatches to, so the location they cover is "foreign" to both themselves and their audiences at home. This distinction is illustrated by the experience of NPR foreign correspondent Jason Beaubien, who at one point was stationed in South Africa, covering twenty-seven countries in the sub-Saharan region of the African continent. While he was there, South African officials wanted to replace the foreign correspondents in their country with local reporters. It was very difficult for NPR to convince them to give up this idea. "It was this lack of understanding of what we, as foreign correspondents, do. Part of what we do is to be *the* foreign person in that country and view it with foreign eyes. NPR doesn't necessarily want just the South African perspective on South Africa. They want someone to come in and be able to relate what it is about South African politics, South African life that would be of interest to an American audience. That's what they want," Beaubien explained in an interview (Cozma, 2009, p. 91).

Foreign correspondence takes its name from the letters that travelers, at a time when travel abroad was rare, slow, and cost-prohibitive, would send back home describing exotic sights and exciting adventures encountered while on visits or expeditions overseas. But modern foreign news-gathering is a far cry from the glamorous shots you might see on, say, a travel Instagram account. The stakes in foreign correspondence are extremely high and have important implications for national security and foreign policy. Former *Baltimore Sun* and CBS foreign correspondent Tom Fenton (2005) argues that the responsibilities of foreign correspondents, especially during times of war, include alerting U.S. audiences to dangers within and outside our borders, monitoring the government's performance abroad in securing Americans' safety and making sure it doesn't abuse its powers, informing Americans about what the government is doing abroad in their name, and educating them in the historical and cultural contexts behind the news. To do this successfully, foreign correspondents must acquire expertise that home-based reporters might take for granted, such as an understanding of local cultures and customs, foreign language proficiency, and an ability to translate complex issues to an audience with limited experience and often little interest in world affairs. If they cover wars or crises, they literally risk their lives in conflict zones, sometimes being embedded with the combatants and often being censored, intimidated, or even targeted by the local governments.

Like all forms of journalism, foreign correspondence has evolved over time. Early stories would focus on topics such as piracy, diplomacy, crimes, and the doings of European royalty (Hamilton, 2009). Judging by the media obsession with the latest fashion or offspring of Catherine, the Duchess of Cambridge, and Meghan, the Duchess of Sussex, you might say that contemporary foreign correspondence hasn't changed dramatically. During the colonial period, foreign news "coverage" consisted mainly of stories plagiarized and translated from European newspapers that travelers would bring on ships from their travels or of letters from Americans visiting other countries (Hamilton, 2009). Given the limited technologies and means of transportation available at the time, gathering and reporting any type of foreign news took considerable time. It could take several weeks or months before news of major events in Europe would reach the United States. For example, during the War of 1812 between the United States and the United Kingdom, Americans didn't receive word of the December 1814 signing of the Treaty of Ghent until seven weeks later, in February 1815.

AN EXPENSIVE OPERATION IN LOCKSTEP WITH TECHNOLOGY

For media owners, historian John Maxwell Hamilton (2009) argues, foreign correspondence is the most difficult type of reporting to finance, which explains why fewer and fewer news organizations maintain foreign bureaus. Foreign news is an expensive commodity. Former correspondent Jill Carroll (2007), in a study for Harvard's Shorenstein Center, estimated that an average foreign newspaper bureau costs $200,000 to $300,000 a year, depending on whether a reporter's salary is included. As foreign news cannot generate the type of revenue that would sufficiently cover production costs, such reporting is typically subsidized by profits from other departments of a newspaper or broadcast operation (Willnat & Martin, 2012). During the Mexican-American War of 1846–1848, which was the first U.S. armed conflict mainly fought on foreign soil, daily newspapers on the East Coast would have to pay a lot of money to get news from the battles taking place 4,000 miles away. They used riders, steamboats, and railroads to gather updates. Newspaper owners soon realized they could save money by sharing resources and stories. This led to the formation of the Associated Press, a cooperative not-for-profit news agency is still in existence today (see chapter 15).

With the rise of the modern nation-state, publishers started to see value in foreign news. They wanted and were willing to invest in original coverage rather than just rewrite wire service copy. Compounded with the fact that it was also getting easier to travel and report the news thanks to technological innovations like the steam ship and the telegraph, foreign correspondence picked up steam as well. The emergence of radio networks in the mid-1920s, which made it easier to spread news from various corners of the world, led foreign news coverage to peak and reach its golden age. It also helped that American audiences became less isolationist and developed an appetite for global politics following World War I. During this time, newspapers started sending more and more correspondents overseas. But journalists ran into difficulties reporting due to access restrictions and military censorship. Foreign correspondents sought to cover serious and substantive issues, such as political turmoil brewing in Europe, war developments, peace talks, and the rise of Hitler and communism. They spent less time pursuing stories about Americans' travels and adventures, sensing that they were witnessing momentous episodes of history in the making.

EDWARD R. MURROW AND THE GOLDEN AGE OF FOREIGN CORRESPONDENCE

It was war, the medium of radio, and the astute news judgment of a particular foreign correspondent that ushered in the golden age of foreign news coverage. David Hosley (1984) describes the foreign correspondence heard on American radio in the summer of 1940 as a Camelot—a time when the men, the medium, and the moment created a perfect storm. While the major American radio networks had been experimenting with broadcasts from abroad since the early 1930s, the bulk of this programming consisted of entertainment, music, and cultural curiosities. When Edward R. Murrow (1908–1965) was sent to London in 1937 as CBS's European Director, he had no journalism experience and was expected to continue to steward the network's cultural programming (his background was in public speaking and drama). Having a front seat at the theater of European politics, including the German annexation of Austria and then of the Sudetenland (a region of western Czechoslovakia), Murrow felt compelled to break rules, innovate, and use his platform for intrepid reporting rather than for entertainment. With the help of William Shirer in Vienna and Bob Trout in New York, he essentially created modern broadcast journalism, airing the first CBS World News Roundup in March 1938, with updates from across Europe about the Nazi Anschluss. The new format was a success and still exists today. CBS coordinated sixteen such roundups during the annexation period, using live telephone interventions from seasoned print correspondents in Berlin, Paris, and Rome. Following the roundup's success, the network mounted its foreign news operation by hiring several expert correspondents who became known as the *Murrow Boys* (a group that included one woman, Betty Wason, reporting from Stockholm). By the August 1940 German bombing of London, CBS had a corps of a dozen correspondents in Europe (NBC, which mounted serious competition and broadcast informative programs about foreign affairs, had four). The London Blitz prompted Murrow to use the speed and dramatic appeal of radio to air his "This Is London" series, often recorded on a rooftop, which further showcased his narrative genius and cemented his legend status. His live broadcasts brought the British plight into Americans' living rooms and were prototypes of all his short-wave reports of the war to come: they provided facts about what was happening, used human interest to highlight how regular people felt inside the city, and explained how the news related to the Americans (Bliss, 1967). The way Murrow manipulated his reassuring voice, accents, pauses, timing, and nuances of words made David Culbert (1976) call him a "musician of the spoken word" (p. 185). Another detail that contributed to Murrow's legend was his courage in literally facing death while performing his job in London. Although his studio was bombed several times, Murrow never retreated to an air raid shelter, thinking it was unmanly not to risk his life on a daily basis. "I was afraid of myself: I feared that if I did it once, I could not stop doing it" (Murrow cited in Sevareid, 2019, p. 19).

After the war, CBS's foreign bureaus around the world were staffed with skilled correspondents that rivaled the foreign services of the most successful newspapers. David Hosley (1984) challenges the general conclusion that radio contributed to the decline of newspapers. The fact that radio increased public interest in international news during the Munich crisis made listeners go to newspapers to find out more, as surveys at the time showed (Hosley, 1984). Nonetheless, Murrow and his correspondents became the standards against which excellence of foreign reporting was measured. Erik Barnouw (1990, p. 154) argues that as a result of radio's extraordinary power to inform, America would be one of the world's most "news conscious and internationally-aware" countries by the end of 1941.

DECLINES IN FOREIGN NEWS COVERAGE

International news coverage declined steadily since the end of the Cold War, being sporadically revived during international crises—the types of events that also made Murrow a household name. In 1987, Dan Rather, who had worked as both a White House and a foreign correspondent and was at the time the *CBS Evening News* anchor, condemned this trend and lamented foreign-correspondent layoffs in an op-ed in *The New York Times*, headlined "From Murrow to Mediocrity?" A census of full-time foreign correspondents conducted by American Journalism Review in 2011 found that twenty newspapers and companies had cut their foreign bureaus entirely since AJR conducted its first census of foreign correspondents in 1998 (Kumar, 2011). This brought the total down to only 234 correspondents to serve as eyes and ears to global events for American audiences. This number includes journalists working for agencies like the Associated Press and Bloomberg News, which covers mainly financial news and represents a decline of 24 percent from a decade earlier. In the 1980s, American TV networks maintained about fifteen foreign bureaus each. Today, they decline to report the number of bureaus they have, only stating that they have an "editorial presence." Cited by AJR, Dana Hughes, the ABC correspondent based in a one-person foreign bureau in Nairobi, said of her job, which consists of covering the entire African continent, "We are fixers, shooters, reporters, producers, and bureau chiefs. Five jobs, one person."

The drastic cuts in foreign bureaus, explained partly by decreased public interest in world affairs and by news executives' concern for increasing revenue, led scholars to deem foreign correspondents an endangered species and to warn about a potential journalistic void that can leave audiences blindsided by world events, such as the September 11 terrorist attacks in 2001 (Wilnat & Martin, 2012). A survey by the Pew Research Center (2008) found that the majority of Americans (56 percent) follow international news when major developments occur, but far fewer (39 percent) consume foreign news on a regular basis. One bright spot in the AJR census was the growing international presence of National Public Radio (NPR), which had seventeen foreign bureaus in 2011, up from six foreign bureaus a decade earlier. Research comparing NPR's coverage of the Iraq War to the CBS coverage of World War II brings further reasons for optimism, showing that the NPR correspondents outshine the golden-age foreign correspondents in both breadth and depth of coverage (Cozma, 2010). Moreover, 48 percent of NPR's foreign correspondents are women, a percentage that is higher than even that among all full-time journalists in the United States, where only 30 percent are women.

One consequence of the reduction in foreign bureaus maintained by U.S. news organizations is a shrinkage in the scope and depth of international news coverage. The news hole (space and time) dedicated to international news in the U.S. media has consistently declined in the past few decades, a trend that has not been reversed by dramatic events like the terrorism of September 11 or the Iraq War. When they do focus on foreign affairs, though, American news outlets favor stories of conflict and disasters. In a 2008 TED Talk, Alisa Miller, head of Public Radio International, showed a map where countries are not represented by physical size but rather by amount of news coverage by American cable and network news organizations. The result is a distorted view of the world, where geographic areas like South America, India, and Africa are almost nonexistent. Representation and portrayals of countries in the media are crucial for public perceptions and understanding of the world and can affect public diplomacy as well as the external recognition and self-identity of nations within the world system (Wu, Groshek & Elasmar, 2016). Citing the fundamental shift of gatekeepers for international news from traditional to social media, a recent study (Wu, Groshek, & Elasmar, 2016) set out to examine if country representation is fairer and more accurate (by landmass and population) on Twitter. The content analysis found that mentions about the world's countries differ dramatically on social media compared to traditional news outlets. The only traditional Western powers among the ten most frequently mentioned in the tweets were the United States and France and, notwithstanding the fact that Twitter is banned in China, four populous and economically dynamic Asian countries (Indonesia, China, Japan, and India) dominated the list of ten most tweeted countries. Smaller countries like Venezuela, Jordan, and the Philippines were mentioned more times on Twitter than the United Kingdom. The researchers found that mobile phone diffusion in each country and social and political crises were the variables that most significantly predicted country mentions on Twitter. They did not examine news valence, or the tone of the information circulated on Twitter about these countries, which is the focus of the following section.

PATTERNS IN THE FRAMING AND SOURCING OF CONFLICT NEWS

Foreign correspondence is often criticized for being event- and violence-driven, at the expense of topics like the environment, education, science, and the arts, which are rarely the focus of attention. With conflict being a central news value, Gans (1979) identified seven dominant types of international news stories in the U.S. media, most of which focus on violent political disorder: (1) American activities in foreign countries, including military interventions, foreign trade, and presidential visits; (2) foreign activity that affects American interests, including killing and kidnapping of U.S. nationals; (3) relations with totalitarian countries, especially China and Russia; (4) foreign elections, transfers of power, and royal ceremonies; (5) civil wars, revolutions, and protests; (6) disasters with great loss of lives, like floods, earthquakes, and famines; and (7) atrocities committed by foreign dictators. Conforming to the old journalism cliché, "If it bleeds, it leads," regions around the world expand or shrink in news coverage "depending on where people are shooting each other" (Hess, 1996, p. 41).

Wars and disasters produce gripping visuals, and their coverage is brief and intense, often provided with little context or explanation of causes and potential solutions. This is what scholars call episodic framing, where news is presented as a "fleeting parade of events" (Dimitrova & Strömbäck, 2010), and its effects on audiences and political accountability can be significant.

Iyengar (1994) found that audiences who watch episodically as opposed to thematically framed news stories are more likely to blame issues like poverty, unemployment, social inequality, or crime on individuals rather than on society as a whole or on systemic factors. When correspondents dramatize events, they produce emotion-driven foreign policy preferences and decisions. For instance, when analyzing the news coverage of the Persian Gulf crisis, Iyengar and Simon (1993) found that episodic, military framed television news coverage increased the public's support for the military as opposed to a diplomatic solution. Similarly, Seib (2016) argues that embedded journalists' reports during the Iraq War were overused by networks, and context was often sacrificed for drama. Indeed, an analysis comparing foreign correspondence by journalists embedded with the U.S. military during Operation "Iraqi Freedom" to coverage by non-embedded correspondents found that the former was more likely to be episodic in nature and more favorable in tone toward the military (Pfau et al., 2004). This sense of "camaraderie" that may have affected the objectivity of reporters in favor of the troops they were covering illustrates a larger tension in war foreign correspondence, stemming from correspondents' dual identities as detached professionals and civilian patriots. While such dual identities might occasionally affect sports journalists, who are expected by their audiences to be fair but also exhibit a sense of local-team boosterism, Philip Knightley (2004) reminds us that the goals of the media and the military are ultimately irreconcilable. While the military aims to win the war as swiftly as possible, ideally hiding the horrific realities of its violence and destruction from the public eye, the media have a responsibility to bear witness and report the military's actions as objectively and accurately as possible, or else they risk turning into propaganda tools.

In a comparison of United States and Swedish television news coverage, Dimitrova and Stromback (2010) found that only about 11 percent of U.S. newshole was dedicated to world affairs compared to 27 percent in its Swedish counterpart, and almost nine out of ten news items on U.S. television were episodically framed in contrast to Swedish television news, where (a third of Swedish stories are thematically framed) about one-third of the stories were thematically framed. The authors concluded that American television news programs offer limited opportunities for their audiences to learn about and understand current affairs in general and foreign affairs in particular.

In addition to its focus on episodic versus thematic framing, research on foreign correspondence has also identified war and peace journalism as two competing frames in the news coverage of conflict (Galtung, 1998). War journalism framing embraces conflict as a central news value to attract audience attention. It is sensational, superficial, and action-oriented. It focuses on immediately visible ground developments, such as bloodshed, damage to property, and casualties, it relies on the voices of leaders and elites, and dichotomizes between the good guys and the bad guys or between victims and villains. Such coverage promotes an us-versus-them narrative that tends to demonize the enemy and blame the party that "threw the first stone." In contrast, the same events can be covered through a peace journalism frame, where war is seen as a challenge to the world and the focus is on the areas of agreement. This type of coverage promotes understanding, conflict resolution, and reconciliation. Peace journalism takes "the high road" and can be achieved by toning down political and ideological differences, by exploring the conflict's historical and cultural context, and by giving voice to all parties (not only to the two opposing sides). Not surprisingly, peace journalism tends to be more thematic in nature, while war journalism is episodic, focusing on the here and now. The framing of conflict by correspondents has important, potentially life-and-death consequences, as it can contribute to conflict escalation or, conversely, promote peace. Research has found that about a third of the Murrow Boys' foreign correspondents used the war journalism frame in their coverage of World War II, while the default mode of operation for the more modern press "is to cover tension, conflict, and violence" (Wolfsfeld, 2004, p. 156). Similarly,

Siraj (2008) found that elite U.S. newspapers favored a war journalism lens when covering the Pakistan–India conflict over Kashmir.

Philip Seib (2016) also points to another worrying trend in foreign correspondence brought about by increasing competition among news organizations but also by what he calls "gadgetry" (p. 3), such as ever-smaller and more mobile technologies (satellite uplinks, telephones, and videophones): speed of coverage. The advent of platforms like social media has pressured news organizations to deliver *real-time* news coverage, which can undercut what should be a deliberative process of judging newsworthiness and assessing accuracy. This has led to occasional inaccuracies, which can have important consequences and undermine the trust of audiences, especially during crises. Seib gives the example of the first fast reports during the Iraq War, many of which did not hold up.

Hess (1996) calls attention to another pattern resulting from the news value of conflict and the appetite for war and disaster news in foreign correspondence. When news of crises breaks in other parts of the world, television networks take advantage of these newsworthy events to promote their signature performers, the anchors, who are expensive to fly abroad. The networks want to amortize the cost of their presence overseas by expanding their airtime at the expense of others (Hess, 1996) such as CNN sending Anderson Cooper to Haiti following the earthquake in 2010, where he spent about a month and had several live interventions. He even became the story during a riot, when he rescued an injured boy in front of the cameras.

In part to avoid endangering their lives, in larger part to increase their efficiency, and to some extent because they see themselves as "emissaries" or "diplomats" in charge of covering high politics (Cozma, Hamilton, & Lawrence, 2012), foreign correspondents tend to herd together in world capitals and rely on sources they feel comfortable with and with whom they develop routinized interactions. This leads to groupthink or "pack journalism" and to less diverse sources making their way into foreign news reports. News sources are a vital component of journalism, and often the messengers are more important than the message itself, providing evidence, legitimacy, and credibility to reporters' work. Leon Sigal (1973) documented an over reliance on international officials in foreign correspondence, finding that they account for more than 70 percent of sources in major newspapers' foreign news coverage. Journalists generally do not give non-official sources the same attention and privileged presence in the news, because their legitimacy can be more easily contested and their perspectives are not automatically authoritative. This pattern is supported by research on news about the U.S. military action, which found that during wartime, foreign correspondents rely heavily on sources from their home governments and are disinclined to challenge them (Hamilton & Lawrence, 2010). Take the example of *New York Times* senior correspondent Judith Miller, who in the days leading up to the Iraq invasion wrote several reports, relying heavily on official sources sympathetic to the administration, warning that Iraq had weapons of mass destruction (WMDs). No such weapons were ever located, but by the time the record was corrected, the course of national policy was forever altered.

In better news, research comparing CBS coverage of World War II with NPR's coverage of the Iraq War found that, while the rate of source attribution has doubled, the use of official sources decreased by 50 percent (Cozma, 2010). This might explain NPR's success, which maintained the highest broadcast ratings of all time as recently as 2018. Indeed, a less cozy relationship with officials and a propensity to cite more non-official sources such as regular citizens, NGOs, experts, or activist groups, seems to be a recipe for journalism excellence. An analysis comparing Pulitzer-winning foreign correspondence at *The New York Times* to routine stories (which did not win the highest award in the field) over eight decades revealed that in award-winning stories less than one-third of sources are officials, whereas about two-thirds of sources are officials in run-of-the-mill stories (Cozma, Hamilton, & Lawrence, 2012), mirroring Sigal's findings in the 1970s.

THE NEWS COVERAGE OF THE SYRIAN CRISIS

The Syrian civil war and refugee crisis offer an ideal setting to examine many of the international news coverage patterns reviewed above. According to Chang, Shoemaker, and Brendlinger (1987), U.S. media coverage of foreign events is dictated by four variables or news values. These determinants are normative deviance (or the unusual nature of an event), relevance to the United States, potential for social change, and geographical distance (proximity). The Syrian civil war, which started in March 2011 and lasted more than a decade, met many of these conditions. While the Assad regime's military crackdown to disperse the anti-government protests in 2011, at the heels of the so-called Arab Spring, attracted immediate attention from media organizations around the world, developments in August 2013 were particularly relevant to the United States. A United Nations investigation at the time revealed that the Syrian government used chemical weapons (sarin gas) against its own citizens, which is a war crime. This prompted the Obama administration to seriously consider a military intervention. During this time, when the possibility for the United States to enter the war was extremely high, U.S. media dedicated an average of two stories a day to the region (Cozma & Kozman, 2015).

Content analysis of *New York Times* and *Washington Post* coverage of the 2013 episode found that U.S. newspapers favored thematic framing in 80 percent of reports from Syria, but relied extensively on the U.S. and foreign official voices, at the expense of more diverse sources like Syrian rebels, citizens, or experts (Cozma & Kozman, 2015). This reliance on official sources is problematic since it corresponded to a propensity for conflict-framing. The use of rebel voices, on the other hand, correlated with morality or responsibility frames.

Another aspect of media coverage is the use of visuals. Greenwood and Jenkins's (2015) analysis focused on the visual portrayals of the first year of the Syrian crisis in photographs published eleven U.S. news and public affairs magazines, including *Newsweek, Time, The Atlantic,* or *The New Yorker*. They found that the conflict was primarily covered through war journalism frames, focusing on violence and disaster, rather than on scenes that would promote the peace frame proposed by Galtung. Men in combatant roles tended to dominate the visuals from the war, and when women and children were present, they were depicted with a sense of hopelessness.

As the war evolved, media research expanded its focus to coverage of the conflict and the refugee crisis by news outlets in other parts of the world (Dimitrova, Ozdora-Aksak, & Connolly-Ahern, 2018), showing that media framing of refugees differed significantly across European nations. Next time you read a report about developments in Syria, pay attention to the visuals, frames, and sources used to see if you notice any changes in coverage patterns since the first days of the conflict. You can also take a moment to ponder what countries are mentioned and what can be added to the coverage to offer a more comprehensive picture of world affairs. As we live in an ever-shrinking global village, it's important to be more media literate and internationally aware than ever.

Another criticism leveled at foreign correspondence has to do with cultural biases and stereotypes that can sometimes color foreign coverage of different regions, cultures, or religions. Take the example of Islam, whose news coverage, especially after September 11, 2001, has evolved from equally problematic Orientalist representations of Arabian sheikhs, belly dancers, and desert savages, into portrayals of religious fanaticism (Ibrahim, 2010). Compounded with the already documented appetite for violence and episodic framing, void of context and background, this distorted reporting of Islam may fuel prejudice, hysterical fear, and aggression (Said, 2008).

Despite these shortcomings, often the result of budget pressures and time constraints, foreign correspondence can have a significant positive impact on the world by bringing attention the important information the public wouldn't otherwise know about. For example, in the 1990s, *Newsday*'s Roy Gutman exposed a network of concentration camps run by Bosnian Serbs, where Muslims were not only beaten and starved, but often murdered. The United Nations High Commissioner for Refugees estimated that 5,000 to 6,000 lives were saved as a result of his coverage. Not surprisingly, Gutman won a Pulitzer for international reporting in 1993. Now, more than ever, we need quality foreign correspondence to make sense of events beyond our borders. But covering crises and conflicts is dangerous, and few journalists are willing to cover war zones. The Committee to Protect Journalists keeps a tally of correspondents who have been kidnapped or even killed while doing their jobs. Even if they get away with their lives, many suffer from post-traumatic stress disorder. Given these realities, such correspondents are hard to recruit and expensive to insure. A correspondent can be worth upward of $4 million to kidnappers who target westerners, and while at one time, reporters were considered noncombatants like the Red Cross, nowadays they are no longer perceived as independent civilians by extremist groups. This has led the president and CEO of the Associated Press, Gary Pruitt, to call in 2015 for changes to international laws that would make it a war crime to kill journalists or take them hostage.

Current Trends and Practices in Foreign Correspondence

Hamilton and Jenner (2004) recognize that the emergence of social media, citizen journalism, and alternate sources of international news as well as increased economic pressures and global interdependence have challenged traditional foreign correspondence. Rather than being an endangered species, they argue, the genre has morphed and adapted to the new media realities, and the systems of people who bring us foreign news continue to evolve. To account for these transformations, the authors propose that international news is nowadays produced by eight types of journalists.

(1) *Traditional foreign correspondents* are full-time foreign correspondents who are nationals of the country that is home to their news organization, similar to Edward Murrow's globetrotting boys. They work for large national newspapers, networks, or news agencies that can still afford them. But, the authors caution, "the traditional elite foreign correspondent no longer has hegemony over foreign news" (p. 312).

They are joined by (2) *parachute foreign correspondents*, a new breed of journalists that are sent, as needs arise, to report short-term events overseas. Like traditional foreign correspondents, they are usually nationals of the country that is home to their news organization, but such opportunistic assignments are easier to finance compared to permanently stationing a reporter abroad.

Moving away from the traditional view that Americans are best equipped to be the public's eyes and ears abroad, more news executives are hiring (3) *foreign correspondents,* foreign nationals who typically command lower salaries and arrangements for family accommodation compared to traditional American correspondents.

International news consumed by American audiences can also originate from (4) *local correspondents* at smaller U.S. broadcast stations and newspapers, under the premise that any local news story has the potential to have an international angle.

Increasingly many news outlets are mining local connections and hiring (5) *foreign local correspondents.* These are foreign nationals who work for foreign news organizations that make their work available online.

Large organizations like the World Bank or Ford or even smaller enterprises with interests and operations abroad can hire (6) *in-house foreign correspondents* as part of their staff to collect valuable information about local markets, making them more globally competitive.

Specialized media such as Bloomberg or Reuters hire (7) *premium service foreign correspondents,* full-time, highly skilled foreign correspondents whose work is syndicated across several news outlets that can't afford their own foreign news corps.

Finally, (8) *amateur correspondents* are unaffiliated and untrained citizens who become de facto journalists when they witness events and can share their accounts thanks to technological advances like smartphones equipped with cameras and mobile applications. They can report live from the scene via Facebook, Twitter, or YouTube.

CHAPTER SUMMARY

The amount of international news coverage has declined steadily since the end of the Cold War, moving further away from an earlier "golden age" of foreign correspondence. Both domestic and global media organizations are faced with declining budgets and staff to cover what happens in other parts of the world. Interest in foreign news tends to spike and is temporarily revived during international crises such as military conflicts and natural disasters. Foreign news coverage, which often favors elite perspectives and episodic framing of events, affects how people around the world perceive other nations. Thus, the media have a responsibility to provide a diverse set of sources and avoid stereotypical visuals and frames in their foreign news reporting. It is recommended for domestic audiences to be critical news consumers and consult multiple sources to get a range of perspectives about international issues, actors, and events.

DISCUSSION QUESTIONS

1. What three factors ushered in the golden age of foreign correspondence?
2. What are some of the main challenges facing foreign correspondence today?
3. What are some problematic patterns that you see in the coverage of international news, and how could they be corrected?
4. How is peace journalism framing different from war journalism framing in conflict news coverage?
5. Where do you get your foreign news from, and what kind of correspondents are producing those stories?

BIBLIOGRAPHY

Barnouw, E. (1990). *Tube of plenty: The evolution of American television.* Oxford University Press.

Bliss, E. (1967). *In search of light: The broadcasts of Edward R. Murrow, 1938–1961.* Knopf.

Carroll, J. (2007). Foreign news coverage: The US media's undervalued asset. *The Joan Shorenstein Center on the Press, Politics and Public Policy Working Paper Series,* 1. shorensteincenter.org/wp-content/uploads/2012/03/2007_01_carroll.pdf.

Chang, T. K., Shoemaker, P. J., & Brendlinger, N. (1987). Determinants of international news coverage in the US media. *Communication Research, 14*(4), 396–414.

Cozma, R. (2009). *The Murrow Tradition: What Was It, and Does It Still Live?* (Unpublished dissertation). Louisiana State University, Baton Rouge, Louisiana.

Cozma, R. (2010). From Murrow to Mediocrity? Radio foreign news from World War II to the Iraq War. *Journalism Studies, 11*(5), 667–682.

Cozma, R., Hamilton, J. M., & Lawrence, R. (2012). NYT Pulitzer stories show more independence in foreign sourcing. *Newspaper Research Journal, 33*(2), 84–99.

Cozma, R., & Kozman, C. (2015). The Syrian crisis in the news: How the United States' elite newspapers framed the international reaction to Syria's use of chemical weapons. *Journalism Practice, 9*(5), 669–686.

Culbert, D. H. (1976). *News for Everyman: Radio and foreign affairs in thirties America.* ABC-CLIO.

Dimitrova, D. V., & Strömbäck, J. (2010). Exploring semi-structural differences in television news between the United States and Sweden. *International Communication Gazette, 72*(6), 487–502.

Dimitrova, D. V., Ozdora-Aksak, E., & Connolly-Ahern, C. (2018). On the border of the Syrian refugee crisis: Views from two different cultural perspectives. *American Behavioral Scientist, 62*(4), 532–546.

Fenton, T. (2005). *Bad news: The decline of reporting, the business of news, and the danger to us all.* Walter de Gruyter.

Galtung, J. (1998). High road, low road: Charting the course for peace journalism. *Track Two: Constructive Approaches to Community and Political Conflict, 7*(4), 7–10.

Gans H. J. (1979). *Deciding what's news.* Vintage.

Greenwood, K., & Jenkins, J. (2015). Visual framing of the Syrian conflict in news and public affairs magazines. *Journalism Studies, 16*(2), 207–227.

Hamilton, J. M. (2009). *Journalism's roving eye: A history of American foreign reporting.* LSU Press.

Hamilton, J. M., & Jenner, E. (2004). Redefining foreign correspondence. *Journalism, 5*(3), 301–321.

Hamilton, J. M., & Lawrence, R. G. (2010). Foreign correspondence. *Journalism Studies, 11*(5), 630–633.

Hess, S. (1996). *International news and foreign correspondents.* Vol. 5. Brookings Institution Press.

Hosley, D. H. (1984). *As good as any: Foreign correspondence on American Radio, 1930–1940.* Vol. 2. Praeger.

Ibrahim, D. (2010). The framing of Islam on network news following the September 11th attacks. *International Communication Gazette, 72*(1), 111–125.

Iyengar, S. (1994). *Is anyone responsible?: How television frames political issues.* University of Chicago Press.

Iyengar, S., & Simon, A. (1993). News coverage of the Gulf crisis and public opinion: A study of agenda-setting, priming, and framing. *Communication Research, 20*(3), 365–383.

Knightley, P. (2004). *The first casualty: The war correspondent as hero and myth-maker from the Crimea to Iraq.* JHU Press.

Kumar, P. (2011). Foreign correspondents: Who covers what. *American Journalism Review,* January, 318–331.

Pew Research Center. (2008). *Audience segments in a changing news environment: Key news audiences now blend online and traditional sources: Pew Research Center Biennial News Consumption Survey.* www.pewresearch.org/wp-content/uploads/sites/4/legacy-pdf/444.pdf

Pfau, M., Haigh, M., Gettle, M., Donnelly, M., Scott, G., Warr, D., & Wittenberg, E. (2004). Embedding journalists in military combat units: Impact on newspaper story frames and tone. *Journalism & Mass Communication Quarterly, 81*(1),74–88.

Said, E. W. (2008). *Covering Islam: How the media and the experts determine how we see the rest of the world*. Random House.

Seib, P. (2016). *Beyond the front lines: How the news media cover a world shaped by war*. Springer.

Sevareid, E. (2019). *Not so wild a dream*. Diversion Books.

Sigal, L. V. (1973). *Reporters and officials: The organization and politics of news reporting*. D. C. Heath and Company.

Siraj, S. A. (2008). War or peace journalism in elite US newspapers: Exploring news framing in Pakistan-India conflict. *Strategic Studies, 28*(1), 194–222.

Willnat, L., & Martin, J. (2012). Foreign correspondents—An endangered species? In Weaver, D. H. & Willnat, L. (Eds)., *The global journalist in the 21st century* (pp. 495–510). Routledge.

Wolfsfeld, G. (2001) The news media and the Second Intifada: Some initial lessons. *Harvard International Journal of Press/Politics, 6*(4), 113–118.

Wu, H. D., Groshek, J., & Elasmar, M. G. (2016). Which countries does the world talk about? An examination of factors that shape country presence on Twitter. *International Journal of Communication, 10*, 1860–1877.

17

Public Diplomacy and International Communication

Suman Lee

Technological globalization has erased national barriers and, in many cases, flattened the global playing field. What happens within national borders affects audiences across the world. The importance of controlling news and communication messages and creating favorable public opinion toward nations has increased in the age of social media. This chapter discusses the notions of soft power and public diplomacy and offers relevant examples that highlight the fine line between strategic communications and propaganda. The chapter addresses these issues with a focus on the importance of public diplomacy efforts in the context of economic and technological globalization.

The world has completely changed since the global outbreak of COVID-19 and the level of fear and anxiety people felt has been unprecedented. While the numbers of confirmed cases and deaths increased day by day, hospitals were overwhelmed, businesses shut down, and schools closed. The entire world just stopped its normal operations to halt the spread of this deadly virus and our daily lives entered an abyss of never-ending uncertainty.

Under this dire global pandemic situation, every country made tremendous efforts to save people's lives and minimize damages to healthcare systems. The whole world had an opportunity to observe how countries would successfully handle or drastically fail in mitigating the global pandemic. This seemed to be a hard test for many countries in the court of global public opinion. Some countries were praised for their active engagement and containment, but others were criticized for failed leadership and poor judgment. China, for example, an early epicenter of the virus, was heavily criticized for its mishandling of the pandemic outbreak (Pew Research Center, 2020). Japan was also criticized for its delayed testing and engagement when a cruise ship with some confirmed patients arrived and stationed ashore unexpectedly (Essig, Swalls, Wakatsuki, & Westcott, 2020). The situation in the cruise ship quickly worsened, reportedly due to the Japanese government's decision to downplay the number of confirmed cases and deaths in order to minimize concerns for hosting the Olympic games, which were postponed soon after. The U.S. leadership was in denial of the severity of pandemic at its early stages when the number of cases moved the country to the top worldwide as the number of infections and deaths skyrocketed. Premature reopening after shortened lockdown, politicizing public health responses, and the privatized healthcare system were largely blamed for tainting the global reputation of the United States.

In contrast, other countries handled the situation well and gave positive impressions to the world. South Korea, for example, quickly flattened the curve of infections by implementing aggressive engagement tactics and public campaigns, which included massive drive-through testing, a web application tracking system, government-controlled quarantines, and nation-wide mask-wearing mandate. Germany also followed the footsteps of South Korea and achieved positive outcomes for containment of the virus.

Whether facing a national crisis like a pandemic outbreak or doing business as usual, countries do care about how people in other countries evaluate them. National reputation and national image are common terms to indicate this evaluation. National reputation is an intangible but valuable asset of a country, and countries are eager to create and maintain a positive national reputation by applying a means of communication called *public diplomacy*.

PUBLIC DIPLOMACY AND NATIONAL REPUTATION

Public diplomacy plays an important role in communicating with publics in other countries and is defined as the purposive and comprehensive activities of a country to influence and build relationships with foreign publics (Gilboa, 2008). Tuch (1990) defined it as "communi-cating with foreign publics in an attempt to bring about understanding for its nation's ideas and ideals, its institutions and culture, as well as its national goals and policies" (p. 3). In short, public diplomacy aims to build and maintain relationships with foreign publics to achieve the host countries' national interests.

Foreign publics are important on many different fronts since they include consumers who purchase foreign goods and services, as well as tourists and students who visit and study over-seas, and investors who build factories or hold shares in other countries. Public diplomacy aims to communicate and engage with these multifaceted groups of people in other countries. For example, Kotler and Gertner (2002) asserted that national reputation affects people's decisions about purchasing, investing, residence, and travel. Lee, Rodriguez, and Sar (2012) found a posi-tive relationship between national reputation and people's willingness to visit another country. Papadopoulos and Heslop (2002) found that strong nation branding attracts foreign investment.

In order to serve national interests and policy goals, countries conduct public diplomacy through a variety of activities. Cull (2009) suggested these five categories: (1) listening, (2) advocacy, (3) cultural diplomacy, (4) exchange diplomacy, and (5) international broadcast-ing. Listening is gathering information about foreign public opinion before policy decisions and active listening is highly regarded as effective two-way communication. Advocacy is to help for-eign publics better understand a country's policy position and its rationale. Cultural diplomacy shares a country's cultural attraction and heritage with foreign publics (e.g., the Goethe Insti-tute). Exchange diplomacy enhances direct experience of other countries as foreign students and visitors (e.g., the Fulbright Scholarship). International broadcasting communicates with foreign publics via different channels using television, radio, and online media (e.g., Voice of America).

Others have used more simplified categories for public diplomacy (Leonard, Smewing, & Stead, 2002): (1) daily communications, (2) strategic communications, and (3) relationship building. Daily communications involve rationalizing foreign policy in the global news sys-tem. Strategic communications are promoting the country as a whole by delivering strategic messages through innovative actions. Relationship building refers to developing sustainable relationships with key people through a variety of events, trainings, and cultural exchanges.

While government plays an important role in public diplomacy, recently more attention has been given to the role of non-state actors in contemporary public diplomacy (Melissen, 2005;

Ross, 2003). Publics in other countries could perceive the public diplomacy activities of foreign governments as propaganda because people might doubt the true intentions of foreign countries, wondering whether foreign countries only pursue their national interests, or the mutual interests of both countries. Non-state actors such as corporations, educational institutions, and non-governmental organizations (NGOs) interact with foreign publics in the form of public–private partnership, which separates authentic public diplomacy from propaganda (Fitzpatrick, 2009).

HARD POWER VS. SOFT POWER

"Soft power" is a commonly used term in public diplomacy literature. Power is defined as an influence to change others' behavior. According to Joseph Nye (2004), a renowned international relations scholar at Harvard, a country's world influence can be explained by two factors: hard power and soft power. Hard power is coercive and forceful influence to change other countries' behaviors, using military threats or economic sanctions. Think about the conflict between the United States and Iran (or North Korea). To counter the security threat presented by these countries' nuclear ambitions, the United States used hard power resources by increasing the U.S. military trainings in the regions and/or placing economic sanctions on their trade and financial transactions. Soft power, in contrast, is cooperative power to influence others' behaviors through appeals such as values, culture, and policies. The common forms of soft power resources are political systems, leadership on international issues, technology/innovation, country reputation, quality of products, tourism, language, history, and so on. When other countries agree with or admire your country's values, culture, and leadership in policy, you do not have to force them to change their behaviors. Rather, they may voluntarily change themselves. This is the influence of soft power, to which public diplomacy contributes a great deal.

The United States has been enjoying a special status in soft power as well as hard power. Democracy, freedom of expression and press, rule of law, innovative entrepreneurship, and global leadership in and contributions to world organizations attract many other countries and they voluntarily follow or collaborate with the United States in global affairs. More recently, however, the United States has lost a great deal of soft power equity developed over many decades because the current administration chose a unilateral approach to isolate the United States from the rest of the world.

Public Diplomacy and International News

International news is a major source of information where people get to know about what is happening in the world. A large number of world events get through the selection process of editorial decision-making and only a few newsworthy events are lucky enough to be covered by the news media. Also, the way a news story is constructed in details and perspectives depends on individual journalists, journalistic routines, organizational constraints, as well as the social and cultural environment. Media researchers observe that some countries are more frequently or positively covered in international news than others (Lee, 2007). This propensity of international news coverage affects how people think or feel toward those countries.

Since the 1960s, many studies have explored the characteristics of international news coverage. Researchers generally agree that there have been two perspectives, gatekeeper and logistical. The gatekeeper perspective is concerned with how the psychological factors of news professionals affect the process of selecting news items. The logistical perspective focuses on the socioeconomic characteristics and physical logistics of news processing. Based on these approaches, a great number of variables have been identified and tested.

The global power structure influences the coverage one country receives in another country's news media. Because a few global media such as BBC, CNN, AP, and Reuters have dominated the international news system for decades, the biases and perspectives from Western countries (the center) can transfer to the less powerful countries (the periphery). This dominance of the Western paradigm and news flow from the global North to the global South can be explained by different factors, including structural barriers as well as newsworthiness values such as impact (Galtung & Ruge, 1965).

Other researchers (Shoemaker, 1996; Shoemaker & Cohen, 2006; Shoemaker, Danielian, & Brendlinger, 1991) suggested an international newsworthiness model based on two main constructs—deviance and social significance. Deviance refers to news items that are unusual by socially accepted values and beliefs. The deviance construct has three components: statistical deviance, potential for social change deviance, and normative deviance. Statistical deviance or the likelihood of a news event actually happening, potential for social change deviance refers and normative deviance, which refers to a news event violating social norms or rules, can be applied to a country. For example, in the eyes of the U.S. media, North Korea has been regarded as a deviant country where there is cult-like generational obedience to a dictator family, nuclear development, and a failed economy.

Social significance is defined as the degree to which a news item is important to a society. Social significance has three dimensions—economic significance, political significance, and cultural significance. Economic significance refers to the business-dominated links between two countries. The key indicators are Gross Domestic Product, direct investment, and trade volume. The magnitude of economic interaction between countries is related to the amount of media coverage in a target country. Political significance entails government-dominated links between two countries. The indicators are military alliances between countries. Countries with closer political ties are likely to interact more frequently and their media are more likely to cover them. The U.S. news media cannot ignore the political importance of other nations in terms of U.S. national interest. Cultural significance is defined as similarities between countries in terms of values and beliefs. Countries that are homogeneous in religion and ethnicity can communicate more effectively than heterogeneous counterparts. Mass media tend to cover culturally similar countries. In summary, the countries with high social (political, economic, and cultural) significance with a target country are more likely to be covered prominently by the news media of the target country than those with low social significance.

As globalization has grown over several decades, the international news system has been diversified. There are more global news organizations in the field, such as the Al Jazeera offering perspectives from the Middle East and CGTN airing Chinese viewpoints, for example. These news organizations as well as the traditional Western media organizations compete with each other for global public opinion. It is noteworthy to discuss China's rise to a global power and the rapid growth of Chinese public diplomacy.

CHINA'S PUBLIC DIPLOMACY

Unlike his predecessor, President Trump explicitly labeled China as a serious threat to U.S. values and interests. The Trump administration tried to reduce the sheer volume of trade deficit with China by trying to negotiate a new trade deal. Global audiences have heard

President Trump blame China for the COVID-19 outbreak by calling it the *China virus*. The Trump administration has also blamed China for threatening regional security by provoking territorial conflicts with neighboring countries such as Taiwan, Vietnam, and the Philippines. Stealing U.S. intellectual properties through Chinese espionage is another frequently heard accusation. As an iconic event of this conflict, the U.S. government ordered a mandatory shutdown of the Chinese consulate in Houston, and China immediately responded with the same measure, closing the U.S. consulate in Chengdu, China. It is widely believed that the United States is not comfortable with China's rise as a world superpower, and sees the country as a threat to U.S. interests.

U.S. public opinion of China has been increasingly negative, reflecting uneasiness and unfavorable sentiment toward China. According to a survey conducted by the Pew Research Center (2019), 60 percent of Americans said they have a negative view of China, the highest percentage since 2005. Americans' positive opinion of China also reached a low point at 26 percent in 2019, showing a steady decrease in favorable opinions of China among the U.S. public. In regard to the concern about regional and national security matters, more than 80 percent of Americans said China's rapidly growing military capability and threat to neighbors are negative factors for U.S. national security.

The U.S. and global news coverage of China is largely negative, and this unfavorable coverage is believed to influence what people think of China and its global influence. One study (Liss, 2003) found that there are recurring negative themes about China in the news coverage of four major U.S. newspapers. These themes include: (1) rivalry/conflict with the United States, (2) system breakdown (e.g., law and order), (3) human rights abuses and political repression, and (4) social unrest and corruption. Another study found a correlation between the U.S. news valance and Americans' opinion of China over a 30-year period (Wang & Shoemaker, 2011). Nye (2004) explains this negative sentiment toward China from a soft power perspective. China's hard power (economy and military) is relatively strong on a global scale, but its soft power (attractive values and culture) is relatively weak. He notes, "In the United States, the attraction of an authoritarian China is limited by the concern that it could become a threat sometime in the future" (Nye, 2004, p. 89).

When comparing global soft power influence between the two countries, the United States is far ahead of China. According to the 2019 Soft Power Ranking, which is based on macro-level data and public opinion surveys regarding government, education, engagement, culture, digital, and enterprise, the U.S. soft power ranked fifth overall with top rankings in culture, education, and digital innovation (McClory, 2019). China, in contrast, ranked at the bottom—at twenty-seventh out of thirty countries.

The Chinese government seems aware of the negative trend in terms of China's national reputation among foreign publics and news media, and has tried active engagement strategies and tactics to respond this soft power challenge. In 2014, President Xi Jinping emphasized the importance of China's public diplomacy to influence world public opinion and initiated many public diplomacy activities. Reportedly, China spends $10 billion per year on improving its national reputation and soft power around the world (Shambaugh, 2015). Government offices and institutions are leading public diplomacy efforts to elevate its soft power and to mitigate the unfavorable perceptions toward China. The State Council of Information Office (SCIO), the Information Department of Ministry of Foreign Affairs, the Xinhua News Agency, and the CGTN (China Global Television Network) are the leading institutions, to just name a few. The message they want to deliver is that China is a responsible global citizen pursuing mutual prosperity with other countries and that China should not be viewed as a threat to the world.

One of the major target countries of China's public diplomacy is the United States, certainly because the United States is the most important country to Chinese national interests. The Chinese government has made extensive public diplomacy efforts on the U.S. soil. The Confucius Institute, for example, a symbol of Chinese cultural diplomacy, has built more than a hundred institutes at U.S. universities, where 1,360 teachers and volunteers have worked with over 400,000 language and exchange program participants (Confucius Institute U.S. Center, 2018). China's government-controlled news agencies like Xinhua and CGTN have increased the number of journalists in foreign offices, including in the United States (Shambaugh, 2015). Interestingly enough, there are some negative voices warning about the rise of China's public diplomacy in the United States and the world. For example, some faculty members openly criticize the universities that host the Confucius Institute on campus because they claim that U.S. higher education may be influenced by a foreign government in the name of cultural exchange.

The question, then, is whether China's public diplomacy can deliver the expected outcomes. Does China exemplify what the global public can genuinely admire and respect? There is no doubt that China's military and economic power are strong and will continue to be competitive for many decades to come. When it comes to soft power and public diplomacy, however, there is still a big question mark.

Observing what happened in Hong Kong in the early twenty-first century, many people in the world may be likely to rethink China's role internationally. When Hong Kong protesters demanded freedom and citizen rights, their movement was violently crushed by the police, and a new security law was enforced by the Chinese government. Months-long street demonstrations and violence were prominently covered by global news outlets. The Hong Kong story was perceived as a significant human rights violation in the eyes of the global public, even though the Chinese government claims that Hong Kong is an internal matter with no room for interference by foreign countries. The soft power assets that China's public diplomacy has aimed to develop for many years were heavily eroded by this incident. The lesson we can learn here is that actions speak louder than words. Public diplomacy and policy action should not be contradictory, but complementary.

JAPAN'S PUBLIC DIPLOMACY AND THE TOKYO OLYMPICS

After World War II, Japan's public diplomacy tried to reestablish its national reputation from ground zero as a country of war criminals. A key message to the world was that Japan had been reborn as a globally responsible leader with a strong economy and attractive culture. About two decades later, Japan did accomplish its mission and the world recognized a new Japan as a host country of the Tokyo Olympics in 1964.

Many state and non-state actors are the leading players of Japan's public diplomacy efforts, including the Ministry of Foreign Affairs (MOFA), the Japan Foundation, and the Japan Broadcasting Corporation (Nihon Hoso Kyokai: NHK) as well as multinational corporations and private institutions (Ogawa, 2009). The MOFA and the Japan Foundations are the two main vehicles of Japan's public diplomacy and initiate many programs, foreign media events, arts and cultural exchanges, Japanese language education, Japanese studies, and intellectual exchange. According to the Japan Foundation (2017), its annual budget in 2016 was JPY 24 billion ($224 million).

Global public opinion toward Japan has been largely positive. According to a national survey conducted by the Chicago Council on Global Affairs (Kafura & Friedhoff, 2018), more than 91 percent of Americans said that Japan is important to the U.S. economy and 79 percent of Americans agreed that Japan is important to U.S. national security. Based on another survey by the Pew Research Center (2018), Americans generally carry positive feelings toward Japan based on a feeling thermometer scale (61 degrees on the 0-to-100 scale). Japan was one of the top three countries with the highest ratings among the American public as of 2018.

It is likely that the year 2020 will be remembered as one of the worst years for Japan's public diplomacy. Japan had been preparing to host the second Tokyo Olympic Games since 1964 and wanted to send a message to the world that Japan has fully recovered from the Fukushima nuclear disaster caused by the earthquake and tsunami in 2011, which damaged Japan's national reputation. The Olympic Games is a sporting mega event that captures the attention of billions of global viewers. As the host country, Japan was ready to promote its intended image to the global community.

Unfortunately, the COVID-19 global pandemic changed everything at the blink of an eye. About a month after the pandemic outbreak in China, thousands of passengers aboard a ferry ship called the *Diamond Princess* were locked down for several weeks under desperate conditions. Because cruise ships are considered floating petri dishes for virus infection, people expected the Japanese government to quickly hand out necessary tests and impose quarantines to prevent the virus from spreading. The Olympics were just months away.

Japan did not meet this expectation and was passive and secretive to the eyes of Japanese people and the global publics. COVID-19 tests in Japan were criticized as not proactive with a lack of contact tracing (Takahashi, 2020). Information seemed to be tightly controlled by the government, and anger and frustration mounted from passengers and their families. Many people suspect that the Japanese government downplayed the severity of the pandemic because it was concerned about a negative effect on the upcoming Olympics. Under growing uncertainty and fear about the global pandemic, the possibility of postponing or canceling the Olympics was raised anyway by the news media and many stakeholders like the IOC (International Olympic Committee). Japanese Prime Minister Shinzo Abe repeatedly denied this possibility and firmly insisted that the Olympics should open as scheduled. However, the Japanese position did not gain much support from the global community. Many countries canceled their participation or boycotted the Tokyo Olympics, blaming Japan's insensitivity to the health of athletes and visitors, and charging that it was myopic to its economic loss as a hosting country.

This story of the 2020/2021 Tokyo Olympics turned out to be a nightmare for Japan's public diplomacy. First, Japan did not listen to the legitimate and reasonable voices of the global publics. Every country has suffered from this unprecedented global pandemic, and it seemed impossible to run this public mega event without sacrificing people's lives. People understood the massive economic damage Japan would take when the Olympics were postponed or canceled. Denying a compelling reality, however, was a fast track to a failed public diplomacy. Second, Japan missed many opportunities on several fronts of action and communication. The Japanese government failed to act and communicate effectively when handling the ferry ship passengers. Because the Japanese government passively reacted to the situations and wished for the best without acknowledging the harsh reality, they were forced from the outside to reverse their decision and postpone the Olympics. Lastly, if Japan had responded to the situation proactively, the outcome could be dramatically different from what we have observed. Japan could have earned more respect and admiration from the global community when showing a true caring mind as a host. You can please guests when they are willing to visit, not when they are forced to come.

THE DECLINE OF U.S. SOFT POWER

Since the collapse of the Soviet Union in 1991, the United States has been the single domi- nant player in world politics. Even though China has recently risen as a competing power, the United States has long had a special status with well-balanced hard power and soft power recourses. The U.S. global leadership depends on a strong military, robust economy, demo- cratic system, rule of law, and multiculturalism, which other countries admire and envy. U.S. soft power, in particular, has been highly respected by the global community and many coun- tries want to learn from the U.S. successes.

Under the Trump administration, the United States has been widely criticized for losing its soft power equity (Handley, 2020). People around the world have expressed disappointment with the unilateral moves of President Trump in many policy decisions: breaking interna- tional collaborations and alliances, tightening immigration laws and increasing restrictions on free trade are just a few highlights. Even though these policy actions were sometimes blocked by the judiciary system, the administration has not given up and continues to try to implement more changes. In the eyes of the global publics, this is not the United States they have known for decades. These policies and the ways in which they have been executed directly contradict the values and beliefs the United States has represented for a long time. According to a Gallup (2020) survey on rating world leaders, the average approval rating people from 135 countries gave U.S. leadership was 33 percent, the lowest rating in decades. This rating is similar to China (32 percent) and Russia (30 percent), while Germany is placed at the top (44 percent).

The COVID-19 pandemic played a critical role in making U.S. global leadership more elusive and vulnerable. The world expected the United States to organize individual countries together and to fight against the exceptionally dangerous virus. The U.S. performance in the COVID crisis, however, was far from meeting such expectations. The initial response to the pandemic failed not only to protect the American people from the spread of the virus, but also to lead the global response by blaming other countries. Xenophobic sentiment and violent acts targeting foreigners frequently appeared in the news. Foreign students were threatened with losing their visa status if they took their classes online, a necessary mode of learning under the life-threatening pandemic situation. This new rule was legally challenged by universities and revoked by the courts. Considering the frustration millions of foreign students and their families felt during this mishap, however, it is not an exaggeration to say that these cases may have contributed to declining U.S. soft power. It is fair to say that the United States has lost some soft power equity, which the country had developed over many decades. It takes a long time to build national reputation, but losing one can happen quickly.

DIGITAL PUBLIC DIPLOMACY

The digital communication environment has drastically changed all forms of communication, and public diplomacy is no exception. Technological developments and media convergence, the blurred line between content generation and consumption, machine learning, ubiquity, network connection, virtual and augmented reality, can all influence the strategies and tactics of public diplomacy. To achieve public diplomacy goals, communication experts are expected to maximize the benefits of these new technologies and minimize the risks.

Like social media, digital technologies will accelerate the level of public engagement. Listening is one of the main activities in public diplomacy and communicators can learn valuable insights from various sources of user data. Gathering social media data will help tailor messages and media strategies for public engagement and relationship building in the future.

There are many new challenges to public diplomacy practitioners in the digital era, especially when it comes to disinformation campaigns initiated by foreign countries and subtle psychological messaging that can be embedded on social media channels. Learning from the U.S. presidential election in 2016, Russia was believed to interfere with the U.S. election by providing disinformation to micro-targeted voters to help elect their preferred candidate (Bump, 2020). This is an example of a malicious act coordinated by a foreign country using digital technology. Identifying and responding to disinformation and misinformation in cyber space has become a challenging frontline that nations will need to monitor in order to protect national interests.

While protecting one's own country from malicious and outlandish foreign propaganda, countries should communicate with foreign publics with authenticity and truthfulness. Responding to malicious foreign actors with the same propaganda tactics is not a sustainable solution. Mutuality is a key value in public diplomacy, which does not aim to win over other countries but to gain respect from others who admire your value leadership. The true nature of public diplomacy is in line with Michelle Obama's famous phrase, "when they go low, we go high." Indeed, the best way to earn respect and admiration from other countries is to communicate with authenticity and fairness and to make sure a nation's actions remain consistent with its rhetoric.

CHAPTER SUMMARY

This chapter provides an overview of the conceptual meaning of public diplomacy, its role in enhancing or damaging national reputation, soft power, and the influence of digital communication. The ubiquity of online information sources and social media platforms has made public diplomacy even more vital in national image building. By reflecting on the most recent developments in China, Japan, and the United States, this chapter shows how these countries have gradually lost some of their soft power equity and national reputation through misguided policies and inconsistent global communication. The mutuality principle does matter for the quality of public diplomacy. When countries lose the perspective of mutual interest, public diplomacy stands still as self-serving prophecy, which does not inspire the hearts and minds of global publics.

DISCUSSION QUESTIONS

1. How does public diplomacy differ from propaganda?
2. Pick a country and share your experience of how your perceptions about this country were created.
3. Do you agree with the claim that some countries are covered more frequently or more positively in international news than others? Why or why not?

BIBLIOGRAPHY

Bump, P. (2020, October 7). Four years ago today, the U.S. saw the wildest hour in presidential election history. *The Washington Post.* www.washingtonpost.com/politics/2020/10/07/four-years-ago-today-us-saw-wildest-hour-presidential-election-history/

Confucius Institute U.S. Center. (2018). *Building the global community: Growing lifelong connections 2018 Annual Report.* www.ciuscenter.org/wp-content/uploads/2018-CIUS-Annual-Report-en.pdf

Cull, N. J. (2009). *Public Diplomacy: The lessons from the past.* Figueroa Press.

Essig, B., Swalls, B., Wakatsuki, Y., & Westcott, B. (2020, February 27). Top Japanese government adviser says Diamond Princess quarantine was flawed. *CNN.* www.cnn.com/2020/02/27/asia/japan-diamond-princess-quarantine-crew-intl-hnk/index.html

Fitzpatrick, K. R. (2009). Privatized public diplomacy. In P. Seib (Ed.), *Toward to a new public diplomacy* (pp. 155–172). Palgrave.

Gallup (2020). *Rating world leaders: The U.S. vs. Germany, China and Russia.* www.gallup.com/analytics/315803/rating-world-leaders-2020.aspx

Galtung, J., & Ruge, M. H. (1965). The structure of foreign news. *Journal of Peace Research, 2*(1), 64–91.

Gilboa, E. (2008). Searching for a theory of public diplomacy. *The Annals of the American Academy of Political and Social Science, 616*(1), 55–77.

Handley, L. (2020, February 25). The US is the world's top 'soft' power—but Trump has damaged its reputation, survey says. *CNBC.* www.cnbc.com/2020/02/25/the-us-is-the-worlds-top-soft-power-but-trump-has-damaged-its-reputation.html

Japan Foundation. (2017). *Annual report 2016/2017.* www.jpf.go.jp/e/about/result/ar/2016/04_05.html

Kafura, C., & Friedhoff, K. (2018). As China rises, Americans seek closer ties with Japan. *The Chicago Council on Global Affairs.* www.thechicagocouncil.org/sites/default/files/report_china-rises-americans-seek-closer-ties-with-japan_20181210.pdf

Kotler, P., & Gertner, D. (2002). Country as brand, product, and beyond: A place marketing and brand management perspective. *Brand Management, 9,* 249–261.

Lee, S. (2007). International public relations as a predictor of prominence of US news coverage. *Public Relations Review, 33,* 158–165.

Lee, S., Rodriguez, L., & Sar, S. (2012). The influence of logo design on country image and willingness to visit: A study of country logos for tourism. *Public Relations Review, 38,* 584–591.

Leonard, M., Smewing, C., & Stead, C. (2002). *Public diplomacy.* The Foreign Policy Centre.

Liss, A. (2003). Images of China in the American print media: A survey from 2000 to 2003. *Journal of Contemporary China, 12,* 299–318.

McClory, J. (2019). *The soft power 30: A global ranking of soft power 2019.* softpower30.com/wp-content/uploads/2019/10/The-Soft-Power-30-Report-2019-1.pdf

Melissen, J. (2005). *The new public diplomacy: Soft power in international relations.* Palgrave.

Nye, J. S. (2004). *Soft power: The means to success in world politics.* Public Affairs.

Ogawa, T. (2009). Origin and development of Japan's public diplomacy. In N. Snow & P. M. Taylor (Eds.), *Routledge handbook of public diplomacy* (pp. 270–281). Routledge.

Papadopoulos, N., & Heslop, L. (2002). Country equity and country branding: Problems and prospects. *Brand Management, 9,* 294–314.

Pew Research Center. (2019). *U.S. views of China turn sharply negative amid trade tensions.* www.pewresearch.org/global/2019/08/13/u-s-views-of-china-turn-sharply-negative-amid-trade-tensions/

Pew Research Center (2020). *Americans fault China for its role in the spread of COVID-19.* www.pewresearch.org/global/2020/07/30/americans-fault-china-for-its-role-in-the-spread-of-covid-19/

Ross, C. (2003). Pillars of public diplomacy. *Harvard International Review, 25,* 22–27.

Shambaugh, D. (2015). China's soft-power push: The search for respect. *Foreign Affairs, 94*(4), 99–107.

Shoemaker, P. J. (1996). Hardwired for news: Using biological and cultural evolution to explain the surveillance function. *Journal of Communication, 47*(2), 32–47.

Shoemaker, P. J., & Cohen, A. A. (2006). *News around the world: Content, practitioners, and the public.* Routledge.

Shoemaker, P. J., Danielian, L. H., & Brendlinger, N. (1991). Deviant acts, risky business, and U.S. interests: The newsworthiness of world events. *Journalism Quarterly, 68*, 781–795.

Takahashi, R. (2020, April 30). Japan and its policymakers search for light at end of COVID-19 tunnel. *The Japan Times.* www.japantimes.co.jp/news/2020/04/30/national/state-emergency-extension/

Tuch, H. (1990). *Communicating with the world: US public diplomacy overseas.* St. Martin Press.

Wang, X., & Shoemaker, P. J. (2011). What shapes Americans' opinion of China?: Country characteristics, public relations and mass media. *Chinese Journal of Communication, 4,* 1–20.

Notes

2. INTERNATIONAL NEWS FLOW IN THE DIGITAL AGE

1. As always, I would like to thank Regula Miesch, who not only read and commented on earlier drafts, but also shared with me her news consumption habits that were used in the introduction of this chapter. A special thanks to Maya Lahat Kerman, who gave me the idea to link between news and searches as two reciprocal flows that complete each other.

15. THE DIGITAL TRANSFORMATION OF INTERNATIONAL AND NATIONAL NEWS AGENCIES: CHALLENGES FACING AFP, AP, AND TASS

1. We have used agency websites for factual information: afp.com, ap.com, and tass.com. Where possible, we have asked representatives of the agencies to confirm our facts and figures. We are also grateful to Dr. Andrei Vyrkovsky for confirming data pertaining to TASS. All data were collected in 2020.

Index

Page references for figures are *italicized*.

Twitter, 23; accounts removed for disinformation, 34; emergency declarations effect, 53; false information, 34; international news flow on, 34, 207; in Latin America, 172; media threats, 169; push and pull principles, 23; Sub-Saharan Africa, 102–4; Transparency Report, 168; Twitter diplomacy, 32

Uganda, 97–101, 103–4; *Uganda Media Centre*, 100
Ukraine, 10, 126; slidstvo.info, 9
UNESCO, 18; disinformation and, 10; domain names and, 20; International Commission for the Study of Communications Problems, 19, 21; Model Curricula for Journalism Education, 72; New World Information and Communication Order (NWICO), 19–20, 26, 33, 154; World Summits on Information Society, 20
Union of Soviet Socialist Republics. *See* Russia
United Kingdom, 49, 51, 72, 137–38, 142; Communicorp U.K., 48; National Union of Journalists' maxims, 145; Scoopt, 191
United Nations, 7, 52, 118, 210–11
United Press International (UPI), 190
United States: digital and online communication, 179–80; Fairness Doctrine, 178; freedom of speech, 44; global public opinion and, 222; investigative journalism, 179; journalism education, 71, 74, 77; journalistic role, 59–60, 62; media bias charges, 182–83; National Public Radio (NPR), 178; press freedom court rulings, 178; press scandals, 179; Public Broadcasting Station (PBS), 178; Telecommunications Act (1996), 180; voter fraud lies, 184–85
Uruguay, 163, 167–68, 171
USAID, 4, 11

Valde, Katherine S., 86
Valentini, Laura, 83
Vallone, Robert P., 75
Van Aelst, Peter, 22
Vartanova, Elena, 195–96
Venezuela, 166–69, 207

Vlad, Tudor, 77
Vliegenthart, Rens, 22
Vujnovic, Marina, 82, 86
Vyrkovsky, Andrei, 195–96

Waisbord, Silvio, 174
Waleed Al-Ibrahim, 116
Walid ibn Talal, 116
Wall, Kim, 41
Wallerstein, Immanuel, 18, 26
Wall Street Journal, 180
Ward, Adam, 41
war journalism, 205–9, 212
Washington Post, 11, 179–80, 211
Weischenberg, Siegfried, 64
Western Europe: codes of journalism ethics, 145; digital and online communication, 138; journalism education, 145; media culture, 142–43; mixed press models, 136–37; newspapers and partisan politics, 137; niche journalism venues, 141; political stability, 137; press freedom, 135, 137; social media and, 140
WhatsApp, 102–4, 114, 117
Whedbee, Karen E., 86
whistleblowers, 37, 41, 50–51
Wilkes, John, 44
Williams, Walter, 74
Winters, Wendi, 41
Wired, 117
women in journalism, 6, 51, 146, 174, 194, 206
World Association for Community Radios, 167
World Press Freedom Index, 61
Worlds of Journalism, 6, 11, 59–60
World System Theory, 18
Wylie, Christopher, 37

Xi Jinping, 219

Yanatma, Servet, 192
Yemen, 111, 114–15, 118–19
YouTube, 48, 51, 87, 102–3, 118, 172, 191, 196, 211
Yugoslavia, 125

Zambia, 18, 98, 100, 104

Contributors

D. Jasun Carr (PhD, University of Wisconsin—Madison) is an associate professor at Idaho State University. He teaches courses in social media, content creation, and research methods. His ongoing research interests focus on persuasion, consumer culture, and civic engagement; the interaction of source and generational cohort in new media; and the changing journalistic and persuasive practices within social media platforms.

Ioana A. Coman (PhD, University of Tennessee) is an assistant professor at Texas Tech University, USA. She teaches courses in public relations, journalism, and entrepreneurship. Her research focuses on how different actors engage and interact in risk and crisis communication situations. Coman has received national and international awards and grants for her research, including the Page/Johnson Legacy Scholar grant.

Raluca Cozma (PhD, Louisiana State University) is an associate professor at Kansas State University. Her research examines foreign correspondence and political communication and the role of social media in these fields. Her work has been published in venues such as the Newspaper Research Journal, Journalism Studies, Journal of Broadcasting and Electronic Media, and the International Journal of Press/Politics.

Daniela V. Dimitrova (PhD, University of Florida) is a professor in the Greenlee School of Journalism and Communication at Iowa State University and editor-in-chief of *Journalism and Mass Communication Quarterly*, the flagship journal of AEJMC. Dimitrova has published research articles in the areas of global journalism and political communication in journals such as *Communication Research, New Media & Society*, and the *European Journal of Communication*. She is the recipient of multiple awards, including AEJMC Senior Scholar and LAS International Service Award, and grants from the International Research Exchange Board and the Arthur W. Page Center for Integrity in Public Communication.

Elisabeth Fondren (PhD, Media and Public Affairs, Louisiana State University; MA, International Journalism, City University of London; BA Humanities, Heidelberg University) is an assistant professor of journalism at St. John's University. She teaches courses in global journalism and media history. Her scholarship explores the history of international journalism, propaganda, media-military relations, and freedom of speech during wartime.

Zac Gershberg (PhD, Louisiana State University) is an associate professor at Idaho State University. He teaches courses in screenwriting, journalism, and media history, law, and ethics. His research examines the history of media, the ethics of journalism, and political communication.

Manuel Alejandro Guerrero (PhD, European University Institute) is the director of the Department of Communication at the Universidad Iberoamericana in Mexico City, and a member of the Mexican Academy of Sciences. His research focuses on media's role in new democracies, media, and political attitudes, as well as social media, emotions, and participation. He has published a number of book chapters, journal articles, and books on these topics and currently serves as Vice President of UNESCO's Chairs in Communication (ORBICOM).

Lea Hellmueller (PhD, University of Fribourg) is an assistant professor at the Valenti School of Communication at the University of Houston. She also worked as a visiting research fellow at the Reuters Institute for the Study of Journalism at the University of Oxford in 2018 and as a visiting professor at the University of Zurich in 2017. Her research focuses on digital news innovations from a global perspective; political polarization on digital news platforms; right-wing populist journalism as transnational phenomena; and media and terrorism.

Yusuf Kalyango, Jr. (PhD, University of Missouri-Columbia) is a media scholar, consultant and trainer and a former foreign correspondent. He is the author and co-editor of three scholarly books and has published more than fifty peer-reviewed journal articles and book chapters. His research focuses on African media, international journalism, conflicts, democratization, rule of law, and global public diplomacy.

Christopher D. Karadjov (PhD, University of Florida) is an associate professor at California State University, Long Beach. As a former journalist in Bulgaria and the United States, he teaches courses in reporting, data journalism, media law, and global news media. His research concentrates on newsroom practices, online comments, media effects, and global patterns of mis/disinformation. Karadjov continues to contribute to news and educational projects.

Anthony Kelly (PhD, London School of Economics and Political Science) is a digital anthropologist at L'Atelier BNP Paribas. He has conducted research on participatory political communication, affective polarization, and the commercialization of news. His recent publications examine the performativity of online outrage and the discursive production of institutional authority among European news agency executives.

Nakho Kim (PhD, Journalism and Mass Communication from the University of Wisconsin-Madison) is an assistant professor in Communication at the Pennsylvania State University Harrisburg. His primary research interests are news ecosystems and participatory journalism.

Claudia Kozman (PhD, Indiana University) is an assistant professor of multimedia journalism at the Lebanese American University. Her research primarily focuses on news content, with particular attention to news values, sourcing, and framing in Arab media. She is interested in media coverage of conflict in the Middle East as well as public opinion and perceptions during political turmoil.

Dean Kruckeberg (PhD, University of Iowa), APR, Fellow PRSA, is co-author of *This Is PR: The Realities of Public Relations*; *Public Relations and Community: A Reconstructed Theory*; and *Transparency, Public Relations,* and *the Mass Media: Combating the Hidden Influences in News Coverage Worldwide.* His honors include the PRSA Atlas Award for Lifetime Achievement in

International Public Relations, the PRSA Outstanding Educator Award, the Pathfinder Award of the Institute for Public Relations, and the Jackson and Wagner Behavioral Research Prize.

Suman Lee (PhD, Syracuse University) is an associate professor at the Hussman School of Journalism and Media, University of North Carolina at Chapel Hill. He has published numerous articles and book chapters on international public relations, public diplomacy, and international communication. Before joining academia, Lee worked for Samsung as public relations professional.

Patric Raemy (PhD, University of Fribourg) is a senior researcher at the Swiss Federal Institute for Vocational Education and Training (SFIVET) and also worked as a visiting scholar at the University of Missouri School of Journalism and as a lecturer at the Zurich University of Teacher Education. His research interests focus on journalistic roles, professional identity, professional education, vocational training, learning cultures, and didactics.

Terhi Rantanen (LicSc, DocSc, Helsinki University) is a professor in Global Media and Communications at the London School of Economics and Political Science. Rantanen's research areas include global news media organizations. She has published extensively on media globalization and global news transmissions.

Elad Segev (PhD, Keele University) is an associate professor at the Department of Communication, Tel Aviv University. He studied the relationship between information and power from cross-national perspectives, focusing on global information flows, country image, Americanization and globalization, international news, information search and search strategies, and the digital divide, often utilizing data mining and network analysis techniques.

Katerina Tsetsura (PhD, Purdue University) is internationally known for her work in media transparency and global public relations. She has over eighty peer-reviewed publications, is a co-author of *Transparency, Public Relations, and the Mass Media: Combating the Hidden Influences in News Coverage Worldwide* (Taylor & Francis, 2017), and a co-editor of *Strategic Communications in Russia* (Taylor & Francis, 2021). Tsetsura serves on editorial boards of *Communication Theory* and *International Journal of Strategic Communication,* among others.

Tudor Vlad (PhD, Babes-Bolyai University, Romania) is the director of the James M. Cox Jr. Center for International Mass Communication Training and Research at the University of Georgia. He has been a consultant to Gallup, *The New York Times*, Freedom House, and the Russian Journalists Union. His research focuses on journalism education, press freedom evaluations, the role of media in emerging democracies, and the relationship between mass media academic curricula and the labor market.

Jane Whyatt is a veteran broadcast journalist, journalism educator, and press freedom campaigner. She has taught journalism at London's major universities and published research on the female news agenda and the news habits of teenagers. Whyatt's recent experience includes work at the European Centre for Press and Media Freedom, an independent cooperative that monitors media freedom across Europe.

H. Denis Wu (PhD, University of North Carolina at Chapel Hill) is a professor of communication at Boston University, USA. He conducts research in international and political communication and has co-authored three books on the interplay between media and p His recent research focuses on the roles emotion and social media play in cross-nation communication and electoral process.

Milton Keynes UK
Ingram Content Group UK Ltd.
UKHW050634040224
437221UK00012B/94